D0207519

Legacy of the Ludlow Massacre

A Chapter in American Industrial Relations

Legacy of the Ludlow Massacre

A Chapter in American Industrial Relations

H. M. Gitelman

upp

University of Pennsylvania Press
Philadelphia

Funding for publication of this volume was provided in part by Adelphi University.

Library of Congress Cataloging-in-Publication Data
Gitelman, Howard M.
   Legacy of the Ludlow Massacre ; a chapter in American
industrial relations.

   Bibliography: p.
   Includes index.
   1. Company unions—United States—History—20th
century.   2. Coal Strike, Colo., 1913–1914.   3. King,
William Lyon Mackenzie, 1874–1950.   4. Rockefeller,
John D. (John Davison), 1874–1960.   I. Title.
HD6490.C612U65 1988   331.89′2822334′0978851   87-35843
ISBN 0-8122-8099-7

For Claudia

Contents

Illustrations • ix

Preface • xi

1. Call to Arms • 1

2. New Counselors • 32

3. Enduring Bonds • 51

4. Half-Empty Words • 68

5. Charity • 90

6. The Truth About Colorado • 114

7. Tangled Motives • 148

8. Selling the Plan: The East • 163

9. Selling the Plan: The West • 181

10. Pulpits and Profits • 198

11. The War • 222

12. Chaos and Constancy • 264

13. On His Own • 305

Epilogue • 331

Bibliography • 341

Index • 349

Illustrations

John D. Rockefeller, Jr., January 1915 • 6

Ludlow tent colony before the battle • 12

A militia unit • 13

Armed miners at the U.M.W. Military Headquarters, Trinidad • 15

The Hole • 18

Ludlow following the battle • 19

Ivy Lee, 1934 • 34

W. L. Mackenzie King, September 1914 • 42

John D. Rockefeller and John D. Rockefeller, Jr., 1914 or 1915 • 48

Frank P. Walsh, c. 1918 • 73

John D. Rockefeller, Jr., following his testimony before the U.S. Commission on Industrial Relations, January 1915 • 76

Seth Low, undated • 107

Horace Hawkins, Mother Jones, and John R. Lawson, c. 1914 • 118

John C. Osgood, president of the Victor-America Fuel Company • 120

Jesse F. Welborn, president of the Colorado Fuel & Iron Company • 128

W. L. Mackenzie King and John D. Rockefeller, Jr., with C. F. & I. employee, September 1915 • 188

Raymond B. Fosdick, 1918 • 224

The Ludlow Monument • 240

John D. Rockefeller, Jr., and Starr Murphy, October 1919 · 293

Franklin K. Lane, Elbert H. Gary, Samuel Gompers, William B. Wilson, and John D. Rockefeller, Jr., at the President's Industrial Conference, October 1919 · 314

Preface

The Ludlow Massacre of April 20, 1914, is one in a painfully long list of violent incidents in American labor history. The details of the tragedy, its setting in the midst of a violent coal strike in Colorado, its many and diverse participants, and their reactions to the massacre all have been recounted a number of times. Another detailed account hardly seems warranted, and I do not intend to provide one. This is a book about consequences. More particularly, it is about the impact of the Ludlow massacre on the course of American industrial relations.

In the years leading up to World War I and immediately after, the labor question loomed as the most intractable problem of the age. The great conundrum that perplexed conservatives and progressives alike and that no one seemed able to resolve asked: Can some way be found to accommodate the interests of Capital and Labor, or is their conflict—often violent and almost always incendiary in its emotional charge—bound to breach the existing order? The massacre provided the most powerful evidence of how desperately an answer was needed.

Trade unions provided one answer, but this was acceptable only to some workers and their allies. Most employers and sizeable majorities of practically all other social groupings feared and opposed unions. As is true today, unions were more commonly viewed as a part of the problem than as the means to its solution. Yet few thinking people supposed that employers, left to their own devices, could produce the industrial peace that had thus far eluded them.

From the start of the century, a handful of individual employers experimented with employee organizations limited to their own workers. The hope was that such organizations would facilitate better company–employee relations without the adversarial challenge that seemed central to unionism. Whether individually successful or not, these experiments proved of little practical consequence. They did nothing to alter the indifference toward employee relations that most employers displayed, except, that is, when touched either by a strike or a union organizing threat.

In contrast, the employee representation plan that Mackenzie King designed in the wake of the Ludlow massacre, and then helped John D. Rockefeller, Jr., install at the Colorado Fuel & Iron Company, became the model for almost all subsequent company unions. At first, few employers seized on King's plan as the antidote to labor unrest. But, the deep personal meaning that employee representation held for the Rockefeller heir led him to push for its adoption in companies in which his father had substantial holdings. Following America's entry into the World War in April 1917, the spread of representation plans accelerated. In the chaos that followed the war, employee representation enjoyed even wider acceptance. It was heralded as the nonunion yet forward-looking answer to both the labor problems and the threat of Bolshevism. By the end of the roaring twenties, serious scholars were wondering whether company unions, in tandem with employer welfare programs, hadn't permanently displaced the labor movement.

The development and spread of company unions, and the place they occupied in thinking about industrial relations until about 1930, provide one major strand of my narrative. The second strand, which is inextricably interwoven with the first, concerns Mackenzie King and John D. Rockefeller, Jr., and their relationship. Since both strands are open to various interpretations, it may prove helpful to bare my leanings at the outset.

The notion that a company might create an organization among its employees, and then confer upon that organization a parity of power in setting employment terms and conditions, may seem too fanciful ever to have been taken seriously. The first, organizational, step seems comparatively simple. It is also telling evidence of the disproportionate power of the employer vis-à-vis the employees. For where employers routinely and forcefully oppose the organization of workers by themselves or others, as they always have in this country, leading employees into an employer's own organization is manipulative.

The next and more controversial step, that of empowering the employee organization, rests on a dubious assumption about the nature of industrial conflict. The belief that elected worker representatives, using only the organization conferred on them by their employer, can effectively counterpoise the interests of their employer, assumes that conflict stems only from misunderstanding or flawed communications. It supposes that worker representatives need only complain and that employers need only respond by putting things right for conflict to be avoided. The very existence of the employee organization, as a means of keeping open the channels of communication, is assumed to obviate any real need for worker power. However, if for any number of reasons, the worker representatives prove reluctant to press worker interests too hard, or if the employers are reticent to make concessions to the disadvantage of their status or balance sheets, something other than misunderstanding or flawed communication is at work.

In this country today, company unions are extinct for all practical purposes, rendered so by the force of the Wagner Act of 1935. With perfect hindsight, we can see that they were a misadventure, the false step of an earlier generation. But the questions they once raised about the nature of worker organization and its role in securing social justice remain very much alive. Although many employers long for a union-free environment, one often hears conjectures about the possibility of reintroducing company unions in emulation of the successful Japanese model. That would be truly ironic for, as we will see, it is quite likely that the Japanese imported their model from this country.

The evidence that the personalities and life circumstances of Mackenzie King and John D. Rockefeller, Jr., played an integral role in the development and diffusion of company unions presents a different set of interpretive problems. Lacking either the professional background or the inclination to undertake a deep psychohistorical analysis of the two men, I have nonetheless been obliged to examine their characters and to attempt to explain their behavior. For better or worse, I have tried to build up my portraits of each man as the evidence permits. Fortunately the papers and personal diaries of King were available to me, as were the extensive record files of the Rockefeller Archive Center. Both collections are marvelously rich, and yielded much of what is new in my account.

The active period of the King–Rockefeller relationship lasted only from mid-1914 to the end of 1919. In view of the length and fullness of each man's life, this interval is but a fragment. King (1874–1950) was forty years old in 1914 and already had an illustrious career as a civil servant, labor mediator, member of Parliament, and Minister of Labour. Ahead lay the leadership of his party and the longest-tenured service as Prime Minister in Canadian history. Rockefeller (1874–1960) was also forty years old in

1914. As the head of his father's staff, he oversaw the management of both a complex portfolio of assets, valued in the hundreds of millions of dollars, and an equally complex variety of philanthropic activities. He would be involved in many of the major social and humanitarian movements of the twentieth century, from preserving antiquities to supporting Negro colleges, from Prohibition to medical research.

In dealing with King and Rockefeller during the 1914–1919 period, I have relied extensively on primary source materials. For the pre-1914 and post-1919 years, I have leaned heavily, but selectively, on published materials. Within the active period, my coverage is intentionally limited. For example, I have little to say about King's family affairs, his social life, his health, or his maneuvers on behalf of his political career. Similarly, Rockefeller's family life and much of his philanthropic activity are introduced only when they have a bearing on the main themes of the narrative.

Readers familiar with the career of Mackenzie King as Liberal Party leader and Prime Minister will not be surprised to learn of his exceptional capacity for rationalizing his actions. With no trace of cynicism or deceit, he could transform the dross of self-interest into the finest gold of reasoned humanitarianism. Yet, he was not a mere opportunist. He had fairly clear preferences against which he weighed his choices, and he regarded himself a man of passionate, profound commitments. Seeing him at work in the period covered here, it would have been impossible to predict that his accession to political power would be accompanied by the abandonment of his aspirations for social reform. It seems, forces were at work within him that, though he little understood them, forged his destiny as surely as the ambition he thrived on. If ever an historic figure cried out for close psychological investigation and provided many of the means in an extraordinary set of diaries, King is such a one.

Much the same may be said of John D. Rockefeller, Jr., who, for all of his influence on so many aspects of twentieth century life, has been the subject of only one largely celebratory biography (as compared to more than half a dozen on King). Although I feel that, despite its limitations, my portrait of King is accurate and rounded, that of Rockefeller is sketchier. This results partly from the lack of comparable diaries and critical biographies, but partly also from a certain wooden quality in the man that proved difficult to work through.

Some readers will find the portrait of Rockefeller troubling for entirely different reasons. For purposes either of politics or sanity, we prefer to believe that those who wield power have interests and ends toward which they shape their means accordingly. The Devil is thus an organizing principle of sorts. To find that the powerful may themselves be manipulated, and that they too may be ignorant of the consequences of their actions and inactions, introduces a disquieting element of uncertainty into the order we seek to impose on the world. My effort to strip away the force field of power surrounding Rockefeller renders him all too human, that is to say, believable.

Though worker rights are the central issue around which the narrative revolves, workers themselves play little part. This is a story of power wielded *over* workers not by them. In a similar vein, no effort has been made to estimate the conseqences of company unions for worker productivity. The record reveals that not one of the firms that adopted employee representation at the urging of Rockefeller or with the assistance of King, did so with productivity or any aspect of work performance in mind. Power more than profits appears to have been their primary concern.

I am indebted to many people for their assistance. Among my colleagues at Adelphi University, Gloria Beckerman, Dominick Cavallo, and James Fennelly provided valuable criticisms and suggestions. In early stages of the work, Joan Catherwood and Timothy Costello generously assisted me. Pat DeLucia was ever helpful and patient through many drafts. The archivists I encountered were wonderfully helpful without exception. The late Margaret Rowden at the Public Archives of Canada and Joseph Ernst at the Rockefeller Archive Center were particularly kind and resourceful. To my daughters, Lisa, Hillary, and Alix, I owe a special note of thanks.

H. M. Gitelman

June 1987

Legacy of the Ludlow Massacre
A Chapter in American Industrial Relations

1. Call to Arms

From the start of the Colorado coal strike in September 1913, John D. Rockefeller, Jr., followed a course of business as usual. This meant permitting company officials, some two thousand miles from New York, their accustomed and virtually complete freedom of action. Profoundly ignorant of workers, unions, and industrial relations, Rockefeller depended entirely on the officers for information about the strike and for his understanding of the issues at stake. Neither he nor his advisors sensed the shallowness and vulnerability of his position. The words he uttered in defense of the company and its policies were fed him by distant agents. The strings that pulled him were worked by his iron-willed father. No wonder the heir apparent to the Rockefeller fortune sometimes felt that his life was not altogether real.

As the strike dragged on, violence erupted and lives were lost. Units of the Colorado militia entered the coalfields. Representatives of the Wilson Administration made several attempts to foster mediation. A growing sentiment developed in Colorado, in Washington, and around the nation that the Rockefellers bore primary responsibility for the strike and its attendant violence. This sentiment hardened into an enduring judgment of history when, on April 20, 1914, a pitched battle, followed by widespread rioting, took the lives of twenty-four men, women, and children.

Neither the senior Rockefeller nor his son ever acceded to the view that responsibility for what has come to be known as the Ludlow Massacre rested with them. Instead, the younger Rockefeller tortured logic until it yielded him exoneration. Simultaneously indignant and perplexed, he also took steps to set the public straight. One step led him to Ivy Lee and public relations; the other to Mackenzie King and company unions. The following sketch of the strike affords the opportunity to characterize the industrial relations of the era in its most extreme form and to observe, in John D. Rockefeller, Jr., a prime mover moved.

In an effort to expand and ensure the stability of its organization in the coal fields of northern Colorado, the United Mine

Workers, in the summer of 1913, began to organize the miners in the state's southern camps. Despite intense employer opposition and the constant harassment of law officers, union organizers made considerable progress. Among their new recruits were numbers of men who had taken the places of other miners during a strike ten years earlier; now they were the aggrieved.

Late in August 1913, the union invited the coal operators to confer about the grievances of the men. The operators ignored the letter. A second request for a conference also was ignored. So, on September 15, when the delegates from the various mines assembled in the city of Trinidad, it was clear that they had a struggle on their hands. They agreed to strike for a seven point program:

1. Recognition of the union.
2. A ten percent increase in wages.
3. The eight hour day.
4. Payment for deadwork. (Miners were paid on the basis of the weight of the coal they mined. Deadwork was work necessary to mining that did not directly or immediately result in mined coal.)
5. The right to elect checkweighmen (i.e., miners who could verify the weight of the coal mined).
6. The right to trade in any store, board anywhere, and hire the services of any doctor.
7. Enforcement of Colorado mining laws and the abolition of armed mine guards.

Items 3, 5, 7, and elements of item 6 were due the miners under existing state laws. They were bargainable only in the sense that these laws had been ignored. The purely economic demands, items 2 and 4, were important, but not critical. Everyone understood that the central issue was union recognition. The fate of the other demands hinged upon whether the U.M.W. would be present to compel concessions and compliance.

Eight thousand miners struck on September 23 and, with their families and possessions, moved out of the company camps and into tent colonies provided by the union.

Every wagon was the same, with its high piled furniture, and its bewildered, woebegone family perched atop. And the furniture! What a mockery to the state's boasted riches. Little piles of rickety chairs. Little piles of miserable looking straw bedding. Little piles of kitchen utensils. . . .[1]

Any knowledgeable observer could have predicted tragedy, for armed conflict was almost certain to occur. Coal mining imposed a degree of vassalage so inconsonant with the American ideal of freedom, that the resort was to arms practically was inevitable. The mining camps were situated in isolated canyons. Everything therein, the roads, streets, land, houses, churches, stores, bars, jails, schools, and governments belonged to the company. The people in the camps were company property, too, in a very real sense. Anyone who would not do the company's bidding at work, at home, or in public was compelled to leave, "to go down the cañon."[2] Discipline was maintained by intimidation and, if need be, by physical assault.

As will be shown, the coal companies openly flouted state mining laws, rigged elections, and suborned local public officials. Local law officers served them as a private army, enforcing the law selectively in the interest of both the companies and their own perquisites. Even in peaceful times, the civil rights of the miners had been routinely ignored. Once the strike began and miners were openly cast as enemies, all restraints were dropped. The companies imported several hundred additional deputies and mine guards, among them Texas desperadoes and thugs provided by the Baldwin-Felts Detective Agency. As the closest contemporary observer put it: "the operators hired an army for the purpose of making war upon, and if necessary, killing their employees."[3]

The miners also armed themselves. In many ways, it became impossible to distinguish the strike from a war. "Troops and armed workers and armies of company goons marched, bivouacked, deployed, and exchanged fire in open warfare. Murder, arson, and dynamiting took their toll."[4] Mackenzie King would later estimate that two hundred lives were lost in the strike.

Most of the employers who received and rejected the miners' demands owned small, independent mining companies. The three largest operators produced almost three-quarters of the total output. The largest company, the Colorado Fuel and Iron Company, accounted for thirty five to forty percent of production and for an equal proportion of total employment. One of its officers served on the operators' committee that directed the fight against the union.

Apart from its size, Colorado Fuel & Iron differed from the other companies in a number of ways. Whereas coal mining was the major business of the others, it was a subsidiary enterprise for C.F. & I., which mined coal primarily to provide coke for its steel mills. This made the company's officers more rather than less interested in repulsing the union, for it placed them in double jeopardy. The continuous operation of the steel mills required a steady flow of coking coal. Since coke could not be stored or inventoried, control over the supply of coal meant control over the steel mills as well. If the union was permitted to gain a foothold in their mines, company officers feared they could be forced to agree to almost any terms by the threat to their steel-making operations. As one officer pointed out to an investigator from the U.S. Commission on Industrial Relations, "not a single captive mine" (i.e., steel company owned and operated) in the country was unionized.[5] C.F. & I. had no thought of becoming the exception to the rule—an intention quite possibly derived from its earlier participation in those feasts of steel industry collusion known as the Gary dinners.

Of the struck companies, C.F. & I also was the only one publicly associated with out-of-state interests. Hired managers conducted its affairs in the name of absentee owners. John D. Rockefeller was the most well known of these, and his complete control over the actions of the company was taken for granted by everyone. Rockefeller (hereafter called "Senior") owned forty percent of the firm's stock as well as a significant portion of its bonded indebtedness. He was represented on the board of directors by the members of his personal staff: his son, John D. Rockefeller, Jr.; Starr J. Murphy; and Jerome Greene.

In an era when private affairs remained privileged and no one, whether newspaper reporter or representative of the public, had a claim to information beyond what private parties chose to divulge (or were obliged to under subpeona), even in 1914, it was not widely known that the senior Rockefeller had retired from the active management of his affairs in 1896. A staff, headed until 1912 by Frederick Gates and subsequently by John D. Rockefeller, Jr., directed his extensive business and philanthropic interests in his name. Since the relations of Senior to his staff and of the staff to the officers of C.F. & I. play crucial roles in what lies ahead, some clarification is necessary.

Senior's retirement proved vastly premature. He was 56 years old in 1896 and lived to the age of 97. His retirement was also incomplete. Though he stayed away from the office and left day-to-day decisions to his staff, he had to be kept abreast of and consulted about major decisions until at least 1916. In dollar terms, a major decision was one with a price tag in excess of two million dollars. But there were nonpecuniary major decisions as well. In the context of the Colorado strike, Senior opposed the unionization of the mines. He did so as a matter of personal, as opposed to ideological or strategic business, preference.

Senior's informing encounter with unionism had occurred some years before, when the men working on the grounds of his estate formed a union and tendered demands for improvements. He thought them so ungrateful for the opportunities that he had provided, that in true autocratic fashion, he fired them and hired replacements. As his son would inform Mackenzie King, "his father had become so bitter against the way the unions had acted he would not have a union man on his estate."[6] Whether his reaction to unionization was that of a self-righteous man who could not accept the implication that he had acted unfairly or that of a prideful man who would brook no constraint on his judgment is not clear. What is clear is that all of the action and inaction of his staff during the Colorado strike rested on the bedrock of Senior's antiunionism.

John D. Rockefeller, Jr., had joined the staff at 26 Broadway in 1897, fresh from Brown University. The fact that his father had just withdrawn from the office, perfectly symbolizes their curious relationship. For however strong the bonds of affection between them, father and son had considerable difficulty relating to one another. They often resorted to intermediaries when they wished to pass on information about themselves or broach a new idea. Mrs. Rockefeller frequently acted as their go-between, as did Frederick Gates.

This low level of direct communication accounted for young Rockefeller's bewilderment on entering the office. He was given a desk, but no one told him what he should do, or learn, or pay particular attention to, or what his role was to be. He felt himself left to sink or swim.

It fell to his father's right-hand man to shepherd the heirling through his apprenticeship. In the process, Gates, a former Baptist minister, regaled the young man with what were his first authoritative accounts of Senior's actions, motives, and accomplishments. As a result, the son felt more keenly than ever the lack of understanding and appreciation by the public for his father's con-

John D. Rockefeller, Jr., January 1915. By permission of the Rockefeller Archive Center.

tributions to American industrial growth. Someday, somehow, he
hoped to find a way to make the truth known to all.

When Rockefeller first entered the office, the staff was engaged
in two distinct activities: making money and giving it away. The
emphasis clearly was still on the former. In 1902, for example,
when Senior's income totaled $58 million, the sum of his dona-
tions, expenses, and losses amounted to $4 million. His wealth at
the time exceeded $200 million. Then, as the demand for petro-
leum increased sharply over the ensuing decade due to the devel-

opment of the automobile, the flow of income became a veritable flood. By 1914, Senior's assets closed upon a billion dollars. As Gates defined it, and as both father and son agreed, the burden of the young man's life was to survive this inundation. The ark of his salvation was to be philanthropy.

From the very outset of Senior's career as a store clerk in Cleveland, Ohio, he had tithed from his income for worthy causes. It was only the scale of his giving and the attendant need for careful planning that were subsequently to differ. His practice of handing out coins was also a long-standing habit, one that the glare of publicity later turned into a gaucherie. He, his son, and Gates subscribed completely to Andrew Carnegie's "Gospel of Wealth," wherein the duties of wealth were enumerated as

> To set an example of modest, unostentatious living, shunning display or extravagance; to provide moderately for the legitimate wants of those dependent upon him; and after doing so, to consider all surplus revenues which come to him simply as trust funds, which he is called upon to administer in the manner . . . best calculated to produce the most beneficial results for the community . . .

Senior's major philanthropic interests initially centered on religion. He strongly supported the Baptist Church and the temperance movement. The funds given for the establishment of the University of Chicago in 1889, for example, were primarily aimed at creating a training ground for the Baptist ministry. Under the influence of Gates, he was subsequently led to philanthropic efforts in medicine and education as well. The Rockefeller Institute for Medical Research was established in 1901. Two years later, the General Education Board was created to provide support for Negro and white colleges. A decade later, the Rockefeller Foundation would be organized to channel support to a wide array of cultural, environmental, and artistic projects.

Young Rockefeller learned the art and the pitfalls of philanthropy under Gates's tutelage. In the wrong hands money was a dangerous weapon. Even in the right hands, it might do more harm than good if too easily come by. (Large numbers of people were nonetheless prepared to sustain whatever loss of initiative or self-esteem might attend a Rockefeller handout. Pleas for assistance usually peaked soon after the announcement of a large gift.

In the thirty days following one such announcement—we do not know the year—almost fifty thousand appeals for assistance were received.)

Gifts were usually directed toward nonprofit organizations whose objectives the staff found worthy. At the time of the Colorado strike, for example, Rockefeller support was going to such organizations as the American Association for Labor Legislation and the National and New York Child Labor Committees. Most gifts were calculated to serve only as seed money. One reason for this was the belief that any organization with worthwhile objectives ought to be able to find a constituency within the body politic that would support it. Assistance was to be given until new adherents enlisted in sufficient numbers to ensure financial stability. Organizations that were under some pressure to attract supporters could also be expected to retain their vitality. They would find it necessary to keep their objectives rather than the comfort of their officers foremost in view. Finally, gifts that provided only partial support would reduce the likelihood that the issue of Rockefeller domination would arise.

The staff regularly reviewed the progress of the organizations that it supported and used these reviews as the basis for deciding whether contributions ought to continue and in what amounts. As all of this suggests, the philanthropic guidelines developed by Gates were well thought out and fairly sophisticated. The same cannot be said of the procedures developed with regard to Rockefeller business interests.

The staff employed two different strategies for monitoring the performance of the companies in which Senior had substantial holdings. Either they relied upon periodic financial reports from company officials or they personally attended meetings of the board of directors. The overarching strategy that guided them in deciding when to buy and when to sell holdings, is not known. But, obviously, theirs was not a short-run, profit-maximizing outlook or they would have abandoned C.F. & I. as a loser at an early date.

Insofar as the management of the companies was concerned, the staff saw itself in a position to offer suggestions but never to command. This may seem bizarre to those who assume that powerful people are bound to exercise their power, particularly in rigid hierarchies like the modern corporation. The Rockefellers, however, were committed to the separation between ownership and management well in advance of its discovery by Berle and Means.

The staff rationalized its hands-off policy with the arguments that the managers on the spot knew better than they what the business required, and that the managers were trusted and proven agents. The latter of these arguments was the more important. It was subscribed to even though it could not be verified and, in one sense, was known to be false. This inconsistency lay very near the heart of the staff's responses to the Colorado strike.

The younger Rockefeller believed that good men were hard to find. Once found, such men could be given free reign because they could be trusted to do the right thing. Rockefeller undoubtedly adopted this view from Gates, for his own experience ran in the opposite direction. To be sure, he had been raised in the insular, half-paranoid world in this country so often reserved for the offspring of the notoriously wealthy. But from the moment he had entered the more public world, he regularly encountered men in whom he placed his trust. Thus, a number of classmates from Brown University followed him into positions at 26 Broadway. He "found" Raymond Fosdick while serving on a grand jury and Edward Cowdrick on a trip to Colorado. Good men appeared wherever he turned. But, since he was not a particularly keen observer of the world, the junior Rockefeller was more disposed to embrace cliches than to overturn them.

Rockefeller also knew from personal experience that the trusted agents who headed some of his father's business interests acted wrongly. As part of his apprenticeship, he had taken up seats on a number of boards of directors. To his chagrin, he learned that the managers of most of these companies wished to use him. Would he give testimony at legislative hearings? Or talk to Senator So-and-so? Or make known his support for a friendly congressman's reelection? When he refused, indicating that he thought it improper for companies to seek to influence or dominate the political process for their own ends, he was written off as idealistic and naive. In consequence by 1910 he had resigned from almost all of the company boards. The seat he retained on the Colorado Fuel & Iron board was the only one he had held in 1914.

These acts of resignation had the effect of exposing the Rockefellers to charges of which their agents were sometimes guilty but of which they were themselves ignorant. Since the senior Rockefeller had also withdrawn from directorships at an earlier time, the question naturally arises as to whether ignorance of their agent's actions was a conscious defensive strategy. Did father and son pointedly not wish to know what was done to win their profits?

Although both Rockefellers withdrew from corporate boards, their closest advisors often retained seats. This indicates that the withdrawals were not aimed at providing deniability. The resignations of the younger Rockefeller were instead calculated to shield his integrity from compromise. As such, the resignations may be seen as an evidence of strength of character. But they were also an embarrassing admission of personal weakness. They demonstrated that the Rockefeller heir lacked the strength either to dominate or decisively influence most of the boards on which he sat. In consequence, the actual power of the Rockefellers was considerably more limited than outsiders had any reason to suppose.

Of equal importance, the resignations also indicate Rockefeller's awareness that his trusted agents were not always to be trusted. For if they asked him to engage in objectionable behavior, could it be doubted that others of their actions might also prove objectionable? Yet on the grounds that good men were hard to find, and that once found they were not to be commanded but only persuaded, Rockefeller and his advisors trusted their agents practically without reserve. Seeing no contradiction, they failed even to guard against the burdens of blame that the actions of errant agents might impose on them.

Lamont M. Bowers was the key Rockefeller agent on the scene in Colorado. For almost a decade prior to the strike, Bowers had served ably in various executive posts at C.F. & I. During his tenure, the company had gained wide recognition for its welfare work. Within Colorado, the company had also built a favorable reputation. Employees were provided with some services that the smaller mining companies could not afford, and company wages topped local scales.

In addition to this record of dependable, effective service, Bowers possessed the added distinction of being the uncle of Frederick Gates. Known for his peppery disposition, he was the very model of an agent: a distinctive man of strong will and character, with kinship ties and executive ability. Since his decision to fight off the United Mine Workers coincided exactly with Senior's preference, there was little reason to question his actions.

At the first rumor of a union organizing drive, Bowers had been quick to make concessions that he hoped would please the miners and thwart the union organizers. So certain were the company's officers of the favored status of C.F. & I. that when their miners actually joined the walkout they could not accept it. They concluded that their men must have been forced to join the strike out of fear for their personal safety.

Seated in their Denver offices, Bowers and Jesse Welborn, the company president, actually knew very little about what went on in the southern mining camps. They presumed that their directives were obeyed and that their intentions of liberal treatment were realized in practice. They were mistaken, and had no inkling of it. Their immediate subordinate, the manager of the fuel department, had his offices in Pueblo, and he also rarely visited the isolated camps. Information came to him from the camp superintendents who, quite naturally, had every reason to tell him only what he wanted to hear. With a little embellishment, he reported to Denver, and Denver reported to New York. Thus, the New York office received accounts of company conditions and the strike that were significantly distorted. The irony of this was that when the Denver officers refused to talk with union representatives for fear of conferring recognition, they unwittingly lost the best opportunity to learn about actual conditions.

In the remote, ramshackle camps, the miners experienced day-to-day vulnerability to the abuses of any of the petty officials who held sway over them. Camp superintendents, pit bosses, company store managers, company doctors, law officers, company housing managers, and their favorites had the power to exact conformity to their wishes at the threat of losing job, income, and home. Not all of the officials abused their power over the miners, but those who did made life hellish—from the pit boss who made his men buy insurance from him to hold their jobs, to the store manager who threatened to have fired those who didn't trade at his store. The worst of it was the complete lack of opportunity for redress. The miners, many of whom were recent immigrants with little English, had good reason to believe that the supervisory and administrative people would stick up for one another. Quitting was sometimes the only recourse. At some mines, any who dared complain were beaten up. Thus the chain of command, from the officers in Denver, to the manager of the fuel department in Pueblo, to the superintendents in each of the camps, to the pit bosses, to the miners, only worked to move directives downward and with considerable variation in interpretation and enforcement. The chain of command was nonexistent for passing information from the miners upward.

Ludlow tent colony before the battle. By permission of the Colorado Historical Society.

In New York, the Rockefeller staff rebuffed all requests to intervene in the strike. Unaware of the true state of affairs in Colorado and slavishly committed to the existing division of authority, the younger Rockefeller took every opportunity to affirm his support for Bowers and Welborn. Even before the strike had begun, Ethelbert Stewart, of the U.S. Department of Labor, attempted to see the senior Rockefeller but had been refused. He was informed that the officers in Colorado were in complete charge of the situation. In November, when the strike was almost two months old and after the state militia had been ordered into the field to maintain order, William B. Wilson, Secretary of Labor, wrote asking if the senior Rockefeller wouldn't use his influence to arrange a meeting between the operators and representatives of the miners. In both instances, the agents of the federal government mistakenly addressed the elder Rockefeller, unaware of his retirement. The younger Rockefeller's icy reply indicated his total acceptance of Bowers's view of the strike:

> The action of our officers in refusing to meet the strike-leaders is quite as much in the interest of our employees as of any other element in the company. Their position meets with our cordial approval and we shall support them to the end. The

A militia unit. By permission of the Colorado Historical Society.

failure of our men to remain at work is due simply to their fear of assault and assassination. The Governor of Colorado has only to protect the lives of the bona fide miners to bring the strike to a speedy termination.[8]

As the strike dragged on and drew its first blood, Bowers and Welborn increasingly began to picture the conflict as a battle of principle between the open shop and the closed shop. "[Many] have become alarmed since the uncalled for and vicious demand of the union leaders in this state for recognition of the union and suppression of the open shop," Bowers wrote.[9] When Secretary Wilson entered the dispute at the invitation of the Colorado governor, Bowers warned New York that Wilson, a former United Mine Workers official, was behind the efforts to end the open shop in the United States. President Welborn, in his yearend report to stockholders, asserted that a closed shop contract was "practically the sole purpose of the [union] in calling the strike."[10]

The New York office readily accepted this argument. When Rockefeller appeared before a congressional investigating committee on April 6, 1914, he supported the open shop as the main line of his defense:

> Mr. Rockefeller. We believe that the issue is not a local one in Colorado; it is a national issue, whether workers shall be allowed to work under such conditions as they may choose. And as part owners of the property, our interest in the laboring men in this country is so immense, so deep, so profound that we stand ready to lose every cent we put in that company rather than see the men we have employed thrown out of work and have imposed upon them conditions which are not of their seeking and which neither they nor we can see are in our interest.
>
> The Chairman. And you are willing to go on and let these killings take place—men losing their lives on either side, the expenditure of large sums of money, and all this disturbance of labor—rather than go out there and see if you might do something to settle those conditions?
>
> Mr. Rockefeller. There is just one thing, Mr. Chairman, so far as I understand it, which can be done, as things are at present, to settle this strike, and that is to unionize the camps; and our interest in labor is so profound and we believe so sincerely that

Armed miners at the U. M. W. Military Headquarters, Trinidad. By permission of the Colorado Historical Society.

that interest demands that the camps shall be open camps, that we expect to stand by the officers at any cost. It is not an accident that this is our position—

The Chairman.   And you will do that if it costs all your property and kills all your employees?

Mr. Rockefeller.   It is a great principle.

The Chairman.   And you would do that rather than recognize the right of men to collective bargaining? Is that what I understand?

Mr. Rockefeller.   No sir. Rather than allow outside people to come in and interfere with employees who are thoroughly satisfied with their labor conditions—it was upon a similar principle that the War of the Revolution was carried out. It is a great national issue of the most vital kind.[11]

Rockefeller's defense of the open shop was as conventional and derivative as most of his views. The union was an organization of outsiders and agitators that, through intimidation and false promises, lured otherwise contented employees into conflict with their employers. The union's object in fomenting trouble was to increase its dues paying membership, thus enriching the leadership. These perfectly selfish ambitions endangered the interests of both the employer and his employees; the employer because union demands were made without knowledge of, or even concern for, the company's economic situation, and the employees because they stood to lose their liberty, since in a closed shop everyone would have to join the union and pay dues in order to remain at work.

Rockefeller confessed to the Congress that he knew absolutely nothing about the actual conditions of work and life in the C.F. & I. camps. He was later to admit that he knew as little about trade unionism or the United Mine Workers. In no other aspect of his varied business and philanthropic career would he have leaned so heavily upon his ignorance. Any organization coming under his consideration for a gift, as a matter of routine, was subjected to a thorough examination of its objectives, finances, and staffing. The office staff investigated the prospects of every business transaction with equal attention to specifics. Indeed it was a point of pride with the younger Rockefeller—one in which he believed he emulated his father—that he mastered even the finest details and minutiae of his dealings. Yet, on the say-so of agents two thousand miles away, discussing a holding he had not visited in a decade, he was prepared to defend a situation about which he knew nothing and to support a principle he had not previously considered.

One reason he knew so little about the C.F. & I. miners was that, despite his protestations to the contrary, he didn't care at all. Like most businessmen of the day, he thought matters concerning labor unimportant compared to questions of sales, finances, and profit. Thus he fretted about the adequacy of the interest C.F. & I. earned on its surplus cash and, just four days after the strike began, had asked Bowers to provide him with a monthly accounting. But six months into the strike, he confessed that he did not know that C.F. & I. provided company housing. Telling himself that he couldn't possibly become familiar with the details of every enterprise in which his father held an interest, he chose to learn only those details he deemed it crucial to know. Like most corporate businessmen, when he gave any thought to labor matters, he simply assumed that those in charge of hiring and overseeing workers employed sound practices and fair play. That was their duty, just as it was the duty of those in charge of production to use the most economical and efficient processes. *Duty* was the handmaiden of the reigning social philosophy of the era to which the younger Rockefeller subscribed. As he would describe it to his biographer:

> Our attitude was due entirely to Mother, who talked to us constantly about *duty*—and displeasing the Lord—and paining your parents. She instilled a personal consciousness of right

and wrong, training our wills and getting us to want to do the things we ought to do. There were never any punishments that I recall. We did what we did from a sense of duty and right.[12]

Since *his* intentions were to be as liberal and fair toward workers as possible and since he believed Bowers and Welborn shared these intentions, they and he were blameless in the present trouble. Union leaders were the culprits, with their threats against loyal miners, their purchases of arms and ammunition, and their incendiary talk.

In the week following his appearance before the congressional committee, Rockefeller received a number of letters from bankers and industrialists congratulating him on the stand he had taken. Charles M. Schwab of Bethlehem Steel was among his correspondents. So was the senior Rockefeller, who gave his son ten thousand shares of C.F. & I. common stock (valued at approximately $300,000), saying: "I want you to have an active interest personally in the property. I hope we can make it worth more money."[13] To which the son in his thank you letter replied, "if we are only left in peace to conduct what is a legitimate and necessary business, it is to be hoped that some return on the investment may be realized before many years."[14]

The younger Rockefeller also received a very courteous letter from Frank J. Hayes, vice president of the United Mine Workers, requesting a meeting. Hayes suggested that the trouble in Colorado owed little to outside agitators. The strike had occurred because company officers refused to take the miners' grievances seriously.

Frederick Gates happened to visit the office and was asked what response should be given the Hayes letter. Although he appears to have been strongly opposed to unionism during his active career, Gates now counselled moderation and recommended a meeting. Before anything further developed along these lines, however, calamity struck in Colorado.

During the preceeding months, most units of the state militia had been withdrawn from the coal fields. No serious disturbances had occurred for some time, and the troops had become as restive to return to their families and jobs as the state was to have them off the payroll. The few units that remained in the field were composed largely of mine guards and company hirelings, who had taken the places of departing militia men.

On April 20, shooting between the militia and the miners broke out at the Ludlow tent colony. As commonly happens in such situations, conflicting reports leave unresolved the question of who fired the first shot. The gun battle raged throughout the day and reached its climax when the militia overran the colony, looted the tents, and, after dousing them with kerosene, put them to the torch. Ten men and one child were killed in the shooting. The following day, two women and eleven children who had sought refuge from the gunfire in a room dug under one of the tents, were found dead of suffocation; the burning tents over their heads had denied them oxygen. The subterranean room was reported to have served as the camp's confinement/birthing place.

When the bodies of these hapless victims were discovered, the strikers erupted in a retalitory frenzy. Armed miners occupied the city of Trinidad. Others moved as mobs through the coalfields setting fire to mine buildings and engaging mine guards and militia men in gun battles. From Denver, the Colorado Federation of Labor issued a call to arms:

> Organize the men in your community in companies to protect the workers of Colorado against the murder and cremation of men, women and children by armed assassins in the employ of

The Hole. By permission of the Archives of Labor and Urban Affairs, Wayne State University.

Ludlow following the battle. By permission of the Colorado Historical Society.

coal corporations, serving under the guise of state militiamen.

Gather together for defensive purposes all arms and ammunition legally available. . . . Hold all companies subject to order. . . . The state is furnishing us no protection and we must protect ourselves, our wives and children from these murderous assassins. We seek no quarrel with the state and we expect to break no law; we intend to exercise our lawful rights as citizens, to defend our homes and our constitutional rights.[15]

Responding to urgent pleas from all segments of the state's population, President Wilson reluctantly ordered federal troops into the strike zone, and only with their arrival, on April 30, was order restored.

The pressures upon Rockefeller in the days following the Ludlow Massacre were as varied as they were formidable. Battle reports from Colorado made daily front page reading in New York papers. Reporters pressed the office for statements, while editors canvassed the meaning of Ludlow in their columns. Pickets, including the writer Upton Sinclair and his wife, paraded and protested outside of 26 Broadway. A fracas between the pickets and police made still more newspaper copy. President Wilson dispatched Congressman Martin Foster, chairman of the congressional committee that had heard Rockefeller's testimony, to New York to confer. Hundreds of letters poured into the office carrying every message from congratulations to threats of revenge. Rockefeller, Sr., fearful for the safety of the family, took the precaution of retaining a force of private detectives.

In his talks with Congressman Foster and his communication with President Wilson, the younger Rockefeller conceded nothing. He wrote the President:

Dr. Foster was unable to make any suggestion which did not involve the unionizing of the mines or the submission of that question to arbitration. We stated to him that if the employees of the Colorado Fuel and Iron Company had any grievances, we felt sure that the officers of the Company would be willing now, as they had always been, to make every effort to adjust them satisfactorily, but that the question of the open shop namely, the right of every American citizen to work on terms satisfactory to himself without securing the consent of the union, we regarded as a question of the principle which could not be arbitrated.[16]

When Foster, on returning to Washington, learned that the Mine Workers leadership was prepared to waive the issue of recognition, he wired to ask if Rockefeller would not be prepared to open negotiations. Rockefeller responded that he would forward Foster's information to the company officers in Denver for their consideration. Foster wired back, "Your telegram somewhat disappointing. Thought you would deem the issues important enough to intervene personally to achieve settlement and prevent more deaths."[17] President Wilson personally chided Rockefeller for having missed "a great opportunity" to reach a settlement.[18]

Congressman Foster and the President could not understand this reluctance to intervene. But Rockefeller refused to become involved out of loyalty to Bowers and Welborn and to a system of divided authority that had always proved effective. He believed his agents on the scene were knowledgeable about the situation in Colorado and that he was not. Their interest in the welfare of the miners and their commitment to the owners was a matter of record. In their fight against brutal and criminal union forces, his duty was to provide unwavering support. Those who approached him requesting intervention had it in mind that there was some concession he might make that would end the strike. But he could not betray his subordinates and his modus operandi in this way.

There were other commitments as well, but these were so elemental that they remained unspoken. He blindly approved of the actions of the Colorado managers, actions about which he had only their word, because they pursued a course consistent with his father's opposition to unionization. Had the officers chosen to embrace the United Mine Workers, he might have found it expedient to get rid of them. For all of his talk of the appropriate delegation of authority, he found it harder still to be crossed, especially when his father had taken a stand.

Of these two forces—the will to be obeyed and the need to obey his father—the latter was incontestably the stronger. As the very model of the dutiful son, Rockefeller at 40 remained completely, and it must be said comfortably, indentured to his father's wishes. Lacking originality either in his ideas or in his person, his name alone conferred distinction on him. When Walter Lippmann first observed him, his strongest impressions were of his limitations and conventionality:

Those who listened to him would have forgiven him much if they had felt that they were watching a great figure, a real master of men, a person of some magnificence. But in John D. Rockefeller, Jr., there seemed to be nothing but a young man having a lot of trouble, very much harassed and very well meaning. No sign of the statesman, no quality of leadership in large affairs, just a careful, plodding, essentially uninteresting person who justifies himself with simple moralities and small-scale virtues.[19]

Foremost among these "simple moralities" stood the belief, shared by father and son alike, that their wealth was deserved only so long as it was used for right. Any wrongdoing or error on their part threatened to nullify their title to fortune and power. Moreover, since that title was God-given, wrongdoing and error were the embodiment of sin. Consequently, they felt their accountability to be of the most exacting order. Aware of no ulterior motives save to do what was right, both with the fortune and in their personal lives, father and son saw themselves as stewards of a divine trust. Such beliefs made it very difficult for either of them to admit to error.

That the Rockefellers had so strong a need to feel worthy of their material success, in a country so largely given over to the worship of success, may seem strange. One might mistakenly conclude that Senior's achievement was lined with guilt rather than silver. But because their God was more than merely a C.P.A., piety weighed very heavily in their reckonings. Success without good works would have been as unthinkable as salvation without prayer.

Intuitively, the younger Rockefeller agreed with the idea that power is "the production of intended effects"[20] and saw himself striving to produce only desirable effects. But many of his and his father's problems were borne of the *un*intended effects of their power and these he could not comprehend. Both the shallowness of his training and the unquestioned conventions of his morality blocked any view of the contingencies that lay beyond good intentions. Nowhere were these limitations more evident than in his response to Ludlow..

In his first public statement, one week after the tragedy, he denied any responsibility whatever. He pointed out that the battle had been fought between the miners and the militia, not the operators. Moreover, C.F. & I. was but one of many companies involved in the dispute and for its part had satisfied all of the miners' demands except the wage increase and union recognition before the strike had even begun. No blood was on his hands; his conscience was clear.

In spite of this disclaimer, his contemporaries and all subsequent writers on the subject (whether friendly or not) have assumed that Rockefeller's actions in the months and years following Ludlow were the acts of a penitent, motivated by deep feelings of contrition. It may now be said without equivocation that this was not so. He deplored the events at Ludlow but never ever acknowledged any responsibility for them. The facts as he saw them absolved him of all blame. And it was only the facts that counted in his eyes. Everyone else might suppose that a person as powerful as he always guided events so as to produce desired outcomes. Since he was powerful, he was responsible ipso facto. But, in Rockefeller's view, his power had not been deployed in Colorado; he had done nothing. Hence he, and his agents as well, were blameless. In a memorandum prepared several months after Ludlow, he made his case in the following manner:

> There was no Ludlow massacre. The engagement started as a desperate fight for life by two small squads of militia, numbering twelve and twenty-two men respectively, against the entire tent colony, which attacked them with over three hundred armed men. There were no women or children shot by the authorities of the State or representatives of the operators in connection with the Ludlow engagement. Not one. . . . There was but one child shot in this engagement, who having, contrary to the instructions of his parents, gone outside of the tents, was shot by a stray bullet of the strikers. The two women and eleven children who met their death in a pit underneath the floor of one of the tents, where they had been placed by the men, apparently for safety, were smothered. That such an outcome was inevitable as a result of placing this number of human beings in a pit 8 × 6 × 4 1/2 feet, the aperture of which was concealed, without any possible ventilation, is evident. . . . While this loss of life is profoundly to be regretted, it is unjust in the extreme to lay it at the door of the defenders of law and property, who were in no slightest way responsible for it.[21]

In asserting that there was no massacre, Rockefeller stressed the point that the deaths by suffocation hadn't been willfull or intended. As he saw it, they were the result of a tragic accident for which no one was directly responsible. His insistence on the most precise definition of the word "massacre" was not another manifestation of his passion for accurate detail, as he supposed; it was a means of evading blame. For even if the militia had had no intention whatever to cause death, questions remain about why they were in the field at all, and why women and children were hiding in fear for their lives underground in a tent colony.

Along with its petulance of spirit, Rockefeller's defense revealed a steely determination not to be wrong. For his facts, he relied upon a report prepared by a Board of Inquiry created and staffed by officers of the Colorado militia. In *their* version of the events at Ludlow, the militia was attacked first and fought back in self-defense. A striker's bullet killed the child. And the tent colony may have caught fire accidentally. While accepting the report's facts as accurate, Rockefeller pointedly ignored its central conclusion; namely, that the ultimate responsibility for the violence of the strike rested with the coal operators.

Most other observers, then and since, have discounted the accuracy of the militia report because of the clear conflict of interest involved in its preparation. Its final assessment of blame, however, has been widely accepted. John A. Fitch, the most careful and thorough contemporary analyst, came to a similar assessment after a detailed examination. Even Mackenzie King would eventually come within a hair's breadth of admitting that if the miners had carried on more in the fashion of revolutionaries than strikers, theirs was a reasonable response to the situation created by operator domination of housing, weaponry, law enforcement, and public officials. But Rockefeller exonerated himself on the "facts" and refused altogether to entertain the question of his responsibility on larger, more abstract grounds.

As a condition of survival as his father's son, he had become perilously well equipped to ignore the catcalls and hostile opinions of the world. He was an immune to threats to his person as he was to critical editorial comment or the suasive efforts of the President of the United States. This implacability made the subsequent turn of events all the more remarkable, for when his defenses were breached they fell before a single letter to the editor appearing in the *New York Evening Post,* written by a total stranger.[22] The writer accused Rockefeller of making false and misleading statements in the press release he had issued following the massacre. Colorado Fuel & Iron and Rockefeller, the writer maintained, deserved no kudos for having met the miners' noneconomic demands prior to the strike. Their supposed concessions had long been obligatory under Colorado mining laws. The truth of the matter was that C.F. & I. and Rockefeller had seen fit to honor the law only when they came under the threat of union organization.

Troubled by the accusation of deceit, Rockefeller directed Starr Murphy to write to Bowers for immediate confirmation of C.F. & I.'s compliance with state mining laws. He enclosed a copy of the *Evening Post* letter, captioned "Mr. Rockefeller's Concessions." When Bowers failed to reply within a few days, a second letter urging clarification of the issue was dispatched. When it became clear that the facts were as the *Evening Post* letter writer had asserted, Rockefeller decided, finally, to become personally involved in the strike.

But why, it may be asked, with so many opportunities for learning about the true situation in Colorado, did it take so fugitive a form of communication to touch and engage him? The answer to this question is bound up in the answer to another question. Just what was it that Rockefeller learned?

The erroneous press statement that had gone out under Rockefeller's signature had been prepared by clipping and pasting together segments from Bower's letters to him. (This penchant for recycling words will be examined more fully at a later point.) Bowers continued in his position at C.F. & I. until some eight months later when, at age seventy, he retired. Rockefeller also continued thoughtlessly to accept at face value the often erroneous reports of his partisan Colorado managers. These passive commitments to the status quo imply that Rockefeller did not learn to doubt Bowers's reliability or to discount the accuracy of previous or subsequent strike reports emanating from Denver. Nor did he learn to see the strike from a new perspective. It was still, as Bowers and Welborn had repeatedly told him, an effort by a small group of outside agitators to hold up the company and its miners for tribute. Hence, he still had no wish "to conciliate the forces now hostile to the company as the price of calling off their cut-throats and murderers." [23]

Nor did Rockefeller recognize or assume any share of the responsibility for the violence and loss of life associated with the strike. In point of fact, his views on the strike, the union, and the management of C.F. & I. were untouched by the discovery that he had erred. Even the evidence that, prior to the strike, C.F. & I. had stood in violation of state mining laws, escaped his attention.

All that he concluded was that he would have to take a personal hand in the dispute, which suggests that his pride rather than his intellect was engaged. Convinced that he must intervene to preclude further embarrassment, he entered the fray with his hand-me-down perspectives and prejudices fully intact.

The month of May was spent casting about for possible approaches to the problem. He wrote Jesse Welborn suggesting that the strike might be settled along lines recommended by the Colorado governor. Advisor Jerome Greene asked a Boston friend to solicit some frank private opinions about the strike from his Colorado acquaintances. The proferred services of a press agent were refused, while copies of an antiunion, antiradical paper, *The Home Defender,* were sent out West to be considered for distribution. Bowers replied that he had already distributed about twenty thousand copies of two issues. Greene's informants concurred in the opinion that the Colorado strike leaders were an unscrupulous lot.

"That we must beat the unions in the wicked game they are playing goes without saying," Greene advised Rockefeller in one of a series of mid-May options memoranda.[24] We could stand pat, Greene wrote, or work through public opinion until the United Mine Workers "will have to slink off and acknowledge itself beaten." As to launching an assault upon larger game, the American Federation of Labor itself, Greene thought that task best left to such organizations as the National Association of Manufacturers and the Anti-Boycott Association "for whose activities in resisting labor unions there has been very ample excuse and which may continue to serve a very useful purpose." The "greatest good," he concluded, "can come from some movement which has a *raison d'être* that is more positive and constructive than that of an organization formed for combat."[25]

The total inexperience of the office staff in dealing with the question of unionism was nowhere more graphically revealed than in a memo (probably written by Greene) entitled "An Ideal Labor Organization." That anyone might have seriously entertained such thoughts is a measure of the staff's isolation from the real world of workers and their concerns.

An Ideal Labor Organization

An ideal labor organization, should include among other things, the following:

Some plan by which men would be stimulated to do the best work possible and such work would be recognized.

The greater ability or the greater application of one man as against another should be appreciated and rewarded.

Every legitimate incentive towards improving the character and quality of a man's work, as well as its amount, should be held out, and men of ambition and parts should not be held back or kept to the level of slothful, lazy or incompetent men.

All members of such an organization should agree that they would never take part in any strike unless they had an individual or personal grievance.[26]

Fantasizing of this sort came to an end with an unannounced visit from Franklin K. Lane, U.S. Secretary of Commerce. Rockefeller met with Lane on May 26 and heard President Wilson's proposal to create a strike settlement board, whose members would be named from the federal judiciary by the Chief Justice of the Supreme Court. Rockefeller promised to convey the plan to Welborn in Denver and did so. His attitude toward the proposal remains unknown. Welborn's rejection of it was forwarded through him to Secretary Lane early in June. Welborn maintained that the company was already the subject of a state and a federal investigation and could not handle yet another inquiry.

On the day following Rockefeller's meeting with Secretary Lane, the U.S. Commission on Industrial Relations convened in New York City to hear testimony on the Colorado strike. Two young women, the wives of miners, fresh from an interview with President Wilson at the White House, were the star witnesses. In simple affecting terms, they described the rigors of life in the Ludlow tent colony, and portrayed for a highly sympathetic audience the depredations of the coal companies and the militia. Following their appearance, the women were scheduled to tour the East Coast speaking in behalf of the strikers in an effort to raise funds.

The witness who followed them on the witness stand was also in the East to carry a message. Lieutenant Colonel Edward J. Boughton had served in the field with the Colorado militia during the strike and had headed the militia's self-appointed board of inquiry. He had been sent East by the governor in an attempt to counter the very negative impression of the state that the governor attributed to misinformation and misunderstanding about Ludlow. As Boughton related the details of the Ludlow engagement for the benefit of the commission, the responsibility for the tragedy rested squarely with the strikers.

The fourth and final witness of the day was Denver jurist Ben B. Lindsey, the founder and developer of the juvenile court system. Judge Lindsey had also been to see President Wilson and had come to New York hoping to meet with the senior Rockefeller. He supposed that Rockefeller would not knowingly accede to what was being done in his name in Colorado, but he had been unable to gain an interview. He detailed for the commission some of the things he wished the Rockefellers to know. He recounted that the coal companies were the leading opponents in Colorado of progressive, humanitarian reform. They led the opposition against safety legislation, against the enactment of workmen's compensation, and against the regulation of the hours of work and child labor. He told of corporate violence and of corporate dominance of political life, characterizing the situation in southern Colorado as a new feudalism. In concluding, he faulted the Rockefellers for their unwillingness to assume any responsibility for what happened and condemned them for their continued indifference to the plight of the miners, saying

> Kings have gone down among their people . . . lending then succor and help and not being so impersonal and above them that they would not listen to their woes . . . willing to lend something of themselves to really find the cause of these things, and help to solve them, and surely Mr. Rockefeller is no bigger than the President of the United States. He isn't any bigger than Kings, who have done it. But in the new feudalism that exists in Colorado, where towns are built up and owned by private corporations . . . these men refuse any present relation to conditions like these, refuse—those at the top—to listen to the wails and pleas and explanations and facts. . . . And I say that that attitude . . . is doing more to produce lawlessness and talk about confiscation and what they call anarchy than all the anarchists I know . . . [27]

Stung by these remarks and groping for some way to strike out in defense of his father and the family, Rockefeller now resolved upon two lines of action. He would launch a publicity campaign to explain the events in Colorado to the public. In so doing, the operators and his family would be exonerated. Simultaneously, he would support a long-term scientific investigation into labor-management relations that would identify the best means of achieving industrial harmony and peace in the future.

The idea of a publicity campaign had been considered earlier in the strike but had been rejected. Senior's view that any response to hostile criticism was of greater value to their opponents than to themselves had again proved persuasive. Now, however, Rockefeller reconsidered and broke with precedent. Ivy L. Lee and Herbert Casson were among the publicists recommended to him by newspaperman Arthur Brisbane. Lee just then was directing a unique publicity campaign for the Pennsylvania, New York Central, and B & O Railroads, trying in an unprecedented way to persuade the public and the Interstate Commerce Commission of the need for higher freight rates. Samuel Rea, president of the Pennsylvania Railroad, refused Lee's services to Rockefeller but agreed to permit him to provide advice so long as it didn't interfere with the rate campaign. Rockefeller accepted these terms and Lee was retained on June 4.

Brother-in-law Harold McCormick in Chicago thought Casson was not the best man for the kind of work Rockefeller had in mind and recommended James P. Brown in his stead. Brown was also retained. The amount and kind of work he did in the next several months is unknown. The largest part of the publicity program—a series of bulletins favorable to C.F. & I. that were mailed to influential figures in every city and state—was developed and executed by Lee and his assistants.

Jerome Greene had meanwhile contacted Charles W. Eliot, the president of Harvard University, who recommended Mackenzie King as a highly qualified labor relations expert. After two meetings with Rockefeller, Murphy, and Greene (the second of which took place at Senior's Tarrytown estate where the elder Rockefeller met King and participated in the discussions), King agreed to direct a broad and long-term investigation into labor–management relations under the auspices of the Rockefeller Foundation. He would begin on October 1, 1914, by which time he would have fulfilled his political commitments at home. In the interim, he would be available for consultation.

The terms of Rockefeller's arrangements with King, most particularly the October starting date, indicate that he had no idea how helpful King might be in dealing with the Colorado situation. He continued to consider other lines of action. He weighed the idea of asking Dr. Simon Flexner and Raymond Fosdick to conduct an investigation of the Colorado mining camps at first hand.

Both men were in Rockefeller's circle of advisors and had previous experience in conducting scientific inquiries. Whatever the reason, he decided not to ask them. Next, he asked his aides what they thought about giving the widest possible circulation to an antiunion diatribe that had recently appeared in *Popular Science Monthly*. Although even the most conservative of his advisors, Starr Murphy, found the language of the piece too strong, the article was eventually distributed through Ivy Lee. (Written by Professor John J. Stephenson of New York University, the piece suggested, among other things, that if workers had difficulty making ends meet the problem was of their own design: too many mouths to feed. All would be well once the surplus children died off.)

As he prepared to quit New York for the Maine seashore in late June, Rockefeller may have reflected upon the weight of mental baggage the Colorado strike obliged him to pack. Never had the family name been in lower repute. Never had he personally been a direct party to such controversy. The clamor following the Ludlow massacre still hadn't abated. During the previous two weeks, various contingents of anarchists, socialists, and Wobblies, had come up to Tarrytown from the city. As a precautionary measure, he had hired private detectives to keep a watch. On one occasion, Tarrytownsmen "took matters into their own hands" and abused anarchist Alexander Berkman and his comrades in true vigilante fashion.[28] When would it all end, and how?

Notes

1. From the eyewitness account of Don MacGregor of the *Denver Express*. Quoted in Beshoar (1942), p. 64.
2. Ibid., p. 2. The story of the strike has been told many times, most recently in Boemke (1983). In addition to the materials presented in volumes VII, VIII and IX of the *Final Report and Testimony* of the U.S. Commission on Industrial Relations, see McGovern and Guttridge (1972) and West (1915). A portion of the sketch presented here also derives from King diary entries that are explored more fully in Chapter 6.
3. John A. Fitch to Harris Weinstock 2/14/15. Charles McCarthy Papers, Box 19.
4. Gitelman (1973): pp. 1–23.
5. M. McCusker, "Report on Colorado Situation." Dated February 3, 1915, p. 35. U.S. Commission on Industrial Relations Papers.
6. W.L.M.K. Diary, 12/8/14. W.L.M.K. Papers, M. G. 26, Series J13,

p. G2539 118. The King Papers have been reorganized since my use of them. The page numbers cited throughout this volume are to the initial archival pagination while the dates given are those of the original diary entries and correspondence.

7. Carnegie (1965[1889]), p. 250. The major biography of the senior Rockefeller remains Nevins (1953), and that of his son, Fosdick (1956).

8. J. D. R., Jr. to William B. Wilson, 11/21/13. J. D. R., Jr. Papers, Business Interests, Box 21.

9. L. Bowers to J. D. R., Jr., 11/12/13. J. D. R., Jr. Papers, Business Interests, Box 23.

10. J. F. Welborn to Stockholders, 1/2/14. J. D. R., Jr. Papers, Business Interests, Box 13.

11. U.S. Congress, House of Representatives (1914) vol. II, p. 2, 874.

12. Fosdick (1956) p. 43.

13. J. D. R to J. D. R., Jr., 4/13/14. J. D. R., Jr. Papers, Personal, Box 26.

14. J. D. R., Jr. to J. D. R., 4/18/14. Ibid.

15. Beshoar (1942), p. 183.

16. J. D. R., Jr. to Woodrow Wilson, 4/27/14. J. D. R., Jr. Papers, Business Interests, Box 21.

17. M. A. Foster to J. D. R., Jr., 4/30/14. Ibid.

18. Jensen (1974), p. 74.

19. Lippmann (1970[1915]), pp. 264–65. Reprinted from the *New Republic* (January 30, 1915).

20. Bertrand Russell's definition (1938), p. 35.

21. Memorandum, 6/10/14. J. D. R., Jr. Papers, Business Interests, Box 21.

22. "Mr. Rockefeller's Concessions." *New York Evening Post* (May 1, 1914).

23. Undated draft of letter to L. M. Bowers and J. F. Welborn. J. D. R., Jr. Papers, Business Interests, Box 22.

24. J. D. Greene to J. D. R., Jr., 5/21/14. Ibid.

25. J. D. Greene to J. D. R., Jr., 5/21/14. Ibid. (A different memorandum from the one previously cited.)

26. Unsigned memorandum, 5/22/14. Ibid.

27. U.S. Commission on Industrial Relations (1916), vol. VII, p. 6,404.

28. J. D. R., Jr. to James P. Brown, 6/30/14. J. D. R., Jr. Papers, Business Interests, Box 23.

2. New Counselors

In retrospect, neither of the steps Rockefeller took in early June 1914 yielded the results he anticipated. His major strategem for dealing with the Colorado situation, Ivy Lee's publicity campaign, backfired to produce new difficulties. The long-term investigation into labor problems for which Mackenzie King was retained, also fell flat. It resulted in the publication in 1919 of a book that, whatever its merits, was without practical or lasting effect. Yet Rockefeller, King, and Lee would look back on their association as one of the most gratifying in their lives. Each of them came away with warm memories of enduring comradeship and vital achievement.

This seeming paradox of fulfillment in the face of failure dissolves on noting that the three men shared unanticipated successes of such grand proportions that their setbacks were trivialized. Each man reaped a windfall from the association, different in each instance but no less potent as a force of affirmation. The creative energies released in developing and introducing employee representation altered each man's destiny at least as much as it did the course of American industrial relations.

The younger Rockefeller had long acquiesced in the policy of avoiding publicity in disputes affecting his father. Though both he and his mentor Frederick Gates believed in the power of publicity, they had consistently bowed to Senior's judgment that any response would prove counter-productive. Better to suffer attacks in silence than give credence to the attackers by responding.

From his earliest days in the office, when Gates had provided the anecdotal evidence that vindicated his father, Rockefeller supposed that, if only the true story could be presented to the public, much of the hostility toward Senior would disappear. As he saw it, discord and animus sprang from misunderstanding or misinformation, whereas publicity meant the dissemination of the truth. This view had led him, at one point, to encourage publisher Frederick N. Doubleday to interview Senior and publish his reminiscences. Now, in the wake of Ludlow, it led him to set Ivy Lee to work. How self-satisfied he was as he added the names of friends and acquaintances to Lee's mailing list, as if each new name redeemed another sinner.

It never occurred to Rockefeller that the truth might be both more inaccessible and less monolithic than he supposed. His tidy universe of moral absolutes afforded little room for the scattering properties of either relativism or ambiguity. When coupled with his and his advisors' complete ignorance of industrial relations, this simplistic outlook led to a number of fresh embarrassments. The one man who might have been expected to shield him from such blunders was instead a party to them.

Ivy Lee made a highly favorable impression on Rockefeller from the start. The Georgia-born son of a Methodist minister, Lee was younger by three years but seemed much more knowledgeable and worldly wise. Though he took himself as seriously as Rockefeller, he combined a certain modish flair with an element of southern courtliness that added to his affability without detracting from the confidence he inspired. When they met in the spring of 1914, Lee was not quite a self-made man.

Lee's career had been highly checkered. Following graduation from Princeton, he had entered the Harvard Law School only to find himself without the financial resources to continue. He then worked for a number of years as a newspaper reporter and subsequently as a free-lance press agent. Between his easy spending habits and the vagaries of fee-for-service publicity work, feast and famine were equally familiar companions. This was probably why he eventually accepted the security of salaried employment with the Pennsylvania Railroad. But his professional commitments were so unsettled that in 1909 he took a flyer and moved abroad to organize European branch offices for a New York brokerage firm. On his return several years later, he rejoined the Pennsylvania Railroad as executive assistant to its president.

When Rockefeller approached him, Lee was directing a publicity campaign that was as novel in its objective as it was in its tactics. The railroads had a request for a freight rate increase pending before the Interstate Commerce Commission. In an unprecedented maneuver, Lee was attempting to enlist public support for the increase. Initially, he had relied on conventional releases to newspapers. But as the campaign wore on, he prepared leaflets and more elaborate bulletins for distribution to Pennsy stock and bond holders, employees, and customers. In the effort to win over an even broader and more influential body of opinion, his bulletins were next circulated to a national mailing

Ivy Lee, 1934. By permission of the Library of Congress.

list that included professionals of all sorts, public officials, and businessmen. Lee and the officers of the railroad also made numerous public appearances before civic and fraternal groups in their bid for support.

When the Interstate Commerce Commission eventually approved the rate increase, in December 1914, Lee's reputation as an effective publicist was assured. But even prior to this victory, he had won the confidence of the Rockefellers. They invited him to become a full-fledged member of Senior's advisory staff, which he did on January 1, 1915. The personal and corporate contacts he made through this association assured his future in public relations. Which of these overlapping successes was the more consequential for his subsequent career is impossible to say.

When Lee was retained on June 4, 1914, he was authorized to employ a confidential assistant and another aide who was to go out to Colorado to collect and transmit materials. These arrangements were required because, it will be recalled, Lee's own services were available to Rockefeller only on a spare-time basis. While continuing to direct the railroad campaign, Lee was supposed to develop a publicity program that would win a favorable public opinion for the Colorado coal mine operators. Not surprisingly, he simply adapted one of his rate campaign strategies.

Fifteen bulletins labeled "Facts Concerning the Struggle in

Colorado for Industrial Freedom"[1] were prepared through the summer and autumn of 1914 and sent to the roughly forty thousand influential individuals and organizations on Lee's mailing list. As their title indicates, the bulletins were supposed to present factual information about the strike. The presumption was that the facts would enable readers to make their own determination of right and wrong in the strike, and lead them to support the operators' position. A committee of the operators provided practically all of the material content of the bulletins from Denver, while Lee, from Philadelphia, oversaw the editing, production, and distribution.

That both Rockefeller and Lee viewed publicity as a way of disseminating the truth was entirely consistent with that aspect of the Progressive ethos that sought reform through exposure. In this sense, public relations was surely a creature of its age. Where the muckrakers, for example, strove to provoke change by baring the hard-edged truth, public relations sought a similar end through a similar, but soothing, means. The crucial distinction that seems so obvious, that self-interested publicity is much more likely in its selectivity to distort the truth, escaped Rockefeller because he thought himself above petty self-interest. Ivy Lee, on the other hand, had no equivalent filter to shield him from this awareness.

To Lee, the presentation of facts meant putting the client's best foot forward. While he might on occasion admit that that foot had perhaps a minor blemish, it would never do to admit that the other foot might be gangrenous. The facts, which he equated with truth telling, were effectively selected to serve the purposes of the client. As his otherwise uncritical biographer concluded, "Most of the bulletins contained matter which on the surface was true but which presented the facts in such a way as to give a total picture that was false."[2] Even this judgment will be shown to be too forgiving.

Early responses to the bulletins from chambers of commerce, manufacturers associations, churchmen, educators, and the like were highly encouraging to the Rockefeller camp. The bulletins thus appeared from the start to have precisely the effect wished for them. Rockefeller was delighted, and began to weigh the possibility of adding Ivy Lee to his father's staff.

At the same time, Rockefeller was also party to an effort to block the publication of a report on the strike hostile to his interests. Under the auspices of the Federal Council of Churches, the Reverend H. S. Atkinson had prepared *The Church and Industrial*

Warfare: A Report on the Labor Troubles in Colorado and Michigan. At the end of July, Jerome Greene informed Rockefeller that his attempt "to bring pressures from various sources . . . to prevent them from publishing the superficial, inaccurate, and unjust report" had proved unsuccessful.[3]

The record files are silent about how Rockefeller and his advisors rationalized their effort to suppress an opposing view. Nor would this be the only such incident. Rockefeller attempted to block another critical report several years later. The sponsor of this later report was also a philanthropic organization, which may help explain his apparent double standard toward the truth.

In overseeing his father's business interests, Rockefeller repeatedly demonstrated a reluctance to intervene. In most instances, because his father's stock represented a minority holding, he was even unsure about his *right* to intervene. He also thought himself lacking in sufficient personal authority to have influence with most of the corporate managers. Such constraining doubts were nowhere in evidence in his management of his father's philanthropic interests. In this realm, he had all the confidence of an expert manager and the influence of a major donor. Consequently, he possessed both the authority and the power to have his say—if not always his way—in matters philanthropic.

This does not explain, however, why he chose to use his power in so partisan and self-serving a manner. Since he could never admit to intentionally committing a wrongful act, the question is: What story did he tell himself to justify his actions? Of the several plausible explanations, the most obvious one is the one best supported by the fuller evidence surrounding the second attempt at suppression. Here it may be sufficient to note that both attempts at suppression were rationalized by assertions that the points of view adopted by the authors reflected biases unfair to the true (i.e., Rockefeller's) understanding of the matter. Either the bias must be removed or the report blocked; otherwise, the good for which he and philanthropy strove would be undermined.

The extraordinary consistency with which the truth coincided with his own point of view sprung not from Rockefeller's greater understanding—in all humility he would have denied any such claim—but from his lack of bias. Believing himself selflessly at work in the service of humanity, he thought himself immune to the distortions of self-interest or partisanship. His was the commonplace arrogance of righteousness. It was only the mildest of manners and a lingering doubt about his own self-worth that saved him from an excess of hyprocrisy.

On the first day of August, Rockefeller wrote to Mackenzie King to ask him to develop more fully some ideas expressed at their first meeting. At that time, Rockefeller had wondered if there wasn't some way, short of unionism, for an employer to maintain close contact with his employees. Now, during Ivy Lee's vacation from the Pennsylvania Railroad, Rockefeller had arranged to have the publicist visit Colorado. He had asked Lee to survey the scene and come up with suggestions for developing the future labor policies of C.F. & I. King's ideas might prove helpful to Lee, and so Rockefeller wrote to request an outline for

> some organization in the mining camps which will assure to the employees the opportunity for collective bargaining, for easy and constant conferences with reference to any matters of difference or any grievances which may come up, and any other advantages which may be derived from membership in the union.[4]

By the terms of their June agreement, the study of industrial relations that King was to conduct was not to get underway until October. He had consented, however, to provide Rockefeller with counsel during the interim. Now, in reply to Rockefeller's query, King responded with a six-page memorandum in which he sketched his thoughts about employee representation. He apologized profusely, saying that only hours after receipt of the request, the declaration of war between Great Britain (and therefore Canada) and the Central Powers had been announced. In the ensuing excitement, he had hardly found time to compose more than a hasty sketch of his ideas. Little did he or his reader sense how profoundly his "rough outline" would alter their lives.[5]

In May, just days before his first communication from Rockefeller, William Lyon Mackenzie King had despaired of his situation. In the solitude of his diary he had cried: "How terribly broken down on every side is the house of life around me!"[6] For three years now, since the 1911 rout that had swept the Liberal Party from office and cost King both his seat in Parliament and the Labour portfolio, he had been unable to find a suitable outlet for his talents or his ambition. The party leaders encouraged him but proved unable to make possible his return to Parliament. Adequate employment hadn't come to hand either, so he had found it necessary to do a bit of this (speaking and article writing) and a bit of that (editing the party magazine) to get by. But none of it was sufficient. The challenges, the income, and the satisfactions of these days failed in every measure to content him. The unhappy parallel he drew between his own personal plight and that of the war-menaced world only intensified his feelings of futility and helplessness.

Such were King's ambition and desire for useful service that he tended to look upon his already considerable achievements as mere prologue. Like a man half his age, at 40, he was certain that his future accomplishments would easily overshadow his past attainments.

All his life King had told himself and known in his bones that he was destined to lead Canada and accomplish great things. He would reclaim the honor of his family, enhance the lives of working people, win public recognition of his abilities and virtues, and earn a welcomed degree of financial security. His enormous self-confidence emanated partly from an awareness of the obstacles surmounted thus far. But he was also convinced that providential forces directed his life. The present underemployment of his energies was distressing, not merely because so much remained to be accomplished, but because he feared Providence had forsaken him. So complete was the marriage of his ambition with his piety that, without the slightest hint of self-consciousness or sacrilege, Mackenzie King took himself to be an instrument of God.

Born and raised in the town of Berlin (now Kitchener), Ontario, King's beginnings were unremarkable save for the fact that his family had achieved historical notoriety. Both the Kings and Mackenzies had come to Canada from Scotland after 1820. Grandfather Mackenzie had prospered with the growing country, rising from printer to newspaper proprietor and public figure. He served as the first mayor of Toronto and sat in the legislative assembly. Then, in 1837, his role in an abortive rebellion against the colonial government brought his undoing. Fearful for his life, he fled with his family across the border and into exile. The American authorities promptly clapped him into prison. Only with the granting of an amnesty was he able to return to Canada, but never during his lifetime did he or his family erase the scars of his downfall. His youngest daugher, stung with the hurt of privation and diminished station, nurtured in her first son the hope for vindication.

The son, for his part, absorbed everything he could about his grandfather and accepted his mother's dream as the burden of his life. He sought to deserve and fulfill his destiny by paying scrupulous attention to the purification of his body and mind. But in this he was not entirely successful.

A devout Presbyterian, he read scripture daily and annotated his Bible with reflections on passages that moved him. He eschewed tobacco and card playing entirely, and permitted himself only the smallest amount of social drinking. Little of his self-discipline touched him with either rancor or the vanity of self-denial. On the contrary, he positively enjoyed the elements of his regimen. He found both solace and great wisdom in the Bible; sermons and hymns moved him deeply. In cautious moderation more secular pleasures also appealed to him. He loved the theater, opera, social dancing, and the company of women. Had he been less serious in life purpose, he feared such enjoyments might have led him to fritter away his talents.

There had been a time when self-indulgence threatened his doom. As a young man, he had vainly striven to master his sexual impulses. Then, following the accidental death of his best friend, he appears to have overpowered and repressed his sex drive. It was as if he bound himself in a compact with God, in the manner of a covenanting southern (U.S.) Presbyterian. Though ever attracted to women, he would subsequently remain celibate. His deepest attachments would be to married and therefore inaccessible women.

The law, the ministry, social work, and college teaching had each held some attraction for young Mackenzie. All were callings through which he thought he might render useful service to humanity and achieve personal success. One by one he had rejected them; miraculously, it seemed to him. For although he knew well enough why he turned his back on one possibility or another, he rarely had any immediate alternative to take its place. He abandoned the study of law despite his father's hopes and urging to the contrary. A short residency at Hull House in Chicago convinced him that settlement house or social work was not his forte. As if guided by a plan beyond his ken, he resisted each career possibility only to end up in the most promising one of all. In 1897, he transferred from the graduate program in sociology at the University of Chicago to the economics program at Harvard. He became a student of labor problems and very quickly made an impact.

While still a graduate student, he influenced the policies of the Canadian government by exposing the sweatshop conditions under which its militia uniforms were produced. The Liberal government responded by requiring fair wages and working conditions of all suppliers wishing to do business with it. Then, at the request of the Consumers League of Massachusetts, King undertook a similar factfinding survey of the working conditions of sales people in Boston department stores. Again exposure resulted in reform. As his course of studies drew to a close, he was faced with the choice of joining the Harvard faculty or returning to Canada to organize and edit the government's new *Labour Gazette*. Given his sense of destiny, the decision was not a difficult one to make. He returned to Ottawa.

The next eight years, from 1900 through 1907, were filled with practical experience. Under his direction, the *Gazette* built a reputation for the fair and accurate reporting of labor statistics and the coverage of a wide array of work-related topics. In the course of this endeavor, King came to know the situation in many industries at first hand. He frequently served as a mediator in industrial disputes. With this background, he drafted the dominion's primary labor law, the Industrial Disputes Investigation Act of 1907. In this innovative legislation, he sought to establish the state as "an impartial umpire"[7] in industrial relations.

King's diversity of talents rendered his services increasingly valuable to the Liberal government. When a labor expert or an especially tactful negotiator was required for a royal commission, an international or imperial conference, King was often selected. In recognition of his service, the government placed him on the King's Honours List and the party leadership actively encouraged him in his decision to plunge into politics. In 1908, he stood for Parliament and easily carried what had been thought a doubtful district. Soon after, when an independent Labour Ministry was created, he was given its portfolio. At 35, he was a recognized authority in industrial relations, an experienced bureaucrat, and an influential figure in Canadian politics. These accomplishments he viewed as but a prelude to the loftier goals of the premiership and the liberal reform of society.

Although he probably preferred to think of himself as a Christian Socialist, Mackenzie King was a thoroughgoing liberal. His position is to be explained partly by what he opposed and partly by what he favored. From either perspective, his liberalism was something more than a purely intellectual stance. It reflected his tastes and his ambition as well.

The conservative admonition to allow social forces to run their own course, devil take the hindmost, struck King as purely self-serving. Society had good reason to wish to intervene to limit the power of private persons. For such power, bound up in great concentrations of wealth, was likely to severely reduce the opportunities available to the people. Yet the common people composed the great mass from which sprang the talented and ambitious. Unless society made certain that such people found ways to pursue and realize their goals, it would stagnate. The upward mobility of the gifted and able (like himself) was the dynamo of capitalistic society and human progress.

King's second, more temperamental, objection to the conservative position stemmed from the contempt in which he held the conspicuous consumption of its wealthiest supporters. Their lavish displays and diversions he knew to be purchased at the expense of struggling working people. He was equally certain that their gratification of every whim and fancy robbed them of strength of character. The stakes here went well beyond the individual. As King saw it, the character of those who served as society's standard bearers shaped its destiny. Leaders of honesty and integrity provided the one best, possibly the only, guarantee that social injustices and inequities would be corrected. Weak and corrupt leaders, in contrast, reduced cohesion by making cynics and revolutionaries of those who perceived the growth of and inattention to social wrongs. The reform of the social order and its cohesion were thus predicated on the character of its leaders.

King possessed a strong and persistent desire for economic security. He worried most of his life about money, even after it was no longer a problem, thanks largely to his association with Rockefeller. As he repeatedly told his diary, he was less concerned for creature comforts than for the immunity from the pressures and temptations inherent in public life, that economic security would provide. He also wanted to be free to subordinate gainseeking private activity to more consequential public affairs.

In this, perhaps more than anywhere else, King seems to have deceived himself. His taste for social pleasures and his habit of fussing with his surroundings (the folly he built at Woodsmere, for example) suggest how dearly he valued creature comforts. Perhaps the great puzzle of his biography—the question of why a man who all his life aspired to reform society, eschewed reform in favor of the blandest expediency once he attained power—is to be unravelled here. Perhaps, the fuel that economic insecurity provided for his ambition was spent once he banked his Rockefeller dollars. This and several alternative explanations are indicative of how much work remains toward understanding King.

The Socialist position held as little attraction for King as the Tory one. The prospect of an all-controlling State suggested a tyranny no less destructive of the independence and initiative of

W. L. Mackenzie King, September 1914. By permission of the National Archives of Canada.

common folk than concentrated wealth under capitalism. There was, moreover, no reason to believe that the demonstrably productive incentive of private property could be replaced by another as hazy as that on which the socialists counted. He thought them particularly guilty of the fallacy of endowing the collectivity of men with dominant motives, of selflessness and cooperation, not obviously dominant in individuals. They patched over this logical chasm with faith, he thought, and then took great pride in being scientific. Nor did it help their cause in his eyes that the personal behavior of some socialists was as objectionable as that of some industrial barons. On King's first visit to England, while still a graduate student, he had been particularly offended by the way several of the women in the Fabian Society flaunted their freedom from bourgeois conventions. Among other things, they smoked, and in public.

As this suggests, King was quite firmly attached to traditional social mores. While on social questions—trade unionism, equity in the distribution of income, and limiting corporate power—he took positions in advance of many of his contemporaries, in behavioral matters—questions of manners, decorum, and character—he was if anything more old-fashioned and unbending than most. Quite possibly, it was the opposing pulls of these tastes and intellectual commitments that lay at the heart of his liberalism, reining in his ardor for change while at the same time pushing him beyond the complacency of his somewhat dusty gentility. He wished for social reform, sensed that it was bound to come, and hoped to lead it. But he also believed that it was essential to preserve some aspects of present society. Thus, unlike the conservatives, he wanted change, and unlike the radicals, he wanted to save some things. The balance of these discordant preferences was resolved in the name of social reform by his ambition.

King's liberalism bore a remarkable resemblance to the progressive views of his older American counterpart, John R. Commons. Both men were among the foremost students of industrial relations in their respective countries. They both regarded unions as necessary structural components of industrial society, seeing in them the workers' primary means to fairness and equity. Both men also welcomed the intervention of the state into economic and social affairs, provided only that the intervention was clearly delimited. And both tempered their strong preferences for private property by favoring expansions of public ownership into the realms of natural resources, transportation, and communication.

These ideological similarities are largely explained by the evidence that King and Commons drew their intellectual inspiration from the identical mix of sources. In Commons's case this meant German historicism filtered through and coupled with the Christian Socialism of Richard T. Ely. King absorbed many of the same precepts through the teachings of Arnold Toynbee and his students.

In practice, King diverged further from his liberalism than Commons from his progressivism. Since practice often renders theory imperfect, such a result might have been expected. First as a bureaucrat and then as a politician, King became actively involved in industrial dispute settlement and policy implementation. Commons, in contrast, retained his status as a scholar and experienced less vulnerability to his career. A particularly crucial divergence developed around King's ideas about union formation.

While King always believed the organization of unions necessary and desirable, he developed an antipathy toward strikes for recognition that was highly incongruous if not contradictory. P. Craven has shown that King began his career with a serious underestimate of the value of "recognition strikes."[8] As the result of his experience as a mediator, he grew increasingly opposed to them. He came to believe that recognition strikes afforded little or no opportunity for compromise. Either one side conceded defeat or the other had to; a mediator was bound to fail. To a strong-willed romantic like King, this frustration was enervating. It not only thwarted his need for achievement, but belied his presumption that reason and intelligence could always overawe conflict. Recalling King's revolutionary heritage, it seems likely that his thoughts about conflict and accommodation also had a deep and personal edge to them.

In any event, King's idiosyncratic attitude toward recognition strikes served as the linchpin of his relationship with Rockefeller. At their first interview, Rockefeller had talked about the Colorado strike and mentioned the union's demand for recognition. King responded with his condemnation of such strikes. From that point, we may understand why they got along famously.

But consider the luck of Rockefeller's draw! The likelihood of finding another expert who both favored worker organization and deplored recognition strikes from among such contemporaries as Commons, John Graham Brooks, Earl Dean Howard, William Leiserson, Joseph Willets and Robert Valentine, bordered on the impossible. It was not because they appreciated these

odds, however, but because they imagined their lives directed by
Providence that both men attached so much meaning to their discovery of one another.

At their first meeting, Rockefeller had asked King to prepare
an outline for a broad study of industrial relations, and to provide
the names of people he thought best qualified to direct such a
study. King initially agreed only to do the latter. On returning to
Ottawa, he received first a wire and then a letter from Jerome
Greene, urging upon him the position of study director.

> We are now prepared to go so far as to invite your earnest con-
> sideration of the proposal that you should enlist under the aus-
> pices of the Rockefeller Foundation in the great problem of
> industrial relations, with a special view to the discovery of some
> organization or union, or at any rate of some mutual relation-
> ship of capital and labor which would afford to labor the pro-
> tection it needs against oppression and exploitation, while at
> the same time promoting its efficiency as an instrument of eco-
> nomic production.[9]

Only with the receipt of this offer did King have to weigh the
pros and cons of associating himself with Rockefeller. The obvious benefits were the boost to his income, and engagement in an
eminently worthwhile project. The negatives were all tied in with
that name, Rockefeller.

Like a Rorschach inkblot, the name was subject to any interpretation the imagination and social background might suggest.
It carried a staggering number of free and random associations.
It was the object of hate and fear, of envy and adulation—almost
every sentiment save neutrality. At the very least, the name presented a three-dimensional problem. One dimension turned on
the judgment of whether the Rockefeller fortune had been accumulated through means (1) foul, corrupt, and rapacious; (2) un-
savory but legal and shrewd; or (3) fair, sound, and uncommonly
astute. A second problem that arose, no matter how the first was
resolved, turned on the *power* of the fortune: How much power
and of what kinds and for what purposes and through what channels? These were matters about which very few knew anything
concrete but on which many held strong opinions. And last, a
third problem turned on the moral and political judgment of
whether such a concentration of wealth and power was at all con-
sonant with democratic ideals. Many people had good reason to

suppose that those who commanded great wealth and power used them to their own advantage and not in the interest of society.

The Rockefeller name had become notorious through more than two decades of federal and state investigations, court and muckraking exposures. Most influential among the latter were Henry Demarest Lloyd's *Wealth Against Commonwealth* in 1894; Ida M. Tarbell's *History of the Standard Oil Company*, which first appeared in serial form in *McClure's Magazine* in 1902; and Thomas W. Lawson's *Frenzied Finance*, serialized in *Everybody's Magazine* in 1904. Each of these works roundly condemned the business practices of Standard Oil and its leading figure, John D. Rockefeller. Balanced unevenly upon the scales of public judgment were Rockefeller's philanthropy, his *Random Reminiscences of Men and Events*, appearing in 1909, and his personal achievements: Standard Oil, wealth, and power.

The Colorado strike and the tragedy at Ludlow were thus only the latest supplement to the provocations of the Rockefeller name. Quite naturally, King wondered whether an association would besmirch and destroy his reputation. He traveled to New York for a second meeting. Again Rockefeller disarmed him by appearing so utterly uncomplicated and well intentioned. The depth of his religious feelings proved decisive. King concluded that there could be no evil or deviousness in so simple and unpretentious a man.

But Mackenzie King was also intoxicated with the possibilities for doing good that lay within Rockefeller's power. Such headiness was not an uncommon response among those coming within the aura of seemingly limitless wealth. Of course, King discounted the importance of mere monetary rewards in his own motivation. He needed to see himself as a man above such concerns, even if he was not. It was the nobility of the cause and the purity of Rockefeller's character that he felt determined his course. He said yes.

In contrast to the deliberate calculation by which King was led to his decision, Rockefeller embraced King immediately. In this, he surprised himself more than anyone, for he rarely experienced strong surges of emotion or acted spontaneously. Almost forty years later, in interviews with his biographer, he continued to express amazement at his response. Returning repeatedly to the subject of his first meeting with King, he recalled: "Seldom have I been so impressed by a man at first appearance," and "My first impression of him was overwhelming."[10]

Perhaps what Rockefeller saw in King was his alter ego. The two men were exact contemporaries, aged forty, about the same height and weight, with King perhaps a few pounds heavier. Rockefeller was the handsomer of the two, his square jaw and aquiline nose conferring an air of decisiveness altogether absent from King's almost pudgy features. Whatever their physical similarities and differences, their personalities were in many ways perfect counterpoints to each other. King's sensitivity to the feelings of others and his poise put most people at ease, while his clever conversation by turns charmed and impressed them. In contrast, Rockefeller placed a stiff formality between himself and the world. His practiced defenses made it impossible for him to let himself go even with those he trusted most completely. Mackenzie King would never be Bill or Rex but always Mr. King, as Raymond Fosdick would never be Ray but always Mr. Fosdick. And he was to everyone, always, Mr. Rockefeller, Junior. When he first entered his father's office, he was for a time referred to as Junior but never to his face. Only a very few family friends addressed him as John.

Bereft of a sense of humor, Rockefeller seemed colorless and introverted. He would have seemed uninteresting, too, but he was far too rich for that. Instead, he was regarded by most acquaintances as a serious and humble young man. In contrast, King exuded a lively self-confidence that came across less as arrogance than as the by-product of a serious involvement with weighty ideas. Though both men would have acknowledged themselves duty-bound servants of humanity, King's brand of service, like his life, was of his own original robust design. Rockefeller's life and service, at 40, remained impositions of his family. As he later recalled

> Our attitude was due entirely to Mother, who talked to us constantly about *duty*—and displeasing the Lord—and paining your parents. She instilled a personal consciousness of right and wrong, training our wills and getting us to do the things we ought to do . . .[11]

Rockefeller and his three sisters had been raised in comparative isolation, with private tutors and a narrow circle of approved friends. His devout Baptist parents adhered to a rigid behavioral code that forbade not merely the vices (e.g., drinking, smoking, and gambling) but most forms of amusement as well. Music alone

John D. Rockefeller and John D. Rockefeller, Jr., Easter 1914 or 1915.
By permission of the Rockefeller Archive Center.

among the arts met with their approval. The young Rockefeller did not venture onto a dance floor or into a theater until he was in college. His matriculation at Brown University exposed him to a wider circle of people than ever before, but left his quite conventional prejudices intact. From college, he went directly into his father's office. His tutelage under Gates, and then his marriage to the cultured and spontaneous Abby Aldrich in 1901, expanded somewhat the narrow range of his training and tastes.

His father's role in young Rockefeller's upbringing appears to have been highly indirect. The children heard him talk with their mother and sometimes with business associates. But Senior appears to have been taciturn in the extreme in his personal dealings with the children. John, Jr. always knew that as the only male heir, his father's fortune would one day be his. However, apart from encouraging him to keep accounts of his allowance and expenditures, his father made no personal effort to prepare him for this responsibility. Fortunately, Frederick Gates would prove an excellent teacher. Yet this coldness in Senior had its price. His son admired and respected him immensely. He also feared him a good deal. In contrast, his mother was his ally and his affection for her knew no bounds. When, years later, he was asked to explain why he and Mackenzie King had hit it off so well together, he began with, "First, we had mothers whom we both adored."[12] Rockefeller never acknowledged—perhaps, he never understood—that King's greatest contribution would be to free him from the grip of his father.

Notes

1. A file of the bulletins is included among the C.F. & I. papers, J. D. R., Jr. Papers, Business Interests, On the retention of Lee's services, see Jerome D. Greene to I. L. Lee, 6/4,14; Starr Murphy to J. D. R., Jr., 7/8/14; and J. D. R., Jr. to J. D. R., 11/4/14. J. D. R., Jr. Papers, Business Interests, Boxes 22, 20; Friends and Services, Box 15.
2. Hiebert (1966), p. 101.
3. Jerome D. Greene to J. D. R., Jr., 7/31/14. J. D. R., Jr. Papers, Business Interests, Box 22.
4. J. D. R., Jr. to W. L. M. K. 8/1/14. Quoted in Fosdick (1956), pp. 154ff.
5. W. L. M. K. to J. D. R., Jr., 8/6/14. W. L. M. K. Papers. Mg 26, Series J1, vol. 24.
6. W. M. L. K. Diary, 5/12/14. W. M. L. K. Papers, MG 26, Series J13.
7. The phrase is from Craven (1980). In addition to this valuable work,

see Dawson (1958), Hardy (1949), Stacey (1976), and English and Stubbs (1978).

8. Craven (1980), pp. 66, 235, 266, and 270. On Commons, see his autobiography (1963).

9. J. D. Greene to W. L. M. K., 6/19/14. W. L. M. K. Papers, Series J4, File 187.

10. Raymond B. Fosdick, "Conversations with J. D. R., Jr." Typescripts dated 9/17/52 and 1/1/53. J. D. R. Jr. Papers.

11. Fosdick (1956), p. 43.

12. Fosdick, "Conversations with J. D. R., Jr." Typescript dated 10/23/52. J. D. R., Jr. Papers.

3. Enduring Bonds

In early August 1914, King responded to Rockefeller's request for advice by outlining a scheme of employee representation. King proposed that the miners at Colorado Fuel & Iron elect representatives from among their ranks. These representatives, in turn, would meet periodically with company officials. In this way, the company would create a direct link to the miners and vice versa. Both parties would thus have the opportunity to learn about any problems and to respond before these could escalate into disagreement and conflict. King proposed that this arrangement cover all questions affecting the terms and conditions of employment, as well as any grievances. Moreover, if it proved impossible for the company and the representatives to reach agreement, he proposed that an appeals procedure extending outside the firm be provided, as a guarantee of fair dealing.

Although King never publicly admitted it, the germ of the ideas he transmitted sprang from a "practice of the Royal Mounted Police."[1] In the more sparsely settled districts of Canada, the Mounties did not wait for crimes or conflicts to be reported. Instead they travelled through the frontier areas and called on the inhabitants to learn of any difficulties. In this way, they both gave visible presence to the forces of law and order and served the peace-keeping needs of the settlers.

If Rockefeller reflected on this representation scheme at all, he may have been swayed to it by King's use of a rhetorical device that he himself often employed. This involved portraying the ideas that were to be rejected as polar extremes, so that the preferred position could be made to appear to occupy a sensible middle ground. King, in defending collective bargaining, argued that the individual contract and a union contract incorporating recognition were undesirable extremes. In the one case management held all of the power, while in the other the power resided with the union officers. True collective bargaining, he maintained, should provide capital and labor with an equal footing. A company bargaining with representatives drawn from among its own employees seemed the fairest arrangement. As he put it,

> Between the extreme of individual agreements . . . and an agreement involving recognition of unions of national or international character . . . lies the straight acceptance of the principle of Collective Bargaining between capital and labour immediately concerned in any certain industry or group of industries and the construction of machinery which will afford opportunity of easy and constant conference between employers and employed . . . [2]

The crucial point for both Rockefeller and King was that the representation scheme avoided unionism. For this reason Rockefeller went along even though, as later developments would reveal, he never fully accepted the idea of collective bargaining. From King's point of view, his scheme would give the miners everything except what he regarded as the hollow victory of union recognition. They would have their union in fact, a bargaining agent and grievance machinery, without having it in name.

Rockefeller sent copies of King's letter to Denver for the consideration of company officers. In independent responses, Bowers and C.F. & I. president Welborn indicated the unwisdom of any action along the lines proposed. They thought such a move would make it appear that they were trying to repair grievances that they had all along contended did not exist. Moreover, they noted, the union now seemed prepared to waive the issue of recognition in exchange for a three-year trial of some sort of grievance machinery. If the operators were to take any of the steps recommended by King, the union would claim a major victory and the miners would join in droves.

From his vantage point in Denver, Ivy Lee concurred. Although he agreed with King on the need for some sort of grievance machinery, the timing was not propitious. His brief survey of C.F. & I., he informed Rockefeller, had revealed that

> The men are very well paid, and the policy of the management is most enlightened as to all important subjects. But the mine superintendents and petty bosses have all the faults of their kind and the Company has no assurance that its policies are being carried out. There is no appeal (in practice) from the de-

cision of the pit boss . . . the men are afraid to complain or appeal . . .³

Though this was the first word Rockefeller had received from one of his own people, indicating that the C.F. & I. miners may have had some real grounds for complaint, Lee's revelation produced no change in his views on the strike. He simply deferred to the judgment of the Denver officers and decided that for the present nothing would be done along the lines of King's suggestion.

Lee also forwarded the first evidence of the critical role played in the strike by John C. Osgood. Osgood, Lee reported, was the dominant voice on the committee that directed the operators' strategy. He had previously owned C.F. & I. and now directed the Victor-American Fuel Company. Welborn had once served under him as a bookkeeper, and rumor had it that he permitted himself to be bossed by Osgood. Lee reported that Osgood was rabidly antiunion and inflexible to the point of being oblivious to the consequences of his actions for others. This was particularly undesirable since it was the Rockefellers who had ultimately to answer for whatever was done in the operators' name. Local sentiment, Lee advised, was strongly biased against the Rockefellers. Many people believed they were exploiting Colorado for their own pecuniary gain. Lee recommended that they give some attention to the question of how to correct this false impression.

Rockefeller sent the letters of Welborn, Bowers, and Lee along to King so that he would understand why changes could not be introduced at this time. He made no reference to Lee's comment about the mine superintendents and pit bosses. In his response, however, King fixed on this portion of Lee's letter, citing it as proof of the need for grievance machinery. He gave no more than the merest suggestion that he thought the origin of the strike lay here. But he too agreed that nothing should be done that might convey an impression of victory for the union.

Intelligence that the union was reformulating its position reached Ivy Lee through the commanding officer of the federal troops in the strike zone. According to this source, the local U.M.W. leaders were going to inform President Wilson's conciliation commission that the union would waive the demand for recognition in exchange for the creation of some sort of grievance machinery. The national officers of the union also were going to endorse this new position and transmit it to the President. The implication of these developments, Lee noted, was that should the President's commission adopt the union's proposition, it would reach the operators and the public as if it were an impartial proposal from a public body. This would make it hard to resist.

Actually, Lee was badly misinformed by his confidante. The proposal he reported as a union strategem was part of a more elaborate plan developed by the two-man commission itself, "after consultation with the Secretary of Labor."[4] This plan provided for a three-year truce accompanied by strict enforcement of Colorado mining and labor statutes; the reemployment of all strikers not guilty of a crime; the prohibition of intimidation of either union or nonunion miners; and the establishment of miner-elected grievance committees at each mine. The plan further required that the union waive its recognition demand and suspend all militant organizing tactics, and called for the creation of an arbitration commission with power to resolve all issues on which the parties could not reach agreement.

The President's conciliators, through much of the summer of 1914, found their way to a settlement blocked by an internal union dispute. The local U.M.W. officers were not as prepared as the national officers to cede the recognition demand. When the local officers finally agreed, the conciliators carried the proposal to the operators only to encounter implacable resistance.

So matters would rest until late August when U.M.W. president Frank Hayes pressed the Secretary of Labor for some measure to end the costly strike. In response, Secretary Wilson, along with the two conciliators, modified the original proposal slightly and sent it along to the President. President Wilson, in turn, on September 5, forwarded copies to the union and the operators and asked for their acceptance. Even the antiunion *New York Times* thought the proposal so eminently fair that any rejection of it "would justify stronger measures."[5] In fact, the President had already weighed the option of closing the mines but had been informed by the Attorney General that he lacked authority.

Rockefeller's reaction to the proposal, delivered from his summer home at Seal Harbor, Maine, was entirely negative. Misinformed about the origination of the proposal, he expressed particular concern that President Wilson would name a union sympathizer to the public seat on the proposed tripartite arbitration commission. This would give the union a two-to-one majority.

C.F. & I. president Welborn shared this fear. He wrote from Denver that such a commission "would virtually have charge of the conduct of our business."[6] He also objected strongly to the proposal on rehiring strikers, since in the present circumstances that would necessitate firing men who had taken their places. The President, Welborn thought, could not know the facts surrounding the strike or he would not display so obvious a leaning toward the mine workers union. This comment prompted a telegraphic discussion about whether Welborn should go to Washington to personally discuss the situation with the President. It was decided that he should.

Starr Murphy at the office in New York prepared the draft of a response to the President that he sent along to Welborn and to Rockefeller for their consideration. He argued that the President's proposal afforded C.F. & I. the perfect opportunity to cut itself loose from the other operators without in any way endangering their position. The decision to have C.F. & I. go it alone appears to have been a direct result of Lee's remarks about Osgood's role in the operators' committee. Murphy particularly urged Welborn to seize this opportunity, so that in the future, C.F. & I. would be free to chart its own course.

Like his colleagues, Murphy was wholly disinclined to accept the President's proposal. He did, however, include in his draft a passage indicating that C.F. & I. intended in the near future to create some sort of arrangement that would involve workers in the settlement of internal problems. Frederick Gates, who seems to have visited the office more frequently at this time, heartily approved of Murphy's tack. He was especially pleased that no suggestion would be given the President that C.F. & I. policy was influenced in any way by the union.

By the time Welborn received Murphy's letter, he and Ivy Lee had already drafted a response, but he signified that they were happy to incorporate some of Murphy's suggestions into their version. Welborn initially objected to making any mention of the future development of grievance machinery. He informed Murphy that he thought this matter best left for his face-to-face meeting with President Wilson. Before he left for Washington though, he received another letter from Murphy bearing on this issue. Noting that the U.M.W. had just signified its acceptance of the President's proposal, Murphy reflected:

It seems to me clear that public opinion will demand either the acceptance of the President's proposition or some constructive suggestion from the operators. A mere refusal to do anything would be disastrous. It appears from the correspondence, that we have all been considering certain constructive suggestions, notably in the line of a plan for enabling the different interests in the company to exchange views with one another and to peacefully adjust any troubles that may arise. It has seemed wise to defer these during the pendency of the strike, lest any action should be deemed a concession to the union. In view, however, of the President's action, and particularly in view of the fact that the plan which he suggests is stated in his letter to be tentative, I think the time has come for the operators to bring forward their constructive suggestions . . . [7]

Welborn's response to the President consequently mentioned the current development of plans for dealing with grievances and misunderstandings. At best, this was a half-truth; the current plan was to do nothing. But, in publicly committing C.F. & I. to create some means for dealing with grievances, an unretraceable step along the path marked out by Mackenzie King had been taken.

Following his late September meeting with President Wilson, Welborn traveled to New York to report that it had proved fruitless. Welborn described the interview over lunch with Rockefeller, Murphy, Greene, Lee, King, and Gates. That evening he visited the Rockefeller estate, Pocantico, for dinner in the company of Rockefeller Senior, Lee, King, and Rockefeller Junior. The following day, he met with Hywel Davies, one of the conciliation commissioners, and Charles P. Neill, the former U.S. Commissioner of Labor. Davies was of the view that if matters were handled quietly, he could gain a substantial modification of the President's proposal. Nothing is known to have come of this. In this connection, it should be noted that Ivy Lee had been a student of Woodrow Wilson's at Princeton. A personal friendship had developed between them. No evidence has been uncovered that suggests that Lee made any use of this relationship in Rockefeller's behalf.

President Wilson was not nearly so favorably disposed toward unionism as Rockefeller and his advisers feared. Nor was he so ignorant of the facts as Welborn presumed. It was rather that the information that had reached him through his conciliators, the Secretary of Labor, the Colorado governor, and both sides to the dispute had led him to the conclusion that the mine operators were responsible for the stalemate in efforts to reach a settlement. It was this stalemate that was uppermost in his mind. So long as the strike continued, federal troops would probably have to remain in the field. Wilson viewed this extraordinary situation as undesirable in the extreme. Consequently, his recent (and subsequent) intervention had less to do with preferring the victory of one side over the other than with his ardent wish to recall the troops as soon as possible.

The operators' rejection of the President's proposal doomed any hope of a settlement. Although by this time all parties earnestly wished for an end to the dispute, the terms of an acceptable solution remained beyond reach.

Coming as it did in the wake of the collapse of these settlement efforts, the public announcement of Mackenzie King's affiliation with the Rockefeller Foundation was read in some quarters as evidence that hostilities were about to resume. Rumors of the wildest sorts circulated among labor's allies, and almost always bore the implication that King was hired to design some means for destroying organized labor. The staff of the U.S. Commission on Industrial Relations also perceived a threat in the announcement. As a result, Rockefeller and King would find themselves the target of a searching public inquiry into their motives and actions.

On October first, fortified as was his custom by reading scripture, Mackenzie King formally assumed his duties for the Rockefeller Foundation.

> I thought I would begin with reading the gospel of Luke, Luke being of the apostles the physician. . . . If I can only translate into methods of administration and adjustment that will compel a recognition of the underlying principle of brotherhood . . . the contribution I seek for most will be obtained.[8]

For the next two weeks, he worked steadily on the design of his investigation into industrial relations. Then, on October 15, the Colorado strike intruded. He was served with a subpoena obliging his reappearance before the U.S. Commission on Industrial Relations. He had previously given expert testimony on the Canadian Industrial Disputes Investigation Act.

King was furious both to be subpoenaed when he would have answered a simple request, and to be recalled at all. He thought the labor people on the commission probably wanted to embarrass him. Rockefeller and most of his associates were also subpeonaed, and Rockefeller was also furious; the process server had followed him to Providence, where he was attending a college reunion. He too believed that the labor people, and perhaps his former Brown classmate, Charles McCarthy, now the research director for the Commission, had played a hand in this affair.

Both King and Rockefeller believed they knew what their subpoenas augered. They would be badgered and grilled in an attempt to expose the Rockefellers as powerful and grasping. The Foundation would be made out to be a tool of their villainy. They expected that the Commission would openly side with the United Mine Workers Union because the Wilson administration wanted the votes of workingmen.

In fact, Commission chairman Frank P. Walsh and research director McCarthy held suspect King's appointment to the Rockefeller Foundation and the Foundation's sudden interest in labor relations. They wondered if the Rockefellers proposed to compete with the Commission by bringing some predetermined antiunion position before the public as if it were the finding of scientific research.

A.F. of L. president Samuel Gompers responded to the public announcement of King's appointment by raising similar questions in the columns of *The American Federationist*. Recalling Rockefeller's testimony before the House investigating committee in April, Gompers asked:

> Have the American people forgotten that strange, sinister witness, his dogmatism, his absolute unyielding indifference to public sentiment, his cynical ruthless disregard for the effects of his policies, his terrible concentration of purpose, his assumption of infallibility?[9]

Charles McCarthy was aware that among radicals, rumors were circulating to the effect that the Foundation was going to attempt to enlist the nation's colleges in a campaign against the labor movement. Discounting such talk, he and his allies were much more alarmed by the evidence that the Rockefellers were trying to buy a favorable public opinion through the use of false and misleading propaganda. For several months it had been known that the bulletins circulated by Ivy Lee contained numerous distortions and errors of fact. As one leading Progressive characterized them to McCarthy, the bulletins were "an utterly unscrupulous and mendacious . . . campaign of publicity."[10]

Lee and his staff had not verified the information supplied for the bulletins by the Colorado operators. In the most glaring error, they reported the annual salaries and expenses of United Mine Workers' strike leaders as the amounts paid for nine weeks. Although discovered soon after it appeared, through yet another mix-up, this error was allowed to stand for four months before a correction was attempted. In another bulletin, much was made of the fact that few of the striking miners had made withdrawals from their substantial company-held savings accounts. This was put forward as evidence of prestrike high wages and of the intention of the miners to return to the company's employ once the union agitators had been dealt with. However, most of the savings accounts were owned by nonmining employees, and were not subject to withdrawal on demand.

Inaccuracies such as these, which were a matter of common knowledge in labor circles well before their public exposure late in January 1915, sparked the interest of the commission in the Colorado strike and the Rockefellers. The flawed bulletins appeared to provide prima facie evidence of the contempt in which industrialists held both the public and the truth when the question of unionism was at issue. Chairman Walsh believed the situation tailor-made for exposing the overweening power of great private fortunes. He seized upon the opportunity to capitalize the political and publicity value of such an exposure.

Lee's biographer thus had ample reason to conclude that his initial effort for the Rockefellers was "one of the greatest errors of his career."[11] And if Lee has any claim to regard as the founding father of public relations, the Colorado fiasco may help explain why practitioners have ever since been held suspect in their legitimacy. Certainly, the literary fraternity never permitted Lee to forget his shortcomings. Poet Carl Sandburg wrote of "Ivy L. Lee—Paid Liar," and Upton Sinclair of "Poison Ivy." More than a decade later, Lee was still the object of verbal brickbats. Before John Dos Passos created J. Ward Moorehouse in his image for *U.S.A.* in the 1930s, Robert Benchley delivered this classic thrust:

Mr. Lee, for those of you who lead sheltered lives, has long been the press agent *de luxe* for such radical organizations as the Standard Oil Company, and has devoted his energies to proving, by insidious leaflets and gentle epistles, that the present capitalist system is really a branch of the Quaker Church, carrying on the work begun by St. Francis of Assisi.[12]

But Lee not only survived the contretemps over the bulletins, he positively flourished. Both the senior and junior Rockefellers found him charming and serious. They valued his counsel. The younger Rockefeller was particularly fascinated by his apparent grasp of public opinion and by his knowing and cordial relations with the press. He also prized Lee's mailing list, for this afforded him a direct personal link with those people around the country whose opinions mattered most. In sum, Lee combined in his professional skills and talents precisely the means for Rockefeller to realize a long-cherished goal: to clear his father's name and have him celebrated for the far-sighted builder he knew him to be. Weighed against this objective, the stir created by a few regrettable mix-ups in the bulletins seemed to Rockefeller but a minor irritant.

In contrast, Rockefeller resented with some vehemence the unwelcome counsel of Charles McCarthy of the commission staff. Writing as a personal friend (McCarthy had been the captain and star of the Brown University football team when Rockefeller served as its student manager), McCarthy attempted to persuade him that his family's reputation would continue to suffer so long as their affairs were conducted secretively. The public, McCarthy argued, was bound to equate secrecy with malicious intent. He urged that the Rockefeller Foundation be cut loose from family domination and restructured as a more representative quasi-public institution. Even in their private affairs, McCarthy advised, the Rockefellers could gain the public's trust only if they were more trusting and open. They were peculiarly accountable to the public because their wealth and power contained so much potential for the subversion of democracy.

McCarthy pressed his message home along every avenue available to him. He called on mutual friends—Brown classmates, several of whom worked at 26 Broadway—to explain his intentions and reiterate his thoughts. He strongly supported Frank Walsh in bringing commission and public pressure to bear. Although Rockefeller cannot have felt too kindly toward so taxing a friend, McCarthy was more understanding than he had any right to expect. For McCarthy knew what a complete stranger might only have guessed; that Rockefeller tried hard to be honest and well intentioned. McCarthy also believed, however, that Rockefeller had been "enmeshed and educated in a system which is entirely wrong" and was "surrounded by a group of men who are simply wooden."[13] Had he known of Jerome Greene's recent attempt to have the Federal Council of Churches suppress a damning report on the Colorado strike, his worst suspicions would have been confirmed. On the other hand, had he known Mackenzie King better, he might have been more sanguine about Rockefeller's future.

In the period between the receipt of the Industrial Relations Commission's subpoenas in mid-October 1914, and their appearances before it late in January 1915, King tutored Rockefeller in the rudiments of economic history and trade unionism. At her request, he also provided Mrs. Rockefeller, Jr., with reading materials on unionism. In conversations at the office, while walking to the Rockefeller home on West 54th Street from the 14th Street subway station, and via the mails, King shared his knowledge and experience. He explained common misunderstandings, such as why the open shop meant one thing to employers and quite the opposite to workers, and why employer concerns over the "right to work" weren't of the slightest interest to workers who cared more that those who benefitted from union bargaining efforts should bear a fair share of union expenses. He stressed collective bargaining, the need to deal with workers as a group rather than one by one, as the only equitable arrangement in a world of large-scale industry. He also asserted the belief that unionism was a necessary adjunct of modern industry. When the time was ripe, he thought it would be useful for Rockefeller to meet some labor leaders and learn for himself what dedicated and able people they often were.

As the date initially set for the hearings approached, the Rockefeller staff spent hour upon hour debating and drafting the responses to be submitted to the commission's questionnaire. With painstaking care, every answer was examined to ensure that Rockefeller's position would be reflected accurately, that the language and tone were most likely to win public acceptance, and that the fewest openings were provided for criticism. The task seemed to call for the skills of a parliamentary minister and, more often than not, it was King who spotted the danger lurking in a particular expression or who volunteered the correct thought or turn of phrase. Since King's political experience hadn't figured in Rockefeller's consideration of him as an advisor, it came as a very pleasant surprise to discern that public life had equipped him with an understanding and feeling for public opinion every bit as useful as his grasp of industrial relations.

But something much more important also emerged from these sessions. Although King's services had been sought as a result of the Colorado strike, he had not been retained to settle that dispute. His assigned task was to prepare a general study of industrial relations. Partly because Rockefeller could not separate his role as trustee of the Foundation from that as leader of his father's staff, and partly because of the Commission investigation, the Colorado situation kept intruding on this arrangement. King came to recognize that Colorado would have to be dealt with before he could proceed with his larger study. The staff meetings over the Commission's questionnaire provided him with the further insight that everything associated with the Rockefellers— their reputation, the program of the Foundation, Rockefeller's career and peace of mind, and even his own future—hung on the balance of what was done in Colorado. The intervention of the Commission had transformed the public interest in the strike into a broader and more fundamental challenge to the responsibility with which the Rockefeller's used their wealth and power.

The challenge in these terms suited King's taste perfectly, since it permitted him to construe the stakes at issue in grandiose proportions. He argued convincingly that all of the good that the Rockefellers had done and could do in the world turned on the outcome. To Rockefeller and to the rest of the staff, King's perspective was irresistible. He had redefined their problem, the Colorado strike, into their splendid opportunity to do good and noble works.

King found an additional high purpose for himself in his investigation into industrial relations. Living in Canada as he continued to do, he was more preoccupied with the European war than the Americans he encountered on his periodic visits to New York. He keenly regretted that there was so little service he could render his country in the crisis. This was probably why he came to see a parallel between the political war on the continent and the industrial war in Colorado. In coming to understand the causes of and remedies for the latter, he believed, he would expose the sources of and cures for the former. Reasoning in this manner, his adventitious association with the Rockefellers came to bear the overtones of a special sort of patriotic war work, over and above the more obvious humanitarian objectives toward which he believed his efforts were directed. Though denied a role in the war-

time councils of his country, he hoped through his work for the
Rockefeller Foundation to contribute to an understanding of the
prerequisites for peace. This understanding in turn would pave
the way for harmony and stability in both modern industry and
international affairs.

On a number of occasions, Rockefeller and King mused on the
question of which of them was the more powerful. Rockefeller
maintained that King's ideas were the critical ingredients of their
endeavor, while King took the position that Rockefeller's ability to
implement ideas and achieve results mattered most. This was not
a purely idle exchange of flattery nor a self-deprecatory game the
two men played. At the time, they both had good reason to feel
ambivalent toward power. Rockefeller possessed the status of a
powerful person but lacked a proper title to the influence and resources as his disposal. Senior had only just begun to transfer bits
of his fortune into his son's name. King, on the other hand, possessed the intellectual capabilities that might furnish an entitlement to power but lacked office or recognized status. Prizing
power as both men did, these assymetries in their lives troubled
them. Each envied the other's strength.

Rockefeller was troubled by the knowledge that nothing he had
accomplished on his own had earned him the status he held. In a
revealing exchange recorded in King's diary, he gave expression
to the self-doubt that his lack of accomplishment nourished:

> "But," he said, in an almost pathetic way, "I must learn to
> handle big business affairs myself. If I do not the business men
> of today will not pay any attention to what I may say in financial
> matters." I said none of them could afford to underestimate his
> judgment already. His reply to this was that none of them did
> think anything of it; that he was not taken seriously on financial
> and business matters.[14]

Rockefeller was undoubtedly alluding here to his earlier experiences as a member of a number of corporate boards of directors. The penumbra of his name had then proved his only asset.
The telling assumption of his plaint was that he *should* be playing
a leadership role in business affairs, as if there were desirable
goals toward which he felt obliged to lead. But there were not; he
was desirous of leading for no other reason than that as a Rockefeller he thought he should.

By the time of the Colorado strike, Rockefeller had done everything in his life as he should and yet, in his own eyes and perhaps in his father's as well, he remained somehow incomplete. His existence was still a test to prove something rather than an expression of his nature. Mackenzie King's impact on him would change this, for the Canadian's shrewd counsel and warm regard, like the bright hot rays of the sun, would bring forth the flower of his being.

> I advised him strongly to nail his colours firmly to the mast at the hearings of the Commission, and said that he must recognize that we were living together in a different generation than the one in which his father had lived, that it was possible, in building up an industry such as Standard Oil, to maintain a comparative secrecy as to methods of work, etc. and to keep business pretty much to those who were engaged in it. Today, there was a social spirit abroad, and it was absolutely necessary to take the public into one's confidence, to give publicity to many things, and especially to stand out for certain principles very broadly.[15]

As the Rockefeller staff at 26 Broadway searched for the best responses to the Industrial Relations Commission, additional pressures were thrust upon it. On December 1, President Wilson issued a statement publicly blaming the coal operators for their failure to settle the strike on the terms recommended by his conciliators. He noted that, so long as federal troops remained in the field, he had an obligation to try to end the dispute. He had, therefore, resolved to create the grievance commission called for by his conciliators. His wish was that the operators would come to rely upon it as a means for settling outstanding issues between themselves and the miners. As commissioners, he named Seth Low, president of the National Civil Federation, representative of the public interest; Charles W. Mills for the operators' interest; and Patrick Gilday for the miners' interest. Henceforth, this would be known as the Low Commission.

The following day, in Denver, the Commission on Industrial Relations reopened public hearings on the strike. Reports of testimony incorporating subpoenaed correspondence between 26 Broadway and the C.F. & I. officers were regularly featured in eastern newspapers. These developments served to rekindle the issue of who was responsible for what had happened and again pointed to the Rockefellers.

Only several weeks later would Rockefeller and King learn that Frank Walsh had led the commission to renew its investigation over the objections of President Wilson. The President hoped for a strike settlement through the Low Commission. He wanted to remove federal troops from Colorado at the earliest possible date. Walsh, however, was determined to expose the employers' abuses of power. Writing to McCarthy soon after the Denver hearings, he had little doubt of what had been accomplished:

I had hoped that you would seize upon the fundamental character of the hearings in Colorado, as you have done. Almost everything of industrial unrest, that means clash of power, with its attending bloodshed and bitterness, is exemplified there. The efforts of the unions to get in; what might be called "high handed demands" on the part of the unions; absolute refusal on the part of employers to deal with employees; these employers backed up by the combined power of all the money of the East; venal local officials; nonenforced laws; controlled legislative, judicial and executive officers; and the whole traced from the pit boss with a hand full of dirty money, controlling the elections, and the money followed right into the offices of the coal company.

We succeeded in putting the finishing touches upon the evidence that brings all of this home to the owners, and the Rockefeller letters, carefully phrased as they were, locates the power in the hands of the Messrs. Rockefeller, and explains the emptiness of the pretensions to power upon the part of the manikins surrounding the throne.[16]

Meanwhile the financially drained United Mine Workers Union took the opportunity provided by the creation of the Low Commission to call an end to the strike. The miners were advised to seek employment wherever they could find it, but many found no work. Either their jobs had been taken by others or the general decline in business activity limited job openings. As winter deepened, so would the hardships of the unemployed and their families.

The coal operators responded to President Wilson's action by condemning his interference and announcing their unwillingness to cooperate with the Low Commission. For the second time since the onset of the strike, the Colorado Fuel & Iron Company acted independently of the other operators. Under King's guidance,

Rockefeller urged C.F. & I.'s president Welborn to show every courtesy to the President's commission. He argued that the development of King's employee representation plan would be aided considerably if it could win the approval of the Low Commission. Welborn agreed. As suggested in their September meeting, he had already begun to introduce improvements along the lines King had suggested.

Senior had also to be dealt with, for he was most apprehensive that the course being charted by King would deliver them into the hands of the union. Aware as they were of his views, Rockefeller and King made a studied effort to explain their actions and objectives to him in detail. He listened, but he was not entirely convinced. Subsequently, when he gave his son eighty thousand shares of C.F. & I. common stock (with a market value of approximately one million dollars) following the latter's appearance before the Industrial Relations Commission, it was less because he agreed with the views he espoused, than for the dignity with which he faced the ordeal.

The opposition Rockefeller and King encountered in various quarters, gave them little pause. On the contrary, since the two were absolutely certain of the correctness of their own motivations, resistance only stiffened their will to prevail. And, because in King's employee representation scheme they had a positive alternative to act upon, their essentially defensive maneuvers would have the ultimate and ironic effect of casting them in the role of innovative reformers. Such a role, in turn, was so highly congenial to their individual ambitions, that both men enjoyed the luxury of having their cake and eating it.

Notes

1. W. L. M. K. Diary 10/24/16, W. L. M. K. Papers, Series J13.
2. W. L. M. K. to J. D. R., Jr., 8/16/14. J. D. R., Jr. Papers, Business Interests, Box 23.
3. Ivy Lee to J. D. R., Jr., 8/16/14. Ivy Lee Papers. This is the only surviving letter in the collection that bears on Lee's earliest relations with the Rockefellers.
4. Boemke (1983), pp. 194ff. provides a detailed account. The commissioners were William R. Fairley, a former U.M.W. official, and Hywel Davies, president of the Kentucky Mine Operators' Association.
5. Ibid.
6. Jesse F. Welborn to J. D. R., Jr., 9/10/14. U.S. Commission on Industrial Relations (1916), vol. VII, p. 6692.

7. Starr J. Murphy to J. F. Welborn, 9/16/14. Ibid.
8. W. L. M. K. Diary, 10/1/14. W. L. M. K. Papers, Series J13.
9. Gompers (1914), p. 985.
10. Amos Pinchot to C. McCarthy, 11/13/14. McCarthy Papers, Box 17.
11. Hiebert (1966), p. 100.
12. Ibid., p. 299.
13. C. McCarthy to F. P. Walsh, 12/14/14. McCarthy Papers, Box 17.
14. W. L. M. K. Diary, 3/14/15. W. L. M. K. Papers, Series J13, p. G2539, 303.
15. W. L. M. K. Diary, 1/12/15. Reprinted in McGregor (1962), p. 131.
16. F. P. Walsh to C. McCarthy, 12/20/14. McCarthy Papers, Box 18.

4. Half-Empty Words

On January 25, 1915, John D. Rockefeller, Jr., presented himself as a witness before the United States Commission on Industrial Relations. Originally subpoenaed to testify in October, his appearance had been postponed at the request of the Commission. Several developments during the intervening months materially reduced the vulnerability of his position. For one, the strike in Colorado had officially come to an end. The federal troops deployed in the wake of the Ludlow Massacre had also been withdrawn, and President Wilson had created the Low Commission. The Colorado Fuel & Iron Company was the only company cooperating with the Commission. Consequently, much of the pressure for action that might have been brought to bear on Rockefeller in October had been dissipated by January. Commission chairman Frank Walsh nonetheless counted on the recentness of the strike and the wide publicity given the Ludlow tragedy to aid him in the effort to expose the virulent antiunionism of American employers.

The hearings took place before capacity audiences in the New York City Council chamber. An army of newspaper reporters and journalists attended hoping to find good copy. The police also were present in numbers. The atmosphere was charged with expectancy as if any minute there might be drama, revelations, or even fireworks.

For three days, Rockfeller occupied the witness chair and fielded the questions fired at him by Frank Walsh. The confrontation proved anticlimactic. Rockefeller especially seemed a disappointment: "wary and bland" were the words the *Times*[1] used to describe his performance.

The hearings nevertheless marked a turning point in Rockefeller's life. The positions to which he committed himself before the commission, though he hardly grasped their significance at the time, bound him to a course that would yield a new sense of life purpose and eventually catapult him into the leadership of the avant garde among corporate employers. He would cease to serve merely as the passive exchequer of social reform and become one of its architects. In following the path marked out by Mackenzie King, he encountered the wholly unanticipated opportunity to recast his life so that it was less an extension of his father's will and more nearly his own.

Although the Commission had heard and would hear from a number of leading capitalists—including Andrew Carnegie, J. Pierpont Morgan, Jr., August Belmont, Henry Ford, and the senior Rockefeller—none was subjected to the protracted and hostile examination Rockefeller sustained. They testified; he was more nearly on trial. For, from the perspective of Commission chairman Frank Walsh, the appearance of the younger Rockefeller provided an unparalleled opportunity to educate the American public to the warfare between capital and privilege on the one side and trade unionism and democracy on the other.

From all he had learned from staff investigations thus far, Walsh had concluded that the Rockefellers' power over the Colorado coal industry was complete. They enriched themselves even as they denied the most fundamental civil rights to their miners. In addition, their repeated refusal to bow to the urgings of President Wilson to bring about a settlement revealed an arrogance of dangerously aristocratic proportions. Walsh believed that the exposure of such power and arrogance would impel the public to give its support to unionism and to progressive reform. He wished also to force the Rockefellers, if possible, to moderate their present position in Colorado. For these reasons, he was determined to give Rockefeller no quarter. A prior meeting in private, arranged by King, did nothing to alter this intention.

In his opening statement, Rockefeller noted that he was accused by some of exerting complete control over the Colorado coal industry and of seeking "to dictate a policy of non-recognition of unions."[2] He denied these accusations unequivocally. Other critics, he noted, accused him of being too indifferent to the situation in Colorado and of failing to exert his influence as a company director. Both views of him could not be correct, he said, leaving unspoken the implication that he was more inclined to honor the latter criticism than the former.

The facts, he informed the Commission, were that he couldn't have led the fight against union recognition because in principle he believed in unions. In what amounted to a striking about-face from his congressional testimony nine months earlier, he asserted that he regarded unions as entirely legitimate organizations of workers. They paralleled corporations, the legitimate organizations of capital. Unions that devoted their energies to improving the terms and conditions of employment through collective bargaining and that helped to create machinery for settling grievances, were clearly in the interests of the workers. Insofar as unions were alive to the responsibilities they bore vis-a-vis the employer and the public, and so long as membership in them was entirely voluntary, he could endorse them wholeheartedly.

Mackenzie King was, of course, responsible for Rockefeller's new stance. Among other things, the tutor had explained to his pupil why individual contracts between workers and large corporations were untenable. Only collective bargains between workers as a group and management, he argued, could assure some equity in the employment relationship. King had also explained why Rockefeller's support for the open shop was subject to criticism. The employers' defense of the right of workers to work wherever they chose, without regard to whether they were union members, he advised, was usually and correctly understood by workers to imply that no union men were welcome. Moreover, the employers' line of argument was entirely self-serving, since the only so-called worker right that interested them redounded to their own advantage. King maintained that an honest employer was obliged to show through both word and deed that he would not countenance discrimination of any sort that compromised the rights of his employees to form or belong to a union. Rockefeller echoed these lessons in his testimony.

Rockefeller told the commissioners that the issue of union recognition in Colorado had not been his to resolve. Company officials had independently decided their policy and informed him of it afterward. His correspondence with them, which he had been required to produce for the Commission, would make that clear. It would also show that, to the extent that he had intervened, he had merely suggested steps that might be taken to increase the opportunities for the miners to deal with work-related problems. He pointed out that in his dealings with company officials he merely made suggestions and never gave orders.

Defending his father and himself from the charge of self-aggrandizement, he told the Commission that they had received very little in the way of profits on their investment in C.F. & I. Instead, they had permitted company earnings to be reinvested to develop the industry, expand employment, and foster the economic development of Colorado. Although he would be the first to admit that the company had made some mistakes in the past, he thought that now the greatest need was for "all concerned to develop increasing good will and to improve conditions as far as may be possible."[3] It was out of his deep concern for what had happened in Colorado that he had asked the Rockefeller Foundation to launch a study of industrial relations. Following a suggestion of the study director, Mackenzie King, steps had now been taken to create within C.F. & I. a system of representation among the miners. This system would give the miners an orderly and regular means for discussing their problems with company officials. The first elections of representatives had just been held earlier in the month. The first meeting between the representatives and company officers had occurred only within the week. Rockefeller held out to the Commission the prospect that the fullest development of this system might yield a lasting solution to the labor problems of C.F. & I.

In his examination of Rockefeller, Walsh first attempted to sort out the details of Senior's holding in C.F. & I. and to clarify the composition and role of Senior's advisory staff. Prompted by Rockefeller's assertion that his father had not profited from C.F. & I. but had plowed the earnings back into the company, Walsh unsuccessfully pressed him to admit that his father had indeed profited but had simply deferred current dividends in favor of future capital gains. Walsh next turned to the leitmotif of the hearings, the issue of corporate responsibility.

As in his questioning of other business leaders, Walsh's object was to lead Rockefeller to the admission that he knew little or nothing about the labor policies and practices of the companies in which he held an interest. And Rockefeller, like most of his business colleagues, had to confess as much. Walsh contrasted this situation with the regular flow of reports and discussions that came to Rockefeller about corporate financial matters. His point was to demonstrate that no aspect of business enterprise was as remote from the concern and responsibility of corporate owners and directors as was labor policy. In this area alone, managers were entirely free to do as they wished.

Rockefeller disputed this conclusion, arguing that directors customarily limited their involvement to finances and left *all* other areas of decision making to the discretion of the managers. The primary duty of the directors was to place their enterprise in the hands of executive officers who were qualified by their character and ability to conduct it in an appropriate manner. But, Walsh queried, if the directors did not know what the officers were doing, how could they evaluate their performances?

> Chairman Walsh.   How do the executive officers of the Colorado Fuel and Iron Co. deal with those activities?
>
> Mr. Rockefeller, Jr.   That I do not know. That is left in their hands.
>
> Chairman Walsh.   How can you judge if they are proper people to deal with those activities unless you know how they deal with them.
>
> Mr. Rockefeller, Jr.   I can only judge by what I know of the men.
>
> Chairman Walsh.   Their general characteristics?
>
> Mr. Rockefeller, Jr.   Their general characteristics and their general experience and training and so forth.[4]

Rockefeller concluded by requesting that the Commission supply him with any information bearing on worker abuses perpetrated by C.F. & I. He said he would do everything in his power to right any wrongs of which he was made aware. On that note, the first day of his testimony came to an end. The audience applauded.

King found every reason to be pleased as he reviewed the events of the day in his diary. It was now clear to him that Rockefeller had erred seriously at the very onset of the strike by failing to inform himself of the actual state of affairs. His rigid adherence to the conventions of delegated authority in business had led him astray—to the point of abdicating his responsibility. In spite of his growing dislike for Walsh, King credited him with having compelled Rockefeller to recognize this. King believed the testimony provided a clear public acknowledgment of the undesirability of too wide a separation of ownership from management. In a more positive vein, Rockefeller's statements in regard to unionism and collective bargaining heralded a new era of respect for working people. His pledge to go to Colorado at an early date served perfectly to announce a new, active stance on his part. King was especially impressed by the tact and good judgment Rockefeller had shown in parrying Walsh's questions. Only twice had he felt obli-

Frank P. Walsh, c. 1918. By permission of the New York Public Library, Frank P. Walsh Papers.

ged to pass notes suggesting that Rockefeller modify something he had said; otherwise, his responses had been just right.

Frank Walsh thought differently. Time and again as he had questioned Rockefeller about the practices and some of the charges leveled against C.F. & I., Rockefeller had responded that he knew too few facts to speak with any confidence. When Walsh asked more general questions in the effort to elicit Rockefeller attitudes toward trade unions, grievance machinery, and company towns (among many others), Rockefeller had either referred him to his opening statement or demurred from expressing an opinion on the ground that, since he had neither thought about nor given serious study to the issues raised, his opinion would be of little or no value to the Commission. In the course of one of these attempts to avoid an expression of opinion, Rockefeller had indicated that he saw no serious objection to the seven-day workweek.

King felt the exercise of caution in this instance had been excessive and potentially damaging. He passed a note that prompted Rockefeller to come out a bit further along in his testimony in favor of one day of rest in seven.

Walsh opened the second day of the hearings by quoting Rockefeller's last words to the effect that he would gladly receive any information uncovered by the Commission that pointed up failings on the part of C.F. & I. Was he aware, Walsh wanted to know, that over the past ten to twelve years, labor strife in the Colorado mining industry had prompted twenty-seven distinct public investigations? Rockefeller had no idea of the number. How, Walsh queried, could the Commission bring the information contained in all of these investigations to Rockefeller's attention, so that the reforms he declared himself so willing to introduce could be set in motion? Rockefeller couldn't say. Walsh suggested that perhaps if Rockefeller took the trouble to read through testimony he would find an adequate basis on which to act. Rockefeller parried with the reply that he hoped the Commission would provide him with concrete suggestions for the improvement of conditions at C.F. & I.

In the course of his interrogation, Walsh posed three crucial questions about the employee representation plan. Was it to be expected, he asked, that an organization of employees created and maintained by their employer would ever raise serious questions about company policy or conduct? He also wanted to know whether it was reasonable to believe that the workers' elected representatives would fight for the resolution of grievances, when the supervisors with whom they had to contest held absolute power over their livelihood. Finally, could an organization of employees limited in its membership to one company exert a telling influence on that company if a good many of its policies were shaped by industrywide forces and relationships?

In his responses, Rockefeller repeatedly emphasized the newness of the representation plan and the absence of any evidence of its workability or unworkability. He hoped it would prove effective and said he was personally prepared to encourage continued experimentation until a clear verdict could be reached. He went on to say that he did not intend the company's sponsorship of the plan to squelch disagreements but rather to bring disagreements out into the open where an effort could be made to find mutually acceptable solutions. If the plan were found to be of little or no value to the miners, he had little doubt but what they would simply refuse to continue to participate. That would be the end of it. However, assuming that the miners had as large a stake in the efficient operation of the company as did its managers, he believed it reasonable to expect that the creation of a formal system of joint consultation would go far toward building harmonious industrial relations. Rockefeller tried to leave little room for doubt that he wished to foster just such harmony.

Rockefeller's testimony evoked widely divergent responses. Those closest to him whose opinions are known were unequivocally pleased and even proud of his performance. Frank Walsh and several members of the commission staff, on the other hand, believed he had been evasive and uncooperative. Indeed, several months later, Walsh would seriously weigh the possibility of asking Congress to hold him in contempt for refusing to answer many of the questions put to him. Walter Lippmann, writing in the *New Republic,* expressed amazement at the intellectual helplessness that Rockefeller revealed on the stand. His reluctance to answer questions, coupled with the opening statement, which clearly had been prepared for him by others, prompted Lippmann to write with his customary prescience:

> I should describe Mr. Rockefeller as a weak despot governed by a private bureaucracy which he is unable to lead. He has been thrust by the accident of birth into a position where he reigns but does not rule. . . . The failure of the American people to break up his unwieldy dominion has put a man who should have been a private citizen into a monstrously public position where even the freedom to abdicate is denied him.[5]

Yet, there was something about Rockefeller's performance that elicited applause and won for him the respect of most of Walsh's fellow commissioners. Even the redoubtable Mother Jones was impressed. She hailed Rockefeller as he left the stand for the noon recess on the first day of the hearings. King introduced them. The white-haired octogenarian hardly looked the part of a labor agitator, yet it was well known that the miners of the country would follow her anywhere, and she was feared for this reason. She told Rockefeller how very much she admired his manner and what he had had to say. He might achieve lasting industrial peace, she thought, if he knew more about the actual state of affairs in Colorado. King took the opportunity to suggest that the three of them arrange a meeting in a more private setting in the next day

John D. Rockefeller, Jr., accompanied by an unidentified aide, and followed by W. L. Mackenzie King (right) and Starr Murphy (left), January 1915, following his appearance before the U.S. Commission on Industrial Relations. By permission of the Rockefeller Archive Center.

or two. They would talk, and Mother Jones could describe the Colorado situation as she knew it. She agreed. From this sprang a series of private, but nonetheless well-publicized, meetings between Rockefeller and the national and Colorado leaders of the United Mine Workers.

The spectacle of a leading American businessman sitting down and holding discussions with trade union leaders undoubtedly contributed to the favorable impression Rockefeller made on many people. Nonpartisan observers saw the meetings as a reasonable, and maybe even a courageous thing for the Rockefellers to do. Their willingness to meet showed that for all their money, they would not stand aloof, indifferent to the concerns and problems of common people. The U.M.W. leaders, for their part, were pleased to have the opportunity to discuss the situation in Colorado. Only the Colorado mine owners, some employers' associations, and those radicals who viewed any compromise as a barrier to the attainment of genuine social transformation viewed the talks with hostility.

Mother Jones never fully resolved her thoughts about the hour she spent talking with Rockefeller and King. Her intuitive judgment seems to have been that Rockefeller was honest and sincere, and could be trusted to correct the problems of the Colorado miners now that he was informed. But, on more than one subsequent occasion she would be induced by the arguments of her comrades to denounce him and his plan of reforms. The pattern of this struggle between the judgment of her feelings and that of her politics emerged almost immediately. Following her interview, she expressed to reporters her confidence in Rockefeller's integrity and her trust in his intention to do the right thing by the miners. The next day, stung by a rebuke from Upton Sinclair, she railed that the young Rockefeller was full of promises when what she wanted was action. She denounced his scheme of employee representation as "a fraud."[6] These reversals were only slightly less surprising than her approval of Rockefeller in the first instance.

Though not everyone was thrown into the depth of confusion Mother Jones evinced, it must be supposed that many others who came into contact with Rockefeller experienced similar crosscurrents of feeling. Not about him, of course, but about themselves. For Rockefeller's supposedly limitless power placed him in the center of a magnetic field that pulled with greater or lesser force upon everyone who came near. Since he was not in the least prepossessing or charismatic, his personality cannot have been the source of this effect. His character undoubtedly contributed something; King certainly believed it did. Meeting with Walsh in advance of the hearings, King had attempted to disarm him by arguing, among other things, that Rockefeller was uncommon among rich young men, not at all the playboy but a serious and hardworking businessman and philanthropist. Yet, Rockefeller had to do nothing, had to exert no will whatever, to have effects upon others. Few things were denied him. Most people were disposed to find themselves in agreement with him for he was a Midas of possibilities. He might make anything happen.

The positions Rockefeller took on trade unionism and collective bargaining in his opening statement may have helped to sway many of the commissioners to his side. He gave every appearance of being reasonable and even forward looking, as if he accepted unions and bargaining as necessary adjuncts to modern, large-scale corporate enterprise. Those commissioners who were themselves sympathetic toward organized labor could take his remarks as a positive endorsement of unionism, while those who were dubious about the value of unions could be touched by his evident good intent. Walsh was not at all moved, however, because he was less interested in Rockefeller's thoughts and intentions than in his actions during and since the strike.

That Rockefeller himself did not believe in what he said was to prove of little moment. He simply recited King's point of view, supposing it to be the right one and supposing, for that reason, that he must agree with it. Subsequent events would amply demonstrate that he did not, but subsequent events also would shield him from any recognition of his inconsistency. In time, it would become possible for him to fulfill Finley Dunne's stereotype of the open-shop employer:

> "But,"—said Mr. Hennessey, "these open shop min ye menshun say they are f'r unions iv properly conducted."
>
> "Shure," said Mr. Dooley, "iv properly conducted. An' there we are: an' how would they have them conducted? No strikes, no rules, no contracts, no scales, hardly iny wages, an' dam few mimbers!"[7]

Yet, he would simultaneously regard himself and be widely regarded as the chief spokesman for a new wave of sophisticated corporate leaders whose employee representation plans and liberality promised a future of industrial peace. Part of the explanation of this seeming paradox lies hidden in the shifting attitudes toward unionism between 1915 and the postwar era. The following sketch provides a base line against which such changes can be gauged.

The American political spectrum in 1915 was as broad and as variegated as it had ever been in the history of the nation. Although this political variation turned upon a host of issues and allegiances, no great distortion results from employing the single issue of trade unionism to refract the major strands of opinion. Unionism aroused such strong feelings that most groups felt compelled to take a stand. In so doing, they revealed something of their valuation of the present condition of American society and something of their preferences for the future.

At one extreme, on the far right of the spectrum, there were those who viewed unionism as an antisocial menace, requiring an active, militant opposition if it were to be eradicated from American life. Some adherents of this school believed unionism a criminal conspiracy aimed at extorting funds from employers as the price for labor peace and from employees, in the form of dues, as the price for their continued employment. Others saw in unionism an alien institution brought into the country to foment a revolution against the institution of private property. Still others could not fathom the presumptions implicit in unionism: that complete strangers to an enterprise—that is, union leaders—should presume to tell businessmen how they were to deal with their employees; that workers, the obvious losers in the race for success, should presume to dictate terms to the winners; that businessmen were presumed to be willing to accede peaceably to the usurpation of their right to manage their businesses as they saw fit. Employers who held such views tended to support organizations like the National Association of Manufacturers, the American Anti-Boycott Association, and the numerous associations organized to speak for the interests of individual industries. These were the employer combat organizations, support for which relieved individual companies of many of the burdens of battle except where unions attempted to gain a footing in their own factories.

In 1915, the leaders of this militant antiunion grouping were fearful of losing their battle. Never, in their estimation, had the labor movement been so strong. Never had it and its allies among the social workers and the intellectuals held so much sway over the President, Congress, and public opinion. The European war would only exacerbate the situation, since the interruption of the flow of new labor force recruits would make labor scarce and all the more demanding. In mid-1915, "Twenty-three gentlemen representing various industrial experiences and viewpoints" met by invitation to discuss their plight and to develop strategies that would preserve the threatened hegemony of the American businessman.[8] Rockefeller was among those invited to this private conclave, but he refused to attend.

Most of the conferees agreed that some sort of public relations effort was desirable, suggesting how widely diffused the idea of self-advertisement had already become. They could not, however, agree on what position to put forward. Viewpoints ranged from the extremes of one delegate who supposed unions and government intervention a natural response to the growth of large corporations to another who, in the context of the discussion of various means of "educating" working people, advocated

> the preparation and issuance of one or several short stories in which the cruelties of the present interference with healthy industrial development through autocratic provisions of legislation and arrogant methods of labor combinations would be depicted in dramatic style and manner, in the hope thereby to arouse the people at large to a saner attitude toward industry and its leaders. What the story of Uncle Tom's Cabin has done for the abolition of slavery, a novel as suggested might accomplish in bringing equitable industrial conditions to pass.[9]

The parallel drawn here was clearly preposterous. The conferees may have had good reason to be unhappy with the trend of events but, as spokesmen of the single most powerful group in society, for them to liken their situation to that of the slave population oversteps the bounds of sensibility. It reflects a paranoid strain among American employers. It must be recognized, however, that staunch conservatives outside of employer circles shared many of their fears. Such conservatives saw the republic imperiled by the growing strength of a labor movement nurtured by a Democratic administration. Speaking at the banquet of the N.A.M. that spring, former president William H. Taft had warned:

> The power that the leaders of the American Federation of Labor exercise has become excessive and detrimental to the public weal and the good of society, and especially that of the mem-

bers of the labor unions. I fully approve the principle of labor unions. . . . What is needed to produce a sobering effect upon the truculent labor leaders, intoxicated with their sense of political power . . .[10]

Ironically, Taft would be teamed with Frank Walsh just a few years later, to serve as cochairman of the National War Labor Board.

The opposite end of the political spectrum was occupied by the Industrial Workers of the World (I.W.W.). Like all partisans of the left, the Wobblies regarded capitalism as an exploitive and inhumane social construct. They differed with the socialists over how the inevitable destruction of capitalism was to be brought about, as well as the shape of the new social order to be erected in its place. Primarily, the Wobblies disdained the socialist fascination with the ballot box. They pinned their revolutionary hopes on the general strike. One day, any day, they believed, a struggle between ordinary working people and an ordinary (i.e., exploitive) employer would spark widespread unrest. Workers nearby and then further afield, at first spontaneously and then contagiously, would lay down their tools and fold their arms. Everything would stop. Nothing would move. It would suddenly become apparent that workers alone had the power to make society tick. Filled with a new consciousness of their power and of their destiny, workers would start the wheels of industry turning again only after a complete transformation of work, government, and society had begun. They would themselves create the new world through the agency of their democratic work organizations; a world that was classless, equitable, and just.

As the famous Little Red Song Book proclaimed, a primary mission of the I.W.W. was "To fan the flames of discontent."[11] In most places, the organization refused to enter into contracts with employers, believing such an act would concede *them* recognition! The leaders also did little to build or sustain a dues-paying membership. They weren't much interested in "pork-choppers" —those who joined hoping only to improve their terms and conditions of employment. They were interested in strikes, in displays of militancy and worker solidarity. Somewhere, somehow, they expected a spark to ignite the tinder of oppression and produce the general strike in which capitalism would perish.

Unconstrained by either the norms of capitalist society or by the need to build a lasting, bureaucratic organization, the I.W.W.

became the most daring and unpredictable of American radical groups. It often acted with telling, imaginative effect, as in the Lawrence strike of 1912 and the thousand-mile picket line thrown up at the points of entry into the midwestern harvest fields in 1914 and 1915. Because of their militant conduct of strikes and demonstrations, the Wobblies often elicited a violent—and in the West, a characteristically sadistic—reaction. Yet, it would probably be incorrect to suppose that the Wobblies were any more feared by their enemies than the socialists.

Socialism was an ascendent movement in the United States in 1915. A steadily rising tide of members, votes, and successful candidacies for public office, gave the Socialist Party a record so congruent with theories of evolutionary growth that it was not at all unreasonable to think in terms of the party's eventual triumph. Unlike their more flamboyant counterparts in the I.W.W. leadership—whom they had recently purged from their ranks—the leaders of the Socialist Party were committed to parliamentary politics and to building a stable, mass-membership organization, one capable of generating election victories. The party promised to displace capitalism peacefully, by voting it out of existence. Blood would be spilled only if representatives of the bougeoisie refused to accept the fair judgment of the polls and chose to fight to preserve their privileged position. The end of private property in the means of production and its attendant exploitation would pave the way for a benign state socialism in which justice and equality were the dominant and flourishing virtues.

In keeping with Marxian theory, the Socialist Party looked upon the working class as its primary constituency. It found considerable support among some groups of organized workers. Yet, the labor movement, as embodied in the A.F. of L., was openly hostile toward it. This long-standing cleavage on the left was without parallel among all other industrial nations.

In other industrial countries, the labor movement was regarded as the defensive economic arm of the working class, while the socialist movement was its aggressive political arm. Committed to the same objective, the overthrow of the capitalist system in the name of Socialism, the two movements depended on one another and coordinated many of their activities, so that in their larger purposes they were indistinguishable. The variance in the American situation stemmed from the unique philosophy to which the A.F. of L. and most of its affiliated national unions were committed.

When Samuel Gompers responded to the question of what union members wanted with the now-famous answer, "More, more, more,"[12] he lent strong support to the judgment that the A.F. of L. was bereft of any philosophy worthy of the name. However, a whole train of assumptions and implications was pulled along behind the "more, more" engine. The A.F. of L. viewed itself as a successful adaptation to a new and unprecedented society. This society could not be compared with those in which continental socialist and labor movements functioned. American institutions freely endowed workers with political and civil rights that nurtured strong feelings of equality and independence. The openness of the country and its heterogeneous people, along with its rich resources and their burgeoning development, extended opportunities to many and put a premium upon results. Largely for these reasons, the leadership of the A.F. of L. believed that there was no need to struggle for the displacement of existing institutions—American or capitalist. Workers already possessed rights and opportunities that gave them all the freedom they might wish for. The problem instead, was one of protecting and enhancing the positions of workers so that they and their children could exploit their rights and opportunities on a footing of equality with others.

The beauty of the ideology of pure and simple unionism was that it was entirely in harmony with prevailing American ideals and values. It required no new pulpit or prayer book. Solidarity was limited by discernible self-interest. Gompers, though himself a socialist at one time, came to look upon the promise of a blissful, cooperative commonwealth off in the future as a cruel hoax. He knew, of course, that the socialists desired to unseat him and turn the Federation into an appendage of their party. Their boring from within was no less an act of hostility than the I.W.W.'s efforts to build a dual movement. Alienated in this manner from labor's conventional allies on the left, the A.F. of L. moved along an uncharted, friendless track. It was perhaps only natural then that when an opening appeared on the right, in the form of the National Civic Federation, the A.F. of L. leaders moved in that direction with alacrity.

The National Civic Federation had been formed in 1900 as the successor, on a national scale, to the Chicago Civic Federation. In both incarnations, the Federation was dedicated to building an alliance of influential political moderates. Its members were recruited and self-selected from among the top echelons of business, labor, and public and professional life. The Federation's innovation of tripartite representation gave expression to one of its guiding premises, that the often conflicting interests of different groups in society were amenable to peaceful resolution through communication and the development of mutual understanding. Ralph M. Easley, founder and executive secretary of the organization, believed not only that such an accommodation of interests was possible but that it was imperative if American society was to be preserved. He and many of the men who over the years participated in the Federation shared the judgment that should they fail to address and solve, or at least moderate, some of the most nettlesome social problems of the day—the labor problem foremost among them—the way would be clear for a socialist take-over. Reform was required if revolution was to be avoided.

In many business circles, nonetheless, the Federation was regarded as a radical, if not traitorous, organization. The legitimacy it conferred on unions and their leaders was often bitterly resented. As John Kirby, president of the National Association of Manufacturers, once put it to Seth Low, the president of the Civic Federation, I cannot "in conscience wink at the great danger to the best interests of our common country that lies hidden in the endorsement, by your organization, of these men and the doctrines they preach." [13]

By the nonsocialist political standards of the day, the Federation's open acceptance of union leaders *was* a radical step. Many progressives of the Bull Moose and Wilson varieties could not even bring themselves to go so far. They kept their distance, put off by misgivings about industrial conflict, union corruption, and the choice between the A.F. of L.'s brand of self-serving unionism and the revolutionary syndicalism of the I.W.W. The irony of this was that the reluctance of the progressives to forge an alliance with the labor movement obliged them to work through the Civic Federation whenever they wished to deal with labor. As the Roosevelt Administration had turned to the Federation in its effort to settle the anthracite coal strike of 1902, so the Wilson Administration turned to it for help in selecting the members of the Industrial Relations Commission. In consequence, eight of the nine members of the commission were also members of the Federation. President Wilson again turned to the Federation in naming the members of the Low Commission. Not until 1916, on the eve of the country's entry into a war that threatened to create internal division, did Wilson feel it necessary to give formal recognition to the labor movement. He spoke at the groundbreaking ceremony of the A.F. of L. headquarters and then named Gompers to the Council of National Defense.

Among socialists and their sympathizers, on the other hand, the participation in the National Civic Federation by union leaders, including Gompers and one-time United Mine Workers president John Mitchell, was decried as *their* betrayal of class. For the Federation's assumption of a fundamental harmony in the interests of labor and capital ran counter to the precept of class struggle. Only capital, it was thought, stood to gain from this illusory ideology and from the false relationship built upon it. In the curiously self-deprecating logic of would-be heirs to power, radicals warned that the Federation would coopt the unionists and rob them of whatever militancy they possessed.

If there were co-opting, however, much of it was to the benefit of the A.F. of L. Which is why, in anticipation of the gains to themselves and to their members, union leaders eagerly had assisted in the creation of the National Civic Federation in the first instance. The Federation was the earliest, and for many years the only, organization through which unionists could reach business leaders and influential community leaders in a setting disassociated from strikes, boycotts, and the hot rhetoric of conflict. Federation conferences and committees provided them with opportunities for projecting themselves as they wished to be seen, as conservative and reasonable men. This feature of their participation gained in importance with the emergence of the militant anti-union employers' associations. The willingness of some employers to interact with union leaders implied that they couldn't be as bad as the militants made them out to be. The Federation also conferred a modicum of recognition and status that neither unions as institutions nor their leaders as individuals could find elsewhere in society. Money also changed hands. Several leaders surreptitiously supplemented their union salaries by consulting for the Federation. One such individual, John Mitchell, on losing his union office, went to work for the Federation on a full-time basis.

Clear expressions of the Civic Federation's ideology were provided by Seth Low, who served as its president from 1907 until his death in 1916. A former mayor of Brooklyn (1882–1885) and New York (1902–1903) and president of Columbia University (1890–1901), Low believed that the stability of American society was contingent upon countervailing power. He reasoned that, as agglomerations of capital grew larger and larger, they would override all other interests unless counterbalanced by equally strong contesting forces. The labor movement was to play this role in his judgment for, if it did not, either the government would have to step in to control capital or the socialists would come to power with the same result, an equivalent loss of individual freedom. Although this view of things cast the labor movement in the role of the savior of capitalism, Low, his predecessors in the office, and Easley especially hoped for enlightened action on the part of capital as well. They hoped that businessmen could be induced in their own self-interest to support reforms aimed at modifying or eliminating some of the more glaring abuses visited upon working people.

The workmen's compensation issue provides a case in point. Until the first compensation law was passed and sustained in the courts, in 1910–1911, workers hurt or killed on the job were held liable for whatever accident befell them. The courts quite consistently shielded employers from liability by holding either that accidents resulted from the negligence of the worker or fellow workers. A widely publicized campaign for safety on the job, however, demonstrated that many accidents were avoidable if appropriate precautionary steps were taken by employers. A cry was then raised that the courts were being unfair and that legislation was needed to make employers liable for industrial injuries and deaths. The National Civic Federation suggested to employers that if they wished to minimize the financial burdens imposed by such laws, they would do well to participate in drafting them. There was more to be gained by supporting such reform than by opposing it. The Federation's suggestion, in this respect, was a mincing meliorism.

Much of the same was true of its advocacy of welfare work. Despite the earlier evidence from Pullman, where George H. Pullman's efforts to build a model town had come crashing down upon him, and from Dayton, where National Cash Register's well-publicized program of employee benefits had similarly failed to forestall strikes, the Federation boosted welfare work and counseled in its favor as if it were more than an expedient. Easley was well-informed about both the motives for and limitation of welfare programs. He knew that most welfare programs were motivated by a desire to exclude unions. And although this meant that, in supporting welfare work, the Federation supported a potential rival to unionism, no inconsistency was recognized. Nor was Federation support of welfarism a source of friction with the unionists.

From Easley's position, welfare work was, like unionism, another bulwark against radicalism, less effective than unionism perhaps but another weapon nonetheless. For their part, the unionists condemned welfare work as a sham at almost every opportunity. Their reluctance to force the issue within the National Civic Federation suggests, however, that they were not really much concerned about the effectiveness of welfare work as a deterrent to organization. When, for example, the Federation asked Gompers to express the attitude of the A.F. of L. toward profit sharing, he replied that the subject had "never seriously been considered."[14]

The inherent flaw in welfare work lay in that most companies unilaterally decided what they would do for their employees. They imposed programs and retained control over their operation. Workers were expected to return the favor through high productivity and loyalty, the latter a euphemism for steering clear of unionism. As in most forms of paternalism, both the gift *and* the response of the recipient were thought to be at the disposal of the giver.

Because welfare work was viewed by some employers as a relatively cheap solution to their labor problems, the National Civic Federation was considerably more successful in this realm of its advocacy than in its advocacy of unionism. In contrast to the widespread adoption of some aspects of welfare work in many of the companies affiliated with the Federation, not one member company ever voluntarily opted for the high cost alternative of sharing power with a labor organization.

Nor did Rockefeller have any such intention when he supported the ideas of unionism and collective bargaining before the Commission on Industrial Relations. As he saw it, his general statement of principles found no application in Colorado because the union leaders there were not to be trusted. He believed them a ruthless and unscrupulous lot, implicated in strike-related crimes ranging from arson to incitement to riot to murder. By simply qualifying his endorsement of unionism with the word "responsible" he thought in one stroke to keep himself free of both hypocrisy and the United Mine Workers. Unaware of the intent of this reservation, the commissioners had found Rockefeller's statement in broad agreement with their own sentiments. All of them, except Frank Walsh, were impressed by the ringing declaration of beliefs he had read to them. In time this declaration would be gotten up as the Rockefeller creed:

> I believe that the ultimate object of all activities in a republic should be the development of the manhood of its citizens, that such manhood can be developed to the fullest degree only under conditions of freedom for the individual, and that industrial enterprises can and should be conducted in accordance with these principles.
>
> I believe that a prime consideration in the carrying on of an industry should be the well-being of the men and women engaged in it, and that the soundest industrial policy is that which had constantly in mind the welfare of the employees as well as the making of profits, and which, when the necessity arises, subordinates profits to welfare. In order to live, the wage earner must sell his labor from day to day. Unless he can do this, the earnings from that day's labor are gone forever. Capital can defer its returns temporarily in the expectation of future profits, but labor cannot. If, therefore, fair wages and reasonable living conditions cannot otherwise be provided, dividends must be deferred or the industry abandoned.
>
> I believe that a corporation should be deemed to consist of its stockholders, directors, officers, and employees; that the real interests of all are one, and that neither labor nor capital can permanently prosper unless the just rights of both are conserved.
>
> I further believe that, in matters pertaining to industrial relations, the public, quite as much as the parties engaged in industry, is entitled to confidence and consideration. Industrial relations are essentially human relations, and human relations should be not less the concern of the State as a whole than of individuals engaged in industry. My appreciation of the conditions surrounding wage earners and my sympathy with every endeavor to better these conditions are as strong as those of any man.
>
> I believe it to be the duty of every citizen to do all within his power to improve the conditions under which men work and live.
>
> I believe that that man renders the greatest social service who so cooperates in the organization of industry as to afford the largest number of men the greatest opportunity for self-development, and the enjoyment by every man of those benefits which his own work adds to the wealth of civilization. If, with

the responsibilities I have and the opportunities given me, I am able to contribute toward promoting the well-being of my fellow men through the lessening of injustice and the alleviation of human suffering, I shall feel that it has been possible to realize the highest purpose of my life.[15]

The man who uttered these words neither completely understood nor believed them—they were half empty. He knew enough, however, to want both to understand and to believe, and to a degree, he would succeed. This was perhaps his saving grace.

Notes

1. *New York Times* (January 26, 1915), p. 1.
2. U.S. Commission on Industrial Relations (1916), vol. VIII, p. 7764.
3. Ibid., p. 7766.
4. Ibid., p. 7815.
5. Lippman (1970), p. 265. The article originally appeared in the *New Republic* (January 30, 1915).
6. *New York Times* (January 29, 1915), p. 1.
7. From Douglas et al. (1923), p. 611.
8. Magnus W. Alexander. "The First Yama Conference on National Industrial Efficiency, June 5–7, 1915." Typescript, marked "For Confidential Use," W.L.M.K. Papers, Series J1, vol. 29, pp. 26217–26245.
9. Ibid., p. 26237. See also Gitelman (1984).
10. Taft (1915). Taft's position won the approbation of the editors of the *New York Times* (May 28, 1915), p. 12.
11. *Songs of the Workers* (1956). Main sources on the I.W.W. include works by Dubofsky (1969) and Lorwin (1913).
12. Quoted in Hoxie (1924), p. 123. Among the numerous works on socialism and the labor movement see Draper (1957), Chapter 1, Laslett (1970), Salvatore (1982), Perlman (1928), and Bell (1952).
13. John Kirby to Seth Low, 12/27/09. Reproduced in Taft (1957), p. 226. On the National Civic Federation, see Green (1956), Weinstein (1968), and Ramirez (1978). Kurland (1971) provides a biographical sketch of Seth Low.
14. S. Gompers to Gertrude Beeks, 10/8/15. Gompers Correspondence, A.F. of L. Papers, Series 11A, Box 21.
15. U.S. Commission on Industrial Relations (1916), p. 7767.

5. Charity

> You ask why should all this have been possible. Why this endeavor to hold you responsible for matters beyond your control. The answer lies in a sentence and it is worth remembering through the whole of life, and that is, that in the public mind, with whatever you may be associated or have to do *nothing* lies beyond your control. Of course, we know this is not true, but the fact that it is not does not lessen the conviction in the public mind, and that conviction is a factor of which constant account has to be taken.[1]

So Mackenzie King wrote John D. Rockefeller, Jr., in a long personal letter following the Commission on Industrial Relations hearings in New York. No one had ever addressed Rockefeller so candidly as an equal—or, more nearly, as a brother—offering both counsel and warm assurances of affection. No one had ever made his life and his opportunities seem so vital to the world. King's words touched him like a benediction. He treasured the long letter and held the writer his dearest friend. When next they met, Rockefeller conferred the highest accolade, saying "I have put the letter among my own private papers at my home; so it is a personal matter between us." King duly recorded the honor in his diary.[2]

As much as any posthumous evidence can, this letter reveals King's talent for telling people what they wanted to hear, but he also told Rockefeller what he needed to hear. With exquisite tact his criticisms were either implied or delivered as compliments. Even as he provided guidance, his remarks were aimed at his reader's keen desire to prove himself a leader:

> It seems to me you will have to lead, have to be the example, whether you will or no. Your modesty and your humility do not permit you to see this, but those who have your life interests and your life more at heart see it, and it is in the field of industry primarily that this leadership must be conspicuous. . . . The stage is just as large for you as it is for Wilson—larger—because

more people are vitally affected by the industrial outcome than by the political. . . .[3]

Such a line of reasoning and so favorable a comparison hit their mark exactly. Only by convincing Rockefeller of his capacity for leadership would King be able to work through him to achieve industrial reform.

Had Rockefeller been the conniving businessman prefigured by those who assumed he directed the Colorado strike, King could not have perceived such an opportunity. Indeed, he probably would have refused to associate himself with Rockefeller. It was because Rockefeller seemed so uninformed and yet so decent and well-intentioned that King recognized what they might accomplish together under his direction.

Perhaps it was only natural that at this point King should ignore the consequences of success in helping Rockefeller develop as an industrial leader. For to the extent that a leader cannot be led, the Canadian's ambition for his patron would eventually vitiate his own influence. An even more critical lapse occurred in an unsettled area of King's liberal ideology.

The liberal abandonment of laissez-faire was premised largely on the unwillingness or inability of private power wielders to redress the social wrongs and inequities of industrialism. Public intervention was needed to deal with the negative consequences of private gainseeking. As King saw it, the liberal state had to impose limits on the rapacity of the Tories. Yet liberals like himself were ever mindful of the dangers inherent in state power. Too much intervention represented as grave a peril to individual initiative as none at all. The appropriate balance of public–private power, however, remained open to dispute. There were no evident principles on which to separate the two domains.

Now the Rockefellers struck King as sui generis. Though nominally Tories, they sincerely wanted to do the right thing by workers. Moreover, such was their influence and repute, that any example set in their name was likely to become a model for industry generally. Hence, the policies he might develop for them could serve as an alternative to public intervention. As we shall see, King had good reason to be sensitive to charges that the Rockefeller's sometimes usurped the functions of government. In several aspects of their activity, he worked to reduce the basis for such charges. But in the realm of industrial relations he acted as if their power and public power were perfect substitutes—not that there was any reason to expect the enactment of an American public policy toward industrial relations at the time. In fact, the only pertinent legislation to receive serious consideration in Washington and some state houses at the time was modeled after King's Industrial Disputes Investigation Act. But, in early 1915, all of the pressures exerted on the Rockefellers to act emanated from public agencies. In employing these pressures to move the Rockefeller forces in the desired direction, King supposed he was doing a public service when he was actually serving a private interest. He never acknowledged or resolved this confusion.

On the other hand, Rockefeller's acknowledgement of the legitimacy of unions created several more obvious problems. For one, his pronouncement conflicted with the antiunion view held by his father. King was reasonably sure that the son "did not himself entertain the prejudice so strongly."[4] Nevertheless, the younger Rockefeller never relented in his wish to avoid dealing with the United Mine Workers at C.F. & I. So a second problem required that some basis for continuing to reject *this* union be found if Rockefeller and King were to avoid hypocrisy.

Throughout the strike, the C.F. & I. officers consistently had portrayed the local union leadership as criminal and irresponsible. This characterization provided their rationale for refusing to meet and negotiate. Until he decided to become personally involved, Rockefeller had thoughtlessly accepted and endorsed this view. Now a reappraisal of the union leadership was prompted by Mother Jones' cordial remarks at the commission hearings. King arranged interviews with her, with national U.M.W. officers, and with the foremost local leader, John R. Lawson. These sessions proved amicable, but instead of a reappraisal, they led to a hardening of attitudes. Lawson's testimony before the commission in particular caused King such personal discomfort that he joined Rockefeller in refusing to have further dealings with the man.

The private meeting with Lawson had been friendly and without embarrassment. The image of the strike leader as a reckless firebrand—Lawson was still under indictment for murder—was not sustained by his demeanor or his words. But from the meeting, Lawson had gone before the commission with a prepared statement. He delivered a scathing indictment of the Rockefellers and their role in the strike. He accused them of total indifference to the human costs at which their profits were won and of the grossest hypocrisy in using these profits to underwrite benefactions to their own glory. All of the pertinent questions that might have been raised to challenge the Rockefellers from the points of view of the strikers and of Progressives concerned about private concentrations of wealth and power were hurled full fury at them. Their representation scheme was denounced as an antiunion trick. King was also brought under fire and his authorship of the Industrial Disputes Investigations Act deplored as an antilabor action. It was an impressive performance. However, Lawson's biting criticisms provided King and Rockefeller with just the excuse they needed to avoid any future dealings with him.

Soon afterward, as they laid plans for their meeting with the Low Commission, the issue of union recognition was resurrected by Senior. In a letter to his son, he warned that "care should be taken to see that the Colorado Fuel and Iron Company was not drawn, through the plan it had proposed, into recognition of the United Mine Workers."[5] Senior pointed out that Low was on record as being favorably disposed toward unions and might try to use his commission to aid the mine union.

In reflecting on this warning for Rockefeller's benefit, King revealed the wholly unanticipated significance of Lawson's testimony. By drawing their fire, Lawson had given them an excuse for leaving intact Senior's antiunionism.

> I said I could appreciate his father's position in not wanting him to be drawn into any false relationships with the . . . Union; but that I felt very strongly that there was no alternative between either a long and severe and unpleasant struggle with the U.M.W.A. over the question of recognition . . . or a policy that would give for the miners everything that the Union could possibly give them and that would antagonize the union as little as possible in the process; that we could leave to the future the question of recognition. For the present it would be unwise to consider it; that Lawson, by his evidence, had made that an impossible consideration. Mr. R. Jr. approved absolutely of what I said.[6]

The most remarkable aspect of King's rejection of Lawson was that he fundamentally agreed with the latter's critique of power and privilege. This would become clear over the following weeks as he repeatedly used Lawson's arguments as a lever with which to ease Rockefeller and his cohorts along the paths he wished them to take.

King never admitted that he agreed with Lawson or, more properly with Edward Costigan, the Colorado Progressive who served as the United Mine Workers counsel and who, King later learned, had prepared Lawson's statement. King could no more have acknowledged that he agreed with Charles McCarthy on the question of the control of the Rockefeller Foundation, although he did. In both instances, he found himself helping to defend Rockefeller against criticisms with which he was intellectually sympathetic and then using those criticisms within the Rockefeller camp to press for change in the direction he and the critics desired. In acting thus, he saw himself neither as a hypocrite, selling his services to the enemies of his values nor a false friend to Rockefeller. What he *did* believe was that Rockefeller was motivated by the strongest desire to do only what was right, that he was prepared to be guided by King's judgment, and that the power of any example set by the Rockefellers would be sufficient to influence the entire course of industrial relations in the United States. Certain as he was of the correctness of his own vision of society, King saw himself pursuing through the voluntary and private actions of the Rockefellers, many of the same social objectives that men like Frank Walsh, Charles McCarthy, and Edward Costigan hoped to achieve through the compulsion of public law. In time, he would come to admit that the pressures that these reform advocates exerted, and which both he and Rockefeller were too high-strung not to resent, were very useful to him. But the primary factors conditioning his behavior were Rockefeller's decency and his power, attributes that, when combined with his own sense of social justice, guaranteed that the right and the good would prevail.

King's perspective meant, among other things, that he never felt any need to face up to the question of whether an organization of workers put together for them by their employer was more or less desirable than one they initiated independently. The obvious answer to this was moot because of Senior's unwillingness to permit dealings with a labor union. The crucial question, instead, was whether the Rockefellers were prepared to assume the responsibility for ensuring that workers within their sphere of influence were treated fairly and given the opportunity to resolve problems that arose in their employment. Once it was clear to King that the answer to this was yes, his task became that of devising a system of employee representation that would guarantee the desired results.

King supposed that the workers would attach more importance to being treated fairly and having honest grievance-consultation machinery at their disposal than to the issue of whether they were represented by a union. He also believed that as the labor movement matured, it would inevitably capture any employer-sponsored organization that failed to live up to its promises. As he saw it, it didn't matter so much *how* the condition of labor was improved so long as improvements were made. When, for example, he later recommended that, for the benefit of the miners, Colorado Fuel & Iron introduce an element of consumer cooperation into the operation of its company stores, he admitted to a preference for worker sponsorship. But, since he thought the miners too inexperienced and too divided to organize such an effort, he advocated that the company impose the program from the top.

There was more than a little temporizing in such views. King consistently opposed welfare work because it was tainted by paternalism. For much the same reason, he would later oppose screening entrants into the mining camps to keep out professional gamblers. The efforts of employers to protect workers in such ways, he thought misguided. They unwittingly blocked worker opportunities for self-reliant learning and growth. That workers encountered difficulties and occasionally made mistakes, he believed, were necessary parts of the process of developing a mature labor force and movement. Why then should the C.F. & I. miners not learn how to manage a cooperative or be permitted to chose the leadership of someone like John Lawson? In both instances, King let more pragmatic considerations override principle without a qualm.

Toward the end of February 1915, Rockefeller gathered his advisors around him in New York. King came from Ottawa and Mr. and Mrs. Welborn arrived on a visit from Colorado. The staff was particularly eager to learn from Welborn about his first meeting with a group of elected employee representatives. There were many other things to discuss as well. The staff spent almost two weeks talking among themselves, with the members of the Low Commission, and with still other Rockefeller advisors, who had arrived for an executive committee meeting of the Rockefeller Foundation.

At the very first staff meeting, Rockefeller told Welborn, in the presence of King, Starr Murphy, and Ivy Lee:

> Mr. Murphy and I have talked this matter over, and we are decided that there must never be another strike in the mines of the Colorado Fuel & Iron Company. No matter what is to be done, there must never again be a strike. Now, the only way to avoid this is to make conditions so satisfactory that the men in our Company will prefer to be there under conditions in our mines rather than to associate themselves with an organization which may call a strike to suit its own purpose. So we must consider these different features. We must leave nothing undone that can be done to restore the best of feeling, and to make conditions of labour as satisfactory as they can be made.[7]

King told Welborn that the investigation of the Commission on Industrial Relations had supported the view that the Rockefellers were largely, if not entirely, responsible for the strike and its consequences. Hence, whatever actions C.F. & I. took would serve as a mirror of their intentions everywhere. They would not be free to give aid to starving Belgians or assist Negro colleges or create bird sanctuaries or anything of the sort without eliciting catcalls and jibes, such as Lawson had given them, unless they first ensured that conditions in their own backyard were above reproach. Welborn readily acknowledged the point. He indicated that he was pleased that the attitude adopted toward the Low Commission, coupled with Rockefeller's meetings with the strike leaders, had served to set C.F. & I. apart from the other operators. He went on to assert, however, that he personally would have nothing to do with Lawson and his cohorts, since he believed them guilty of inciting murders, if not of committing them.

Throughout that morning, during lunch at the Whitehall Club, and at 26 Broadway in the afternoon, the staff discussed a variety of possible changes in C.F. & I. policy. Questions were covered regarding company clergymen, schools, teachers, and school boards, regarding cooperative features in the company stores, and grievance handling. Rockefeller reported that he had acted upon the suggestion of Professor John R. Commons, a member of the Commission on Industrial Relations, and had attempted unsuccessfully to appoint a labor manager to oversee all labor issues within the company. Such a manager would have reported directly to the board of directors and, although equal in rank to the company president, would have been expected to cooperate with the president to assure a unified policy. The man he had hoped to recruit for this position, former U.S. Commissioner of Labor

Charles P. Neill, had proved to be unavailable, so that the matter was held in abeyance. Welborn protested that no such step was needed since the man he had appointed specifically to deal with the problems of the miners was highly regarded and quite effective. This prompted Rockefeller to reply in a manner so congenial to King's taste that he reproduced the reply in his diary:

> The men say that a union gives them the assurance that when they have a grievance and present it, their standing will be of equal strength in gaining a consideration of it as is the standing of the managers, who represent the stockholders. That seems to me a fair position to take. Now, if you are not going to allow the men this kind of security, something else as effective must take its place, and the men must have the means whereby they can be assured against any kind of arbitrary action.[8]

Welborn's man, he noted, was not an independent advocate. Something more was needed, but what and who were matters for further consideration.

They next talked about Rockefeller's proposed trip to Colorado. He had told the Commission on Industrial Relations that he would visit C.F. & I. as soon as he could, and it now looked as if that would be in April. He confided to King that, with his father about to leave for Florida and his mother ill, he could hardly leave sooner. It troubled him though, that little would be done to prepare for his visit. He had counted heavily on Neill to precede him, learn the lay of the land, and guide him during his stay. Now that it was clear that Neill was unavailable, he was at a loss to know where to turn. Welborn had extended a general invitation to the staff but Rockefeller feared that a visit from any one of them might worsen rather than improve matters. When King offered to go and pointed out that his visit would be quite consistent with his role as Foundation investigator of industrial relations, Rockefeller was greatly relieved. This was one of several actions for which King earned his gratitude during the week. Another came that evening.

Present at dinner that evening were Rockefeller, Starr Murphy, Jerome Greene, and A. Barton Hepburn, all members of the executive committee of the Foundation. They were joined by Wickliffe Rose, the head of the Foundation's International Health Division, who had just returned from a tour of war-ravaged Europe. The evening had been arranged to hear of his travels and recommendations. The group was completed by King and by Mr. and Mrs. Welborn, to "enlarge their view," as Rockefeller had told King.[9]

Rose told of the conditions he had observed on the eastern and western fronts. In Holland and Belgium, thanks in part to the excellent work of the Rockefeller Relief Commission, the critical food shortages facing the civilian populations had been alleviated. Progress had also been made in resettling refugees. Additional aid was needed, however, which he proposed the Foundation should extend. A still more desperate situation prevailed in Poland, now largely occupied by the German army. From his conversations with high German officials, Rose believed that they would consent to allow a private American agency to provide relief to the Poles. He urged that the Foundation move to provide that relief. No other work they had ever performed had given him and his colleagues the powerful experience of their relief efforts. For the first time in his life, he had witnessed starvation, women and children begging for food. The memory would remain with him forever.

The executive committee was preparing to respond to Rose's moving appeal when King spoke up to suggest an alternative course of action. He asked the board members to consider that the policy of the Allies was clearly to starve Germany into defeat and that any food intended for Polish civilians might be appropriated by the Germans for their own use. Wasn't it possible then, that if the relief program vexed the Allies, it would reflect adversely on the U.S. government? At the very least, shouldn't Dr. Rose raise the issue with State Department officials to learn if they had any objections to a program of Polish relief? The point was so well taken that a vote was postponed until Rose could canvass official opinion in Washington.

As they left the Rockefeller home on West 54th Street, King walked with Rose to his hotel and explained himself at greater length. He apprised Rose of Rockefeller's recent encounter with the Commission on Industrial Relations where, among other things, the Foundation had been charged with usurping some of the functions of government. The Foundation had also been accused of engaging in philanthropy at the expense of the workers who produced its income. Just that morning, a telegram had arrived from Colorado pleading for assistance because some miners in the town of Trinidad were alleged to be starving. If the Foundation were to extend aid to the Poles without helping the western miners at the same time, it would lay itself open to renewed criticism that might handicap its activities forever. The possibility that a Polish relief program might inadvertently affect American foreign relations and provoke the wrath of the government in so doing was an additional peril to be avoided. Rose responded that he hadn't known about the hearings and now that he did, he believed he could see the wisdom of King's counsel.

One week later, King was again present when Rose brought his proposal forward, this time for the approval of the full executive board of the Foundation. As before, King was pressed by Rockefeller to state his views, even though he had no right to a place or a voice in the board's deliberations. Since his initial objections had not been met, he renewed his attack upon the proposal. The debate continued through the afternoon until dinnertime. A vote on the resolution consistent with King's reservations was taken and resulted in a tie, with Rockefeller, Starr Murphy, Frederick Gates, and Harry P. Judson on one side and Rose, Jerome Green, Charles W. Eliot, and Charles O. Heydt on the other. Eventually, President Eliot decided to change his vote and the issue was resolved as King and Rockefeller preferred.

From discussions held with Gates, Eliot, and Rockefeller on separate occasions in the next few days, it is clear that King's position on the question of Polish relief was primarily conditioned by his support for Allied war policy. In speaking as he did, he was merely defending the policy of his own country. But this perspective was sufficiently different from that of the Americans to make a considerable impression. King's grasp of the possible international repercussions of the relief program emanated from a global, or at least continental, perspective that must have been quite attractive to a number of board members. Certainly, President Eliot cannot have failed to be impressed when he learned the day following the meeting that King would communicate Eliot's views on Allied policy to the British Foreign Minister. In a similar way, King's proximity to Rockefeller in dealing with the Colorado troubles and federal commissions gave his warnings about the future of the Foundation an added weightiness. Discerning King's influence on Rockefeller, Rose told Eliot that he liked King's attitude and the way he did things, and that he was prepared to be guided by King's judgment in matters affecting the interests of the Foundation and the Rockefellers.

Clearly, Eliot shared Rose's view, for he asked King to use his influence to guide Rockefeller in his mode of living. Having spent the past three days as Rockefeller's houseguest, Eliot confessed himself appalled by what he had observed:

> He is trying to carry all kinds of details and is burdening himself with endless machinery and matters that he should not be concerned with, and considering office affairs which should be left to clerks and others; and all this at the expense of the development of his mind and expansion of his nature. He should be living in the country at least four days in the week, and have people come and discuss matters with him there, instead of putting time in his office over routine of business. He is fearful of his own health, and is dosing himself with medicines and the like: and what he needs is fresh air. With his purpose, it is a pity that a man who can do so much good should gradually destroy his own possibilities by his method of living.[10]

King agreed wholeheartedly with Eliot. He told him that he had already discussed these matters with Rockefeller but would do so again at the next opportunity. He found such an opportunity the following day.

They were talking about an error Ivy Lee had made when King noticed how tired Rockefeller looked. The strain was exacting its toll. King thought that it would take little additional pressure to break him down. He needed a rest, and more and better advisors to assist him. When King broached the subject, Rockefeller admitted that his burden was larger than he would have liked but attributed this to the inexperience of Greene and Lee. "The trouble," he asserted, "is to get men."[11] The suggestion that he decide either to exercise direct control over his father's interests and accept responsibility for their actions or place them totally beyond his control and avoid responsibility for their errors—King was thinking specifically of the Foundation here—was met with equivocation. As for removing to the country, Rockefeller thought that he had to remain in the office because he needed more experience. And, when King urged him to travel more,

> He said he did travel a good deal, and spoke about going to the west much oftener. I said that was not what I had in mind. It was going to China and India and those countries where he was helping big movements at the present time; that I thought he should know men of the stamp of Sir Edward Grey, King Albert of Belgium, leading statesmen in the Orient, scholars and

scientists the world over; that I was far from having any snobbish view of life, but that his place was to be dealing with men who were shaping the vital currents of the world's life, so that he could use his fortune in the way that was sure to give the greatest help to mankind.[12]

In reflection, King saw that several of Rockefeller's mistakes were the very ones for which he had himself been criticized, taking the work in hand too seriously and slavishly devoting energy to a multitude of small details at the expense of breadth of vision. He thought these shortcomings, in Rockefeller's case, were the product of a narrow upbringing and his way of living. Equally important, his overriding sense of duty made a prisoner of his spirit. Mrs. E. H. Harriman had said as much when King had called upon her the previous week. She greatly admired Rockefeller's purposes, but thought his lack of imagination and spontaneity helped nurture the prejudice against him. It was wise to be cautious she agreed, "but unless there was spirit and imagination inspiring everything, money of itself would not perform the service it should . . . in the working out of true ideals."[13]

King was consequently all the more pleased with himself for having pushed Rockefeller so hard for aid to the unemployed Colorado miners. When the first wire appealing for help had been shown to Welborn, the C.F. & I. president had attempted to minimize the problem. Noting that the company had already contributed $1000 for local relief, he thought there wasn't much more to be done. Nonetheless, a message was sent to the director of the company's fuel division asking for his appraisal of the extent of hardship among the miners. His reply indicated that distress was mounting, that unemployment was widespread, and now that union strike funds were no longer available, community relief sources were inadequate. A wire was next dispatched to the Trinidad Chamber of Commerce asking it to assist C.F. & I. in locating any former employees among the needy. Rockefeller told Welborn that he would meet the needs of former employees out of his own pocket rather than burden the company. He did not believe that he had any obligation to help those who had no previous connection with C.F. & I. King concurred in this judgment.

Two days later, however, King changed his mind. Prompted by a newspaper item that suggested that the Rockefellers could do a great work by coming to the aid of all those in need whether associated with C.F. & I. or not, "I made up my mind at once that in this circumstance there lay the most fortunate opportunity of helping to pave the way for the restoration of good conditions in Colorado and of placing Mr. R. in his true light before the miners and the public."[14] Before King could raise the issue though, it came up during a meeting of the staff with the Low Commission. Low and another commissioner praised Rockefeller's generosity and volunteered the opinion that he had no obligation to aid other than former employees. King supposed the matter was now beyond recall. But, as he walked with Rockefeller down Fifth Avenue reviewing the meeting, the subject came up again and he took the opportunity to express his new opinion.

Rockefeller "doubted exceedingly" the wisdom of the course King proposed.[15] He believed it would provoke every village, town, and city with unemployment problems to appeal for his assistance. The miners would regard it as an attempt to buy their friendship. Moreover, who knew what it would cost, for who knew how much actual need there was? King, seeing how completely his suggestion took Rockefeller by surprise, assured him that many of the practical difficulties could be overcome but asked only that he weigh the suggestion in his mind. Putting his own position as forcefully as possible, he said that he could not think of any better opportunity that might arise to prepare the way for his work in Colorado or for Rockefeller's visit there. He concluded that if Rockefeller "were seeking to make an investment for his own future and the future of his . . . children, he could not spend fifty or one hundred thousand dollars or more, more profitably at the present time."[16]

Later the same evening, King visited with the Welborns in their suite at the Vanderbilt. At their very first meeting he had marked Mrs. Welborn as a likely ally in the effort to broaden Welborn's understanding of Rockefeller's intentions and purposes. His intuition was confirmed when she came to his assistance as he tried to bring Welborn around to his point of view on the question of giving aid in Colorado. Welborn argued that he and Rockefeller had reconsidered the matter afresh that morning and had found no reason to alter Rockefeller's initial impulse to aid only those with some previous tie to the company. King responded that a gesture of the sort he was proposing would serve to convince the world that Rockefeller's resistance to the union hadn't been a fight for profits but for principle. Mrs. Welborn agreed and pointed out that so generous an act would make all of their plans for change and improvement in Colorado much easier to realize.

Slowly, they won Welborn over to their side but not before he passed along some surprising information. He admitted that the distress that existed in the Trinidad area was more serious than he had cared to indicate. He confided, in addition, that there was much bitterness toward the Rockefellers in the coal fields and that neither he nor the other company officials on the scene thought that Rockefeller's life would be safe if he visited the region as planned. Welborn reasoned that, perhaps, the move King wished Rockefeller to make would remedy both problems simultaneously.

Reflecting on what Welborn had told him, King was angered that all the while Rockefeller had been giving them his unqualified support, the C.F. & I. officers were keeping secrets from New York. Apparently, they had intended to allow him to come to Colorado without warning him of the danger. Surely, Rockefeller or one of his advisors ought to have been informed some time ago, so that steps might have been taken to counter the hostility that prevailed. King concluded that it was absolutely imperative that his aid proposal be adopted.

The following morning, Sunday, Rockefeller telephoned to provide King with the address of a lady he wished to call upon. He mentioned in passing that he had given King's idea some thought and was more favorably disposed toward it than he had been initially. Rockefeller's change of heart, which King believed to be the result of his wife's prompting and prayer, encouraged King to devote the morning to drafting a message to the Trinidad Chamber of Commerce. This done, he called upon Welborn for his opinion. Mr. and Mrs. Welborn were to lunch with the Rockefellers, and at some urging from King, Welborn promised to let Rockefeller know why he thought King's proposal was sound. Welborn took along a copy of the draft King had prepared and left it with Rockefeller.

Bright and early the next day, King and Welborn arrived at the office bound in friendly conspiracy to have King's way. Starr Murphy was already in and they proceeded to bring him up to date. They showed him the much rewritten message, which by now took the form of an instruction to the Trinidad Chamber of Commerce suggesting that the Colorado governor appeal to the Rockefeller Foundation for funds to aid the unemployed miners. Murphy had just signalled his hearty approval when Rockefeller arrived. Before he had even removed his coat, he was beset by King and Welborn, to whose enthusiasm he responded by producing his own reworked version of King's draft. The discussion that followed proved interesting on several counts. In it, King echoed the sentiments Mrs. Harriman had expressed to him a few days earlier, and Rockefeller revealed the sources of his concern in the matter. As always, there was the shadow cast by Senior.

> [Mr. R.] thought we ought to add words to the effect that "if the suffering were widespread and general." I advised against his making the message too cautious, saying that I did not think he ought to lose the chance of being asked to do this thing by making the message appear . . . so framed as to make it improbable that any request would be sent; besides, in proposing a charitable thing or offering to assist in one, the spirit was all important, and it was well to show a free and cordial disposition. He replied to this that, while it might be true, I had to remember other demands might come to him in consequence of a loosely drafted message. He added further, "You do not know how hard it is going to be for me to get this through the Foundation; that is something I have to consider also. Besides," he said, "I doubt very much if Father would agree to this at all." Then he added, "Perhaps I should not say that. He would be satisfied with it, though his judgment might differ."[17]

They worked on the message most of the morning until they had a version that satisfied them. Rockefeller was about to dispatch it when King suggested that they wait until after the meeting of the executive board of the Foundation the following day. Then, they would know for certain that an application if made would not be refused.

At the meeting the next day, March 2, 1915, King was first asked to explain a letter he had written requesting the board's approval for his trip to Colorado. Gates thought he ought to resist the temptation that Colorado represented and launch his investigation in Europe. Judson suggested Pennsylvania, to which King replied that he would be accused of a willingness to look everywhere except where the problems were the most obvious. He hoped to use his visit to gain the acceptance of certain ideas whose adoption would greatly enhance the value of his investigation. President Eliot supported him; he was particularly taken with the argument that, since the Foundation was a beneficiary of C.F. & I. activities, it had a responsibility to ensure that those activities were conducted in an acceptable fashion. The discussion was brought to an end on a note of general agreement when

Jerome Greene pointed out that it was not up to the Board to decide how King should proceed since he already possessed their
authority to conduct his investigation as he thought best. The
next item of business was the telegram.

As soon as Rockefeller concluded the reading of the message,
individual members of the board expressed their enthusiastic
support. Rockefeller's concern over the possible rejection of the
proposal by the Board was entirely misplaced. Gates and Judson
raised the suggestion that, perhaps, Rockefeller Senior ought to
be indicated more clearly as the donor instead of the Foundation,
since he was the one who suffered the most from the negative
publicity. This would help balance accounts, so to speak. The
group as a whole, however, preferred to have the Foundation receive the request for aid. And so, with one word change of little
consequence, the message was approved as read.

Whatever elation King may have felt over his triumphs that
day—at the afternoon session of the board his views on Polish relief prevailed—was tempered by his sense of how much work remained to be done. That very morning, a bomb plot had been
exposed by a police undercover agent. Two anarchists had been
arrested as they attempted to set off a bomb in St. Patrick's Cathedral, following which they had intended to destroy Andrew
Carnegie and the Rockefellers. The story made banner headlines
in the afternoon papers.

> The paper was lying, with the headlines covering half of a front
> page, at Mr. Rockefeller's feet during the afternoon, as he
> stayed on until seven in the evening discussing what it was best
> to do in the interests of the starving people of Poland. Here is
> part of the tragedy of life . . .[18]

There was more distressing news in the papers the following
morning, this time in the form of a summary of the report of the
House committee that, under the chairmanship of Congressman
Foster, had investigated the Colorado strike. King thought the report grossly unfair because it ignored the other struck companies
and accused Rockefeller of being prepared to use C.F. & I. funds
to buy guns and starve out the miners rather than arbitrate
differences.

> *Knowing all the facts* as I do, I can think of nothing more cruel
> than this. Literally hundreds of thousands will read this report

and accept it as true because of its having an official imprimatur upon it. It will confirm prejudices already entertained, and through the whole of his life Mr. R. will not be able to eradicate the bitterness and hatred which this indictment would produce in the minds of countless numbers, seek to do what he may. He asked me, as he walked along, if I had seen the Foster report. I told him I had, and that I thought it most unfair. His only comment was "Isn't it unfair!" I added that it only helped to emphasize what I had tried to impress upon him, that in the last analysis he would be held responsible for the actions of the others in everything with which he was concerned.[19]

The shortcomings of the Foster report only served to strengthen King's partisanship, his sense of himself as a guide and shield to Rockefeller. The possibility that there might exist an accurate set of facts that sustained the report's conclusions never entered his mind. Before the month was out, however, he would discover that he had not known "all the facts." And before the week had gone by, he reversed his opinion of the report's likely consequences. Perhaps, he remembered how small the reading audience for government documents was; more likely, he was influenced by the progress he had made by then in talks with the Low Commission.

The first meeting with the three Commission members on February 28 proved both cordial and enlightening. The admission of Patrick Gilday, the U.M.W. representative on the Commission, that his union's western leadership was unreliable and reckless was particularly significant. It confirmed King, Welborn, and Rockefeller in their opinion of Lawson et al. and in their desire to avoid dealing with the union. King also understood, from what both Gilday and Low said in the course of the interview, that the commission had no intention to make the recognition of the union one of its objectives. Questions were directed to Welborn about the changes he had introduced at C.F. & I. and about those he contemplated for the future. Gilday suggested that, if the representation scheme was expanded somewhat, C.F. & I. would have the equivalent of the union's pit committee. These committees, he explained, were usually elected by the men to reflect the different ethnic groups present, a feature that the union thought vital to its success. The main task of such committees was to thrash out grievances.

Seth Low was interested in knowing if the object of the representation plan was to deal with grievances or more broadly with

Seth Low, undated. By permission of Columbia University.

all the terms and conditions of employment? Was it to be a complaint system or a system of collective bargaining? Welborn responded that only the first step had been taken in organizing the representation plan. In time, the men would be involved in many of the areas Low had in mind; although, since the wage rate paid was already the second highest in the country, he did not anticipate any issue in that quarter for some time. One problem that he confessed had him stumped was the matter of checkweighmen. This issue had figured in the strike, but all efforts by the company to resolve it had been rebuffed by the miners. Either the men refused to vote in a checkweighman or, having elected one, they changed their minds and chose to work without one. Welborn was fearful that some observers would attribute the absence of checkweighmen to covert pressure by the company. Gilday provided an explanation.

Like many aspects of industrial relations, the true motive here lay hidden to outsiders. The checkweighman was primarily used by the union as a means of securing dues from all the men in a mine, he explained. Only in those relatively infrequent instances where a company cheated its miners on the scales was it the safeguard most people supposed it to be. The C.F. & I. miners, who weren't shortweighted, were probably unwilling to pay for the support of a checkweighman when his presence made no difference in their earnings.

There followed a discussion of the workmen's compensation and industrial commission bills then pending before the Colorado legislature. The National Civic Federation had taken a hand in drafting these bills, so that it must have pleased Low to hear Welborn say that he supported their passage. Welborn surprised King at one point in the meeting by going so far as to say that, although C.F. & I. did not recognize the union and would not so long as its present leadership continued in office, that did not mean that the company would not be prepared to deal with it at some time in the future. Surely, he was being disingenuous in saying this, King thought. Left to his own devices, Welborn would do nothing. For this reason, King took some satisfaction in having persuaded the commission to hold off in its visit to Colorado until the following spring. To his way of thinking, the prospect of this future visit would help sustain the pressures necessary to keep Welborn moving toward reform.

Later that week, Ivy Lee expressed concern that King's own pending trip to Colorado might be mistaken as a rejection of the commission. At his urging, King called on Low to talk the matter over.

King was very favorably impressed with Low, whom he saw playing a role very much like the one he had often assumed in Canada. At this second meeting, he cast himself as Low's ally. In explaining why he was making the western trip, King repeatedly stressed the view of himself as serving the public interest, as if he too were a public servant. He was genuinely convinced that any accomplishments he made in behalf of the Rockefellers would benefit the public. He pledged that one result of his trip would be that, by the time Low and his fellow commissioners visited Colorado, they would find sufficient change to oblige them to write a favorable report. King also asked Low whether it would be wise for him to pay a call on Labor Secretary Wilson. Low thought that since King had occupied a comparable position in Canada, a courtesy call would be expected of him. When King mentioned this to

Rockefeller, Rockefeller expressed the fear that Wilson would try to block his trip. King supposed that his call would have the opposite effect, and he proved correct.

As he made preparations to leave New York for Ottawa, King reflected upon what he took to be the positive results of his visit. Welborn had been made to understand Rockefeller's intentions and was now prepared to consider seriously King's plans for reform at C.F. & I. Amicable relations had been established with the Low Commission and, as a result, the public interest in building industrial peace would benefit. The program of relief to the miners would do more to allay hostility in Colorado and show Rockefeller's true colors than anything else that might be done. Finally, King had a clear field to develop his ideas for reform in Colorado, to put them into practice, and if successful, to use them as the guiding principles in his larger investigation into industrial relations.

With considerable prescience he gauged the temper of the day:

When, after there had been bloodshed in Colorado, Mr. R. testified on the stand that he was prepared to use the Rockefeller millions to stand by the mine operators, this was interpreted to and by the public to mean that the enormous fortune of his father was to be used to help crush trade unionism, and when there followed, after this testimony, further bloodshed in Colorado, the loss of women and children as well as men, with no endeavor on his part to ascertain conditions, but a willingness to accept the operators' word for everything, conditions were just about as bad for Mr. R. and his future as in the history of this world they have ever been for almost any man on earth. . . . To have worked from the situation as it then existed, through the aggravation of it by the refusal of the operators to accept the proposals of the President of the United States, the subsequent publicity of Colorado conditions through the Walsh Commission in Colorado, and the melodramatic exhibition of the Commission in New York, and to have reached a point where a finding by a congressional committee would have sounded as a death knell, to where its effect is little more than that of an exploding rocket, means that a big change has been wrought both in the attitude of Mr. R. and the interests he represents and in the interpretation of that attitude to the public . . . there is reason to feel that the worst of the storm has been weathered . . .[20]

King surmised that as the favorable interim report of the Low Commission, the relief program in Colorado, and Rockefeller's tour of inspection came to the public's attention, each would further enhance the repute of the Rockefellers.

The lone cloud on the horizon emanated from the realization that several Rockefeller advisors were not as able as they should be. It was fortunate that Rockefeller was aware of the limitations of Jerome Greene and Ivy Lee, but that awareness did not compensate for their inadequacies. Rockefeller's complaint about the difficulty of finding honest and capable advisors notwithstanding, he made very little effort to search for good men and depended largely on chance acquaintances or referrals. King was concerned most particularly about the influence of Ivy Lee. On several occasions during his visit he had found Lee's initiatives alarmingly malapropos. When, for example, Seth Low had shown Lee a draft of his commission's interim report, Lee had made two suggestions that ran directly counter to the desires of King and Rockefeller. Where they wished to minimize the public's tendency to mistake the Rockefellers as the sole or dominant employer in the strike, Lee suggested that the Rockefeller name be prominently featured in the report. Where they wished to minimize their dealings with the mine workers' union, partly because of the alarm such dealings would raise among the other mine operators, Lee suggested that Low discuss his report with the union's national officers. Low confessed to King that he had impetuously followed Lee's recommendations but had since come to doubt their wisdom. King assured him that his second thoughts were correct and asked that the report be returned to its original form.

On returning to 26 Broadway, King talked about Lee, first with Starr Murphy and then with Rockefeller. He told Murphy that he distrusted Lee's judgment and thought him capable of getting the Rockefellers into great trouble.

> That I feared, in matters of publicity Mr. Lee had the immediate effect too much in mind rather than the effect in the long run; that I looked on the daily press as a daily curse in some respects; and that while it was well to consider the moulding of public opinion hour by hour, it had always to be moulded in the broader conception of what would best stand the test of time.[21]

King urged that Lee be watched closely and forbidden to act without first consulting Murphy. Murphy confessed that the staff had come to a similar conclusion. An understanding had been reached that he, Murphy, was to be informed prior to any actions by Lee.

In spite of his doubts about Lee's judgment, King permitted himself to be influenced by the publicist's opinion on several occasions. It was at Lee's suggestion that he had talked to Low about the advisability of going to Colorado and of going to Washington to meet with Secretary Wilson. For some reason that he did not understand, Lee did not appear to want him to make the western trip. But Low thought it made sense for him to go and Rockefeller was very keen on his going. If Lee had hoped that Secretary of Labor Wilson would block the trip, he was again mistaken.

After setting his affairs aright in Ottawa, King left for Washington to pay his courtesy call at the Department of Labor. In his talk with Secretary Wilson, Wilson described his early efforts to prevent the strike by having the union drop its demand for recognition. The quid pro quo was to have been the operators' agreement to establish the equivalent of pit committees. The operators, however, were fearful that, if they once permitted the men to organize committees, they would be captured by the union. Wilson thought this fear well placed. As an alternative, he had next recommended that a commission be created to resolve any differences between the mine committees and the operators. The operators again refused. He was of the opinion that had the Rockefellers then taken the position Rockefeller had taken since, the strike would have ended at that point. He said several times how pleased he was that Rockefeller's recent views had changed so dramatically from those he aired before the Foster Committee.

King remarked that Rockefeller had been perfectly sincere in what he had said both before the Foster Committee, when he had defended the open shop, and before the Commission on Industrial Relations, when he had endorsed unionism and collective bargaining, as if the sincerity of his views excused their substance. King told Wilson of the strength of Rockefeller's commitment to improve industrial conditions. In earnest of this, he placed himself at Wilson's disposal should the Secretary ever learn of any sort of labor problems arising in or threatening a Rockefeller holding. As he noted afterwards in his diary, he told Wilson, "I felt it was important that those of us who had our hands on levers that were important, should understand each other, and knowing that our purpose was one and the same, should cooperate whenever a chance offered."[22]

The two men talked of the intense hostility that divided capital and labor in the western states. Wilson thought each side far too eager to take the law into its own hands. So long as this was the case, the prospects for peace and settled conditions seemed extremely poor.

King read in Wilson's words the implication that prevailing conditions justified a refusal to recognize the union. This was the second time within two weeks he had been led to such an understanding by the union or its allies. He related to Wilson that, when Rockefeller finished reading John Lawson's testimony before the Commission on Industrial Relations, he had said he finally understood why C.F. & I. officials had shown the union leader so little courtesy. Wilson responded with the opinion that Lawson's influence had peaked and was on the wane. By his manner, he indicated that such a development was to his liking. This was the second time also that King had heard Lawson disparaged by his supposed allies. He, Rockefeller, the Low Commission, and Secretary Wilson seemed to be of one mind: no one objected to avoiding the union in Colorado since that meant avoiding John Lawson. Inasmuch as those whose opinions counted in New York and Washington were disposed to allow the Rockefellers to avoid the union as they had intended all along, King left Washington convinced of the correctness of his course. He left for Denver and a series of conversations and inspection trips that added wholly new dimensions to his understanding of the strike and industrial relations.

Notes

1. W.L.M.K. to J.D.R., Jr., 2/9/15. J.D.R., Jr. Papers, Friends and Services, Box 72.
2. W.L.M.K. Diary, 2/23/15. M.G.26, Series J13, W.L.M.K. Papers, p. G2539, 208.
3. Ibid.
4. Ibid., 12/8/14, p. G2539, 118.
5. Ibid., p. G2539, 210.
6. Ibid., pp. G2539, 210–11.
7. Ibid., p. G2539, 214.
8. Ibid., p. G2539, 216.
9. Ibid., p. G2539, 222. The words are King's paraphrase.
10. Ibid., 3/3/15, p. G2539, 284.
11. Ibid., 3/4/15, p. G2539, 302.
12. Ibid., pp. G2539, 303–04.

13. Ibid., 2/26/15, pp. G2539, 239–40.
14. Ibid., 2/27/15, pp. G2539, 253.
15. Ibid., p. G2539, 254.
16. Ibid., p. G2539, 255.
17. Ibid., 3/1/15, pp. G2539, 261–62.
18. Ibid., 3/2/15, p. G2539, 276.
19. (emphasis added). Ibid., 3/3/15, p. G2539, 279.
20. Ibid., 3/5/15, p. G2539, 308.
21. Ibid., 3/4/15, p. G2539, 295.
22. Ibid., 3/15/15, p. G2539, 323.

6. The Truth About Colorado

In the thousand miles west from Chicago to Denver, the train speeds along a gradient that carries it from 579 feet above sea level to an elevation of one mile. The ascent is so gradual that the passengers have no sensation of the climb, even though most of it occurs during the last half of the trip. In all directions, the prairie seems unrelievedly flat, the more so once the first glimpse of the Front Range is confirmed. The mountains announce the West and bar the way. By turns stupefying and exhilarating in their majesty, they project the challenges of endurance and discovery right into the streets of Denver.

The shape of Mackenzie King's visit to Colorado changed even before it began. The elder Mrs. Rockefeller died on March 12, causing her son to postpone his departure for the West for one month. On the eve of his rescheduled trip, Rockefeller's father-in-law died, and Mrs. Rockefeller, Jr., then in the last months of pregnancy, fell ill, causing an indefinite postponement. As a result, King in the company of his secretary Francis McGregor, spent an unhurried month and a half learning about industrial relations Colorado style.

On arriving, King advertised in Denver newspapers his willingness to meet with any who might wish to provide information. Subsequently, he interviewed coal company officials, union advocates, public officials, and a number of influential men who had observed the strike at some remove. Later, he toured the Colorado Fuel & Iron Company mining camps, and spoke with miners and their wives, with superintendents, pit bosses, store managers, and anyone who might provide information or insights useful in developing reforms. He visited the parlors of some of Denver's leading citizens, surveyed the saloons and brothels of the red-light district in Trinidad, and traveled into the earth to see the conditions under which coal was won.

King used a portion of his time to guide the development of the work relief program he had advocated in New York. He also devoted considerable time to considering measures for the improvement of C.F. & I. mining camps. Building upon the relationship begun in New York, he called frequently at the Welborn home. He grew in Welborn's confidence to a point where he felt free to speak candidly about the management of the company. With Mrs. Welborn continuing in the role of his "co-conspirator," he came to exercise considerable influence on Welborn's judgment.

King entered in his diary what others told him, his impressions of people and places, and his reflections upon what he learned. Many of his conversations were private ones in which the information and opinions provided were understood to be given in confidence. People revealed things about themselves, about the strike, and about others, that they would not have revealed in public. Consequently, King's diary entries provide an extraordinary opportunity to penetrate beneath the outward show of events to the living tissue of history. A note of caution is in order, however. Few pieces of evidence that corroborate the diary entries could be found in other record files. This is understandable given that much of the information King received was transmitted orally. There is, however, no compelling reason why the entries in question cannot be taken at the same value as others whose substance can be corroborated. The absence of confirming evidence also happens, in this instance, to be an integral part of the story this chapter has to tell.

Much of the correspondence between King and the New York office was destroyed willfully. The letters often ended with some such statement as "Please destroy this letter of which I have kept no copy." Several of these survived by being incorporated into the diary or because one of the parties did keep a copy. Still other letters were exchanged between seconds. Thus, King communicated through his secretary, McGregor, with Rockefeller through the latter's secretary, Charles Heydt. These letters were not preserved in either of the principal's files. Again, evidence of their having been written was found in the diary. Telegraphic messages were exchanged in a private code. The telephone also was employed, leaving no record other than the one King chose to indicate in his diary. These tactics suggest either that King and Rockefeller were seeking to hide something or that they were reluctant to create a pool of information that might be used to embarrass them. Actually, both things were true.

Throughout King's stay, coded telegrams were exchanged to ensure that hostile union people and possibly even antagonistic coal operators would not learn what the Rockefeller camp was

up to. Then, late in April, the strike-related correspondence between Rockefeller and Lamont Bowers, which Rockefeller had
been obliged to turn over to the Commission on Industrial Relations, was made public. At the same time Rockefeller, King, and
Ivy Lee were notified that they would be recalled for further
questioning before the Commission in mid-May. This combination of events provided King and Rockefeller with a clear incentive to minimize the written record between them. They believed
that their exchanges could, and probably would, be distorted in
a way calculated to compromise or embarrass them. If they were
again obliged by subpoena to turn over their correspondence,
they would provide their enemies with as little ammunition as
possible.

It also transpired that some of the things King learned in Colorado *were* scandalous to report and would have compromised
Rockefeller were they generally known. For this reason, King had
no desire to create a written record that might be exposed. His
caution ran to such lengths that, in a tactic made familiar to the
contemporary reader by the exposures of the Watergate conspiracy and the Iran-Contra affair, through McGregor he would advise that no one in New York was to query him about Colorado in
advance of giving testimony before the commission. He sought to
shield Rockefeller by sustaining for the time being his ignorance
of the truth about Colorado.

One of King's very first interviews in Denver was with Mother
Jones. The angel of the miners seemed anxious to make amends
for any misunderstanding that might have grown out of her actions and those of John Lawson in New York. She portrayed Lawson as someone wrongly used, indicating that his testimony before
the commission had been prepared by someone other than himself and that pressure had been applied to make him take a hostile
position. When King asked if that "someone" was Frank Walsh or
Edward Costigan she replied that it was not Walsh. Not that it
mattered much to King, for he concluded at that time that "none
of these people, Walsh included, are entitled to any serious notice,
and were it not for the press would receive little of it."[1] He regarded Mother Jones as an agitator by temperament, given to
making rash statements for their shock effect. Still, he could not
gainsay the evidence of her clear, logical mind and her political
acumen. Her abilities in a man, he reflected, would undoubtedly
have produced a political leader. Almost in spite of himself, he
could not deny his admiration.

Several days later, they had another opportunity to talk and King found himself deeply touched. Out of curiosity, he asked her to tell him how she had come to the role of labor agitator. She related that injustice had always been a presence in her life. One of her earliest memories was of watching British soldiers walking down a street in Cork carrying the head of some poor Irishman at the top of a pike. Her family had emigrated to Canada where she had attended school. In the 1840s, she had taken part with her father in the Grand Trunk Railway strike. Since then she supposed she had been in more strikes than anyone in the entire country. Now that she was 83 years old, the strain of this activity was beginning to tell, she admitted. After each battle, it took her longer and longer to regain her strength. When King suggested that the union owed her a home and some comfort for her remaining years, she disdained any thought for herself, as if she and privilege had an abiding pact to avoid one another. She was content she said to make her home at Terence Powderly's place in Washington.[2]

Seeking to bare what was for him the touchstone of character, King asked her about her religious sentiments. When she revealed a depth of Christian awareness wholly satisfying to him, his last doubts were swept away. He saw in her an admirable heroine, completely honest and dedicated to the cause of justice for the miners, willing to bear any burden and make any sacrifice that cause might impose. In this light he understood that

> Her life illustrates the inevitable working out of moral law in the world, and should teach men who allow strikes to run on over a period of time, and the militia to be called in, to be careful of what they are doing. When I think of the 200 people that have been killed in this recent strike . . . and of the two years in which little children have lived in tent colonies with their daily thought concentrated in hate upon the militia and armed forces and brutal police as the symbols of capital, I shudder to think of what the American people may not reap when the sense of injustice and wrong seething in their hearts and beings breaks forth at some time during the manhood and womanhood of these lives, seeking the vengeance which they believe their natural right and which human nature, being what it is, will certainly demand at some time in some way. Revolution is never born in a day. . . . It is but the graphic expression of volcanic seethings which all injustice and oppression serves to feed.[3]

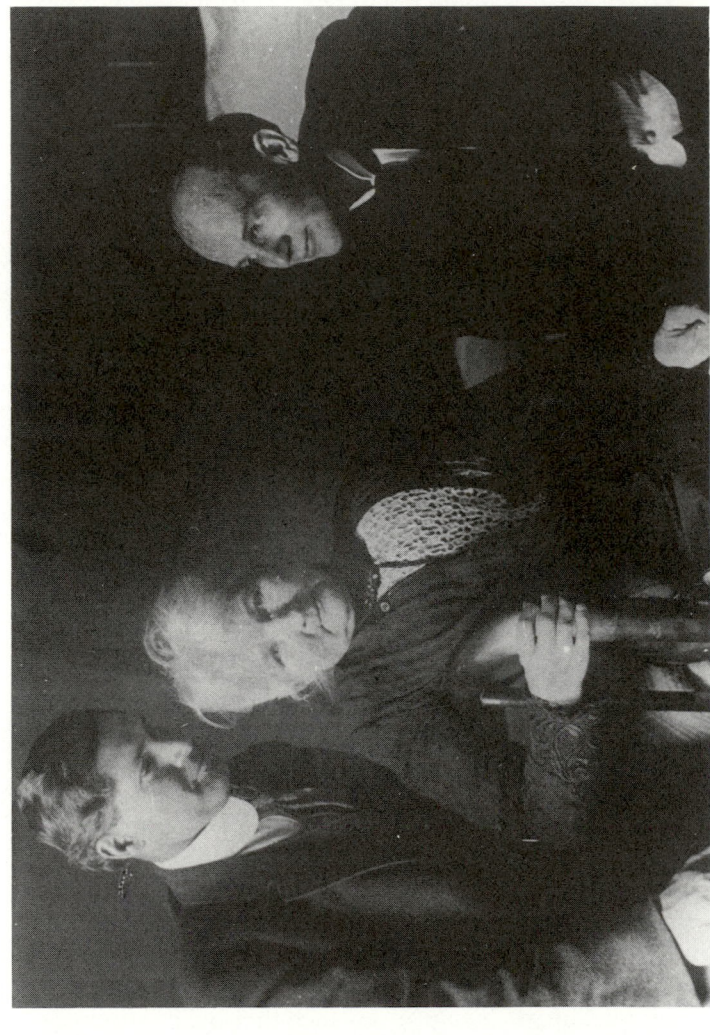

Horace Hawkins, Mother Jones, and John R. Lawson, c. 1914. By permission of the Archives of Urban Labor and Urban Affairs, Wayne State University.

King did not indicate whom he had in mind when he wrote of "men who allow strikes to run on." He certainly did not mean Rockefeller, for his very next thoughts were of him and wholly positive. Mother Jones had expressed to King the belief that now that Rockefeller was taking pains to inform himself about conditions in Colorado, he was certain to set everything aright for the miners. King was delighted at what he took to be evidence of the force of Rockefeller's character at work among those who were once his enemies. It also struck him as noteworthy that not once during their conversation had Mother Jones mentioned the desirability of union recognition. She seemed content to rest her hopes for reform on Rockefeller's goodwill. It was probably John C. Osgood who entered his thoughts, for since his arrival in Denver, Osgood had been portrayed to King on all sides as the villain of the strike. He had seen the man only once, yet the occasion had given rise to the strongest feelings of antipathy.

Quite by chance, Osgood had been pointed out to him just two days earlier. He was in the company of his wife, a strikingly handsome woman, entertaining guests at lunch. King's luncheon companion informed him that although the Osgoods had openly carried on an affair for some years prior to their marriage, they now stood foremost among "the Sacred Thirty-Six," as Denver's smart set was known. King was flabbergasted; nothing he had heard about Osgood thus far was as damning as this piece of intelligence. (He recognized that his information was hearsay but thought it was probably accurate given the reliability of its source.) That the Osgoods and their friends were among the very ones who most loudly condemned Rockefeller for shaking hands with Mother Jones, when they themselves led lives so obviously open to criticism, struck him as rank hypocrisy.

It was not mere prudery that animated his feelings in this regard, but deeply held convictions about the role of character in shaping the world. He believed that social injustice found its rooting-ground in flaws of character. His entire view of life turned on this belief.

Most theories of social conflict are macrocosmic in design and for that reason tend to oversimplify, where they do not altogether ignore, the motivations of individuals. This is particularly true of interest theories of conflict, which picture social classes or interest groups arrayed against one another in a contest for shares of society's assets and privileges. Such theories often assume that the existence of marked disparities in life circumstances is itself suffi-

John C. Osgood, President of the Victor-America Fuel Company. By permission of the Colorado Historical Society.

cient to explain social conflict. Some variants of interest theory do recognize that individuals may differ in the degree to which they are aggressive, risk aversive, or defensive, etc., but they tend to discount these differences as of little importance. Individuals tend to be seen as the instruments through which the social pressures created by inequality find expression. From such a perspective, the individuals caught up in any social conflict are barely responsible for their behavior.

Mackenzie King possessed an altogether different perspective. Although he knew better than most the dimensions of the gulf separating those whose lives were a constant struggle from those who lived in luxury, he did not accept the notion that inequality inevitably bred conflict. Nor did he accept the thought that conflict might have positive dimensions. He believed that conflict sprang from human ignorance or error, that it was hurtful and destructive, and that it was to be avoided insofar as possible without compromising principles. His thinking on the subject was intimately connected with his lifelong desire to serve as the leader of his people, so that his views were not the musings of a detached student of society but the modeling of a world so shaped and ordered as to permit him to realize his dreams.

He began from broad religious premises that were not peculiarly Presbyterian. A reverence for the teachings of Christ was the foundation of all else. By his standards, this was the clearest talisman of good character. He meant by good character the acceptance of a force in life superior to one's own will, a force that bound one to think of others and to rise above oneself through the disciplines of work and purification. Good character constrained egotism with high purpose and hard work. However, high purpose and hard work are often the major ingredients of ambition, as they clearly were in King's life. How then was ambition divorced from egotism when the two seem so intertwined? For King the answer lay in character. High purpose reduced life's many temptations to trivial proportions at the same time that hard work humbled vanity. So separated from selfishness, ambition was transformed into service. And to serve as a leader of the people was the noblest of human callings.

King believed that the good repute of leaders was vital in a democracy if the prevailing social order was to be accepted and sustained. Should there be inconsistency in this, with undeserving men occupying positions of power and influence, the people would have evidence of social malaise, and some among them would adopt cynical attitudes conducive to conflict. For if some men dominated without an entitlement at once legal, moral, and reflective of merit, they would provoke the belief that the prevailing distributions of power and reward were arbitrary and unjust and, therefore, might be attacked with impunity.

The threat to social stability created by inadequate leaders had its twin in misinformation. King possessed an abiding confidence in the public's capacity for sound judgment, but he was troubled by the ease with which that judgment could be misdirected by inadequate or inaccurate information. One of the aspects of his relationship with the Rockefellers that he found most challenging, and sometimes most disheartening, was the gap he perceived to exist between their intentions and their public reputation. So critical was the adjustment between what was true and what the public took to be true, that King's interest in political leadership may be seen to have emanated from his passion to show the truth to his people.

Character and correct information were as necessary to justice as they were to social stability. King believed that leaders of good character, whatever the sphere of their activities, could be depended upon to work to redress any wrongs afflicting those people touched by their authority. Their desire and their duty to make the practices of the world conform to their good intentions necessarily made them the standard bearers of life-enhancing change. No one deserving of the responsibilities of leadership would ever knowingly allow injustice to persist within the scope of their power. In contrast, men who thought themselves bound by no higher authority than their own will owed no debt to their fellows and were more likely than not to use them poorly. King was so affected by what he learned of Osgood's personal life because it seemed to illustrate this. It was as if a deep and universal truth had been called up from within him for confirmation. He noted in his diary: "This brings the solution of the labor problem back again to the question of character."[4]

The public at large, and public officials as well, had assumed that the Rockefellers controlled events and directed the strike. Knowing this to be untrue, Rockefeller and King had assumed that Lawson was to blame. This assumption now seemed less and less tenable. The longer he remained in Colorado and the more people he spoke to, the stronger the conviction grew in King that Osgood was the culprit. He, and not John Lawson, had all along been the central figure in the strike.

Henry Cohen, a lawyer for the United Mine Workers, was among the first of those with whom King talked. Recommended to him by a labor member of the Commission on Industrial Relations, King found Cohen well equipped to present labor's side of recent events. He was most impressed with the broad context that Cohen developed for his understanding. The labor history of the state, as Cohen saw it, bore intimately upon the recent strike. At the turn of the century, the first mine workers' union in the region, the Western Federation of Miners, had alarmed the mine operators by advocating state ownership of the mines. The operators had responded to this threat swiftly and brutally, crushing the union. When the smoke of battle cleared, the operators found themselves with only token union opposition and in complete control of the political machinery of the state. Unchallenged, they proceeded to employ the state to their own ends. The rights of workers were suppressed, union organizers arrested, and the coal fields kept clear of any whom the companies deemed undesirable. In Cohen's judgment, the recent strike was an uprising against this oppressive regime.

Two days later, much of what Cohen told King was confirmed by Horton Pope. Pope was also a lawyer, but one whose services had been at the disposal of the coal companies. What Cohen surmised or could only speculate about, Pope knew from direct experience. He admitted to enough compromising behavior to convince King of his sincerity. King, however, took the precaution to seek independent confirmation of what he was told.

Pope readily admitted that for years, while serving as counsel for the Victor-American Fuel Company under Osgood, he and the counsel for C.F. & I., Cass Herrington, had manipulated the state's political affairs. Since leaving Victor-American, he had devoted his energies almost exclusively to securing the election and reelection of Simon Guggenheim to the United States Senate.

> He said that when they were seeking to have Senator Guggenheim elected . . . [by] the State Legislature, and to have appointments controlled in the manner they wished them, there was not a part of Las Animas and Huerfano Counties which they did not absolutely control; that an abundance of money was spent in gaining this control. In two years he thought it had cost Senator Guggenheim about a half a million dollars. This had not been spent in bribing individual voters directly, so much as in controlling every situation and position. In the counties mentioned they began with the county judge, the district attorney, the sheriffs and county officers, with the result that any man whom they wished to get rid of because he was an organizer or for any other reason, they could readily free themselves of. They could get convictions where they wanted them, and exemptions from convictions where they wanted them.[5]

In his judgment, Pope confided, the true cause of the recent strike lay in the fact that the money required to maintain control over this political machine had given out. The asking prices of the local bosses had risen so high that the coal companies, including C.F. & I., were loath to meet them. One of the bosses, Jesse G.

Northcutt, in an effort to provide an object lesson in the value of his services had turned traitor and aided the union. His encouragement, Pope believed, had been instrumental in luring the union into the attempt to organize the southern field. This was not to deny the existence of very real grievances among the miners. Had there been no grounds for complaint, Pope averred, the union would have found much less support than it did.

In Pope's mind there was no question that Osgood had been the dominant figure in the strike. He characterized him as "a complete reactionary, unrelenting and unmovable."[6] Pope held an equally low opinion of Lamont Bowers. Welborn, he believed, was too passive to either free himself from Osgood's influence or to lead C.F. & I. along a new and independent course. He had been a first-rate salesman, but he lacked the breadth and the boldness required for leadership. He would probably never free himself of once having worked under Osgood. When King asked about the steps Welborn had taken to establish a system of representation among the miners, Pope laughed and said that Welborn and the men under him managed the company like an army: they gave orders and expected them to be obeyed. Any worker who complained about his superior would get no satisfaction, for the management people shielded one another. It was too much to expect men accustomed to this autocratic style of management to change in the absence of strong, guiding leadership at the top.

The people of Colorado were waiting, Pope told King, to see whether Rockefeller meant what he had said before the Commission on Industrial Relations. The reactionaries in the Osgood group were furious about his testimony. The labor people, on the other hand, were wary; they wanted to see actions confirming the testimony before they would believe it. If actions were indeed forthcoming, Pope was of the opinion that a revolution would be avoided—those were the stakes: peace or revolution.

Pope believed that it would not be necessary to recognize the union to have peace. It would suffice if the union people knew that the company was being absolutely fair and honest in its dealings with the miners. He suggested that getting rid of Welborn and Cass Herrington would demonstrate concretely Rockefeller's intentions. Both men were tainted by their past actions, and neither was big enough to provide the type of leadership that would be required to build an effective, lasting peace. C.F. & I., he reminded King, was the largest enterprise and the single most powerful of all influences in the state. Its future would inevitably shape the destiny of Colorado.

King mused aloud that although he was generally opposed to corporate involvement in politics, he wondered whether, in view of Colorado's adoption of the initiative, the referendum, and recall, it wasn't necessary for C.F. & I. to get involved as an act of self-defense against unwise legislation. Pope's opinion was quite surprising in view of his past. He replied that the very best thing the corporations could do was to stay out of politics. The people, when left to decide matters for themselves, could be trusted to act wisely. This was the second time in almost as many days that a man more or less directly confessed to King that he had lived a lie, acting in a way he knew to be wrong and yet unable or unwilling to cease or withdraw.

Pope indicated that thanks to the generosity of the Guggenheims, he was now financially independent and in a position to speak with perfect candor. He owed an immense debt of gratitude to the Guggenheims and explained that his motive in coming to King and speaking as he had was by way of repaying their favors. He was certain that any reforms and improvements King made on the basis of the intelligence given him would ultimately prove as advantageous to the Guggenheims as they would to the Rockefellers. He also expressed confidence that what he had told King would somehow be used to the advantage of the miners, for whom he confessed to feel a genuine concern. If industrial peace could be built upon a fair and firm foundation, everyone stood to benefit.

Much of what Pope confided about the coal companies' domination of politics and the instruments of government had previously been attested to at the Denver hearings of the Commission on Industrial Relations in December. U.M.W. leaders, Judge Ben Lindsey, Professor James H. Brewster of Colorado University, and State Senator Helen Ring Robinson were among those who had testified about corporate political control. The Rockefeller staff, however, unable to distinguish between fact and politically inspired fancy in this testimony, had adopted the self-serving tactic of discounting it. They simply refused to credit adverse reports of C.F. & I. when they came from people regarded as partisan opponents. Even the criticisms of "acceptable" neutrals, such as the state's attorney general, went unheeded because of the selective distortion enforced by the staff's bias. Hence, King's interview with Pope was something of a revelation. *His* testimony was entirely creditable and made it clear that there were problems within the operations of C.F. & I. that required immediate attention.

King had been drawn to the same conclusion by an earlier interview with Cass Herrington who, along with his brother Fred, served as C.F. & I. counsel. Where Fred fulfilled his legal duties in a more conventional fashion, Cass was reputed (by Pope and others) to be the political wire puller. When questioned by King about the repeated assertion that injured workers and the survivors of deceased workers had no hope of winning a suit for damages brought against the company, Cass was embarrassed to concede that this was so. He admitted that while the decisions of the courts were always legal, they were sometimes unjust and unfair, so much so that the company after winning the verdict sometimes made compensatory payments on its own. King reflected in his diary that treatment of this sort by the courts could hardly promote the workers' faith in either the law or the institutions of government. Nor would it prompt the coal companies to work as hard as they should to prevent accidents. Clearly, in this phase of the problem, the courts and the company were responsible for breeding unrest.

At the very first opportunity, King discussed what Pope had told him with Cass Herrington and, later the same day, with Jesse Welborn. Without revealing his source, King asked Herrington about the company's involvement in state and local politics. Herrington readily admitted to his interest and participation in political manipulation. Just as readily he was led to admit that this might not have been a wise course to follow. He was now prepared to be guided by whatever policies were consistent with Mr. Rockefeller's plans. When asked what he thought about setting up permanent boards of conciliation within the company, Herrington said that he would be glad to help in whatever way he could. There were two obstacles of which King should be made aware, however. The first arose because of C.F. & I.'s past associations with Osgood and the operators' group. It would be difficult but not impossible for C.F. & I. to go its own way. The second obstacle arose from the limitations of Jesse Welborn. Herrington described the latter as a product of the "old school," with narrow, even reactionary views, who could not mingle with his men and, perhaps, liked his ease overmuch. He could be helped to overcome these limitations, Herrington was persuaded, but it would require placing constant pressure upon him and watching him.

Herrington expressed the concluding judgment that Welborn was worth the effort.

Perhaps, this kindly and helpful attitude toward Welborn endeared Herrington to King; or maybe, his saving grace resided in the conscience that prompted him to recommend payments to the injured workers he had vanquished in court. In any event, something about Herrington touched King, for in reflecting on their conversation in his diary, he concluded with reference to him and to Welborn: "One has to learn to work through the powers that be and to take the instruments that lie at hand, not always looking around for dramatic changes."[7]

Welborn, for his part, certainly gave every indication that he was not one for dramatic changes. When King employed Pope's simile and likened the company to an army in which the privates had no voice, Welborn indicated that he had given some thought to visiting the camps and arranging some meetings with the men. King argued that this was not enough. What was required was a regular and permanent structure that allowed the men to discuss issues and guaranteed that they could do so without fear of reprisal. This was the sort of arrangement the Low Commission would be looking for when it came west. Moreover, King noted, if the company didn't permit and even encourage its men to organize themselves in some permanent way, it could not hope to resist future organizing efforts by the union.

King then raised the question of the company's role in politics. Welborn admitted that there had in the past been a considerable involvement, but went on to assert that in the last few years this had not been so. At the mention of Sheriff Farr and Judge Northcutt, however, he became quite defensive. C.F. & I., he maintained, had no control over Farr and would be happy were he retired from office. Admittedly, the sheriff was a source of irritation to the miners, but he was virtually the law unto himself. Only by becoming deeply involved in politics could the company hope to oust him. The company's relationship with Judge Northcutt, on the other hand, was now limited to his role in the prosecutions against those who had violated the law during the strike. Welborn thought him one of the few fearless men who understood the situation. Like Farr, though, he was entrenched and corrupt. It would not be easy to strip him of influence.

Mrs. Welborn contributed the judgment that Farr and Northcutt were both bad men, responsible for more harm than good, and that they should be vanquished. King was bemused when

Jesse F. Welborn, President of the Colorado Fuel and Iron Company. By permission of the Colorado Historical Society.

Welborn then asked him to speak to Cass Herrington in much the same way Herrington had asked him to speak to Welborn. Cass had to learn to restrain his taste for political intrigue, Welborn said, otherwise his activities would lend credence to stories of the company's domination of political affairs.

Taking care that their discussion did not become too heated, King flattered Welborn by likening his situation to Rockefeller's. Just as Rockefeller was misunderstood by many people, so was Welborn. In both instances, it was necessary to correct mistaken impressions by making true purpose and character apparent. Some dramatic action was needed, which in Welborn's case might well take the form of a radical alteration in the company's dealings with its men. Welborn, however, did not suppose that it was wise to move too fast. Undismayed by this attitude, King reflected that, "Welborn has the heart and the purpose, if he can surmount his training; but it is going to be very difficult and the best of schemes will not work out satisfactorily unless they are sympathetically administered."[8]

When, after King had left, Mrs. Welborn asked her husband why he opposed King's representation idea, he told her that he was not opposed but merely trying to point out the difficulties that stood in the way of its adoption. Mrs. Welborn conveyed this to King and assured him that her husband would eventually go along. She invited King to continue to press the issue. As for herself, she confessed to having been profoundly touched by her recent exposure to Rockefeller—called back, as she put it "from the material point of view into which she had been falling, to the spiritual beliefs of her earlier years." Nothing else she might have said could have struck so responsive a chord in King. Smitten, he concluded, "how much better it is to begin to work through people rather than against them in attempting the accomplishment of an ideal."[9]

In addition to his many interviews, King spent a large part of his first two weeks in Denver guiding the development of a work-relief program for unemployed miners. An executive committee was organized and King drafted the grant request for the governor's submission to the Rockefeller Foundation. This was all achieved with such dispatch that, by the end of March, the foundation's pro forma approval was in hand and the relief program under way. The effort attracted favorable comment from all quarters. When even John Lawson praised the program in a newspaper interview, King believed that word had been passed along the union line to give Rockefeller his chance. With the relief program underway and the groundwork laid for Rockefeller's visit in mid-April, King decided to take a vacation and left Denver for Toronto.

On his return, two weeks later, King took up where he had left off. First, he reviewed the activities of the work-relief program. After suggesting some minor modifications, he turned his attention to the grave problem presented by the upcoming trial of John Lawson on the strike-related charge of murder.

King learned that although Lawson's prosecution was in the hands of the district attorney, Judge Northcutt had been volunteered by the operators to serve as one of his assistants. (This implies either that Pope's intelligence concerning Northcutt's prestrike role was mistaken or that the operators had indeed learned the value of his services.) Northcutt was now being paid by the operators' committee, and much of the committee's expenditures were covered by C.F. & I. contributions. King reasoned that Northcutt's role in the prosecution was wholly undesirable. It would be said Rockefeller sought vengeance at Lawson's expense. That Northcutt was simultaneously on retainer from the notorious Baldwin-Felts "detective" agency, would lend further credence to the view that the trial had more to do with persecution than with justice.

Alerted to these dangers by King's probing questions, Welborn attempted to ensure that Northcutt would remain in the background during the trial. Unsatisfied, King suggested to Cass Herrington that he see the state attorney general and have Northcutt replaced by someone unassociated with the companies. Herrington did so but, when the statement announcing the change appeared in the press, King found it not very clear. At the time, this didn't seem to matter greatly because Rockefeller was to arrive in a few days. He had been advised by King to announce publicly that C.F. & I. would play no part in the prosecution. Now, on learning that the illness of Mrs. Rockefeller had caused a cancellation of the visit, it seemed necessary that someone else make a public statement.

On one of his many evenings at the Welborns' home, King suggested that Welborn take the initiative and set the company's position straight in a press interview. At first, Welborn demurred, but his demurral precipitated an argument that, like a cloudburst on a muggy day, did much to clear the air. King goaded him by portraying for his benefit the gulf between how others saw him and how he wished to be seen. In parrying, Welborn dropped his guard and revealed a new dimension of the strike. Mrs. Welborn was present throughout and witnessed the capitulation of her husband to King's will.

There were two damaging impressions abroad, King informed Welborn. One was that he was not his own master but dominated by Osgood and used by him to serve his own ends. The second was that the people to whom he delegated responsibility often took advantage of their positions and acted in ways he would not countenance, but that he failed or was unwilling to know what was going on. Although Welborn confessed that he understood how these impressions might have come to King, he believed them undeserved. King agreed that they were undeserved, just as those directed against Rockefeller were undeserved. In both instances, it was necessary to act in ways that belied mistaken impressions. This prompted Welborn to discuss what he thought to be his limitations. He thought himself fully able to conduct the business aspects of the company but less competent in political matters and in dealing with the relations of the company to the community. He believed he needed an astute legal advisor. During the strike the Herrington brothers had been of very little help ot him. That was why he had leaned so heavily on Judge Northcutt. Northcutt, he continued, was the best lawyer in the state and knew the strike situation better than anyone. Yet, Welborn also believed him thoroughly corrupt and ready to do almost anything for money. He did not believe that Northcutt would go so far as to sell out his client.

The problem with Cass Herrington, he reiterated, was that he couldn't keep clear of politics. Just last week, following the death of a Las Animas County commissioner, Herrington schemed with Weitzel, the manager of the fuel division, to have a company store manager named as the successor. Would King please talk to him, he asked? He found this political dealing entirely disagreeable. He went on to relate how at the most casual reference from that "damned old fool" Bowers, Judge Northcutt had gone out in the most recent election and lined up the southern counties for Governor Carlson.[10] The opposing candidate was much the better man, but he had been beaten by the vote in Huerfano County, where the vote was controlled by Jeff Farr and the liquor interests. No matter the whys and wherefores, developments such as these always came back to plague C.F. & I.

Even the militia could not be trusted, he confided. Except for two officers, all of the others were corrupt and looking for bribes. They were also prepared to sell whatever information came into their hands. That's why he was sure that the Lawson defense had copies of all the material that the public prosecutor and the companies intended to use against him. He bemoaned the fact that every step the companies had taken in connection with the prosecution was probably known to the defense.

In another context, Welborn admitted that during the strike, he himself had bought the support of one of the deputy sheriffs in Las Animas County. The man owned a newspaper that was in financial difficulties. C.F. & I. learned that he would help supply mine guards but only in exchange for help to his paper. Welborn was embarrassed to admit that he had sent Weitzel to make an arrangement with the man, for which there was still an outstanding liability. On recollecting this story in his diary, King wrote:

> The question naturally suggests itself, how can Welborn now change his policies toward Weitzel and other men, if he has been issuing orders to officers of the Company and permitting them to do things which will not bear the light of day. No wonder he hesitates to take a bold stand against the whole lot of them and declare himself for a radically different policy. Did I not believe Welborn acted from honest motives, though from lack of experience of men, I would advise Mr. R. to change the whole outfit here. It's only because I believe that if helped and properly guided Welborn is strong enough to stand for the right thing . . . [that] I believe it better to give him his chance.[11]

In keeping with his apparently unshakeable confidence in Welborn, King pointed out how very necessary it was for Welborn to act independently and decisively. Immediately following this pep talk, Welborn went to the phone and gave a statement to an Associated Press reporter in which he distanced C.F. & I. from the Lawson prosecution. Pleased by Welborn's action, King then brought up his plans for touring the company's mining camps. He hoped that now that they had complete confidence in one another, he could feel free to speak to Welborn with perfect frankness. He vowed he would treat him just as if they were brothers and be wholly open with him. He was highly flattering and ended what must have been a difficult meeting for Welborn on a strong affirmative note.

In an afterword to Mrs. Welborn alone, King urged her to encourage her husband to share his problems with her, and for the two of them together to be guided only by what they knew to be right and in accord with what she knew Rockefeller wished. She responded that she would gladly heed his counsel. Perhaps, she sensed how important her role was in all of this. For it is difficult to entirely ignore the possibility that King's attraction to Mrs. Welborn underpinned his confidence in Mr. Welborn. This was not the first nor the last time he would enjoy the piquancy of an attraction to an inaccessible woman.

In the wake of the postponement of Rockefeller's visit, Rockefeller suggested that Starr Murphy might make the trip. King advised against this and his judgment prevailed. Explaining his reasoning in a long letter to Murphy, King passed along some news of his discoveries and his sense of how things stood at the moment. In regard to the prosecutions of strikers, including Lawson, he advised that there was ample justification for the belief that C.F. & I. was directly involved. What should have been a nonpartisan public matter was warped and tainted by the participation of interested private parties. He reviewed for Murphy's information the steps being taken to extricate C.F. & I. from the Lawson prosecution. In general, he reported, the extent of the company's involvement in politics was "astonishing."[12] This was now recognized as an error and an attempt was being made to withdraw. The miners had been quite right in all they had said about the depredations of political bosses like Judge Northcutt and Sheriff Farr. As far as the relations between the company and its employees were concerned, he indicated the need for a great many changes: "The leaven is beginning to work . . . but many old methods are so deep-rooted, and reactionary forces are so strong, it is going to take time to bring about change."[13]

King indicated that he believed he had gained Welborn's confidence and praised his willingness to consider and adopt changes. He also believed that the union people regarded his presence as a positive development, symbolizing Rockefeller's determination to put matters right. However, much work remained to be done.

King now decided to make a brief social survey of the C.F. & I. coal camps. He greatly admired the Pittsburgh Survey[14] and used it as his model. He prepared a list of thirty-nine questions based on the criticisms that had come to him in the course of his interviews. What he wanted to learn from visits to the camps was how these criticisms might be met, and the likely consequences of any changes he might propose.

As his starting point, King requested information about the composition of the work force. He found the diversity of peoples and cultures staggering. The nativity of the 3500 miners employed on April 1, 1915, was reported to him as follows:[15]

U.S.A. White	506	Roumainian	24
U.S.A. Colored	248	Swedish	12
Italian	896	Irish	7
Mexican	602	Bohemian	5
Austrian	429	Croatian	5
Greek	270	Serbian	4
Hungarian	101	French	3

Slavic	83	Belgian	2
German	56	Cretan	2
Russian	56	Jewish	2
Japanese	41	Danish	1
Polish	40	Macedonian	1
Bulgarian	36	Norwegian	1
Welsh	34	Swiss	1
Scotch	31		

Of the miners, 618 spoke no English.

Several of the people King had interviewed had warned him that the heterogeneity of the miners, coupled with the newness of many of them to the country, created primary barriers to any plans built on their participation. The implication was that this was a population one acted upon rather than with.

King withheld judgment until he could see for himself. During his tour of the camps, he learned to discount the allegation that C.F. & I. deliberately hired a diverse work force in the effort to block its unification. Whatever the biases of the individual camp superintendents, no companywide policy was in effect. Hiring patterns largely reflected the diversity present in Colorado labor markets.

At the outset of the tour, King argued in favor of having miners elected to camp school boards. But on learning in one camp that most of the miners could not read English, he concluded that it would be mistaken for them to have even a voice in selecting board members. When, in another camp, the elected worker representative asserted that many of his fellow miners "had not brains enough" to serve as school trustees, King concluded that "what we have seen convinces us of this as a truth."[16] Thus, although King met a number of miners who impressed him favorably, his overall assessment was negative. He concluded the tour with the sense that this Babel of miners *would* have to be led and that most changes would have to be introduced from the top down.

Neither Welborn nor Weitzel had offered any objection when King initially suggested that he tour the mining camps. On the contrary, both men had seemed eager for him to go. They indicated that they had nothing to hide and would be pleased to receive any recommendations for improvements. In the ensuing discussion, however, the suspicion grew in King that Welborn left the management of the camps to Weitzel; that Weitzel in turn left them in the hands of the superintendents; and that the latter did pretty much as they wished. Later, when King queried Cass Herrington on the accuracy of his surmise, Herrington said that he had found the crux of the situation. Hair-raising stories could be told of how miners who complained of legitimate grievances had been brutally manhandled by some of the superintendents and pit bosses. This sort of thing occurred, he believed, even though Weitzel got along well with the men and was fair minded. He just would not bother himself with discipline, and that is where much of the discontent among the miners arose. Here, at last, King supposed, lay the real cause of the strike: the arbitrary exercise of the power wielded by the miner's immediate superiors.

On first impression, King was troubled by Weitzel's apparent limitations. A second talk brought about a revaluation. Weitzel said just the right things about Welborn, lauding his integrity and sincerity, at the same time that he noted his over dependence on Osgood. He volunteered condemnations of Sheriff Farr and Judge Northcutt and suggested that the sooner the company was free of all connection with them the better. The subject of political activities on the part of C.F. & I. gave King an opening to deliver what had by now become a set lecture:

> I told him . . . that Mr. R. would be displeased beyond words if methods that would not bear the light of day were resorted to in any particular. I then emphasized . . . how impossible it was to separate the doings of the C.F. & I. Company from the future of Mr. R. and his children, and their influence in all they were attempting to do. I pointed out that he was devoting his life to high purposes, and that it was his desire that the industries in which his money was invested should be above reproach, and that this could not be too clearly understood by everyone who had to do with them.[17]

Weitzel responded by saying that he had always been in favor of improving conditions but that Bowers had blocked most of his proposals. He now stood ready to help King in every way and was particularly keen on developing some sort of representation plan among the men as had been proposed. He was also prepared to support King in recommending improvements in camp conditions.

Leaving Denver, King and McGregor traveled south to the city of Trinidad, which would serve as their base for visits to the

camps. Although some of the camps they saw left much to be desired, King concluded that Trinidad itself was the worst place of
all. Strolling along the town's streets with McGregor late one
night, he was impressed that saloons and brothels were woefully
abundant. It seemed to him folly to suppose that a healthy nation
or community could be constructed on a foundation of such ram-
pant corruption. He reflected that the people residing in the isolated mining camps, for all the limits on their development and
social life, were really better off than those living in such a town.

The mining camps varied considerably in the impression they
made. King supposed this was because too little attention had
been given to their appearance and, consequently, too much depended on the taste and character of influential individuals, such
as the superintendent, doctor, or schoolteacher. The most outstanding camp they saw happened to belong to the Guggenheim
interests. Clean, attractive, and well managed, this camp gave
King a model against which to gauge the deficiencies of the C.F. &
I. camps. When he learned that miners were so eager to work in
the Guggenheim mine that vacancies in the camp arose only when
a resident died, he was sure that the effort to make the camp a
physically attractive place was crucial to its success.

On his visit to the C.F. & I. camp at Morley, King was taken underground to witness how coal was mined. The sensation of being
deep underground, the constant hazard, and the dirty nature of
the work made it immediately evident why the miners had to be
paid high wages. That evening, in the safety and comfort of his
hotel room, he reflected on the experience from the perspective
of a student of society:

> One could not help feeling as one looked at the huge seams of
> coal that this wealth of nature was never intended to be pri-
> vately owned, but was intended in reality for society as a whole.
> The only defense there can be for private ownership in natural
> resources is the corruption incident to government ownership
> and the check which would be placed on development if the
> possibility of reaping large fortunes did not exist as an induce-
> ment for the investment of private savings. Were men honest
> and actuated by a sense of duty in their personal relations, pri-
> vate ownership in natural resources would not last for a day. It
> is because men know that human nature is as weak as it is that
> they feel obliged to penalize themselves by permitting a sort of
> natural selection in the matter of cupidity and daring to deter-

mine who are to be the controllers and possessors of great wealth as against its real owners, the people as a whole.[18]

So much for John D. Rockefeller, Senior!

Before King could visit many more camps, developments in New York and Washington demanded his attention. During the past week, he learned, the Commission on Industrial Relations had released to the press the correspondence between Rockefeller and Lamont Bowers. These letters had been turned over to the Commission by Rockefeller in response to a subpoena. Their release was accompanied by a statement by Frank Walsh that implied that something sinister was contained in them. Rockefeller complained that the Commission was acting unfairly in making the correspondence public. Walsh, however, maintained that, since the letters seemed to conflict with previous testimony, it was not only proper that the public should see them but that Rockefeller, Lee, King, and Bowers should be recalled to testify about the discrepancies. They were ordered to appear before the Commission in Washington, D.C., on May 29, 1915.

From his vantage point in Colorado, King immediately understood that Walsh's latest foray against Rockefeller was prompted by the Lawson trial. King reasoned that since Walsh and Lawson had become personal allies, they would be bound to assist one another. The jury selection process had been completed and the trial begun on the same day that Walsh issued his statement. King recognized that the Bowers–Rockefeller correspondence contained materials likely to prove useful to the defense, such as Bower's statement that the operators "would not change their position till their bones were bleached as white as the chalk of the mountains."[19] Such language could not help but win sympathy for Lawson.

Concerned that the connection between Walsh's actions and the Lawson trial might not be recognized in New York, King telephoned and counseled Rockefeller. He advised him in any further statement to the press to cite the Low Commission's interim report calling for a cooling-off period in Colorado. He also should point out the difficulty he faced in attempting to cooperate with two government bodies when they seemed bent on different courses.

While King was substantially correct in linking Walsh and Lawson, he never grasped Walsh's position in its fullest dimensions. Seeing in Lawson's "private life, personality, labor connections"[20] all that was decent and admirable in American unions, Walsh felt duty bound to protect him from the vengeance of the Rockefellers. The Commission chairman believed, as did Lawson, that the Rockefellers *were* directly responsible for whatever happened in Colorado. Walsh was convinced, moreover, that the younger Rockefeller was merely a tool of his father, that he did "not do anything without first getting orders from Tarrytown"[21] and that both father and son shared an attitude toward working people and unions that was patronizing where it was not contemptuous. From Walsh's point of view, the Rockefellers were perfect instruments for the exposure of antiunion sentiments among American employers. As one Commission staff member noted, the newspapers might tire of King, Lee, and Bowers, "but Rockefeller is, of course, always first page news."[22] Publicity and exposure were the primary means by which Walsh hoped to bring about labor reform.

Just as King was conversing long distance with Rockefeller, Horace Hawkins, Lawson's attorney, arrived. King had requested the meeting, to which Hawkins brought along a Mr. McHarg, who was serving as counsel in most of the other suits pending against strikers. The three men remained in King's room for almost four hours, discussing the strike, the Lawson trial, and other strike-related trials and indictments. From King's account, it appears that Hawkins did most of the talking.

The thrust of Hawkins' remarks was that during the strike the miners had been led by their struggles and experiences to believe that they could expect justice neither from the courts nor from the state government. They were convinced that their only hope lay in taking the law into their own hands. So great was their embitterment that those who provided strike leadership constantly had to restrain the men so as to avoid open insurrection.

Hawkins elaborated by sketching for King's benefit the recent histories of the role of the judiciary in industrial accident cases, the role of the employers and the state legislature in foiling efforts to enact meaningful eight-hour day legislation, and the role of the courts and the military in subverting the right of habeas corpus during the strike. As Hawkins talked, King compared his assertions with what others had told him. All that he had learned—from C.F. & I. officials, from the former governor, from Pope, and from others—sustained Hawkins' appraisal. He concluded that, more than anything else, the despair of the workers and their readiness to resort to violence, were the fault of the companies. In fighting every move for improvement in the legislature and in the courts, the companies had reaped the whirlwind. He observed, "It is only the story of privilege through all history. Privilege is always blind and will never make way for justice save by some force which will overthrow it; that is why I hate Toryism with all my heart." [23]

When Hawkins identified Judge Northcutt and Sheriff Farr as the main political bosses in the region, King drew his attention to Welborn's statement in the newspaper, announcing the severance of Northcutt from the Lawson prosecution. Hawkins had not seen this and believed Northcutt was still involved. He informed King that the state attorney general had told him that C.F. & I. had asked him personally to try the case. If the company truly wanted conciliation, Hawkins advised, it should have asked the attorney general to drop all of the outstanding strike-related indictments. King was amazed when Hawkins informed him that between three and four hundred men still were under indictment on various charges of murder, arson, and assault.

King supposed, and Hawkins agreed, that it was too late to attempt to call off the Lawson trial. Hawkins emphasized, however, that once Lawson was acquitted, as he was confident he would be, all of the other cases should be dropped. He viewed that as a necessary first step toward any peaceful accommodation. From the way he said this, King took it that the quashing of the indictments was labor's prime objective. Recalling that Welborn had expressed the same wish, though from a recognition of the inability to win convictions, King told Hawkins that he wouldn't be surprised if the companies asked to have the indictments thrown out. In his own mind, he castigated the lawyers who "have hung as bloodsuckers around industry in this state." [24]

Hawkins suggested that the second change needed to heal Colorado's wounds was to create confidence among the miners that conditions would be improved. The attitude of men like Osgood, who thought the operators so superior to the miners that they had no need to listen to them, was conducive only to hatred and conflict. Hawkins praised by way of contrast the new attitude communicated by Welborn in a statement carried in that day's *Denver Post*. King did not say that he was less impressed with this statement than Hawkins. He valued the new openness the statement symbolized but thought that in its substance it smacked of paternalism. Welborn was not yet ready to make a broad concession of rights or to work for cooperative solutions to problems.

King did take the opportunity, however, to speak of Rockefeller and the sort of man he was. Hawkins replied that others had spoken of him in the same way; Mother Jones in particular had sung his praises at great length.

As they were about to part, King brought up the subject of Lawson's testimony in New York as it reflected on himself and the Canadian Industrial Disputes Investigation Act. He recited for Hawkins's benefit the history of the act and its practical consequences. Hawkins thought that, on the basis of what King said about it, it was an admirable piece of legislation toward which labor should have no objection. Pleased though he was to have this approval, King was vain enough to require vindication from Lawson himself. He expressed the hope that once the trial was over, he could meet with Lawson and discuss the matter with him. Apparently, now that he had heard very favorable things said of Lawson from a number of sources, King no longer considered him a unworthy opponent. It bothered him immoderately to be misunderstood by anyone.

Hawkins expressed such complete confidence in winning an acquittal that King subsequently gave little thought to Lawson's trial. He became preoccupied with the question of how best to improve conditions in the mining camps. With his secretary, Francis McGregor, King visited half a dozen more of the camps; talked with superintendents, store managers, and miners; and collected impressions of what might be done. The news that Lawson had been found guilty came to him as a complete surprise. His first reaction was to welcome the verdict as a needed assertion of the will of the judiciary to stand firmly against lawlessness. Uncharacteristically, he did not consider the impact of the decision on C.F. & I. or the Rockefellers, nor did he weigh it against the many reports that had come to him of how unfair the Colorado courts were. The reactions of Lawson's supporters, however, soon forced him to reconsider his position.

Hawkins wired Frank Walsh as soon as the verdict became known: "Absolutely no evidence sufficient to convict. In any other community an acquittal would have been certain."[25] Walsh endorsed this judgment, for in a letter expressing his regrets to Lawson, he wrote, "I cannot believe that the cruel injustice inflicted upon you will be allowed to stand."[26] Walsh also stepped up his attacks on the Rockefellers. He charged in a press interview that the Rockefellers had all along controlled events in Colorado and were now using their power to take revenge on Lawson.

In New York, at Ivy Lee's suggestion, Rockefeller, Lee, and Starr Murphy busily made preparations to publish Rockefeller's entire correspondence with Bowers and Welborn. Their thought was to place a complete record before the public, so that the public might judge for itself whether Rockefeller had directed the strike from New York, as Walsh alleged. When King was informed of this project, he objected strenuously. Arguing that "designing persons" would exploit the correspondence for years to come, that publication would keep alive thoughts and expressions that would otherwise be forgotten, and that many new issues would be raised, he persuaded his colleagues to abandon the effort.[27] Privately, King worried about Lee's ineptitude and again prophesized that he would one day lead Rockefeller into grave trouble. He reflected that nothing in public life required more sensitive appraisal than the estimate of how much information the public might be trusted with, especially when confidences were involved. Lee seemed seriously lacking in this regard. As always on occasions when his counsel prevailed, King prided himself for having served Rockefeller so well. The earned increment to his self-esteem was more valuable to him than the added debt in which his assistance placed Rockefeller.

No sooner had the New York staff been straightened away than a new complication arose at C.F. & I. King learned that a few days after Lawson's conviction, Hawkins had called on the Herrington brothers to request a formal statement to the effect that the Rockefellers had played no part in the trial. They had refused. When told of this, King said that they had missed a golden opportunity to boast of clean hands. As he pressed to learn more details of the Hawkins visit, and he found it necessary to press each of the Herringtons and Welborn, it became evident that something was amiss.

Hawkins had told the Herringtons that the United Mine Workers' leaders recognized King to be a man of integrity and good will. They wished to believe the same of Rockefeller but found that impossible because of what had transpired at Lawson's trial. The two men whose testimony had convicted Lawson were Baldwin-Felts detectives in the employ of the coal companies, one of whom worked for C.F. & I. Hawkins reported that Lawson's supporters believed these men could not have testified as they did without the company's encouragement, nor could the company have become involved in this way without the approval of Rockefeller. Other aspects of the trial also suggested that someone was exerting undue pressure for a conviction. Hawkins noted that the presiding judge, who in trying the last strike-related case had dismissed the jury quickly when it looked as if it was going to acquit, in the present instance kept the jury at its deliberations in hopes of a conviction. Two of the bailiffs were mine company employees. When the jury reported that it was still divided nine for conviction and three for acquittal, the judge sent word by a bailiff that they were to remain sequestered. The bailiff instead told the jurors that they were to go without food or water until they agreed on a verdict. Hawkins viewed this as intimidation of the jury by a man who just happened to have worked for C.F. & I. as recently as three months earlier.

As soon as he heard of Hawkins' charges, King questioned the Herringtons and Welborn about the company's relationship with Baldwin-Felts. They reported that C.F. & I. was indeed linked to the notorious detective agency, both as a member of the operators' association and as an individual company. Although the latter connection had ended just recently, it was altogether possible that some Baldwin-Felts men were still with the company and that Hawkins' statements were correct. King urged Welborn to act at once to fire any Baldwin-Felts men still in his employ. When he found Welborn unwilling to act promptly, he attributed his reticence partly to his lingering fear of Osgood and partly to an unwillingness to signal his subordinates that he had foresworn the belligerent attitude that he had till now encouraged them to share. King concluded:

> It is singular that during the last hours of our stay here we have really probed the bottom of the situation. I am convinced that this business of hiring detective agencies and allowing them to ferret out information is the wrong way to conduct industry. If men of character are obtained for the responsible positions and the truth is really desired all along the line, detective agencies will not be necessary. It is quite conceivable that this whole strike trouble may have been fomented in part through this method of warfare. Certainly, many of the incidents growing out of it have been, and here, at the last moment, months after Mr. Rockefeller has made plain his position at a public inquiry, is revealed a condition which if publicly known as it will be in Washington next week, is certain to cause the public to disbelieve entirely in the genuineness of all his professions.[28]

From this it would seem that King attributed much of the labor strife in Colorado to the use of industrial spies and goons. What is striking is that he failed to consider why the men of character whom he served had not "really desired" to know the truth "all along the line." Rockefeller, so guarded in his behavior that he felt compelled to supervise the smallest details of office activity, cared so little for the truth that he had depended completely upon Bowers and Welborn for information about the miners. Welborn cared so little for the truth that he had relied upon Osgood, Weitzel, and a body of detectives whose pecuniary interest lay more in making trouble than in preventing it. At each step in the corporate hierarchy, responsibility had been abdicated under the guise of its delegation. Although King recognized this, he appears momentarily to have lost sight of his guiding principle that "Industrial relations were relations between human beings."[29] For the truth of the matter was that no one among the company owners or managers had sufficient respect or regard for the miners to care to know the truth about their condition.

As the result of what he had learned about the causes of the strike and about conditions within C.F. & I., King would take away a distinctly different sense of the problems to be faced from those that he had envisaged on his arrival. Before coming to Colorado, he had attributed most of the responsibility for the violence and disorder of the strike to the union leadership. John Lawson's bitter assault upon the integrity of the Rockefellers and himself at the New York hearings had settled the matter: the union leadership was so irresponsible that dealing with it was out of the question. King's employee representation device would serve to exclude these people and at the same time give the miners a genuine opportunity to be heard by the management. Now, as he prepared to leave Colorado, he understood that much of the violence of the strike had been provoked by the coal companies. Their domination of the mining camps and the coal counties was so complete that in desperation, the miners had been compelled to resort to the force of arms.

King had also learned that John Lawson was not the wild-eyed revolutionary he had supposed him to be. Mother Jones had explained that Lawson's testimony before the Commission on Industrial Relations had been prepared for him in advance of his meeting with Rockefeller and that there had been no opportunity to alter his statement. Horace Hawkins had advised that, far from fomenting violence, Lawson had been a major force for responsible behavior by the strikers. Without his restraining influence, Hawkins was certain there would have been much more bloodshed and devastation. King accepted enough of these explanations to wish to correct Lawson's misinterpretation of the Canadian Industrial Disputes Investigation Act. Yet his initial response to Lawson's conviction on charges of murder was that the verdict would help reconstitute the rule of law in the coal fields, and not that Lawson was being victimized or that justice had miscarried. Nor did King ever stop to reconsider that if Lawson wasn't the villain he was supposed to be, the need to avoid dealing with him and with the United Mine Workers had evaporated.

The question naturally arises as to why King was so little influenced by his new understanding. Simply as a matter of justice, he might have been expected to wish to see Lawson exonerated. There were, however, added and uniquely personal reasons why his deepest sympathies should have been aroused. It will be recalled that King's maternal grandfather had also played a leading role in an armed rebellion. In defeat he too had been hounded and persecuted. King knew the story in every detail. The resonances that Lawson's plight might have been expected to stimulate in him should at the very least have prompted a reexamination of his position, but he did not even go so far as to draw the obvious parallel. Nor did he alter his intellectual and emotional judgment that armed rebellion was always unwarranted. He thought Lawson should be punished.

Negative evidence of this sort suggests that King, as part of his commitment to retrieve his family's honor and standing, had never intended to vindicate his revolutionary forebearer. It points to the alternative likelihood that his drive for success was conditioned by his desire to compensate for his grandfather's political blunder. I leave it to some future clinician to address this matter more fully.

Perhaps the major barrier to any revision or realignment of King's sympathies toward Lawson and the miners arose from the total absorption of those sympathies by Welborn and Rockefeller. For, as his familiarity with the past and present behavior of C.F. & I. officers increased, King came to the conclusion that Rockefeller's problems in Colorado had little to do with avoiding unionization. They had everything to do instead with reforming the management and operation of the company. Clearly, if he was to succeed in his effort to rescue Rockefeller, he would have to rescue Welborn and C.F. & I. in the process. Largely for this reason, his helping hand went out to Welborn rather than to Lawson. Of course, Lawson's connection with Walsh and Walsh's antagonism toward Rockefeller also influenced his judgment. In all likelihood, King's low estimate of the quality of the mine work force also played some part in his thinking.

Whatever the precise balance of the factors involved, it should not obscure the transformation that had taken place. When King came to Colorado, his employee representation scheme was mainly a device aimed at excluding the union from C.F. & I. By the time he left, it was an absolutely vital ingredient in the reformation of the company's management and its labor policy. In this new guise, employee representation was a tool for the modernization of corporate labor relations. More than this, it could be seen and would be adopted by Rockefeller as a righteous cause, a cause aimed at introducing fair play and mutual respect into the otherwise one-sided employment relationship that had accompanied the growth of large scale enterprise.

As he prepared to leave Denver for Washington, King dictated a five-page letter advising Rockefeller, in unusually emphatic terms, how and why he should respond to Walsh when the commission hearings resumed on May 19, 1915. The letter, signed by McGregor and addressed to Rockefeller's secretary, Charles O. Heydt, was designed to communicate through seconds without leaving a trace. McGregor indicated that he made no copy of the letter and asked that it be destroyed once read. King informed Rockefeller that he need not worry that Walsh would try to contravert his New York testimony. Walsh's sole object was to aid Lawson. He would try to show that Lawson and his comrades had been obliged to adopt extreme tactics because of the nature of their opposition. That opposition remained so ardent and so overbearing in its control of the situation that Lawson's conviction ought to be overturned. In an allusion to the role of the Baldwin-Felts men in Lawson's conviction, King warned that "there may be grounds for . . . the prejudice which Walsh will attempt to arouse . . . that Mr. R. knows nothing about."[30] He urged Rockefeller, almost commanded him, to volunteer in his statement that he would personally exert all the influence in his possession to remove any officer or person connected with C.F. & I. who made an attempt to influence the course of justice in Colorado. The letter closed with an interesting postscript:

It is Mr. King's intention to take accommodation at the New Willard, and to be there on Monday next. He thinks it advisable that neither Mr. R., Mr. Lee, nor Mr. Murphy should ask him any questions about the situation in Colorado or his investigations here, until after the Industrial Relations hearings are over. He will volunteer such information as he thinks desirable, but he wishes to be free when he appears before the Commission to say, as he can up to the present, that no questions have been asked him concerning the results of his investigation by anyone connected with the office at 26 Broadway . . .[31]

One wonders whether, if King and Walsh had exchanged places, King would have been outraged at the subterfuges he found it necessary to employ. Such tactics as keeping principals in ignorance, writing through seconds, and destroying communications were adopted as strategies of self-defense, yet at the same time, their intent was to deceive the public authority. King, quite clearly, was not acting as a detached student of industrial relations—that was impossible. He was committed to Rockefeller and, like him, was out to have his way.

Notes

1. W.L.M.K. Diary, 3/23/15. W.L.M.K. Papers, Series J13, p. G2539, 385.
2. Powderly had served as leader of the Knights of Labor, 1879–1893, and was now an official in the Bureau of Immigration.
3. Ibid., 3/27/15, pp. G2539, 448–49.
4. Ibid., 3/25/15, pp. G2539, 408–09.
5. Ibid., 3/27/15, pp. G2539, 430–31.
6. Ibid., p. G2539, 436.
7. Ibid., 3/28/15, p. G2539, 451.
8. Ibid., p. G2539, 458.
9. Ibid., 3/30/15, p. G2539, 478.
10. Ibid., 4/19/15, p. G2539, 506.
11. Ibid., p. G2539, 510.
12. Ibid., p. G2539, 499.
13. Ibid., p. G2539, 500.
14. A multifaceted investigation into living and working conditions in Pittsburgh, Pennsylvania, conducted under the auspices of the Russell Sage Foundation 1907–1909.
15. W.L.M.K. Papers, Series J 4, vol. 191.
16. W.L.M.K. Diary, 4/26/15. W.L.M.K. Papers, Series J13, pp. G2539, 587ff.

17. Ibid., 4/22/15, p. G2539, 524.
18. Ibid., 4/27/15, p. G2539, 596.
19. Ibid., 4/25/15, p. G2539, 566.
20. F. P. Walsh to Edward L. Doyle, 8/22/15. F. P. W. Papers, Box 143.
21. F. P. Walsh, quoted in the St. Louis *Globe Democrat*, F. P. W. Papers, Clipping Scrapbook No. 34.
22. Basil Manly to F. P. Walsh, 4/23/15. F. P. W. Papers, Box 143.
23. W.L.M.K. Diary, 4/25/15., p. G2539, 575.
24. Ibid., p. G2539, 577.
25. Hawkins to F. P. Walsh, 5/4/15. F. P. W. Papers, Box 143.
26. F. P. Walsh to J. R. Lawson, 5/6/15. Ibid.
27. W.L.M.K. Diary, 5/9/15. W.L.M.K. Papers, Series J13, p. G2539, 638.
28. Ibid., 5/10/15, p. G2539, 656.
29. Ibid., 12/8/14, p. G2526.
30. Ibid., 5/10/15, p. G2539, 659.
31. Ibid., pp. G2539, 660−61.

7. Tangled Motives

At the Washington hearings of the Commission on Industrial Relations in May 1915, Commission chairman Frank Walsh aggressively and unsuccessfully attempted to trace the responsibility for what had happened in Colorado to the Rockefeller offices in New York. It is curious that he should have done so, for one of the Commission's central findings was that most owners of large corporations knew little and cared less about the labor practices of their companies. All of the available evidence indicated that John D. Rockefeller, Jr., had done nothing exceptional in giving his hired managers a completely free hand. If he was to be faulted, it was more for acts of omission than for those of commission.

But Walsh was determined, at Rockefeller's expense, to win public sympathy for strike leader John R. Lawson, who now stood convicted of murder. Walsh pressed hard during the examination, trying to prove that Rockefeller had played an active role in directing the strike. Most observers concluded that he pressed too hard. His grilling of Rockefeller was widely criticized in the press. His tactics also alienated some of his fellow commissioners. Feelings ran so high that the Commission became irreparably divided. Even President Wilson became involved.

Fortunately, Walsh's misdirected effort had no adverse affect on the fight to free Lawson. In the weeks following his conviction, the labor leader's allies launched an agitation for a new trial. They sustained this agitation through much of the summer. Mackenzie King sympathized with their effort, though it angered him that Rockefeller was so often misrepresented as the primary obstacle to Lawson's freedom. However, toward the end of the summer, when favorable court decisions made it increasingly likely that a new trial would be granted, the anti-Rockefeller propaganda abated somewhat.

When, in mid-May, King arrived in Washington for the hearings, he immediately set to work to put Rockefeller at ease, for he found him alarmingly tense and dispirited. He purposely diverted much of their conversation away from business, though he did manage to convey some of his new understanding of what had occurred in Colorado. His portrayal of the strike must have been very comforting, for it moved Rockefeller to conclude (with uncommon resort to the royal *we*): "Mr. King relieves our minds very much about Colorado. So many terrible things have been said about us that I was really beginning to think we must be criminals, though we had not known it."[1]

Observing the first afternoon of Rockefeller's grueling examination by Walsh, King took steps to shield him from further harrassment. He prepared a statement to be read to the Commission the following morning. In it, Rockefeller expressed the hope that the course of justice in Colorado would prove to be absolutely fair and above reproach. Since any expression of opinion by him on the merits of the Lawson case might be misconstrued as an attempt to influence the judicial proceedings, he would have to respectfully refuse to answer any questions bearing on the case.

This maneuver proved effective in more than one way. At the time it served to frustrate Walsh's intention to somehow embroil Rockefeller in the Lawson case. For months afterward the statement would also serve as a reference point to which Rockefeller returned whenever he wished to explain his position. He dearly needed such a reference point, for he still had little confidence in his ability to articulate the principles to which King's prepared statements—this one and the one on collective bargaining and unionism he had delivered at the New York hearing—committed him.

As Rockefeller was dependent on King for intellectual and strategic guidance and was truly relieved to have him close by, so King found an equivalent satisfaction in coming to the aid of so needy and deserving a figure. His concern for Rockefeller's health; his admiration of his turning to prayer before each session of the hearing; his disdain for Walsh; his vexation over the fickleness of the public; and his confidence in his own and Rockefeller's desire to do right—all of these feelings commingled to produce an aura in which every move and suggestion he made sparkled with a touch of nobility. In this knight errant spirit, he searched for an opening to do battle with Walsh, when his turn came to appear before the Commission.

King knew that Walsh was in trouble with his fellow commissioners. Several of them had been so deeply offended by his examination of Rockefeller that they had carried a complaint to President Wilson. The press reported that the President was said to be "far from pleased" with Walsh.[2] Wilson had told the commissioners that he would approve of their resigning publicly in protest should Walsh continue his seemingly personal vendetta. Word of the President's position was relayed to Walsh and to the Rockefeller camp. The following day, Joseph Tumulty, the President's secretary, observed the Commission's session, presumably to report on Walsh to his chief.

King thought that Walsh became more moderate in his examination in consequence, although the hearing transcripts suggest no such change. In writing to a close personal friend several days later, Walsh admitted that he had been "rough at times" in his questioning, but excused this as a necessary means "to get at the truth." He confided, "I am sure you will not think it is boastful when I say that I turned the young man inside out, and left him without a single justification for anything that took place in Colorado, or for the Rockefeller attitude."[3]

From King's partisan perspective, however, Walsh appeared irresponsible. Instead of conducting the investigation fairly, with an eye to recommending legislation that would correct industrial abuses, he had set himself up as a one-man judge and jury. In so doing, he had thrown away an unprecedented opportunity to help labor. Moreover, in his attempt to discredit Rockefeller, singling him out as if he were the wellspring of industrial ills, Walsh threatened to destroy a crucial source of future progress and harmony.

When King and Walsh eventually crossed swords at the hearings, the proximate cause was a line of questioning that proved intensely embarrassing to King. Walsh wanted to know if King had from his very first meeting with Rockkefeller understood that any representation plan he might develop would be used to circumvent union organization. King strove to distinguish between the then immediate situation in Colorado, for which he was given to understand unionism was out of the question, and his plan of representation for the poststrike period. His plan, he claimed, was not antipathetic to unionism. Walsh, however, failed to see the distinction and forcefully pressed home two points: that the representation plan precluded unionism and that it had been designed with that intention.

Mr. King. As far as the union was concerned, I was told before I began to discuss that part of the situation, that the question of union recognition was a question the mine managers in

Colorado had a policy on, and Mr. Rockefeller was not going to interfere.

Chairman Walsh. So whatever you did out there had to be something other than recognition of the union?

Mr. King.   No; that was not the suggestion I got; but—

Chairman Walsh.   No; but any plan you might make for the situation in Colorado had to be something other than recognition of the union.

Mr. King.   Understand, what Mr. Rockefeller spoke of then was a plan that would help to bring industrial peace at that time, notwithstanding the position that the operators had taken in Colorado.

Chairman Walsh.   Yes; whatever plan you got up could not include in it the recognition of the union in Colorado in this trouble.

Mr. King.   Well, it is quite conceivable that the plan I suggested then—there was nothing in it whereby, if a company cares to grant recognition to a union, it should not be granted through this plan as well as any other. In fact, the whole plan is a plan of representation.

Chairman Walsh.   Well, but when you started your plan it was with the understanding given you by Mr. Rockefeller that the executive officers had already passed on the question of recognition of the union, and that they would not recognize it?

Mr. King.   As far as that trouble was concerned; yes—as far as that trouble was concerned.[4]

* * *

Chairman Walsh.   The plan you proposed to Mr. Rockefeller the first time you ever had a talk with him was that the men selected to prevent [sic] the grievances should be men actually inside the industry and not called from the outside. Is that correct?

Mr. King.   No.

Chairman Walsh.   Let me look at it please. [Reading:] "This would make it an essential that all members of such boards, excepting possibly persons chosen as chairmen, referees, or umpires, should be persons actually engaged in the industry or connected with it in some way, not persons chosen from outside."

Mr. King.   Yes; what is your question?

Chairman Walsh.   My question is that this presupposes that very thing.

Mr. King.   What very thing?

Chairman Walsh.   That it was an essential that all members of such boards . . . should be persons actually employed in the industry, or connected with it in some way, not persons chosen from outside?

Mr. King.   If they were to be representatives on boards of industry, certainly.

You remember there were certain limitations laid down I tried to have regard for in giving advice, and how, within the industry itself, certain boards could be constituted.

You do me a great injustice—I want to make this plain—you do me a great injustice if you try to infer that this was any attempt not to recognize the union or any attempt to evolve machinery which would prevent the union getting recognition.

Chairman Walsh.   That is what I am asking you as directly as possible; under that could these men have chosen Frank J. Hayes, or Mr. McLennan or any other of the members of the United Mine Workers of America?

Mr. King.   Mr. Chairman, you are a lawyer; when you are called in to advise in regard to a particular situation, you advise with the situation put before you. I was, as an expert, asked to advise as to a particular situation, and I took the situation presented to me, and I gave advice within the restrictions placed upon me. Any attempt to construe that advice to in any way show prejudice against labor unions is something I think would be dishonorable in the highest degree, and I want to make it most emphatically plain, both for my own sake and for—for the sake of my own reputation and for the sake of the reputation of this commission, that any effort of that kind is doing one of the greatest acts of injustice to any man that can possibly be done.[5]

Moments later King and Walsh were exchanging verbal brickbats of a clearly personal sort. Walsh believed that King had been bought by the Rockefellers or at the very least had permitted himself to be used in their effort to stave off unionization. By his own admission, King had designed his plan of representation knowing that the U.M.W. was to be excluded, and his design had conformed to that specification. The requirement that employee representatives be drawn only from workers currently employed effectively barred the participation of professional union officials. Thus, from Walsh's point of view, the verbal acceptances of unionism by both King and Rockefeller were belied by their actions. For however much his aggressive manner opened Walsh to criticism, there is no denying the acuity of some of his perceptions.

King viewed the identical circumstances quite differently. He could not and would not bear the stigma of wrongdoing. The Colorado strike had been one of the lesser matters put before him in his initial meeting with Rockefeller. He had not been called upon to advise about or to settle the strike; he was merely told about it. His decision to accept the role of advisor had been conditioned in the first instance by his positive appraisal of Rockefeller's character and intentions. That, plus the expectation that significant improvements in the relations between employers and employees everywhere could result. Whatever recommendations he had subsequently made to Rockefeller about the strike, and especially his plan for employee representation, had been made well in advance of his recognition that the treatment of the Colorado situation affected all other Rockefeller undertakings. That is, the representation scheme had been broached and discussed while King still regarded the Colorado situation as a minor irritant to be gotten out of the way as quickly as possible. However, the probing of the Commission on Industrial Relations, and Walsh's own eagerness to expose the Rockefellers, had converted what might have remained a small problem into a major stumbling block. Consequently, he had been forced to redirect his energies away from his research to the affairs of C.F. & I. Now, Walsh was attempting to portray the representation plan as an antiunion tactic. This effort stung King because his identification with the plan had become complete. It would not do to have so important a piece of work tainted in this way. Consequently, in the months ahead, he would exert himself to ensure that any overt antiunion overtones in the representation plan were eradicated.

King and Walsh clashed again during the second day of testimony. This time Walsh provided the provocation by attempting rather baldly to distort one of King's responses. Walsh had asked if it wasn't necessary to inform the public about what had been going on in Colorado during the last decade, so that public opinion could be hardened against any repetition of the conflict and violence. King replied that it would take a long time to achieve the education of the public in this way. He suggested that the immediate and pressing problems in Colorado could be resolved more readily by enlisting the conscience of the younger Rockefeller in the effort. Walsh seized upon these words and went to some length to transform them into a statement that ran "the will and conscience of Mr. Rockefeller . . . is more powerful than the will and conscience of all of the balance of the people in the United States."[6] Even though King clarified the meaning and intent of his remark, stressing that it was meant to apply only to the immediate present, Walsh persisted in holding to his interpretation of it. The result was another heated exchange between them.

Later that week, Walsh repeated his tortured version of King's remark in an interview that was widely carried in the papers. He also told reporters that King's testimony sustained the judgment that the Rockefellers were indeed responsible for all that had happened in Colorado. In self-defense, King prepared a rebuttal in which he quoted from the hearing transcript to show that he had specifically refused to place the responsibility for the strike on any person or group and that his remark about Rockefeller's conscience and public opinion could not be made to sustain the reading given it by Walsh. Many of the newspapers that had carried Walsh's interview printed King's statement, and he felt relieved and vindicated.

With the ordeal of the hearings behind them, King, Rockefeller Welborn, and Starr Murphy returned to New York. They immediately took up the question of how to deal with the problems King had uncovered during his Colorado visit. For one thing they agreed that Murphy would go out to Denver in the very near future. He would review the company's legal affairs and ensure that they were in proper order. He was also delegated to put an end to any covert political activity in the company's name or by its officials. The Herrington brothers were to lose their role in company policy making. They would be relegated to the role of legal advisors under Welborn's authority.

Rockefeller and King also importuned Welborn to sever his connection with the operators' association. They argued that C.F. & I. could then follow an independent course, without fear of being compromised by Osgood and his followers. Welborn rejected such a move and offered a variety of excuses. King believed he was still reluctant to stand up to Osgood. Then Rockefeller took Welborn by surprise. He related that Osgood had recently come to New York with an offer to organize a syndicate to buy out the Rockefeller holdings in C.F. & I. Perhaps, he suggested, Osgood's leadership of the operators' group and conduct of the strike might all along have been part of a design to take over C.F. & I. Welborn apparently thought there was some merit in this surmise, for he become angry and intimated that he felt betrayed by Osgood's action. The following day, he announced that he had changed his mind. On his return to Denver he would quit the operators' association.

The group also devoted considerable time to a memorandum King had prepared following his tour of the mining camps. Incorporated in this were a number of policy guidelines. One provided that the company would in no way interfere with the political, religious, and educational preferences and activities of the miners. Another provided that the social life of the camps would henceforth be based on the cooperative efforts of the company and the miners. A third held that, in all matters pertaining to their employment, the miners were to have a voice through their elected representatives. Both Rockefeller and Welborn readily assented to these guidelines. They also agreed to the specific improvements King suggested by way of making the camps more livable. In view of the consensus that emerged, it seemed appropriate for the group to take steps to implement its plans. These led to connections with the YMCA and with the National Civic Federation.

Both King and Rockefeller were strong supporters of the "Y," to which the Rockefellers were also large and influential contributors. They turned to it now as a neutral agency interested in uplifting the lives of working people. Discussion with "Y" officials elicited their positive interest in the management and staffing of the club houses that were to be built in the camps. When asked to recommend someone capable of supervising the new industrial relations program at C.F. & I., the same officials suggested Clarence Hicks.

An interview with Hicks late in June convinced the staff that he was precisely the man they needed. Rockefeller was able through his brother-in-law, Harold McCormick, to persuade International Harvester president Cyrus McCormick, Jr., to release Hicks to his service. It was agreed that Hicks would begin work in August by making a survey of the mining camps. Following this trial period, if Hicks and Welborn were mutually agreeable, Hicks would become the director of all phases of C.F. & I.'s relations with its employees. He would report directly to Welborn to ensure that the latter always knew the drift of employee sentiment.

At 52, Clarence J. Hicks had behind him a career that singularly prepared him for the assignment at C.F. & I. He and Rockefeller had met previously, at a time when he was an official of the "Y" and Rockefeller a member of its board of trustees. Rockefeller thus knew that Hicks had "been the pioneer"[7] in the development of the Railroad "Y," a network of boarding/club houses maintained by the "Y" for the benefit of railroad workers whose jobs carried them away from home. Hicks had successfully persuaded many railroad managers that they owed it to their employees to underwrite the costs of these facilities. This accomplishment, coupled with his demonstrated organizational skills, resulted in his advancement within the "Y" hierarchy. Then, in 1911, after more than twenty years with the organization, he had been hired by the International Harvester Corporation to direct its elaborate welfare program. This new position brought Hicks to the very frontier of large-scale corporate labor relations at the time. As Ozanne (1967) has so ably shown, his welfare department served as the spearhead of International Harvester's ongoing efforts to avoid the unionization of its employees.

When contacted about Hicks, Harold McCormick urged that Rockefeller make the acquaintance as well of Gertrude Beeks of the National Civic Federation. Beeks had preceded Hicks as the director of Harvester welfare work, and might prove helpful. Accordingly, Ivy Lee paid a visit to the Federation's office's, met Beeks and Ralph Easley, and came away with materials on the welfare programs of various companies. King also called on Beeks and Easley. With some misgiving he concluded that it would be useful to cultivate the latter's friendship:

> While Easley is a man in whom I have little confidence, I feel he is in a position to do much harm if an enemy, and much good if a friend, and that to ignore him, in view of the close relations of the Civic Federation to Labor and to Mr. Low and his Commission, would be a great mistake.[8]

When King transmitted his views to Rockefeller, he suggested that it might be wise to pay a visit to Easley's offices in the near future. He was sure that the flattery implicit in a Rockefeller visit would not be lost on Easley.

King took the opportunity of his own call to enlist the Civic Federation Secretary as the go-between in arranging meetings between Rockefeller and Samuel Gompers and John Mitchell. Easley, for his part, was entirely complaisant; he could barely contain his delight at the prospect of eventual Rockefeller backing for the Federation. Aware of this and fearful that Easley's eagerness might override his judgment, Seth Low positively forbade him to accept one cent from the Rockefellers so long as his "Commission continues in existence."[9] (At the same time, Starr Murphy was counseling Rockefeller along similar lines about his giving.) Easley agreed that Low's was the proper stance to take. He contented himself with befriending King against the day that the Rockefeller name and fortune were in the Federation camp. The two men had several talks and carried on a correspondence once King returned to Ottawa.

King may have mentioned to Easley his concern over the continuing verbal brickbats being hurled at Rockefeller. In one of his letters, Easley confided that Gompers believed that it was more important for the labor movement to help Lawson and the other strikers under indictment than to spare the feelings of the Rockefellers. This intelligence confirmed King's suspicion that the sole object of the anti-Rockefeller agitation was to influence the course of justice in Colorado. He urged Rockefeller to take whatever steps he could to see that all of the outstanding indictments were either quashed or acted upon as quickly as possible. He communicated his belief that Rockefeller could only be hurt if the indictments were not out of the way by the time of his visit in September. Should the charged atmosphere that now existed in Colorado continue, he cautioned, their efforts to place C.F. & I. on a new footing might prove futile.

At the suggestion of Ivy Lee, the staff at 26 Broadway responded to King's call for action by drafting a lengthy statement detailing Rockefeller's position on the indictments. They proposed to submit the statement to the Low Commission and, in that way, enter it into the public record. When King learned of this plan, he was astounded by the density of his colleagues. They had entirely missed the point, which was to get the indictments out of the way as quickly as possible *without* calling attention to the Rockefellers in the process. They didn't seem to understand how imperative it was to ensure that Rockefeller was met by an open and receptive atmosphere when he visited Colorado. Their action would only serve to increase Rockefeller's visibility and feed the notion that he was behind the indictments.

It was therefore with some relief that King learned that Seth Low had advised Ivy Lee not to forward the statement. King did not yet know, however, that Lee had said something to cause Low to suspect that the Rockefellers were trying to put something over on him. Low discussed this possibility with Easley, who concurred.

While this minor tempest steeped in the heat of the New York City summer, welcome news reached King from Colorado. The state supreme court had agreed to hear argument for a new trial for Lawson. It had also disqualified the judge who had presided at the initial trial from further participation in any legal proceedings growing out of the strike. King thought Lawson was virtually guaranteed a new trial and that his conviction would be overturned. Calculating the advantage to Rockefeller and himself, without a thought of justice for Lawson, he surmised that the court rulings would significantly reduce the enmity that might be encountered on their visit to Colorado.

In preparation for this trip, King spent much of July drafting a constitution that embodied his plan for employee representation. When he had earlier broached the idea of a written constitution, Rockefeller and the other staff members had responded with enthusiasm. They were largely attracted by the publicity value such a document might have, he thought. His own interests were both more strategic and more substantive. Above all else, he wanted to avoid the charge that the representation scheme was an antiunion device. A written document would accomplish this in several ways. By spelling out rights, responsibilities, and procedures and by listing the prevailing terms and conditions of employment, it would be the moral equivalent of a collective bargaining contract. Because everything would be spelled out in detail, no one would be able to accuse them of attempting anything underhanded. In addition, the miners would find a written contract a tangible gain over past practice, and the C.F. & I. management would undoubtedly do a better job of meeting its responsibilities with an explicit set of rules in hand. King sent the draft constitution off to New York for review, and asked for suggestions on how it might be improved. Although a few suggestions were forthcoming, the New York office was preoccupied with more pressing matters.

Rockefeller and his associates were absorbed just then with a sudden and highly volatile strike at the Bayonne, New Jersey, refinery of Standard Oil. Both the Rockefeller and Standard Oil offices were located across the harbor from Bayonne, in the same building on lower Broadway. In rapid-fire order, the strike displayed all of the attributes of industrial warfare: strikebreakers, armed thugs, riots, and in all, six fatalities. The stance of Standard Oil throughout the dispute was perfectly reflected in a *New York Times* leader: "SO Spurns Strike Mediation."[10] Then, with much the same suddeness with which the strike had come to public attention, it vanished following news of a settlement.

A surprising aspect of the strike was that, despite their intimate connection with Standard Oil, the Rockefellers were neither widely blamed nor criticized. Almost three weeks after the strike, a staff report for the expiring Commission on Industrial Relations led the *New York Times* to run a front page story headed: "Hit Rockefeller in Bayonne Report."[11] But the strike produced no further discernible consequences in the weeks ahead.

In sharp contrast, the subject of Rockefeller's role in the Colorado strike remained very much alive. In August alone, the *Survey* carried a long article by John A. Fitch, "What Rockefeller Knew and What He Did"; the *Independent* carried a piece by Frank Walsh, "Perilous Philanthropy"; and the *Final Report* of the U.S. Commission on Industrial Relations appeared.

The *Survey* article was a remarkable piece of reporting. John Fitch had been in Colorado during the strike, reviewed the testimony given before the Walsh Commission, and read all of the published correspondence between the Rockefeller office in New York and C.F. & I. A skilled analyst, his conclusions were not to be dismissed lightly.

It was evident to Fitch that Frank Walsh was mistaken in his belief that Rockefeller had had a direct hand in the Colorado strike. The record, wrote Fitch, sustained Rockefeller's innocence on that point. On the other hand, the same record clearly convicted him of a failure to act responsibly.

> Where was Mr. Rockefeller when, in the early days of the strike, the papers were telling day after day of machineguns in the hands of deputy sheriffs, of attacks and counter attacks, of men and boys being killed? Granting as we must that the executive officials told him only of the violence of the strikers, he could have read in the papers that civil war was on foot. Whether the cause was just or not, people were dying for it . . .

It was a time when Mr. Rockefeller could have done great and statesman-like things. But he did not do them. He did not take up the responsibility which was so clearly his whether he accepted it or not. By failing to find out for himself he merely evaded this responsibility; by backing up his men without finding out, he weighted it down the more heavily.[12]

Fitch concluded by criticizing the Walsh Commission for refusing to recognize that Rockefeller's failure was less the result of some personal deficiency or malevolence than it was a by-product of the increasing separation between corporate owners and the managers. He thought that the Commission should have riveted its attention and the attention of the public on the problems associated with absentee-owner capitalism rather than on the Rockefellers. Walsh's treatment of Rockefeller had amounted to "unconscionable heckling." In what was almost certainly a veiled criticism of Rockefeller, Fitch concluded by dismissing "platitudinous expressions of good intent" as inadequate either as an excuse or as a remedy for the kind of failure evident in Colorado.[13]

No direct comments on the Fitch article were preserved among the papers of Rockefeller or King. Both men unquestionably read the piece—King mentioned it in his diary. We also know that Ivy Lee sent a copy to Seth Low, marked to call his attention to several points. Low, in turn, wrote to Easley that he thought Fitch's appraisal "rather fair."[14] Frank Walsh, on the other hand, thought that Fitch had "made a Hell of a poor job of it." Lee's action suggests that the Rockefeller camp did not find the article particularly damaging. In fact, King and Rockefeller actively considered reprinting the piece several years later but finally rejected the idea.

The article provided, perhaps, the last genuine opportunity for Rockefeller to face up to his responsibility for some of what had happened in Colorado. Had he done so, he might have been led to examine his subsequent actions and the motives underpinning the representation plan. His and King's elaborate subtrefuge for avoiding dealings with the union might then have been recognized for what it was: his father's will at work. But he did not see, or sieze, the opportunity. The evidence suggests that he and his associates valued the Fitch article because it exonerated them of the charge of evil intentions. They absolved themselves of any responsibility for the unintended consequences of their actions and inactions *because* they had not intended them. The old saw about the road to hell found no application among them.

In his article "Perilous Philanthropy," Frank Walsh raised anew the question of the value of any investigation into labor relations conducted under the auspices of the Rockefeller Foundation. His views provoked a stronger reaction within the Rockefeller camp than the Fitch piece, which suggests that the staff still feared Walsh's power. Frederick T. Gates took the occasion of one of his timely visits to the office to suggest that for a reasonable period the Foundation ought to steer clear of controversial undertakings. The staff readily agreed. Soon afterward, King in his meetings with Easley, and Rockefeller in meetings with John Mitchell and with several national officers of U.M.W., sought assurances that the labor movement was not opposed to King's investigation. Rockefeller went the length of offering to put a halt to the investigation if Mitchell, the U.M.W. leaders, or Gompers thought he should.

The threat Walsh posed to King and Rockefeller was out of all proportion to his actual power. With the publication of the Industrial Relations Commission's final report in mid-August, it should have become clear that for all his ability, Walsh had been a divisive Commission chairman. It was also evident that his views commanded little authority.

The Commission's final report took the form of a majority and a minority report. Walsh, along with the labor members, constituted the minority. There was no little irony in this, for the split within the Commission stemmed largely from the majority's judgment that Walsh had gone overboard in attempting to lay the labor problems of the day at the Rockefeller doorstep. Thus, if King and Rockefeller overreacted to Walsh, Walsh for his part reciprocated.

But the consequences for Walsh and for his interest in labor reform were considerably more costly. The division within the Commission ensured that, as a body, it would leave little imprint on the future development of American labor policies or practices, whether public or private. In contrast, King and Rockefeller had merely had their feathers ruffled. They easily survived Walsh's intellectual challenges and rough handling. Shielded from self-knowledge by their blinding rectitude, they were free to move ahead to have their way with the world.

Notes

1. W.L.M.K. Diary, 5/17/15–5/25/15. W.L.M.K. Papers, Series J13, p. G2539, 672.
2. Quoted from the New York *Sun* (May 22, 1915) in Adams (1966), p. 170.
3. F. P. Walsh to Dante Barton, 5/24/15. F.P.W. Papers, Box 143.
4. Commission on Industrial Relations (1916), vol. IX, pp. 8792–8793.
5. Ibid., p. 8796.
6. Ibid., p. 8816. At times wrongheaded but almost always kindhearted, Walsh deserves a searching and unsentimental biographer. So many of the reform currents of the age touched him, and he reacted to them with such energy and courage, that we may expect a close examination of his life to yield fresh and important insights into the Progressive movement, the Wilson administration, the labor movement, and American radicalism.
7. J.D.R., Jr. to J. F. Welborn, 6/29/15. J.D.R., Jr. Papers, C.F.& I. Files, Business Interests. See also Hicks (1941).
8. W.L.M.K. Diary, 7/1/15–7/31/15. W.M.L.K. Papers, Series J13, p. G2539, 698.
9. S. Low to R. Easley, 6/28/15. Low Papers, Box 146.
10. *New York Times* (July 25, 1915), p. 10. In addition to the *Times* coverage, the strike is treated in New Jersey Bureau of Industrial Statistics (1916), *Survey* 34 : 18 (July 31, 1915), and Gibb and Knowlton (1956).
11. *New York Times* (August 16, 1915).
12. Fitch (1915).
13. Ibid.
14. Seth Low to Ralph Easley, 8/28/15. Low Papers, Box 146. The Walsh quote appears in F. P. Walsh to George Creel, 8/26/15. F.P.W. Papers, Box 143.

8. Selling the Plan: The East

With summer's end, the Rockefeller staff assembled in New York City. King arrived from Ottawa on the same day that Clarence Hicks arrived from Denver. Two days later, C.F. & I. president Jesse Welborn joined the group, which also included Ivy Lee, Starr Murphy, and of course, John D. Rockefeller, Jr. Their agenda was crowded, and each item, including the questions of Hicks's status, King's draft constitution, and Rockefeller's upcoming visit to Colorado, provoked some contention. The process of thrashing out these disagreements ensured that every decision reached by the group was buttressed by an explicit understanding of its assumptions and intentions. Those whose arguments prevailed did as much to clarify their own thinking as they did to win over their opponents.

Polite and gentlemanly as the meetings were throughout, they also embodied elements of coercion. Welborn and Hicks repeatedly found themselves giving way to the positions developed by King and supported by Rockefeller, Murphy, and Lee. The meetings thus effected the transfer of authority over C.F. & I. labor policy from Colorado to New York and from Welborn to Rockefeller.

King first had to be brought up to date on a number of developments. To his dismay, he learned that the latest rulings of the Colorado Supreme Court had done little to ease the situation there. Worse still, the governor, for reasons of his own, had verbally attacked the United Mine Workers, and the coal operators had launched a new antiunion publication. The union, for its part, was busily engaged in an attempt to have a number of mine operators, including Rockefeller and Welborn, indicted on charges of criminal conspiracy. Under these circumstances, King observed, the value of Rockefeller's visit to Colorado was likely to be reduced sharply. The attendant risks would rise.

He persuaded Rockefeller that it was imperative to take steps to defuse the Colorado situation. They would have to convince the union people of their complete sincerity in wishing both to improve the lot of C.F. & I. miners and to avoid further antagonisms. With Rockefeller's consent, King called on Ralph Easley of the National Civic Federation to arrange meetings between Rockefeller and the national leaders of the United Mine Workers and the A.F. of L.

By way of greeting King, Easley unleashed a tirade against Rockefeller and his associates. He charged that Ivy Lee had improperly attempted to use the Low Commission to get the indictments in Colorado quashed. Then, switching gears, he characterized the recent announcement of the creation of an industrial relations department within the Rockefeller Foundation as an attempt by reactionaries like president Eliot and Jerome Greene to usurp the role of the National Civic Federation. Finally, he advised King to cut himself loose from the entire Rockefeller crowd, saying that he and the labor people had no use for any of them, and that King could only injure himself if he prolonged his association.

King laughed and asked Easley what had happened to change his opinion in so short a time. He reassured him that his work for the Foundation was in no way intended to rival the work of the Federation. He was still committed, as he hoped Easley was, to promoting harmony between the Rockefellers and labor.

Easley confessed that he was angry mainly because Walsh had succeeded in winning the solid support of labor for his radical minority report. This success, he felt, had come at the expense of the Federation. He went on to imply that the intransigence of the Rockefellers had helped Walsh make his case. Nonetheless, he agreed to do as King asked. A day or so later, he advised that Samuel Gompers was out of town and would not be available for a meeting. The president and the secretary of the Mine Workers were available, however, and would be pleased to talk with Mr. Rockefeller. Arrangements were made for a meeting later that week. In the interim, King worked to bring several of his colleagues into line.

King must have discussed with Lee the trouble he had created with Easley and Low. No doubt he also lectured him on the need for the greatest delicacy in making any public statements about the Colorado indictments. Chastened, Lee spent the entire week being perfectly agreeable.

Clarence Hicks had come to New York primarily to request funds for improvements that his survey of the mining camps had led him to propose. The cost of some of these improvements was to be met out of company funds, but the outlays for community facilities were thought to be beyond the current means of the company. President Welborn had suggested that Hicks approach Rockefeller to see whether he would be willing to absorb these expenses personally. Welborn promised to back him up; he had to go to New York at about the same time to gain authorization for the new executive position Hicks was to fill.

Hicks' proposal met with the hearty approval of the staff. King and Lee encouraged him to lay his recommendations before Rockefeller, assuring him that they would be accepted, and they were. Rockefeller also took the opportunity to express concern that his gifts might be misconstrued as an attempt to purchase the favor of the miners. King counseled him that if proper care were taken in deciding the form and nature of the gifts, no such problems would arise. The churches, for example, should be built only after a congregation had been formed in a camp and tendered a request. The funds should be applied exclusively for church buildings. In no other way should they be used to impinge on the religious life of the camps. In a similar vein, King suggested that club houses ought to be constructed, but that their staffing and programs should be left to the discretion of the YMCA. Instead of retaining the "Y" staff directly, Rockefeller or his father might covertly increase the size of their annual gift to the international YMCA organization by an equivalent amount. Although King's advice did not resolve the problem Rockefeller had broached, Rockefeller accepted it as if it did. Apparently, he agreed that if he insulated himself from potential charges of dominating life in the camps through his gifts, no one would charge him with using his gifts to buy the favor of the miners. In any event, he wanted to agree to Hicks' recommendations.

King admired the way Hicks carried the day for his improvements. He was particularly pleased when Hicks objected that some of the men in the C.F. & I. steel mills were working seven days a week and recommended that they have one day of rest without any reduction in pay. The staff immediately agreed and turned to Welborn for his opinion. Although he was not reluctant to be the first in the steel industry to take such a step, Welborn said, he was concerned about the rise in costs that would result. Since the staff believed that a way *had* to be found to grant one day of rest, they requested that Welborn explore ways of implementing the change as soon as he returned to Colorado. If possible, the matter would be resolved during Rockefeller's visit. Their discussions and decisions made it quite clear that in the eyes of the staff and Rockefeller, doing good works and the publicity value of such works each outweighed considerations of profitability.

In spite of his admiration for Hicks, King was troubled by a number of his attitudes. Ivy Lee professed to share his concern. They sensed that Hicks attached so much weight to his camp improvements that he failed to appreciate the far greater importance of the employee representation scheme. As forcefully as they could they worked to impress on him the centrality of the scheme to their strategy. Employee representation was the linchpin of all their plans, their main defense against future conflict. They argued that his improvements, though eminently desirable, were palliatives of a far less critical nature. Not only did they expect him to recognize and act in accord with this sense of priorities, they obliged him to pledge before the entire group that he would do so.

King was also quite concerned about Hicks' attitude toward unions. When Welborn came before the C.F. & I. board of directors to request authorization for Hicks' appointment, Lee, as a director, raised an objection. He contended that Hicks' hostility toward trade unions made it unlikely that he could act in the unbiased fashion required of the position they had it in mind to create. Rockefeller left the meeting room to consult with King and, on learning that he was of the same opinion, returned and moved for a compromise. The board voted to create the post of assistant to the president but to defer the appointment of Hicks until he had been given an opportunity to resolve their doubts about him. Rockefeller and his advisors wanted Hicks for the job, but first they had to bring him around to their quite uncommon position on union membership.

In their first discussion of King's draft constitution, Hicks had mentioned that the mine superintendents were enforcing the practice of hiring only nonunion miners. He indicated his approval of this practice, for he believed that otherwise the union would move in and eventually impose a closed shop. If there was to be a clause in the constitution pledging that the company would not discriminate for or against union members, he urged that it be carefully worded to apply only to men already employed and not to new hires.

Alarmed by these remarks, King and Lee were quick to point

out that Rockefeller did not countenance having "one policy in theory and another in practice."[1] The hiring practices Hicks had described, they told him, were not in line with company policy. Although the nondiscrimination clause in the draft constitution applied technically only to those already employed, it was to be understood by everyone in C.F. & I. that hiring practices were to conform to the same principle.

> I told Hicks that if Mr. R. took a position against unionism and the right of men to join the union, I myself would get out and fight against him; that it was fundamentally wrong that a man of his wealth should be placed in antagonism towards the organization of labor . . .
>
> . . . We made it plain that Mr. R's position on the union question was, namely: that men had a right to join an organization just as they had a right to join a church. The Company had a right to say whether it would make an agreement with the union or not, which was a different question; but managers and superintendents had no right to discriminate against men simply because they belonged to unions.[2]

Lee said at one point in the discussion that, if it were to prove necessary to deal with the U.M.W. in the near future, even that would be preferable to a renewal of the conflict. King thought otherwise. In the privacy of his diary, he wrote that the bitter feelings on all sides made it improbable that there could be any relationship with the union for several years to come. The immediate requirements of the situation, as he saw them, were for all forms of hostility to cease, for the company to introduce its planned improvements, and above all, for the rights of the miners to be observed so scrupulously as to preclude any need to turn to the union. This last objective made it imperative that the draft constitution be adopted and lived up to in practice. Yet, here was Hicks, who was supposed to oversee the representation plan, giving expression to antiunion sentiments when nondiscrimination was absolutely vital.

King foresaw major difficulties with Welborn as well, for he supposed that Welborn's decision to hire Hicks owed something to the latter's sentiments. He was much relieved to learn he was mistaken. When questioned soon after his arrival, Welborn indicated that Hicks had erred; there were many union men at work in the company's mines. No policy of discriminatory hiring was in force.

It then came out that Hicks had received his information from a single superintendent and had mistakenly generalized from that instance.

At the group's final luncheon, on King's advice, Rockefeller spoke about his commitment to the positions he had taken before the Commission on Industrial Relations. He said that he would not allow a divergent policy to be enforced. He went on to elicit from Welborn the promise that, on his return to the West, he would meet with each camp superintendent individually to impress upon all the importance of consistency in policy and practice. The same requisite was more forcefully conveyed to Hicks by making his appointment contingent on his willingness to conform.

Aware as Hicks was that C.F. & I. had no intention of dealing with the United Mine Workers, he must have been perplexed to find himself pressed to endorse and implement a policy of nondiscrimination. Was it possible to avoid unionization where union members were freely hired and treated the same as nonunionists? Hicks had come to New York firmly believing, like almost everyone else in employer and management circles, that the answer to this question was no. Yet King, Lee, and Rockefeller insisted that the answer was yes.

By the time he was asked to clarify his views, Hicks knew what was expected of him. He said he had no very strong feelings about unions one way or the other, that he had faced an entirely different set of circumstances at International Harvester, and that he still had much to learn about C.F. & I.'s situation. He candidly admitted that the prospect of hiring miners without regard to union membership troubled him because, he believed, union miners were more likely to create management problems. Nevertheless, he was prepared to carry out the policy of nondiscrimination to the best of his ability. He asked, however, that the board of directors rather than the management shoulder the responsibility for any adverse consequences of the policy.

Everyone was greatly relieved, and Hicks was immediately confirmed in his appointment. Although King had previously detected in him a tendency to say what his superiors wanted to hear rather than what he believed, King thought that in the present instance, he had acquitted himself forthrightly.

This hurdle overcome, Welborn and Hicks were next constrained to accept the constitution King had prepared. When initially given a copy of the draft, Welborn had dismissed the entire idea. Such a document was too elaborate and unworkable in a company like C.F. & I., he declared. If a shorter and simpler version could be prepared, he would look it over and give it some thought after his return to Colorado. Hicks joined him—all too eagerly from King's point of view—in urging simplification and delay. But, King was determined to gain the acceptance of the document so that it could be introduced during Rockefeller's Colorado visit. At the latter's direction, an entire day was given over to reviewing the draft so that any objections Welborn or Hicks might raise could be dealt with.

As the group worked its way clause by clause through the draft, it became clear that Welborn had few practical objections. His reservations stemmed from the novelty of the idea—as if he found it too incongruous to think of the refinement of a formal constitution in connection with his rough, polyglot workforce. The most telling suggestions for modification came from Ivy Lee, who, much to King's satisfaction, made a number of recommendations that they had previously discussed. With the two of them working in harmony, they were able to achieve all of the changes King desired. Lee, for example, suggested the idea of including, after the body of the constitution, a statement of the prevailing terms and conditions of employment. If this were done, he suggested, the entire document would become the equivalent of a contract. They could further enhance this similarity by making provision for the signatures of company officers and employee representatives. The entire document—including, on Rockefeller's recommendation, an organizational chart—could then be printed up and distributed among the men. King was as pleased as Punch.

At the end of the week of staff meetings, King, Rockefeller, and Starr Murphy met with John White and William Green, the national president and secretary-treasurer of the United Mine Workers. Rockefeller thought it would be helpful if he started off by indicating where he stood on the issues of unionism and collective bargaining. He proceeded to read portions of his statement before the Commission on Industrial Relations. Both White and Green praised his stance. He then described the Rockefeller Foundation's investigation into industrial relations and concluded by asking the union leaders if they knew of any reasons why this project should not be continued. He told them that if they and other union leaders believed the Foundation should not undertake the investigation, he would do everything he could to bring it to an end. King added that if he thought labor was opposed to his effort, he too would feel obliged to stop immediately. White and Green reassured them that on the basis of Rockefeller's description of the investigation, and their awareness of King's reputation, they had no objection. Rockefeller then asked what it was White and Green wished to discuss with him.

The unionists wanted it understood that they believed the first requisite of the situation in Colorado was to bring an end to the hatred and bitterness spawned by the strike. They had several suggestions that they believed would accomplish this objective. For one, they thought it would be helpful if Rockefeller would go out to Colorado and learn the situation first hand, visit the camps and talk to the miners. In their experience, personal contact of this sort was highly conducive to the development of good relations. They said that both sides had made mistakes during the strike and that they were not interested in continued recrimination. A fresh start was the healthiest thing that could happen.

Their second suggestion was that Rockefeller enter into a written agreement with his employees, an agreement that stated the terms and conditions of employment and indicated how grievances were to be handled. President White made it clear that they were not asking for a contract with the union but one between the company and "its own employees."[3] He suggested that this contract ought to run for a fixed number of years and indicated his preference for a three- or four-year term. When Rockefeller asked why the agreement couldn't just run on indefinitely, White replied that a fixed term of years made the miners feel more secure about an agreement. White's third suggestion was that any agreement that was developed contain a clause stating that the company did not discriminate against employees because of union membership.

King and Rockefeller coolly played out what now became for them something of a charade. They masked their surprise with an outward show of interest, listening intently, asking an occasional question, and pointing out some of the practical difficulties they might expect to encounter were they to follow White's suggestions. They politely refused to commit themselves one way or the other but promised to give the proposals every serious consideration. In this way, they kept to themselves the knowledge that the concessions the union leaders were asking them to grant were ones that they had already decided were in their own best interests.

The meeting concluded with a discussion of the Lawson case

and the outstanding indictments. Starr Murphy told of the steps that had been taken to ensure that C.F. & I. played no role in the trial or the indictments. Rockefeller then read the statement he had made before the Commission on Industrial Relations in May. He added that he wished it was within his power to bring these legal proceedings to a halt, but that he was afraid that any action on his part would render him guilty of the very sort of manipulation of which he was so often accused. White and Green responded by saying that nothing could be fairer than the statement he had made and that they too saw no action he could reasonably take. For the moment matters had to take their natural course through the Colorado legal system.

Following luncheon with the unionists, as they were being driven to Pocantico, Rockefeller and King reviewed their morning. Both men were delighted with their good fortune and, it must be said, with themselves. They marveled at the perfect conjuncture of the union's and their own position, without stopping to ask themselves why White and Green had asked for what they did. Instead, they discussed the comparative advantages of a long-term versus a short-term contract in Colorado and calculated the benefits that flowed to them from the union's position. King pointed out that all of the initiatives they were about to take at C.F. & I. would be looked upon by White and Green as the product of their own recommendations. This would please them and it would also oblige them to make good on their pledge to help "to right Mr. R. with Labor and the people."[4] Rockefeller concurred and went on to note that perhaps the largest benefit of their interview was that White and Green

"had taken the fangs out of" the one thing we had to fear, namely, that the union would say that the agreement made with the employees was a substitute for unionism. The agreement with the Company's own employees is now the Union's own suggestion as the step to be taken for the present.[5]

Thus, just as they were about to do something at once willfull and deceitful, Rockefeller and King not only were given approval for their action but actively encouraged in it by spokesmen for those they would have deceived. In the face of such good fortune, they could not help sounding a self-congratulatory note as the car carried them northward to Tarrytown.

It seems clear that White and Green supposed that by dealing with the Rockefellers they would get the best settlement possible in the Colorado fields. The terms of that best settlement could then be adopted by the Low Commission as the basis for all other settlements. The specific requests that the union leaders had made were not at all accidental. They conformed exactly to terms included in the settlement of the 1902 Anthracite Coal strike. Since the U.M.W. had gained substantially in membership among the anthracite miners following the 1902 settlement, White and Green undoubtedly anticipated that similar consequences would flow from a similar settlement in Colorado. The congruence of their strategy with that of Rockefeller and King was thus a coincidence of means. For the time being, it did not matter that there was so wide a disparity of ends.

But at some point in their celebration that evening, King and Rockefeller began to entertain doubts that their triumph was as secure as they had initially believed it to be. What if White and Green hadn't been sincere? Suppose Rockefeller arranged to have an agreement made with the employee representatives; what guarantee did he have that the union wouldn't continue to push for recognition? King placed a call to John Mitchell, the former U.M.W. president, and made an appointment for a meeting on Monday.

Since the contact with Mitchell had come through Ralph Easley, King felt he owed something to the National Civic Federation. On arriving in the city on Monday morning, he arranged for Rockefeller and himself to visit the Federation's exhibit on welfare work. Although the ostensible purpose of the visit was to permit Rockefeller to view the exhibit for himself, his physical presence was the way King paid off his debt. As Beeks led them around, King observed that, as he had expected, she showed more interest in the possibility of some connection between the Rockefellers and the Federation than in the exhibit itself. His dealings with Easley and Beeks always left him feeling uneasy. He believed that they cared only for their own recognition and, for that reason, had always to be dealt with with great care. John Mitchell, on the other hand, was easy to like and to trust. King hadn't seen him since his days as a labor mediator, when Mitchell had ably represented a group of striking miners.

In his appearance before the Industrial Relations Commission in late January 1915, Mitchell had been asked for his opinion of the representation plan recently introduced at Colorado Fuel & Iron. He had pronounced it "absurd." Even though the miners might not be overtly forced, he believed there would be "an indirect influence which they cannot resist"[6] impelling them to elect the representatives their bosses preferred rather than the ones they themselves preferred. It seemed clear to him that an organization dominated by the employer could not give free expression to the wishes of workers.

The record leaves unanswered the question of whether Rockefeller or King were aware of Mitchell's remarks. Their approach to him, which they agreed upon in advance, was to indicate that they were seriously entertaining the recommendations of White and Green, and wished to have the benefit of his advice. Rockefeller outlined the recommendations and indicated some of the problems he anticipated in carrying them out. He then asked whether the union was likely to accept his effort to follow through as evidence of a genuine desire to improve working conditions and build industrial peace or was it likely to start fresh troubles and condemn his actions as hostile? Mitchell responded that, if Rockefeller were to make an agreement such as had been recommended, it would probably encourage the men to organize and join the union. He should also expect that, when the agreement ran its course, the miners would seek to gain some modifications.

Mitchell expressed surprise that White and Green had given their sanction for an agreement that excluded the union. He could not understand why they would have done such a thing, which is interesting since he had presided over the union during the 1902 anthracite strike and been party to a similar settlement. King repeated for his benefit White's statements about the errors having been committed on both sides during the strike and the paramount need to bring an end to the rancor that still existed. White, he noted, had also said that the workers involved needed educating in the merits of unionism quite as much as did the employers.

After reflecting for a moment, Mitchell said that, from what he knew of the Colorado situation, it would probably still be impossible for the local union people and the companies to come to any sort of agreement. Passions ran too high. So he thought that he could understand what White and Green had in mind. He told Rockefeller that the course of action they had recommended to him seemed sensible and helpful. He urged him to go to Colorado and have an agreement drawn up. As to the nondiscrimination clause, he said:

> There are many employers . . . who profess to be favorable to the organization of labor and to be willing to allow their men to organize, but they are unwilling in fact to let them do so or to state their position in an agreement. I think if you include in this agreement the clause that there shall be no discrimination so far as unions are concerned, that . . . will give entire satisfaction to the union men and will relieve the situation in Colorado so far as you are concerned.[7]

King interjected the thought that unionism would be treated just like questions of race and religion. But Mitchell suggested that there was a very real difference. He said that it might not matter to anybody to what church a man belonged, but union men could not afford to be indifferent to the union status of their fellow workers. The worker who benefitted from the union's efforts but bore none of the sacrifice was a source of understandable concern to unionists.

Mitchell went on to recall that in the anthracite coal strike of 1902, the commission that effected the settlement also had avoided the formality of union recognition. He had signed the agreement simply as John Mitchell, without any reference to his standing as the U.M.W. president. In his view, the Low Commission would probably be guided by the precedent set by the anthracite commission, since the latter's efforts had resulted in a substantial improvement of industrial relations in the anthracite industry. He wondered if Rockefeller would be prepared to support such a settlement.

King responded that they would not favor any recommendations from the Low Commission that treated C.F. & I. as one among an undifferentiated group of coal companies. Much of their time and energy over the past months had been directed to cutting the ties between their company and the others. By way of example, he cited the fact that C.F. & I. had welcomed the creation of the Low Commission and cooperated with it, whereas the others had not. They had also taken every precaution to ensure that the company was no longer involved in the strike-related prosecutions. By charting an independent course, King related, they hoped to so improve working conditions and the relations between the company and its employees that they would attain industrial peace. If they were as successful as they hoped to be, their efforts would provide the Low Commission with a new model for settlements among the other companies.

Mitchell had to concede that this strategy was preferable to passive acceptance of the anthracite settlement formula. He said that he had not known of the actions mentioned by King, which prompted Rockefeller to read to him the statement he had made before the Walsh Commission in May. Mitchell again expressed surprise and wondered that so forthright a statement hadn't been reported more widely in the press. This led to a discussion of the Lawson trial and consideration of what steps might be taken to publicize Rockefeller's desire for fairness and an end to the recriminations growing out of the strike. The problem, Rockefeller confided, was to make his position clear and at the same time avoid any suggestion that he was attempting to influence the Colorado courts. Mitchell assured him that he had done all that might reasonably be expected of him.

Shifting ground somewhat, Rockefeller asked Mitchell for his views on the investigation into industrial relations being sponsored by the Rockefeller Foundation. Saying that the attacks on the investigation and the Foundation by the Walsh Commission seemed to reflect labor's opinion, he extended to Mitchell as he had earlier to White and Green the power of veto. If he or Gompers thought it unwise or undesirable for the research to continue, King's study would be brought to a halt. Mitchell replied to the effect that the attacks on the Foundation were absurd. They were a by-product of the Colorado strike and had nothing to do either with the merits of the research or the integrity of the Foundation. He thought that, by all means, King ought to continue and complimented Rockefeller for having chosen King as his counselor. He had some very nice things to say about King, which the latter duly recorded verbatim in his diary.

Rockefeller concluded the interview by asking if there were any other labor leaders, apart from Gompers, with whom he should meet. Mitchell said that White, Green, and Gompers were the critical figures, and advised that he meet with Gompers. Rockefeller explained that he had tried to arrange a meeting but that Gompers had been out of the city. He himself was going away shortly, so that the matter would have to wait until a later date. Mitchell assured him that his position would prove as satisfactory to Gompers as it had to himself.

Once they left Mitchell's office, Rockefeller told King that it had never been clearer to him that there had to be a written contract in Colorado, and that they must face up to the likelihood that the contract meant unionization in the long run. This conclusion led him to ask if the clause he had suggested, providing for the discontinuance of the representation plan in the event of unionization, had been incorporated into the constitution. King explained why it had not been. Its inclusion, he argued, would sustain the charge that they were trying to create a substitute for unionism. In contrast, the nondiscrimination clause refuted any such charge and was consistent with both the open shop and the position Rockefeller had taken before the commission.

Rockefeller responded by saying that he was sure his father would not approve of their plans if they led ultimately to unionization. King suggested that Rockefeller Senior could be won over if he understood that the representation plan was in every sense a vindication of the open shop. C.F. & I. would continue to deal only with its own employees and without regard to their union status. True enough, Rockefeller replied, but a better response to his father's objection might be to acknowledge that if during the life of the plan "every man [became] a member of the union,"[8] there would no longer be any basis for refusing to deal with the union.

King responded that it was overly pessimistic to talk that way. In four or five years, he thought, the company would have had ample time to so improve its employee relations that unionism would find little or no support. Rockefeller agreed but said that it was necessary to face up to the fact that their strategy contained the very real possibility of their someday having to deal with the union.

Several aspects of this exchange are quite revealing. One clear inference is that Rockefeller remained under his father's shadow. Whether Senior would approve was a crucial consideration in many of his decisions. The colloquy also indicates that Rockefeller still clung to the view that he was morally justified in refusing to deal with the union so long as any number of miners were not members. King's lectures on free riders and John Mitchell's remarks on the same subject had had no effect. This suggests that King's assumption that his expert judgment would prevail was flawed. True enough, Rockefeller read his words like a dutiful schoolboy whenever he wanted to state what was ostensibly his (Rockefeller's) position. But the pupil's complete ignorance of industrial relations did not render him a perfect parrot. His mind was not a blank page awaiting instruction. Instead, any instruction had to compete with preconceived ideas, prejudices, and other pressures. King's instruction sometimes took hold, but, as in this instance, it was sometimes overwhelmed and lost.

Next, consider King's own mental gymnastics. His insistence on the nondiscrimination clause was aimed mainly at appearances. The clause defused potential charges of antiunion intent. But the primary intention of employee representation *was* union avoidance, to organize the miners to deal with their problems so as to preclude resort to unionism. By implication, the course King and Rockefeller were adopting left them free to do whatever they wished just so long as no one could prove it. Thus, it might be said that in worrying about the opinions of Senior on the one hand and Frank Walsh on the other, they had overlooked their all-knowing God. Yet, that they would not consciously stoop to the hypocrisy of adopting the antidiscrimination clause and then agreeing to its violation in practice, suggests how tangled their motives and self-interest had become over the larger issue of the representation plan.

That evening, as King reflected in his diary on the events of the day, Senior and his relationship with his son were uppermost in his thoughts. King told himself that what he and the younger Rockefeller were doing was absolutely right. If C.F. & I. had taken an extreme position in refusing to hire or permit union men to work in its mines, the U.M.W. had also been extreme in hoping to gain a closed shop. Each of these positions, he believed, abridged a fundamental human right. (So he didn't accept the free rider argument either!) In contrast, the policy of a company entering into an agreement with its own employees, coupled with a commitment not to discriminate because of union membership or nonmembership, was entirely fair. Those like Senior who might argue that a nondiscrimination clause necessarily meant the eventual recognition of the union were as mistaken as those who assumed that meeting with union leaders amounted to recognition. A similar mistake was made by those who would counsel against a company making a written agreement with its own employees. Collective bargaining and the liberty to join or not join a union were the twin principles for which Rockefeller would have to fight. Even Senior could not be permitted to stand in the way of this just course.

Although Rockefeller was deeply reluctant to cross his father, he also saw the necessity for doing so in the present instance. With great prescience, King understood that the stakes included Rocke-feller's destiny:

> His remark that his father might not like this, but that he would take it on his own responsibility without conferring with his father one way or the other, makes me feel that he sees it as a step necessary to his own life future, and that it must be taken even though his father might not find it acceptable. I cannot but feel a very great responsibility in urging him to this course . . . if his life is to be worth the living, and any further accomplishments made possible. Besides, it is the right thing, and Time will justify the step as a forward and progressive one, not something wrung from him through despair. Clearly, this is the great crisis in his life . . .[9]

King concluded that everything must be done to ensure the success of their Colorado trip. That very day, he had learned that Rockefeller was being misrepresented among the Colorado coal owners. The prosecutions were a further cause for anxiety. Clearly, it was a matter of acting now or never. He pledged himself to do all he could to help his worthy patron.

Since Senior was at his Cleveland residence, his son had the opportunity to avoid a face-to-face confrontation. He dictated a long letter (nine typewritten pages) in which he recounted for his father's benefit the meetings and decisions of the past several weeks. He concluded with a candid assessment of the advantages and the perils of the line of action he felt bound to take:

> In view, however, of the very explicit and definite expressions of Messrs. White and Green, we can now proceed with reasonable assurance of freedom from opposition. . . . Our thought is to have this agreement run for a period of three or five years, if possible. This will insure industrial peace for that period. It will once and for all absolutely differentiate the Colorado Fuel & Iron Company from all the other coal mining companies in Colorado . . . and . . . will redound all the more to the credit of the company in the public mind.
>
> Of course, we recognize that when this agreement is put into force, if it is lived up to—as it must be lived up to or else be a farce—the United Mine Workers may quietly attempt to unionize all of our employes. This is a danger, however, which we will always be open to, whether the plan is adopted or not, and in

the judgment of us all, the danger will be far less with the plan in operation than without it. . . . Even if however, the men should very generally be brought into the union, we will be assured of quiet operation during the life of the agreement, and at its expiration, if the vast majority of the men who have been giving satisfaction as our employees for some years past should prove to be members of the union, it would be a question then for us to consider whether we should not recognize the union, so long as men who are non-union were not discriminated against. I recognize all the dangers which the proposed program lays us open to. We have discussed them fully here and are acting with our eyes open. All things considered, however, we are of the opinion that the course which is planned is, for the present as well as for the future, the wisest and fairest course . . .[10]

Having thus ensured that his father was fully informed and also that he would have no opportunity to object to the course about to be taken, Rockefeller readied himself for the trip to the West. Members of his family and the staff were apprehensive for his safety, but he appeared unconcerned. He was rather looking forward to his first independent venture as a business leader, his hopes pinned to his ability to convince C.F. & I. managers and employees that the representation plan and the written contract afforded their best chance for a harmonious future. The extraordinary pieces of good fortune that had befallen him in the preceding few days encouraged him to wish for comparable success in the West. Since, in Colorado, he had the power to make his wishes come true, they would.

Notes

1. W.L.M.K. Diary, 9/8/15–9/11/15. W.L.M.K. Papers, Series J13, p. G2539, 721.
2. Ibid., 9/7/15, p. G2539, 714; 9/8/15–9/11/15, p. G2539, 721.
3. Ibid., 9/8/15–9/11/15. p. G2539, 736. Quotation marks in the original.
4. Ibid., p. G2539, 737.
5. Ibid., p. G2539, 739. Quotation marks in original.
6. Colorado Springs, *Evening Telegraph* (February 1, 1915), p. 1. Mitchell's own description of the 1902 anthracite commission award appears in his *Organized Labor* (1903), pp. 392–95.
7. W.L.M.K. Diary, 9/13/15. W.L.M.K. Papers, Series J13, p. G2539, 756–757. Quotation marks in original.

8. Ibid., p. G2539, 755.
9. Ibid., p. G2539, 759.
10. J.D.R. Jr. to J.D.R., 9/15/15. J.D.R., Jr. Papers, Personal Papers, Box 27.

9. Selling the Plan: The West

From the moment John D. Rockefeller, Jr., arrived in Trinidad, Colorado, until his departure three weeks later, a corps of newspaper reporters attended him. His every word and action was recorded and appeared in newspapers throughout the country. During the first week, his progress through the C.F. & I. mining camps and steel mills made front page news in local papers almost every day. In the more cosmopolitan East, the *New York Times* ran only the first day's item on page one, but it provided coverage every day. It also ran a Sunday magazine article that began with the declaration that: "All the world knows what John D. Rockefeller, Jr., was doing last week in Colorado."[1]

It was a royal tour of democratic proportions. The son of the richest man in the world talked amiably with miners, danced with their wives, swung a pick. The miners "were shy and timid" before him.[2] He overawed them be deigning, for all his untold wealth and power, to walk among them. Had anyone anticipated a hostile reception or embarrassment of any sort from the miners or from union sympathizers, they would have been surprised by the warm cordiality with which Rockefeller was received everywhere.

At Rockefeller's request, the first stop on his tour was at Ludlow Junction. He surveyed the setting of the strike tragedy, a silent barren plain stretching limitless to the east, ending abruptly in a series of low ridges to the west—a space that dwarfs humanity. Without speaking, the party drove on to a nearby working mine. There, he conversed with several miners, questioned their wives about the adequacy of the company houses, and visited the schoolhouse.

The following day he and King visited the Frederick mine at Valdez. They donned miner's garb ($2 for the outfit at the company store) and went underground for the first time. It was duly recorded that he several times bumped his head on the low roof of the man-way and that he swung a pick at the coal seam with little effect. He also made an impromptu speech to the miners in which he said, alluding to his pick work, that he obviously needed their help in digging the coal. But, he continued, they also needed his help to provide the mules, the track, and the market for the coal. Anyone who tried to tell them that they were enemies was wrong. They were partners, he asserted, and it was on that basis that he wanted to "do business" with them. As he turned to leave, one of the miners said, "You are not as bad as you are painted." [3]

Much of the newspaper coverage that week "painted" Rockefeller as a sincere and concerned person with many human touches. When he sat in the blazing sun talking with miner Archie Dennison about his role as an employee representative, when he danced one evening with the miners' wives and daughters at the Walsenberg camp, and when a little schoolgirl at the Sopris camp school explained her class work to him, it was newsworthy and touching, largely because of the discrepancy between perceptions of him as a person and the careless stereotypes associated with his name in the public mind. The difference between him as a flesh and blood person and as an object was the unspoken leitmotif of most of what was said.

The *Times* editorially called attention to the physical courage Rockefeller displayed in going among his enemies, and to his moral courage, since his presence amounted to an admission of past error and an attempt to provide the remedy. But Rockefeller was not atoning for any sins. His humility did not run the length of permitting him to admit to serious error. When he met a delegation from the Women's Justice League of Denver at the end of the first week of his visit, he disclaimed any responsibility for the Ludlow Massacre or any other strike violence. He sought to persuade them that he was only interested in building a brighter and harmonious future for all concerned, and they were satisfied.

Although the news stories focused on Rockefeller to his advantage, remarkably equitable coverage of the views of local union leaders was also provided. John R. Lawson, for one, was interviewed in his cell at the county jail shortly after Rockefeller's arrival. His remarks were quoted extensively in the daily wire service dispatch about the tour:

> I believe Mr. Rockefeller is sincere. . . . I believe he is honestly trying to improve conditions among the men in the mines. His efforts probably will result in some betterments which I hope may prove to be permanent.
> However, Mr. Rockefeller has missed the fundamental

trouble in the coal camps. Democracy has never existed among the men who toil under the ground—the coal companies have stamped it out. Now, Mr. Rockefeller is not restoring democracy; he is trying to substitute paternalism for it.

I am glad to assume that Mr. Rockefeller is earnest in his desire to do something for the miners, but Mr. Rockefeller will be here only a week or two. After he is gone, what then? The miners will have neither organization or contracts to protect them. They will be at the mercy of whatever superintendents or pit bosses the company may select.[4]

Lawson, of course, was unaware that Rockefeller fully intended to leave behind both an organization and a contract. Like the general public, the jailed unionist would come to learn his intentions only as they were spelled out in measured doses in the daily press.

During the first week of the tour, all of the reportage was devoted to Rockefeller's visits to the mining camps and the Pueblo steel works. Little mention was made of the representation plan and none of a constitution or contract. During the second week, the human interest stories gave way to reports that Rockefeller was meeting continuously with company officers. It was then announced that a new industrial plan was under discussion. Thus, it was made to appear that a new policy was emerging spontaneously as a result of Rockefeller's tour of inspection. The press corps was told that a constitution and bylaws were being drafted but that everything was still tentative. At the same time, it was made clear to the reporters that the plan under consideration would build upon the successful system of employee representation already in effect at C.F. & I. Rockefeller was asked whether his new plan was an attack upon unionism. He denied the charge in the following manner:

"At the outset of the strike in 1913 the company took the position that every man was entitled to work on his own terms and conditions; that he should be free to join a union or not. The position, when stated by me before the Congressional Strike Investigation Committee in 1914, was misconstrued in some quarters as a statement that we were fighting organized labor.

"What my statement meant, and what the position of the company's officers meant was that we did not think those of our employes who did not care to join a union should be forced to do so, as would have been the case if we had signed the contract tendered by the United Mine Workers of America. This is the position which I always have maintained.

"Do you mean that you will never in the future grant recognition to the United Mine Workers?" Mr. Rockefeller was asked.

"I never have said that I will not recognize the union in the future" was the reply. "If the time should ever come when that course should seem to be the best for the common good of employers and employes, the door is not locked against its adoption."

"Unionism" continued Mr. Rockefeller, "benefits only one class of workmen—those who belong to the union. Our plan takes in all men, irrespective of whether they join a union or not. Unionism benefits one group, not all the working men. Our thought has been to devise something absolutely democratic—something that will take in all workmen whether they belong to the union or not."

Mr. Rockefeller describes his plan as "broader and more democratic than unionism."[5]

In his unquestionable sincerity, Rockefeller believed every word he uttered. He knew his intentions to be honorable. It escaped him that his argument was in part false (at the outset of the strike the company was actively discriminating against union members) in part specious (since the company showed no compunctions about violating the basic civil liberties of its miners, its interest in preserving their "liberty" not to join a union can hardly have been the foremost consideration), and in part self-serving (the benefits of the union could not be shared by all of the miners for no other reason than that the company refused to sign a contract to that effect). This was a rather different aspect of Rockefeller's humanity from the one he and his agents were working so assiduously to project. But, since no one came forward to challenge his statements, Rockefeller could content himself with the fairness and the generosity of his position at the very moment when his frailty was most evident.

The concerted effort to win a favorable public opinion was carried on in a variety of ways. Mackenzie King, in a long letter to Mrs. Rockefeller, likened the tour to a campaign for political office and confessed that as the campaign manager he was responsible for having concocted "all kinds of stunts" for Rockefeller to perform.[6] Going down into the mines in miner's clothes was one such stunt. He wanted her to know, however, that his sole purpose was to use every opportunity to reveal Rockefeller's true nature to the public and to the miners. Her husband, he reported, had caught the spirit of the thing and had come to assume increasing responsibility for the actions and adventures that created such human interest stories in the papers. The impromptu dance at Walsenberg was her husband's doing.

King did not report that they had the press corps eating out of their hands, but such was the case. A spirit of camaraderie developed that Rockefeller remembered fondly long afterward. The Associate Press correspondent in the group, Edward S. Cowdrick, wrote a highly favorable article about the representation plan for *Leslie's Weekly*, a popular national magazine. In titling the piece "The New Freedom for Labor," Cowdrick aped the slogan of Woodrow Wilson's presidency. His very last sentence is of interest here both because of the message it conveyed and because Cowdrick soon afterward was hired as a publicist by C.F. & I. He wrote, "If outside interference is eliminated, there will be peace and prosperity hereafter in the Colorado coal field."[7] He clearly understood that no union was wanted at C.F. & I.

At the same time that daily reports of the visit were appearing in the press, Ivy Lee was busy on another front. During the first week of the tour, the *Times* carried two stories that featured the good works of the Rockefeller Foundation. One of these celebrated the Foundation's role in the fight against hookworm; the other lauded efforts to aid Chinese medical schools. On two different days, the *Times* also carried items about Rockefeller Senior, one a brief reminiscence about his first job, the other relating his involvement in Standard Oil's decision to provide credits to the Allied powers. Coincidentally, Senior's brother William and nephew Percy each received publicity in connection with their separate business ventures.

During the second week of the tour, the *Times* carried a two-page spread in its Sunday magazine. In this, Rockefeller's western activities were grafted on to a flattering biographical sketch to produce the promise of an entirely happy ending for all concerned:

So, after all, John D. Rockefeller, Jr., is much as other men. Being so, the sooner his fellowmen are convinced of what he is and what he means to be, the sooner will be solved those enormous problems on which he so zealously labors. For them it may be that, as he has overcome the golden handicap, those who are to come will say that he had been of service to that world which now ponders on what he means.[8]

All of the staff's efforts notwithstanding, a small amount of unfavorable press commentary emerged. In addition to the items emanating from the union opposition that either accompanied or were incorporated into each day's report on Rockefeller's activities, some editors were less easily swayed in their opinions than was the *New York Times*. Senior was particularly hurt by the charge that most of the trouble in Colorado was the result of his indifference, a charge leveled at him by the editor of the *Pueblo Star-Journal*. He wrote to his son complaining of this slur, and Rockefeller dutifully paid a call on the editor to discuss the matter. He afterward wrote his father that the editor was a fair man who had intended no harm and took the opportunity of his writing to display his strongest suit—filial piety.

> I have wished so many times that you could have been here in Colorado in my place, for all the friendliness and hospitality and cordiality which has been extended to me really belongs to you. I am sure that the kindliness which has been exhibited on all sides would have warmed your heart. Constantly I have felt that I was sailing under false colors in receiving so many expressions of good will myself which are really intended for you.[9]

If it can be said that during the first week of his visit Rockefeller came and saw, during the second and third weeks he made his conquest complete. By the time he left Colorado, the Colorado Industrial Plan, as it came to be known, was approved, signed, and in effect. Most of the credit for this belongs, of course, to Mackenzie King.

King had arrived in Colorado several days in advance of his principal. With all the skill of an experienced political campaigner, he had set about making arrangements for the tour of the camps and planning the human interest stunts that won so much favorable publicity. He also went to work on C.F. & I. managers to ensure that his draft of the constitution-contract would be adopted during the visit.

President Welborn had previously met with the staff, and was able to give King some idea of their questions and reservations about the proposed arrangements. Equipped with this intelligence, King went before the managers and sold them on the plan. No doubt the largest part of their willingness to go along was the obvious determination of New York to impose a change. But instead of dictating the new policy to them, King encouraged them to participate in its design. The result was that the managers approved of the plan as if it were their own creation. How King accomplished this is of some interest since his success at C.F. & I. encouraged him to adopt the same approach in future introductions of employee representation plans.

Knowing that the officers felt themselves under great pressure from New York, King attempted to sweeten the pill they would be obliged to swallow. He began by assuring them that the draft constitution was not an instrument of revolutionary or arbitrary change. On the contrary, it was an effort to make explicit what in largest measure was already prevailing practice within C.F. & I. He related that, when he had first come out to Colorado, he had supposed that he would find much in the operations of C.F. & I. that needed changing. His first-hand examination had proved him wrong, most of what the company was doing in relation to its employees was correct and even admirable. His false impression and the false impression that had grown up in the public's mind as well, he told the managers, grew out of the absence of any clear evidence of company practices, such as the written constitution would now supply. The constitution could thus be seen as more in the nature of an avowal of policy than a change of policy, and everyone, especially the company itself, would benefit from making its position known to all.

The document before them, he continued, was truly a draft. It was subject to any modification that they could suggest and support with cogent argument. He hoped that they would help him, particularly by offering suggestions about how the document could be shortened. And he urged them to help themselves, saying that, since they were the ones who would have to live with the rules and procedures prescribed, they should indicate frankly any objections and make suggestions for changes that would be useful to them in their managerial capacities.

As they proceeded to work their way through the draft, clause by clause, a number of suggestions were made about which King had been forewarned by President Welborn. He accepted these with enthusiasm, acknowledging that the suggested change would strengthen the plan. In one instance at least, he was able to persuade the managers that a change they wanted was likely to backfire against them. By the end of a four-hour session, the group was entirely sympathetic to the constitution and to the program to which it bound them. They were relieved that nothing unpalatable had been forced down their throats. Perhaps more than anything else, they appreciated King's willingness to rely on their judgment in amending the document. King learned from his secretary and from Welborn, both of whom talked independently with the officers that evening, that they now felt the constitution

W. L. Mackenzie King and John D. Rockefeller, Jr., with a C. F. & I. employee, September 1915. By permission of the Rockefeller Archive Center.

and the employee representation plan were theirs, since they had had a hand in preparing them. The fight to win over the C.F. & I. management was won that easily.

In reviewing the meeting and its outcome in his diary, King pinpointed the elements that had combined to produce his success. He had no sense that he was developing a formula he would come to rely upon during the next three years. He did understand, however, that winning over the officers to the constitution and the plan came through involving them in the modification of the draft. This might have become little more than a manipulative technique for converting skeptics in future plan introductions had King not also understood that managers on the spot knew the details of the activities they directed better than any outsider. They were therefore in the best position to suggest how a representation plan could be adapted to their company's circumstances. In fact, the success of the procedural aspects of employee representation depended upon these adaptations. So it seemed that variations in the structure and practices of each firm required that its representation plan be tailored individually; the tailoring was best performed by the operating heads; and the job of tailoring was likely to build acceptance and support for the plan among those managers crucial to its success. The variations in subsequent representation plans would be of this sort, less critical to the nature of employee representation than to its initial acceptance and smooth functioning in different firms. It could not have been otherwise, since, as we shall see, many of the different plans were the handiwork of the same man.

King gave no thought to the need for similar consultation with the miners. Presumably, as the recipients of the gift of the constitution, they had nothing to say about its design. Or, more likely, he thoughtlessly supposed they would have nothing of value to contribute.

During the second week of the visit, this time in Rockefeller's presence, King again reviewed the constitution provision by provision with the managers. Satisfied with their understanding and support of the document, King then arranged for the elected representatives of the miners to come to Denver. A joint meeting of managers and miner representatives was held, and Rockefeller delivered one of the two prepared speeches he gave in Colorado. Most of his words were King's.

He told the assemblage that no one associated with C.F. & I. could afford another strike. Something had to be done to ensure the harmony and peace that they all desired. In his judgment, the constitution before them embodied the best possible means to this end. He urged them to adopt it. At some length he developed the view that the employees, the officers, the directors, and the stockholders were partners rather than rivals. Pointing to a small table that stood nearby, he likened the four parties in industry to the four legs and spun off from this homilies about mutual support, being "on the level," and the "square deal."[10] It probably seemed a clever simile to the audience, none of whom was likely to be as familiar as he was with an address by Andrew Carnegie in which a three-legged stool was employed to make similar points. He reviewed the constitution article by article, indicating how the existing system of employee representation would be retained and embellished.

At the conclusion of his speech, a vote was taken. The new constitution was approved unanimously. The representatives were urged to go back to their respective camps and inform their comrades of the substance of the new agreement. In each of the camps, the miners would have an opportunity to vote the following week.

Denied a union of their own, the miners had every reason to accept the proposal. It gave them as much, and in some respects more, than they had ever asked for and it was theirs for the taking. Nothing was expected of them, they were merely expected to vote occasionally in return for the benefits Rockefeller was prepared to shower on them. Each mining camp would elect two representatives annually. These "reps" would do most of the work. They would represent the miners at the quarterly meetings of their respective districts and serve on the four standing committees within each district: the Joint Committee on Industrial Cooperation and Conciliation; the Joint Committee on Safety and Accidents; the Joint Committee on Sanitation, Health and Housing; and the Joint Committee on Recreation and Education. They would also attend the annual companywide meeting. At these meetings, the reps were empowered to introduce topics for consideration, to bring up complaints, to consider changes recommended by company officials, and to report the results of their deliberations to the president for his consideration. In an effort to guard the integrity of reps, the constitution provided that any representative who believed he was being discriminated against because of his position was free to seek redress at various levels in the company's chain of command and to carry an unresolved complaint outside of the company to the State Industrial Commission.

The constitution also provided what amounted to a bill of rights whereby the company committed itself to observe federal and state mining and labor laws; post its wage scale and work rules; refrain from discriminating on the basis of union membership or nonmembership; grant warning or suspension prior to dismissal from the company; permit employees to hold meetings on company property during their free time; permit employees to shop wherever they pleased; permit the miners to employ a check-weighman; permit employees to press grievances themselves or through their elected representative through all levels of the company to the president and beyond to an arbitrator, if both parties agree, or to the State Industrial Commission. The rights that the company explicitly retained for itself were the rights to hire, to fire, to manage company property, and to supervise work.

At the very moment the company asked the miners to approve these rights, it was engaged in industrial espionage. Someone in the C.F. & I. hierarchy had planted a spy in the Trinidad local union of the United Mine Workers to pass on information about the union's plans. King knew of this, since he received information from the spy's reports at the time. The informer reported that at a joint meeting of several locals, union members were exhorted to get elected as employee representatives so that eventually "Rockefeller's Welfare Plan will be dominated by the union."[11] The informer also passed along the name of a new applicant for admission to the union. Neither King nor Rockefeller acted to bring a halt to this dirty business since subsequent spy reports also were found scattered among King's papers.

Nor does the fact that Samuel Gompers also had an agent on the ground in any way serve to balance the account. Gompers had recently written in confidence to the editor of the *United Mine Workers Journal* that he had few illusions about Rockefeller. Apart from his philanthropic work, much of what Rockefeller did, Gompers said, was calculated to "serve his own interests."[12] Partly for this reason but largely out of loyalty to John R. Lawson, Gompers had authorized a Denver labor leader to stage a demonstration against Lawson's continued imprisonment during Rockefeller's visit. Had such a demonstration occurred, it would have been a perfectly legitimate expression of opinion, violative of the rights of no one. However, Gompers' agent found it impossible to muster the necessary forces and the demonstration never took place. Gompers nonetheless felt obliged to say something when Rockefeller was quoted in the press as asserting that his employee representation plan was broader than a union. He told reporters,

> So Mr. Rockefeller has formed a union—a union of his employes of his Colorado Fuel and Iron Company—and perhaps imagines that he has solved the problem of just relations between himself and his employes. But with all his wealth and all his brains and the brains that he could buy and suborn, he has missed the mark. Imagine an organization of miners formed by the richest man in the world, who employs its members!
>
> What influence can such a pseudo union have to insist upon the remedying of a grievous wrong or the attainment of a real right? . . .
>
> . . . The miners employed by the Colorado Fuel and Iron Company, of which Mr. Rockefeller is the head, have been whipped by means of atrocious brutality and hunger into submission, back to the mines. And these miners have been formed into a union by Mr. Rockefeller's benevolent altruism. But he has organized them, and for that at any rate labor is truly grateful, for when men come together to discuss, even in the most cursory way, their rights and their interests and their welfare, there is afforded a splendid field for development and opportunity.[13]

It is difficult to believe that this statement was much more than a gesture aimed at mollifying Gompers' Colorado allies. Rockefeller, after all, was following a course recommended to him by national U.M.W. officers and approved by John Mitchell, all of whom were close to Gompers.

C.F. & I. miners voted by the wide margin of 2253 to 483 to accept the constitution. In all of the camps save one, the one most heavily populated by union members, a majority of the voting miners elected to go along with Rockefeller. The Colorado Industrial Plan was stipulated to remain in effect until January 1, 1918, a period of about twenty-seven months. As it happened, the plan was renewed periodically with some adjustments of the terms and conditions of employment and remained in effect until supplanted by a union contract in 1933.

The nettlesome problems of Lawson's conviction and the outstanding indictments also prompted King to act. He arranged a private interview with defense attorney Horace Hawkins. By

Hawkins' account of the meeting, he both blamed Rockefeller, saying "You should not have stayed away so long" and praised him, saying "You made a good impression down there [in Las Animas County]."[14] When Rockefeller asked what he might do to help put an end to the legal wrangles, Hawkins recommended that he call on the governor to personally request dismissal of the indictments. This Rockefeller proceeded to do. Even though unsuccessful, this effort by Rockefeller was accepted as conclusive evidence of his goodwill. Soon afterward, John Lawson was asked by a reporter about the fight for union recognition. He replied, "The Rockefeller Plan is recognition in part in that it recognizes many of our demands. . . . I know they are going to recognize the union sometime and this plan will prepare the way."[15]

At the end of his third week in Colorado, Rockefeller appeared before the Denver Chamber of Commerce to give what amounted to his farewell address. He had accomplished all that he had hoped to during his visit. The publicity generated by the trip had been more extensive and more sympathetic than anticipated. He had also learned how very much he enjoyed the limelight of his role as a leader of men. In this triumphant mood, he came before the Denver business community. As he had promised, he employed the occasion to sing his father's praises. With becoming modesty, he concluded this section of his address:

> And if, in their kindness of heart, the people of Colorado have found in me anything that may have seemed admirable, that, and whatever else I am or may be, I owe to my sainted mother and my honored father, whose training and example I regard as a priceless heritage. And so again I say I wish that my father were here that he might meet you men personally and . . . that you, on the other hand, coming to know him, might realize the injustice and the cruelty of the things that have been said and written about him during these many years.[16]

Rockefeller then turned to the views he held toward labor organizations and collective bargaining. As he had on several previous occasions, he set forth his position by reading excerpts from his prepared statements before the Commission on Industrial Relations. Even flush with victory he depended on used words, like an old man who saved string to use over and over again. This was not a form of economy in him but a want of confidence. He found it easier to recycle statements than to trust in his ability to articulate the principles to which King's words committed him. It is possible, of course, that he believed that the official record would carry more weight than any extemporaneous avowal of his position. Yet, he and his associates so prized the virtue of sincerity in him that they would have believed his every utterance of equal probity. On the other hand, some students of religion might find his attachment to the written word of a piece with his training as a fundamentalist Baptist.

In any event, it was bold of him to say favorable things about unions and collective bargaining before *this* audience. He rather enjoyed finding himself in the role of the avant garde leader contending with the forces of reaction. Once he had delivered his plea for labor–management understanding and cooperation, he concluded by offering the plan newly adopted at C.F. & I. as a model worthy of emulation, saying, "And if in any smallest way my coming to Colorado may prove to have been of *service* to you in approaching the solution of this world problem of industrial relations, I shall feel a sense of satisfaction and gratitude beyond expression."[17]

Service was the quintessential word in Rockefeller's lexicon and in King's as well. King's was the service of the Social Gospel, the liberal Protestant teaching that had for its aim the reformation of the lot of humanity, whereas Rockefeller's ideal of service sprang from the Gospel of Wealth. For both men, the benign goal of service held few connotations of humility and meekness. When Rockefeller or King said that they wished to be of service, they meant that they wished to lead. Subsequently, neither man would rest content to solve the labor problems at C.F. & I. Their achievement would have seemed too small in proportion to the influence they wished to wield. They might also have left themselves open to the charge that their solution was self-serving. Instead, King's perception of industrial relations problems on a global scale both magnified the invention of employee representation into a selfless act of service to all humanity and conformed to their desires for achievement and recognition.

Rockefeller was transformed by his experience in Colorado. Not overnight, but henceforth, he would develop and feel himself developing from weakness into strength and from passivity into authority. He would come more and more to speak for himself rather than serve as spokesman for his father, and to place increasing confidence in his own judgment. The tangible achievements of the Colorado visit convinced him not only of the correctness of the representation idea as a new strategy for industrial peace but of himself as an appropriate standard bearer for industrial reform. He won his spurs in Colorado, so to speak, and in winning them gained the sense that he had at last earned the entitlement of his father's fortune.

That Mackenzie King was largely responsible for stimulating this transformation does not mean that Rockefeller lacked designs of his own. Until King entered his life, he had been living defensively, centering his efforts on shielding himself and the family from the adverse consequences of their real and imagined wealth and power. He had developed no very clear ideas about what he might do to place himself and his father on a less volatile, less contentious footing with the world. Philanthropic efforts by themselves were obviously not adequate to the task. He toyed with the illusion that perhaps publicity was. King sparked his transfiguration by bolstering his sense of self-worth and providing him with a pathway to leadership that was both consistent with his desire to be a benefactor of humanity and independent of his father's domination. Rockefeller's coming of age as a man of the world was thus intimately bound up with the innovation of employee representation and with the role of the crusading leader that the introduction of that innovation afforded him.

King, for his part, was fully conscious of his services as the midwife of Rockefeller's rebirth. Given his own ambitions and outlook on the world, he could not help but construe that rebirth in messianic terms. His ecstatic letter to Mrs. Rockefeller describing their triumphal tour was at once all that it would please a loving wife to learn of her husband and an epiphany:

> To me personally, the revelation of Mr. Rockefeller's true character to the American public at large is the most gratifying of all the features of the trip . . .
>
> I cannot but feel that this visit is epoch-making in his own life, as it will also prove epoch-making in the industrial history of this continent. From now on he will be able to devote his life to advancing the vast projects already launched which relate themselves so clearly to human well-being, without being thwarted at every step by the voice of detractors . . .
>
> What it must mean to the world that it has in the person of its foremost captain of industry a man prepared to base his action on fair play and justice and to champion these ideals in all the relations of industry, it is impossible even to surmise . . .

Whereas Mr. Rockefeller met a State, the opinion of which was much divided towards him, he leaves it after a sojourn of barely three weeks, with but one opinion, and that one of undivided praise and affection. Enmity has been changed into good-will; bitterness into trust; and resentful recollections into cherished memories . . .

I hope you will feel that in sparing him from your side, from his home and family for the time you have, your loss has been very much the gain of the many hundreds of those who have been privileged to see and meet him out here. His kindly thoughts and deeds everywhere he has gone have added inspiration and happiness to many unknown lives and humble homes. This capacity to give to others of the best that is in oneself is perhaps the greatest of life's gifts. It is perhaps the best of what has been accomplished here that men generally have come to know that, apart from all else, that gift is his in full and abundant measure . . .[18]

Few heralds have ever carried home to an anxious wife the praise of a conquering hero so artfully crafted or complete.

Several weeks after his return from Colorado, Senior gave his son five million dollars worth of C.F. & I.-related bonds.

Notes

1. *New York Times Magazine* (October 3, 1915), p. 7.
2. Beshoar (1942), p. 327.
3. *New York Times* (September 22, 1915), p. 5.
4. *New York Times* (September 23, 1915), p. 1; and *Colorado Springs Gazette* (September 23, 1915), p. 1.
5. *New York Times* (October 1, 1915), p. 13.
6. W.L.M.K. to Mrs. J.D.R., Jr., 10/6/15. W.L.M.K. Papers, Series J1, vol. 29, pp. 26032-26037.
7. Cowdrick (1915), p. 451.
8. *New York Times Magazine* (October 3, 1915), p. 7.
9. J.D.R., Jr. to J.D.R., 10/6/15. J.D.R., Jr. Papers, C.F. & I. File.
10. Rockefeller (1923), p. 92.
11. Unsigned, unaddressed letter dated 10/5/15. W.L.M.K. Papers, Series J4, Box 191.
12. S. Gompers to Edgar Wallace, 9/14/15. A.F. of L. Papers, Box 21.
13. *New York Times* (October 5, 1915), p. 6. See also Carl Beck to S. Gompers, 10/6/15. A.F. of L. Papers, Box 21.
14. Beshoar (1942), p. 332.

15. Ibid., p. 336.
16. Rockefeller (1923), pp. 111–12.
17. Ibid., p. 120. Emphasis added.
18. King to Mrs. J.D.R., Jr., 10/6/15. W.L.M.K. Papers, Series J1, vol. 29, pp. 26032-26037.

10. Pulpits and Profits

By the autumn of 1915, the war in Europe shaped the main trends in the American economy. The initial wave of uncertainty and pessimism triggered by the outbreak of fighting slowly gave way to a rising tide of business activity. Almost surreptitiously, an economic boom began to emerge. Coupled with an increased demand for goods and services, the war restricted the flood of trans-Atlantic migrants—from one and a quarter million immigrants in 1914 to about a third of a million in 1915. As labor markets became increasingly and uncustomarily tight, industrial workers tendered demands for improved terms and conditions. With increasing frequency, they backed up their demands by walking out on strike. The eight-hour day reemerged as the paramount issue and, as had always been the case in the past, served as a rallying point for unorganized workers as well as unionists. The Schenectady plant of General Electric, the East Pittsburgh plant of Westinghouse Electric, Pratt & Whitney's New Haven plant, and Republic Steel's Youngstown mills were among those struck by unorganized mass-production workers, who surprised managers by their unity and determination.

Industrial employers chafed at the uncommon disadvantage at which they found themselves. If they conceded the workers' demands, what was to preclude still further demands? If they fought off the demands, they ran the risk of pushing their workers into the waiting arms of the unions. Some employer spokesmen argued that this was a false dilemma. They believed that the demand for an eight-hour work day was "in reality a demand for higher wages."[1] In evidence, they cited the experience of firms that had conceded the basic eight-hour day with no reduction in pay. It was found that many of their workers were now eager to work overtime because, under the basic eight-hour day, overtime was paid at time and a half. Hence, it was argued, the workers really wanted more income, not shorter hours. They could be lured away from striking and from the wiles of labor agitators with fatter pay envelopes.

But such a response, as much as any other, obliged employers and managers to share the profits of the economic boom without in any way reducing their future vulnerability. With little agreement among themselves on how to meet the situation, employers improvised. Some quickly acceded to worker demands; others found a basis for settlement only after strikes; still others responded with force and violence. Most corporate leaders had never experienced such a troubled prosperity. Even U.S. Steel's smug Elbert Gary found himself under a strike-related criminal indictment.

In contrast, people who came in contact with John D. Rockefeller, Jr., at the time, encountered a man exuding confidence. He radiated a new vitality in his work and in personal relationships. Much of this new feeling undoubtedly came from the triumph he had scored in Colorado. Some part of it, too, must have come from Mrs. Rockefeller's complete recovery following the delivery of their sixth child, David. (I defer to others the task of attempting to relate the perceived change in Rockefeller to deeper psychological forces; e.g., that his fight for independence from Senior came only after the death of his mother.)

Although he picked up the activities his western trip had obliged him to lay aside, C.F. & I. continued to occupy center stage for Rockefeller. Working closely with Ivy Lee, he supervised each step in the preparation of *The Colorado Industrial Plan,* a booklet containing the texts of the constitution of the representation plan and the contract between C.F. & I. and its miners. Half a million copies were printed and distributed to individuals, organizations, and institutions. Like a first-time author, Rockefeller sent copies to a wide circle of personal and family friends. In his enthusiasm, he pressed a copy on everyone he encountered, from surprised dowagers to new acquaintances. Meeting Baron Yei-ichi Shibusawa, "Japan's leading merchant and financier"[2] during the latter's visit to New York, in December 1915, he promised to send him a copy of the plan and did so soon afterward. It may just be the case that in this way the Colorado Plan came to serve as the model on which Japanese industrial relations were restructured following the war.

Rockefeller also found himself in increasing demand as a

spokesman for the plan and on the subject of industrial relations generally. The *Atlantic Monthly* editor asked him for an article, and he received speaking invitations from such diverse quarters as the YMCA, Chatauqua, and Cornell University. Whenever he mentioned these invitations, King urged that he accept them. King drummed home the message that he could do more to disarm his detractors through public appearances than by any other means. He felt certain that Rockefeller's desire to serve noble ends would shine through to his audiences.

Actually, it took very little prodding to bring Rockefeller before the public. The truth of the matter was that both he and King looked upon these opportunities as eagerly as missionaries might regard so many openings of heathen territory. Convinced that the employee representation idea was an invention of incalculable social value, they hungered to spread word of it. Their ministry, they believed, could only hasten the reign of industrial harmony and social peace. In far off Boston at the time, Robert G. Valentine, a leading industrial relations consultant, might tell a scientific management group that the Colorado plan was "a sociological joke."[3] Such criticism went unheeded in New York. No one could have convinced Rockefeller or King that, at best, they were vicars of noblesse oblige.

Eager for converts though they were, neither man was troubled when few employers came forward to embrace their scheme. Their experiences in ironing out kinks in the operation of the plan at C.F. & I., and in adapting it for use in the company's steel mills, kept alive their own sense of the representation scheme as an experiment, as something tentative rather than complete. They remained certain that they had discovered the basic principle underlying harmonious industrial relations, namely the restoration of personal relations through a representative system. They were also sure that the model they had built on this principle at C.F. & I. would work. They could not demonstrate its effectiveness, however, without the passage of time and the accumulation of experience. Intuitively, they knew they were right. They revealed as much in their correspondence, in the *Atlantic Monthly* article, and in the memorandum that King submitted to the Low Commission. They just could not prove it.

In "Labor and Capital—Partners," Rockefeller did more than explain the Colorado plan for the benefit of *Atlantic Monthly* readers. He also provided an interpretation of modern industrial capitalism that would probably find wide acceptance even today. (King almost certainly played a major role in the preparation of the article, although concrete evidence of this has not been found.) Had Labor in the past been deprived of the benefits of Capital, the argument began, Labor would forever have remained trapped in a subsistence economy. Capital, for its part, was in even greater need of Labor, for without it, Capital was utterly useless. The combination of the two was therefore in their mutual interest. The great question of the day centered on the proper division of the benefits of this partnership. Was capitalist society to be wracked and ultimately destroyed by conflict between Capital and Labor over economic inequality? Or was it possible for the benefits of industrial progress to be shared amicably?

Although Marxian socialism was not explicitly mentioned in the article, it was clearly the target of the argument. The theory of class conflict, the article asserted, was a counsel of despair. It was premised on the mistaken assumption that the wealth of the world was fixed. If this were true, and Labor were to desire a larger share, Capital would have to suffer a reduced share. It would resist, and conflict would inevitably ensue. But the outstanding attribute of modern capitalism was its capacity to add to the wealth of the world. If total income rose, the advancement of Labor did not have to come at the expense of Capital. Instead both parties could harvest the fruits of rising income that resulted from the productivity gains their cooperation made possible.

The partnership of Labor and Capital was thus not an empty figure of speech, the article continued, but an apt description of the proper and most desirable relations between them. The problem of effecting and sustaining this partnership rightly was to be regarded as the most crucial problem facing modern society. With more than a touch of self praise, he concluded that

> the greatest social service is rendered by that man who so cooperates in the organization of industry as to afford to the largest number of men the greatest opportunity for self-development, and the enjoyment by every man of those benefits which his own work adds to the wealth of civilization.[4]

But did King mean to describe Rockefeller Junior or Senior with these words?—the same words Rockefeller had used in his appearance before the Commission on Industrial Relations a year earlier. Presumably, the son was meant, for the father was alluded to and justified in the following passage:

The world puts its richest prize at the feet of great organizing ability, enterprise, and foresight, because such qualities are rare and yet indispensable to the development of the vast natural resources which otherwise would lie useless.[5]

After asserting that the organization of Labor was as necessary to the conduct of modern industry as the organization of Capital and allowing that labor unions had accomplished some good in calling attention to the shortcomings of some employers, the article concluded that the problems between Labor and Capital were largely the product of mutual misunderstanding. The heart of the problem was that business had grown so large that the personal relationships that had once prevailed had been permitted to atrophy. So rapid and so hectic had the growth of industry been that its human aspects had been sorely neglected. With few opportunities for meeting, exchanging views, and coming to know one another, employers and employees found themselves divided by a widening gulf of misunderstanding and mistrust.

The article went on to assert that the Colorado Industrial Plan was aimed at precisely this problem. Its object was to reintroduce personal relationships into industry through a system of representation that was consistent with the much enlarged size of firm. At C.F. & I., the managers would deal with worker representatives and, from them, come to learn the interests and concerns of their employees. The worker representatives, in turn, would come to know the interests and concerns of the managers. They would transmit this understanding to the miners they represented. In this way, the article concluded, both sides would develop an awareness of one another and have a means for airing differences that should preclude misunderstanding and conflict.

So confident were King and Rockefeller of the likelihood of the plan's success, that they quickly pushed Welborn for its adoption in C.F. & I.'s Minnepaqua Steel Works and its limestone quarries. King returned to Colorado to explain the plan to the works' managers. Once again, his adoption of many of their suggestions smoothed the way for their acceptance of the plan.

The Low Commission also was very favorably impressed by the plan. Prior to visiting Colorado, Seth Low wrote to fellow commissioner Patrick Gilday, asking for his opinion of the scheme. Gilday's answer came in the form of a one-line letter that may, by prearrangement, have meant more than meets the eye. The union representative responded, "I am very well pleased with the plan of the Colorado Fuel and Iron Company."[6] Since Gilday almost certainly was in contact with the national leaders of the U.M.W., his reply also signaled their approval. In every respect, the plan conformed to the suggestions White and Green had made.

Low, Gilday, and Charles W. Mills, the third commissioner, visited Colorado in December 1915. On their return, Low began drafting the report the commission would submit to President Wilson several months later. During this period, he met with King and asked him to write up his views on the plan. Toward the end of February, King responded with a ten-page memorandum that was as remarkable in its premises as it was in its conclusions. As Low had requested, he addressed the issues of the plan's relation to trade unionism and its bearing on the development of self-government in industry. Once again, the document reveals King's ability to spin the dross of self-interest into the noblest line of argument.

Workers organize trade unions, King wrote, to help secure, maintain, and advance their terms and conditions of employment. In the best of all possible worlds, such improvements would be forthcoming to workers as a matter of right, and they would not be obliged to struggle and make sacrifices to gain their due. In such a world, their rights would be protected and guaranteed by the State. The Colorado Industrial Plan, he asserted, conformed precisely to these principles. The plan stated that the workers were entirely free to join or not to join trade unions as they saw fit. Their industrial rights under the plan were vested in them without regard to their union status. Moreover, they were entitled under the plan to enlist the power of the state in securing their rights, for it was provided that both grievances that could not be settled within C.F. & I. and bargaining issues that resulted in a stalemate could be brought to the Colorado Industrial Commission for settlement.

How should the unions look upon the plan, he asked? King's answer indicates how far his judgment bowed in the service of expediency. If workers found it necessary to rely solely on trade unions to maintain and advance their rights and standards, the result would be ceaseless social conflict. As at present, militant unions would array themselves against arrogant corporations in a never ending struggle over rights and fairness. The resort to force in the economic sphere would result in industrial war just as surely as the resort to force in the relations between states resulted in international war. The fruits of progress would be endangered and even the trees that bore the fruit, the institutions of society, would stand in jeopardy.

If however, workers could look to the State to secure their rights, internecine conflict could be avoided. Under the Colorado plan, production could continue uninterruptedly while the State resolved differences. A gradual redistribution of income from owners to workers would "take place in accord with popular sentiment and what may be economiccaly (sic) possible."[7]

King concluded that trade unions would oppose the plan only if they mistakenly supposed themselves the sole agency through which workers' rights and employment standards were to be protected and enhanced. Otherwise, they would see in the plan a new ally in the struggle to secure rights and fairness for all working people. He did not say why the unions should welcome an alliance that had the intention of rendering them superfluous.

With undisguised enthusiasm, King went on to explain for Low's benefit the plan's bearing on the development of self-government in industry. He asserted that conscious parallelism between industrial rights and civil or political rights had guided the development of the plan from the start. He and Rockefeller, he wrote (as if the latter had such thoughts), had presumed that the evolution of industrial rights would take a course similar to the evolution of political rights, but with an exception. With the benefit of historical hindsight, much of the conflict occasioned by the expansion of political rights would be circumvented through voluntary concession in the case of industrial rights. The plan itself was such a voluntary concession.

King went on to elaborate four ways in which the plan coincided with the evolution of political rights and simultaneously fostered self-government in industry. Pointing to the British, French, and American constitutions, he suggested that in granting the rights of employees to hold meetings, to purchase supplies where they chose, to employ checkweighmen, to appeal to the company president, to receive a warning or suspension before discharge, and to be free to join or not join unions, comparable rights had been conferred. A second way in which the plan paralleled political history was embodied in the principle of representation. A third similarity was the use of the secret ballot. Finally, the plan paralleled the broad trend away from rule by an all-powerful executive toward participatory democracy. King prophesied that the involvement of workers in the company's affairs would probably expand in the future, until it encompassed all phases of the firm's existence—even to the point of electing representatives to the board of directors.

King sent a copy of the memorandum along to Rockefeller for his information. He expressed the hope that some of his ideas would find their way into the Low Commission's final report. However, Low had already written his report when the memorandum reached him. In any event, some of the views King had conveyed to Low in an earlier conversation found their way into the report. In particular, Low adopted the parallel between the evo-evolution of political democracy and the representation scheme as a step in the evolution of industrial democracy. This placed the plan in a highly favorable light. Consequently, the Commission report proved entirely satisfactory to both King and Rockefeller.

Although nowhere mentioned in the report by name, King felt doubly vindicated. His representation plan was hailed as an important "new departure," adopted "in entire good faith," and conducted "with a single-hearted desire to make it successful."[8] The commission also applauded the passage of Colorado's new labor law modelled after the Canadian Disputes Investigation Act, also of King's invention. The Colorado law, written by John R. Commons, created an industrial commission with the power to delay strikes for thirty days pending investigation. A number of strikes that normally would have occurred already had been averted through the new agency. The Low Commission report concluded that in the face of initiatives taken by C.F. & I. and the state legislature, no further action on the part of the federal government was required.

An important number of positions coalesced in the Low Commission report. Rockefeller, King, Seth Low, the National Civic Federation, John R. Commons (whose authorship of the Colorado law took place under the auspices of the National Civic Federation), Labor Secretary William B. Wilson, and President Wilson were all parties to the report in one way or another. When Secretary Wilson told one of the commissioners that he thought the commission deserved credit for pushing Rockefeller to develop the representation plan ("which he apparently thinks very highly of"[9]), he was also accepting credit for himself and the President. The United Mine Workers Union was also a consenting party. Although the report noted that local union officials in Colorado were skeptical of both the plan and the company's commitment to the rights it had acknowledged, the commission simply discounted these sentiments. Commissioner Gilday, acting in concert with the national officers of the union, apparently had no difficulty in treating the views of his western comrades in this fashion.

The vindication conferred by the Low Commission report gave King and Rockefeller immense satisfaction. Rockefeller's first impulse was to publish copies at his own expense and distribute them far and wide. King counseled against this, however, and his opinion prevailed. As it happened, ample opportunities for publicity arose independently from a number of quarters.

During the spring of 1916, Clarence Hicks notified the New York office that he had delivered an address on the Colorado plan before a YMCA convention in Illinois. A few weeks later, Rockefeller himself addressed a national YMCA conclave. Flattering requests for industrial relations advice were received from numbers of business men. The legal advisor to a number of Cleveland, Ohio, employers' associations wrote that he contemplated recommending that his principals adopt something along the lines of the Colorado plan. The directors of several companies wrote in the hope of retaining King's services as a labor advisor. From Japan, word was received that Jiro Abratani of Tokyo had taken the liberty of describing the plan in a magazine article written for the benefit of Japanese businessmen.

But at almost the very moment that the Low Commission report came out with its characterization of the Colorado situation in settled and optimistic terms, a problem arose that threatened to undo everything. The problem began when an organizer for the United Mine Workers called upon Rockefeller to request permission to enter the C.F. & I. coal camps. Rockefeller advised that the camps were open, public places. He then took the precaution of alerting President Welborn to the organizer's impending visit.

In responding to Rockefeller's news, Welborn enclosed several letters he had received from his staff. E. H. Weitzel, the head of the company's fuel division, anxiously counseled against permitting any union organizers into the camps. He argued that the union had adequate opportunities to talk to the miners when they went into town. He believed it would have a devastating effect on the miners' morale and all that the company had worked for in the representation plan, if organizers were to enter the camps with the company's blessing. Acknowledging the power the company implicitly held over its employees, he wrote:

> We feel that Mr. R. does not realize how much our employees shape their course to comply with the Co's policy . . . we would be slapping [our loyal men] in the face, by openly allowing organizers among them, and virtually saying we wanted them to join the union . . .[10]

Rockefeller wrote to King for his opinion and duly informed Welborn that he had done so. King responded by asserting that the camps were open places and, therefore, had to be accessible to all. Rockefeller urged Welborn to inform the miners of this policy through letters and posted notices and to do the same regarding the company's noninterference with their right to join or not join a labor organization. His response prompted Weitzel to write directly urging that he reconsider. Weitzel contended that the union leaders they had to deal with were corrupt, self-serving preachers of class hatred. They had to be excluded, just as for years he had screened entry into the camps to shield the foreign miners, whom he likened to children, from being gulled by salesmen, sharpsters, and the like. Turning union organizers loose in the camps would be like sending the fox to guard the hen house.

When Rockefeller sent Weitzel's letter along to King for his consideration, King responded by drawing a parallel with newly arriving immigrants. Every year, he pointed out, thousands upon thousands of immigrants landed in New York City where they were preyed upon by all sorts of tricksters and con artists. Yet, in spite of these perils the immigrants muddled through, some of them poorer perhaps but also wiser about the snares and temptations that awaited them. So too must the miners learn what is best for them, even at the cost of some mistakes. Company officers also had some learning to do, King pointed out, if they were to live up to the terms of the representation plan.

With King's counsel in hand, Rockefeller proceeded to write an extraordinary eight-page letter in which he carefully, almost tenderly, recited for Weitzel's benefit, the argument that the camps had to be open; that union organizers could not therefore be denied access; that the paternal interest Weitzel had shown for the miners would have to give way to their learning to stand on their own feet; and that the representation plan was the company's best hope for amicable relations with its employees. He told Weitzel that he was fully cognizant of the risk involved and from which Weitzel wanted to shield him; nonetheless, the policies outlined were the only ones that could be followed, for

It seems to me that every man should have the right to decide for himself whether the Company is his best friend and champion or whether some outside organization is. If the Company cannot convince the men that it is their best friend, that it will cooperate more zealously with them than any outside organization in safeguarding their interests and well-being and securing to them the fullest protection and justice, then the men must and should ally themselves with any organization which they believe gives better assurance of such results.[11]

In spite of Rockefeller's valiant effort at clarification, the problem of two different understandings did not go away. Within the month, a new controversy swirled around Weitzel's stated intention to follow after union organizers to correct any misrepresentations they might make to the miners. It was also learned that Weitzel had been discriminating against unionists when hiring new men. Rockefeller blandly assured King that Weitzel had not known that his action was contrary to the intent of the representation plan and characterized him as a well-meaning, effective manager who could successfully be weaned from his old ways. His patience with the fuel manager's shortcomings bordered on the extraordinary.

King chose not to respond on the matter of discriminatory hiring, though if he recalled the meetings with Clarence Hicks the previous summer, he might have remembered that this very issue had arisen as a sticking point and had been resolved contrary to Hick's liking. He told Rockefeller that Weitzel's plan to form a one-man truth squad reflected both a misunderstanding of what they hoped to achieve through the representation plan and poor employee relations. Company officials should be talking with the men regularly and routinely. Surely, if they were doing so, they would find ample opportunity to hear of and correct any false arguments that were afloat. He concluded by saying that a large company like C.F. & I. had to chose between two possible models. Either it could organize "on the Prussian model of control of everything from above" with an elaborate spy network to gather information, or "as the American commonwealth itself is organized, on a representation of all classes."[12] Although King understood that the line superintendents, who were responsible for introducing the new way of doing things, were themselves a major source of difficulties and the primary obstacle to change, he was not prepared to grapple with this dilemma. Nor was he prepared to forego whatever benefits he might derive from espionage—in this instance, political espionage—as the surviving reports of Agent 426 from Washington, D.C., seem to indicate.

Under the cover of preparing a biographical compendium of some sort, Agent 426 appears to have been collecting information about the activities and personnel of the Committee on Industrial Relations. Since the agent talked with public officials and reported on their attitudes toward the committee, we have here an instance of private parties spying on government. It is unclear from the record who had retained the services of Agent 426 or whether he was affiliated with a detective agency.

The Committee on Industrial Relations had been organized in November 1915, following the termination of the U.S. Commission on Industrial Relations. Frank Walsh (now the publisher of the *Kansas City Post*), the labor members of the commission, and a group of their allies were the prime movers. Their stated objects were to encourage the widest dissemination of the commission's minority report and to "further the work . . . covered in [the] report and [the] recommendations of the Commission."[13]

If the reports filed by Agent 426 are what they appear to be, they indicate that King and Rockefeller continued to attribute influence to Frank Walsh out of all proportion to that which he possessed. During the summer of 1916, on the occasion of a Colorado Supreme Court ruling that overturned as rigged the 1914 election of the Sheriff of Huerfano County, Walsh wrote a pointlessly hostile letter to Rockefeller. It was more a *cri de coeur* than a display of power. Later, in the spring of 1917, Walsh would be party to an unsuccessful effort to have the New York State legislature "revoke the charter of the Rockefeller Foundation."[14] Insofar as Rockefeller was concerned, Walsh was a paper tiger. The espionage was therefore not only outrageous but stupid as well.

Throughout this period, King actively continued to tutor and advise Rockefeller. He rejected all bids for his services as a labor advisor because he believed that he could accomplish more by focusing attention on his study of industrial relations and advising Rockefeller than in any dilution of his energies. He wrote frequently to give his opinions and viewpoint and to send along information about all sorts of labor matters. An enviably efficient postal service eased and encouraged these written exchanges.

Rockefeller often limited each of his letters to King to a single subject. In consequence, he sometimes wrote as many as three letters in a single day when responding to one of King's more ranging letters. Letters that touched on issues of some sensitivity continued to incorporate the injunction to destroy after reading, and the vow that no carbon had been retained. Sometimes this was done, on King's part at any rate, for among his papers are to be found individual sentences and fragments cut out from the body of discarded Rockefeller letters—snippets floating in a sea of words, their once-special significance obscure. Apparently the mentality outlives the siege. More than enough of the correspondence survives, however, to provide a clear view of the kinds of questions Rockefeller asked and of the advice King proffered.

As their exchanges about entry into the camps make clear, both men committed themselves to the most liberal and honest interpretation of C.F. & I.'s new policies. In doing so, they opened themselves up to the possibility that the miners would join the union and abandon the representation scheme. King also recognized that if they could not bring the C.F. & I. managers into line behind their interpretation of the plan, the managers might inadvertently push the miners into the arms of the union. There was also resistance from Senior, a last stand as it happened, in which the father sold short against the son (i.e., sold C.F. & I. stock that he had borrowed from his broker in anticipation of repaying the stock at a future date when he expected its price to be lower). If this rare show of disagreement proceeded from the risks Rockefeller and King were taking at C.F. & I., Senior failed to see that they truly had little choice in the matter. They were not wanton risk takers, at any rate, but careful to a fault as the following examples suggest.

Do not, King advised on one occasion, permit C.F. & I. notices to employees to use the phrase *open shop*, for that will be attacked as antiunion.[15] On another occasion Rockefeller wrote that he believed it unwise for the company to deduct the mens' "Y" dues from their pay because of the precedent this might establish for the check-off of union dues. On still another occasion, Rockefeller informed King that he had decided to change the title of an address he was about to give from "Brotherhood in Industry" to "The Personal Relation in Industry." He was fearful that the first title might be misconstrued as an endorsement of the railroad brotherhoods. King concurred fully.

A particularly revealing exchange took place over what improvements Rockefeller might personally underwrite in the C.F. & I. mining camps. Churches, bandstands, assembly halls, club houses, or pavilions—he confessed himself still at a loss in deciding what he should contribute as against what the company should do. There was also the issue of treating each camp the same or differently. He spelled out the estimated dollar costs of each of the alternative structures and asked King for his views of which gifts would produce the best long-term results by "securing the interest and loyalty and support of the employees."[16]

In his elaborate five-page response, King never mentioned costs but spoke only of the principles that should guide Rockefeller's giving. Generally, he advised, you should treat each camp as nearly alike as possible in dispensing gifts. Alluding to problems that had arisen from Rockefeller's dancing with the miner's wives, he cautioned: "if you dance with one, you must dance with them all or get into trouble with the rest."[17] King continued: Those gifts that come from you should not be mixed up with improvement that the company has a responsibility to provide. Such facilities as club houses, moving picture theaters, and assembly halls ought routinely to be provided by a company that obliges its workers to live in isolated settings. Therefore, you should play no part in providing such things. Concentrate your gifts on bandstands, for along with your contributions toward churches and the gift of hospitals, you will have acted in keeping with the sentiments you express in your *Atlantic* article, namely that "Men do not live merely to toil; they also live to play, to mingle with their fellows, to love, to worship."[18] The bandstands are a part of play, the hospitals a part of love, and the churches a part of worship. King had a marvelous facility for making things sound good even when his reasoning could not stand up to careful scrutiny. His division between company responsibility and Rockefeller philanthropy in this instance was perfectly arbitrary.

King went on to note that he was increasingly of the view that play in the form of sports provided the perfect model for industrial relations. In sports, explicit rules defined what was and was not permitted. The rules were applicable to all players without exception, and any disputes over the rules or their application were resolved by a neutral umpire. These seemed equally the requirements for harmonious employee relations. In his best evangelical style, King concluded his long letter saying:

I should like to see you make a speech on these lines from each of the several bandstands in the camps on your next visit to Colorado. . . . The bandstand is the right sort of pulpit to preach this gospel from, and I think matters have now reached the stage in Colorado where we are justified in beginning to erect the pulpits.[19]

Grace Episcopal Church in Cleveland actually provided Rockefeller with his next pulpit. There, in mid-May, in a brief address to the Industrial Department Conference of the YMCA, he again emphasized the partnership between capital and labor. Society's great need, he told the delegates, was to restore the communication between these two groups that the growth of the large-scale corporation had done so much to erode. He struck an entirely new note by acknowledging that good intentions were not enough, that even the best of intentions of corporate owners and leaders could be nullified by the actions of their agents. Difficulties in the realm of employee relations, he suggested, frequently stemmed from the efforts of such agents, foremen and supervisors, to lord it over subordinates from whose ranks they themselves had risen. As he put it: "Most of us cannot stand success and prosperity; our own heads are turned . . . when we have risen a peg."[20]

This was a novel twist for a onetime Social Darwinist to give to the conventional success story. It suggested that unfairness arose as a negative attribute of social mobility. It also implied that, in contrast, inherited power and wealth were more secure and for that reason less likely to create problems. Rockefeller concluded his talk by asserting that unfairness, arising from this or from any other source, made it absolutely necessary that workers have some means for adjusting their grievances. It was in this connection that, with his customary modesty, he put in a plug for the Colorado representation scheme.

A second less public pulpit opened up to Rockefeller at the Davis Coal & Coke Company, in which Senior had a substantial holding. The available evidence suggests that Davis Company officers appealed to Rockefeller for King's assistance in the face of a union organizing drive. It is known that at the time, spring 1916, the United Mine Workers launched an organizing campaign in the Maryland–West Virginia region where the company's mines were situated. The haste with which Davis officials moved to consider and adopt new labor policies also suggests that they were prompted by pressing need rather than by a new-found interest in experimentation. Finally, there is the evidence that when King reviewed the company's proposed plan of action, he saw union avoidance in every measure.

At Rockefeller's request, King conferred with Davis officials

sometime in May. He learned that the company wanted to introduce an employee representation plan as one of a series of steps
calculated to ensure the loyalty of its miners. The other steps included the formation of an employees' association, publication of
an employees' magazine, and the establishment of training or
educational institutes of some sort. Early in June, Rockefeller
made a quick, unpublicized tour of several Davis coal camps.
Shortly thereafter, Davis Company president, A. W. Calloway,
forwarded for Rockefeller's consideration a synopsis of the actions the company proposed to take. This document was passed
along to King, whose response was remarkable on a number of
counts.

King unequivocally opposed the creation of an employees' association, pointing out that this was precisely the sort of action that
would provoke the union and taint the representation plan as
well. Such an association, he argued, bore the implication that
membership in it was an alternative to union membership. King
reminded Rockefeller that the critics of the Colorado plan often
made the same argument against it, that it was a substitute for
unionism. This criticism fell to the ground, however, once the
nondiscrimination clause was pointed out. He continued:

> My point is that I do not want to see an *Employees Association
> formed by the Company at all.* First because it is unnecessary; and
> secondly, because it conveys an erroneous impression as to the
> significance of the Representation Plan which is exactly what it
> purports to be, namely, *a plan of representation* of employees, ar-
> ranged for, except as to form, by themselves, and in no sense *a
> plan of organization* of the Company's employees affected by the
> Company for them.[21]

None but the true believer could accept the distinction that
King attempted to draw here. The miners at C.F. & I. had been
persuaded to go along with policies that were designed, arranged,
and installed by their employer. Davis officials wished to do the
same. The basic difference between the two was a matter of style.
The Davis company wanted to ward off the union with what King
regarded as clumsy tactics, whereas King was prepared to advise
them to the same end, union avoidance, using the more sophisticated tactic of the plan and a written constitution. Quite possibly,
the difference arose because the Davis officials were reluctant to
live with the risk inherent in the nondiscrimination clause.

King's and Rockefeller's masks again fall away for us in this episode; for us, but not for them. Rockefeller remained blind to his self-deception throughout his life, King for several years to come. They had convinced themselves in Colorado that employee representation was neither a substitute for nor meant to displace unionism. They professed to believe in the necessity of collective bargaining and in the positive contributions that trade unions could and did make in modern industrial society. The representation plan at C.F. & I., they had told themselves, was necessary only because the local union leadership was so corrupt and contemptible that dealing with it was impossible. No similar charges had arisen about the union leaders confronting the Davis Company, yet here they were, eager to help forestall unionization by introducing a representation plan.

The lack of fanfare associated with the introduction of a plan at the Davis Company also suggests that, between helping the company stave off unionization and spreading the gospel of employee representation, Rockefeller still valued the former more than the latter. Believing in the power of publicity as he did and convinced of the great virtue of the plan, he had no need for a silent ministry. Yet, publicity was not given to the adoption of the plan at Davis at the time, nor was any mention subsequently made of it in the biographies of Rockefeller and King prepared by their closest associates. Yet, it would probably be incorrect to conclude that the two were simply hypocrites, saying one thing but doing another. The truest test of their mettle came a few years after the Davis Company episode when unions, in several instances, did displace representation plans. Though they were troubled by these developments, Rockefeller much more than King, they did nothing to reverse them.

Rockefeller intended to return to Colorado in the fall of 1916 on a sort of anniversary visit that would display his continuing interest and afford the opportunity to learn at first hand how the plan was working. When he found himself unable to leave New York, he asked King to go on alone and report back. King took up the assignment with great relief. Work on his book had proved fruitless of late. He had felt himself so nervous and unable to concentrate that he sought medical advice. All summer long, he puttered about his summer cottage, supervising some construction, and playing host to his mother and father. Quite suddenly, on August 30, his father died. The distraction of the visit to Colorado came to him as something of a tonic.

The situation at C.F. & I. toward the end of September 1916 could not have been better, he discovered. During August, union organizers had been active in the camps and had met with some success in signing up new members. Some of their activity, King was told, had been accompanied by intimidation. President Welborn had responded by launching a series of meetings in which he and other officials discussed with the men their rights and privileges under the representation plan. As a result, many miners who had joined the union now withdrew. Welborn told King just before he departed that the most recent meeting of the union had been attended by a mere handful of men. (It must be assumed that this information came to him from a spy.)

In reporting to Rockefeller, King wrote that his original surmise had proved correct; the true object of the union's latest drive had not been industrial but political. The union wanted to be in the position to influence the miners' votes in the upcoming elections. Its leaders had moved too soon, however. They could not sustain their organizing drive so far in advance of election day. King believed that this accounted, in part, for their failure. The other part was attributable to the mobilization of the company officers. He concluded that the entire affair has greatly strengthened the plan, first by revealing more of its potentials to C.F. & I. managers and then by clarifying its terms for the rank and file members. He expressed the judgment that all would be quiet at C.F. & I. for at least another year.

On his return to Ottawa, King looked forward to resuming work on his book. His nervous condition reasserted itself, however, and just as he was becoming obsessed with his inability to concentrate, Rockefeller asked him to come to New York. Two matters required King's presence: Rockefeller's annual report to the Rockefeller Foundation, and a fresh outbreak of labor troubles at the Standard Oil Bayonne refinery. While in New York, King confided in Rockefeller and was urged by him to discuss his nervous condition with Dr. Flexner. Flexner, in turn, advised and subsequently arranged for King to be examined by a specialist at the Johns Hopkins Medical School in Baltimore. Meanwhile, the second strike at Bayonne was unfolding as a replay of the first. Again, there were riots and fatalities. Coming just a year after the previous strike, the latest contest made it evident that something was seriously amiss in Standard Oil's relations with its workers. King believed he discovered where the problems lay after just a brief discussion with F. W. Weller, the vice president who had directed the company's strategy in both strikes. Weller, he concluded, knew practically nothing about labor problems and was, moreover "temperamentally unsuited to appreciate the needs" of workers.[22] Led by such an unseeing person, the board of directors had nothing to guide it but the misleading reports of spies and its own illusions. After two embarrassing strikes, Weller could do no more than concede that, perhaps, in view of the large number of employees at Bayonne, it might be advisable to have someone other than the technical people look after labor matters.

Here, King observed, was a splendid opportunity to extend the representation plan into New Jersey Standard Oil. Knowing that Rockefeller had perceived the same opportunity, he wondered why he had not seized it forcefully. Senior, he surmised was the stumbling block. King recalled that Rockefeller's secretary had confided to him that "severe differences" had developed between father and son and that Senior had become "very bitter and close."[23] He had sold out his holding of C.F. & I. stock and had even sold it short. What King did not know was that this situation had already reversed itself. On October 25, 1916, Senior gave his son a gift of stocks and bonds valued at $7,968,982. Given the way Senior valued money, this could only have been a peace offering. However, as it is unclear from the record precisely what caused the falling out, so is it unclear what brought about the reconciliation. C.F. & I. was undoubtedly involved, since Senior expressed his hostility in terms of that company's stock and its expected future performance. Was he placated by King's report that the union organizing effort had been thwarted and that all was well at C.F. & I.? More likely it was the enormous profits that Welborn reported for the previous quarter. (The younger Rockefeller was himself sufficiently pleased with both of these developments to give Welborn a $15,000 bonus.) In any event, Senior's renewed confidence in his son's judgment opened the way for intervention in New Jersey Standard Oil.

In his report to Rockefeller following his visit to Colorado, King had written of Jesse Welborn that the more he spoke in public about the representation plan, the more he grew in enthusiasm for it. So with King himself. As he read and reread his draft of the speech that Rockefeller was to deliver at Cornell University, he was strengthened in his conviction of the rightness of the representation idea. Several months had passed since the Bayonne strike and yet nothing had come of his talk with vice president Weller. He wrote to Rockefeller urging him to underwrite a social survey of Bayonne by the YMCA and to press for the introduction of an employee representation plan at Standard Oil.

Between this prod, the peace with Senior, and his own resurgence of confidence in the wake of the Cornell University speech, Rockefeller was moved to action. Within the month, he informed King that the social survey was underway. He asked if King would be interested in examining the company's labor practices and making recommendations for their improvement. Since this proposition raised a number of related considerations, he invited King to come to New York for discussions.

On arriving in Manhattan early on the morning of March 7, 1917, King immediately plunged into the round of meetings, interviews, and entertainments that customarily filled his visits. He was hardly ever as comfortable with himself as he was on these hectic trips—using his wits, giving free rein equally to his sensitivity and to his gregariousness, and not less important, living a cut above his usual standard, all expenses paid. Yet, he did not fall victim to the many distractions that his association with Rockefeller afforded. To the contrary, on this particular occasion he departed New York more certain than ever that his destiny lay in service to Canada.

Rockefeller repeated his offer for King to undertake an examination of industrial relations at Standard Oil. He recognized that this would necessitate bringing King's relationship with the Rockefeller Foundation to an end, but he would personally retain him as a member of his staff, or independent of it, as King saw fit. Never had the time been more propitious, he argued, for transforming the company from the "most hated" to the "most loved."[24]

In explaining himself, Rockefeller shared with King a confidence that only his wife and father had known about till now. Some years ago, he related, when he sat on the Standard Oil board of directors, he had learned of some of the methods employed by the company of which "he did not approve."[25] He had spoken up in an attempt to bring about a change but to no avail. The officers and the other board members refused to alter their practices, telling him that he was too idealistic and did not understand what was necessary for success in the world of business. Consequently, he had resigned from the board. His resignation has been "a bitter disappointment"[26] both for himself and for his father, for they were immensely proud of the role Senior had played in building up the industry and would naturally have preferred to continue to participate in its development.

Now, he continued, after years without influence, a new leadership had arisen to replace the old guard within the company. Headed by president A. C. Bedford, the new leaders were a great improvement. They could be counted on in all their dealings to do what was right. A fresh start had already been made in the realm of publicity where, at his urging, Ivy Lee's services had been retained. The new directors would be equally open to recommendations looking to improve labor relations. The time was ripe for change.

Over two days, at the office, at lunch, on their walks uptown, and even at dinner, the matter was discussed from every angle. King felt that he owed it to the Rockefeller Foundation and to himself to complete his book on industrial relations. That was his first priority. He was also committed to stand for Parliament in the general elections in the fall. Even though he had little chance of election, he had pledged himself to contest the seat and was bound to do so. He told Rockefeller that for reasons of his own, he had also decided to end his relationship with the Foundation but only after the book was finished. In his report to the Foundation, he would recommend against the establishment of a permanent program in industrial relations. So contentious an area, he had concluded, would only embroil the Foundation in controversy and detract from the great good it could accomplish. He would also recommend that the less controversial topics of industrial health and safety be added to the concerns of the Foundation's medical program. Then, he would be free to take up the consulting work that Rockefeller wanted from him.

King felt that Rockefeller exerted considerable pressure to have him immediately end his association with the Foundation and assume the role of his consultant. Had Rockefeller understood King better than he did, he would have grasped the true basis of his reluctance. To King, the affiliation with the Foundation gave his work a dimension of disinterested research that, in view of its potential value to society as a whole, justified his involvement. In contrast, consulting for Rockefeller was simply self-serving money making. At any other time it might have been possible to lay such considerations aside. But not now, not while his country was at war. King foresaw that in his political career he might at any time be called upon to justify his lack of wartime service to Canada. His investigation into the principles underlying harmonious industrial relations could be defended as a socially useful contribution, whereas hiring out to Standard Oil and to other Rockefeller interests could not.

King tried to convey these feelings through Mrs. Rockefeller at the theater one evening, but he may have been too indirect for his message to carry. By the time he took his leave of Rockefeller, he was resentful of the pressure to which he had been subjected. For the first time in the almost three years since he had met Rockefeller, he had negative feelings about him:

> He is prepared to crowd, and bring pressure to get his own way, and to be a little petulant when his wishes are not quickly met, —in other words, that he is selfish in his own wishes, like others, not all philanthropist, and that too much cannot be taken for granted on the basis of friendship. . . . He is a dominating type, tho' he seeks not to be, but even to the minute for meals, etc. he likes to have his own way.[27]

Faced with King's refusal to examine Standard Oil labor practices, Rockefeller brought Clarence Hicks from C.F. & I. to do the job. By mid-April 1917, shortly after the United States declared war on the Central Powers, the directors of New Jersey Standard Oil were prepared to respond to Rockefeller's initiatives. President Bedford told Rockefeller that the board approved many of the recommendations Hicks had made and also wanted Hicks to come into the company and implement his ideas. Rockefeller refused unless Standard Oil was prepared to meet one condition: it must introduce an employee representation plan. If the board would agree to this, he pledged to secure Hicks from C.F. & I. and to recommend to his father that he give $100,000 toward the construction of a YMCA building in Bayonne.

Rockefeller kept his father informed about these negotiations. He thought that the willingness of the Standard Oil board to accept some of Hicks' recommendations without adopting the representation idea was shortsighted. They seemed to be more interested in palliatives than in meeting their labor problems seriously, head on. Much was at stake, he confided to his father, his new-found ally in employee representation, for

> What is done at Bayonne will be done eventually in other plants of the Jersey Company, as well as in the former subsidiary companies, and an example set in Bayonne, in the midst of so many

huge industries, if successfully developed, is sure to be followed by industries on many sides . . .[28]

Several days later, Bedford informed Rockefeller that the board was amenable to his terms. At Rockefeller's request, C.F. & I. president Welborn released Hicks to New Jersey Standard Oil. Hicks, by now a firm believer in the efficacy of employee representation, was pleased to take on the new assignment. Rockefeller triumphantly informed King that the introduction of employee representation at Standard Oil would undoubtedly prove "epoch making."[29] No one as yet had much sense of how things would change as the result of the war.

Notes

1. Proceedings of the Second Yama Conference, September 1915. In National Industrial Conference Board Papers.
2. *Leslie's Illustrated Weekly* (December 16, 1915), p. 663.
3. Valentine (1915).
4. The text of the article appears in Rockefeller (1923), p. 41.
5. Ibid.
6. Patrick Gilday to Seth Low, 11/29/15. Low Papers, Box 46.
7. W.L.M.K. to Seth Low, 2/21/16. W.L.M.K. Papers, Series J1, vol. 34, p. 29825.
8. These quotations appear in U.S. Congress, House of Representatives (1916), vol. 145, Part II.
9. Charles W. Mills to Seth Low, 2/11/16. Low Papers, Box 46.
10. E. H. Weitzel to J. Welborn, 2/1/16. This letter accompanies J. Welborn to J.D.R., Jr., 2/3/16. J.D.R., Jr. Papers, Business Interests, Box 14.
11. J.D.R., Jr. to E. H. Weitzel, 3/13/16. Ibid.
12. W.L.M.K. to J.D.R., Jr., 4/27/16. W.M.L.K. Papers, Series J1, vol. 34, p. 29979.
13. Agent #426 reports, 5/31/16. W.L.M.K. Papers, Series J4, File 186, vol. 32, p. C24524.
14. Dante Barton to F. P. Walsh, 4/10/17. F.P.W. Papers, Box 133. See also Beshoar (1942), p. 346.
15. W.L.M.K. to J.D.R., Jr., 3/22/16. J.D.R., Jr. Papers, Friends and Services, Box 18. See also J.D.R., Jr. to W.L.M.K., 6/28/16 and 12/19/16, W.L.M.K. Papers, Series J1, vol. 34.
16. J.D.R., Jr. to W.L.M.K., 4/10/16. Ibid., p. 29940.
17. W.L.M.K. to J.D.R., Jr., 4/13/16. Ibid., p. 29943.
18. Ibid.
19. Ibid., pp. 29944ff.
20. Typewritten "Address by John D. Rockefeller, Jr." Ibid., p. 30076.
21. W.L.M.K. to J.D.R., Jr., 6/19/16. Ibid., p. 30064. See also Harvey (1969), p. 361.

22. W.L.M.K. Diary, 10/24/16. W.L.M.K. Papers, Series J13, p. G2575.
23. Ibid.
24. W.L.M.K. Diary, 3/7/17–3/9/17. W.L.M.K. Papers, Series J13, p. G2690. Quotation marks in the original.
25. Ibid.
26. Ibid.
27. Ibid., p. G2694.
28. J.D.R., Jr. to J.D.R., Sr., 4/13/17. J.D.R., Jr. Papers, Business Interests, Box 134.
29. J.D.R., Jr., to W.L.M.K., 4/17/17. J.D.R., Jr. Papers, Friends and Services, Box 72.

11. The War

On April 6, 1917, the day President Wilson signed the declaration of war, Mackenzie King chanced to meet Raymond B. Fosdick in Ottawa. Fosdick was traveling in his new capacity as an advisor to the War Department, collecting information about how the Canadian military organized and managed its training camps. He would eventually head the department's Commission on Training Camp Activities. He and King were acquainted through their mutual association with John D. Rockefeller, Jr., and the Rockefeller Foundation.

Following dinner that evening, the two men chatted and, almost inevitably, their conversation turned to Rockefeller and their relationships with him. King listened as Fosdick portrayed himself as a true radical, as someone who believed that very significant social changes were required to produce the kind of society he envisaged. When Fosdick confessed that he chafed at the limits imposed on his counsel by the always cautious conservatism of Rockefeller, King identified him as a kindred spirit. Fosdick related that in a recent discussion of the government's proposal to raise the tax rates on large incomes, Rockefeller had expressed the opinion that this was wrong. King joined Fosdick in deriding his attitude. They agreed that in the not too distant future the state would act to level all of the great fortunes. Before the evening was out, they concluded that "socialism was inevitable and desirable,"[1] that workers would one day own the factories in which they toiled, and that society would take proper title to all natural resources.

Such views marked a decided—and temporary—leftward turn in the lives of both men. It was a turn they made with many others who believed that the world would never be the same because of the war. But unlike those many others, King and Fosdick imperiled their own integrity in the process. Not merely or even because they sat in judgment of Rockefeller, but because their standing as his advisors was so much at odds with the future they welcomed in their imaginations. If his privileges and preferment were somehow wrong and antisocial, the servants of his wealth and power also were tainted. Yet, while neither King nor Fosdick savored the irony of their situation, doing good works under a patronage of dubious legitimacy, they were untouched by guilt. They derived too much satisfaction from their access to power for that. Instead, both men held themselves ready to enlist in the nobler service of the public power once that should become puissant. Socialism, they believed, would afford them the ultimate opportunity for selfless public service.

Rather than crushing dreams, the war seemed to many to open up the prospect of a new era. The energy unleashed by the drive to mobilize war resources seemed evidence of this. So did the uncommon experience of a transcendent national purpose. For the first time in the lives of most participants, the interests of the nation took precedence over the purely personal. Lives were altered abruptly by the draft, war work, separations, and relocations. The customary centers of private power in New York, Boston, Pittsburgh, and Cleveland sustained a sharp relative decline, while the activity and authority of Washington officials expanded faster and further than ever before. Raymond Fosdick's position made him particularly sensitive to this shift. Indeed, he was a part of it. And like many of those directly involved in the war machine, he looked upon the changes taking place with the thought that there could be no turning back. Some war-wrought changes undoubtedly would be abandoned at war's end. But insofar as attitudes and aspirations were concerned, he believed that the foundation of a new social order was being laid.

Fearful of just such a result, spokesmen for American business convened that war-tided spring to discuss how they might cooperate with the government without at the same time ceding permanent authority over their relations with their employees. Organized labor had already called upon the Wilson Administration to permit no backward step at labor's expense. The business spokesmen of the National Industrial Conference Board resolved upon an equally conservative response. They urged the government to permit no forward step to labor's advantage.

Most of the government's advisors on labor matters—including Felix Frankfurter, Louis D. Brandeis, and Leon C. Marshall—were decidedly sympathetic to trade union organization. Since the need to ensure that strikes did not disrupt war production carried with it the fairly obvious imperative to organize workers, the spread of unionism seemed a logical means to that end. In the

Raymond B. Fosdick, 1918.

event of a strike, there had to be some agency through which the government could meet with the workers and find the terms of settlement that would get them back to work. Such an agency might also reduce the likelihood of strikes by providing a method for the timely resolution of grievances. Thus, quite apart from anybody's preferences in the matter, the war government had compelling reasons for wanting workers organized. Yet most employers were so vehemently opposed to unions that any attempt to impose them was likely to backfire and result in lost production. What the government needed was a worker organization that would simultaneously serve its own purposes, meet the objections of open shop employers, and satisfy labor's leadership. Employee representation proved to be just the thing. But, first, it had to undergo a vital name change.

The very first proposal for creating wartime labor dispute machinery included a provision calling for the organization of shop committees. Felix Frankfurter, on leave from Harvard Law School to serve as an assistant to the Secretary of War, was the author of this proposal. Samuel Gompers, however, brought it up for the consideration of his colleagues on the Advisory Commission to the Council of National Defense. Gompers' sponsorship of the proposal undoubtedly signified his endorsement. Soon afterward, he tendered a proposal of his own design, which also provided for the creation of shop committees. Such committees, composed of workers and elected by them to represent their interests in dealing with employers and government boards, were looked upon as a vital part of any plans for dispute settlement. Almost all of the proposals subsequently brought before the Council of National Defense provided for them.

The model that Frankfurter and Gompers followed in their proposals was provided by the Whitley Councils in England. In that scheme, works committees were created to fill a void in the structure of British trade unions. In the United States, union members employed in the same trade and by the same employer were very likely to belong to the same local union. Which local union British workers belonged to, however, depended on their places of residence rather than their places of employment. Commonly, workers plying the same trade and employed in the same shop or factory were members of different local branches. For this reason, there were no shop or plant level union organizations to look after the common interests of workers in that particular shop or plant. Works committees, rechristened shop committees on this side of the Atlantic, were designed to perform this function. In so doing, they also provided the organizational base upon which joint labor–management Whitley Councils were established at regional and industry wide levels.

Shop committees were unnecessary in the United States because American local unions were already equipped to deal effectively with shop level problems. This implies that the advocates of such committees intended them mainly for the benefit of unorganized workers. Perhaps, they supposed that these new organizations would develop greater independence from employer influence than seemed true where employee representation prevailed. This would in time prove to be the exceptional case. When shop committee members lacked the outside supportive affiliation of a trade union or radical political party, they were as isolated and as vulnerable to employer pressures as those who served as employee representatives. To all intents and purposes, shop committees were indistinguishable from representation plans. Yet, it would have been impossible for many of the advocates of the former to give their support to the latter. Any scheme so closely associated with the Rockefeller name was suspect and had to be avoided.

Not that the name was to be shunned entirely. When, in May, Gompers selected the members of his labor committee (a committee of the Advisory Commission to the Council of National Defense), the younger Rockefeller was among those invited to participate. His membership, along with that of other business leaders and public figures such as Daniel Guggenheim and V. Everit Macy, made the committee resemble a broadly representative body, in the manner of the National Civic Federation. It also provided a source of funds. The work of the committee, like that of the Advisory Commission, was voluntary and unpaid. There were numerous expenses, nonetheless, and the wealthier participants were expected to cover these. It was the prestige of his name and the size of his purse that prompted Rockefeller's selection and not, as he might have hoped, his connection with employee representation.

Rockefeller permitted himself to be used in this manner because he believed himself knowledgeable about labor issues. He also very much wanted to be of service to his country. Joining the labor committee was one of the several ways he sought to play some part. Through Fosdick and under the auspices of the YMCA, he also toured army training camps and spoke to the recruits about why the country was at war. In New York City, he headed several highly successful Liberty Bond drives. Toward the end of the war, he managed to persuade a number of sectarian charities to conduct a united appeal for funds. The beneficiaries of this unprecedented ecumenical approach to fund raising were servicemen and women.

King was destined to play an equally minor role in the wartime affairs of his country. Through most of 1917, he busied himself with his book on industrial relations. He also ministered to the needs and wishes of his dying mother. Late in the autumn of 1917, he threw himself into the Parliamentary election campaign but to no avail. Then, in December, shortly after his rejection at the polls, his mother died. His relations with Rockefeller at the time were more strained than ever. The end of the year thus found him feeling wounded and bereft. He was still determined, however, to realize his political ambitions.

Even as fate pushed Rockefeller and King to the wings, their idea of employee representation moved toward center stage. In November 1917, the first adoption of shop committees was compelled by the Shipbuilding Labor Adjustment Board. Their idea began to have a life of its own.

It was entirely coincidental that the chairman of the Shipbuilding Labor Adjustment Board was a Westchester County neighbor and lifelong friend of Rockefeller. V. Everit Macy would have been familiar with the Colorado industrial plan solely in his capacity as president of the National Civic Federation, to which post he had succeeded Seth Low. As it happened, apart from his personal relationship with Rockefeller, Macy was also a major stockholder in Standard Oil of New Jersey. He would have known about that company's recent introduction of the representation scheme. But, even if he had been entirely unaware of employee representation, any of a number of his associates in the Board might have brought it to his attention. Columbia University labor economist Henry R. Seager was the Board executive secretary, and labor economists W. Jeff Lauck, Carleton H. Parker, and William F. Ogburn composed the research staff.

In its very first case, the Macy Board had found a situation so fraught with explosive potential that had shop committees not existed previously, they might have been invented on the spot. In the San Francisco Bay area, shipyard owners were accustomed to dealing with unions and the Board was able to effect its policies through existing institutions. But in Portland, Oregon, and Seattle, Washington, the absence of unions and the rabid opposition of the shipyard owners to unions presented the Board with the problem of ensuring that its policies were agreeable to the mass of unorganized shipyard workers and would be adhered to by them. Board members believed that, if they forced unions on the employers, they would exacerbate an already troubled situation. So they chose instead to order the organization of representative committees. This was on November 4, 1917. One week later, Macy, along with Navy Undersecretary Franklin D. Roosevelt, attended the A.F. of L. convention in Buffalo, New York, to explain and lobby for the terms of settlement the Board had imposed. There is little reason to suppose that they had to defend the creation of shop committees.

President Wilson also attended the A.F. of L. convention—the first president to do so—and addressed the delegates. Since his administration had as yet no clear labor program, his talk consisted mostly of generalizations. He promised that in the very near future, steps would be taken to deal with some of the most pressing labor problems. Those he enumerated were all labor market problems, however, rather than problems in the relations between workers and their employers. He made no mention either of shop committees or of the need for worker representation. A memorandum prepared for his guidance on the eve of the convention endorsed shop committees but stressed the continuing need for organized labor's voluntary cooperation. Wishing to "avoid the compulsion of labor,"[2] the President lavishly praised the A.F. of L. for its support of the war effort. He dismissed the tangled issues surrounding the creation of dispute settlement machinery with the bland assertion that face-to-face meetings between workers and employers were desirable.

The honor conferred by the President's visit upon the A.F. of L., and upon Samuel Gompers personally, fulfilled one of the latter's fondest dreams. At last, the labor movement was a recognized and valued partner in shaping the nation's destiny. In keeping with this ascendent role and in direct imitation of British precedent, Gompers and his executive board presented to the convention their thoughts on postwar reconstruction. They characterized the war as a catalyst for social change by means of which the processes of social evolution had been speeded up immeasurably. The alterations produced by the war, they believed, would prove irreversible. Labor had acquired a new standing and a new recognition of its importance. In the postwar future, the labor movement, flying the banner of industrial democracy, was destined to civilize capitalism.

The issue of shop committees and their role vis-à-vis trade unions did not arise directly at the convention; whether by accident or design it is impossible to say. In the closed deliberations of the Advisory Commission and the Council of National Defense, Gompers supported and even advocated the creation of shop committees. With good reason, he may not have wanted the subject discussed on the floor of the convention. For, if some delegates feared that shop committees might serve as alternatives to union organization, they would have opposed them and so cut the ground from under Gompers' position. On the other hand, if some of the delegates saw shop committees as stepping stones to union organization, any statements to that effect would be siezed upon by employers as grounds for rejecting them.

Instead, shop committees received the approval of the convention without a word of debate. Following the lead of Gompers and the executive board, the delegates wholeheartedly endorsed the Whitley Councils' scheme of joint representation. Their purpose in doing so was aimed at shaping the composition of any dispute settlement boards that might be created. In endorsing the Whitley Council scheme, the convention also endorsed the shop committees for which the scheme provided.

From the very first days of the war, a number of disagreements had blocked the Wilson Administration's path to agreement on a war labor program. All of the agencies that had come into being, and their policy positions, had been improvised to meet particular emergencies. A major sticking point in the way of a broad general policy was Gompers' insistent opposition to the creation of a tripartite administrative agency. Not that Gompers was opposed to tripartitism per se. He was an active partner in the tripartite National Civic Federation and had agreed to the 3-3-3 representation of labor, business, and the public in the U.S. Commission on Industrial Relations. But his experience with the latter body, coupled with a similar experience with the Anthracite Coal Commission of 1902, had convinced him that the public representatives were most likely to side with the employers. Because equal representation proved to work against labor, he opposed it.

The alternative Gompers preferred and caused to prevail was the Whitley Council model. In this scheme, the employers named their representatives, the unions named an equal number, and each group in turn named one public representative. These two ostensibly nonpartisan representatives then served as cochairmen of the panel. The A.F. of L. convention endorsement of Whitley Councils can be seen as an effort to strengthen Gompers's bargaining position over the shape of any war labor administration.

The casualness with which the Wilson Administration permitted internal disagreements to block the formulation of its labor program came to an abrupt halt soon after the A.F. of L. convention. A hostile congressional investigation raised serious questions about the effectiveness of the War Department's mobilization efforts and prompted the change. It became clear to the administration that War Secretary Baker had to be relieved of much of the responsibility for labor questions that had been thrust upon him.

On January 4, 1918, the President named Labor Secretary Wilson the War Labor Administrator and authorized him to take whatever steps were necessary to ensure the effective use of labor resources and the uninterrupted flow of war production. Secretary Wilson immediately appointed a group to advise him in the design of his new responsibilities. This advisory group in turn recommended the creation of a War Labor Conference Board, structured along the lines of the Whitley Councils. Secretary Wilson accepted this recommendation and asked the A.F. of L. to name five labor and one public representatives. He asked the National Industrial Conference Board to do likewise for employer interests. Frank Walsh was labor's choice for public representative, while the employers chose former president and now Yale Law School professor, William Howard Taft.

An observer familiar with the announced positions of the two groups would have held out little hope for a viable agreement from the War Labor Conference Board. The A.F. of L. had all along insisted that the rights of workers to organize and bargain collectively must be acknowledged in any war labor policy. The various employers' associations that composed the National Industrial Conference Board were equally adamant in their commitment to the open shop and the prewar status quo. By placing the formulation of its labor policies in the hands of such antagonistic groups, the administration ran the risk of alienating both without providing for its own needs.

Even the individual participants on the War Labor Conference Board entered into their deliberations without much hope of success. Shortly after their sessions got under way, Taft confessed to another former president, Theodore Roosevelt, that

> I have gone into this Labor Commission business not because I have been optimistic as to the outcome of our conference with such men as Walsh and Hutcheson,[3] but because discouraging as this prospect is, I feel I have no right not to help make an effort to secure some basis upon which labor and capital may be kept loyal during the war. I believe labor would be loyal but for the leaders who see the war as an opportunity. Capital can be restrained by taxation and otherwise . . .[4]

Miraculously, after meeting on and off from late February to the end of March, the conferees reached unanimous agreement on a set of guiding principles. The standpat conservatism of the employers' initial position was nowhere in evidence. They had conceded everything in exchange, it seems, for very little. Both sides pledged themselves to no strikes or lockouts. The rights of workers to organize unions and engage in collective bargaining were recognized explicitly. Employers, moreover, were admonished not to interfere with these rights or to discriminate against workers for union membership or union activity. Health and safety measures were not to be relaxed. Women were to receive the same pay as men when they worked at comparable jobs. The basic eight-hour day (i.e., requiring time and a half payment for all overtime work) was to continue where stipulated by law and, in all other instances, the health and safety of workers were to be considered. All workers were to receive a living wage. These were far and away the most generous concessions ever made by American employers.

The Wilson Administration was entirely satisfied with the results of the Board's deliberations. It quickly accepted its report and implemented the recommendations by executive order. In this manner, the National War Labor Board was created. The members of the wonder-working War Labor Conference Board were prevailed upon to accept appointments to the new body.

Overall, the War Labor Board would prove a complete success. No major work stoppages occurred during the war, and much more often than not, the Board members found themselves in agreement on the issues they confronted. Sharp divisions arose only in a few cases, usually surrounding one of two issues: employer antiunionism and the eight-hour day.

The Board's success would not prove to be a lasting one. In part, this was the result of the brevity of its life and its creation through executive order rather than legislative enactment. The activities of the Board also set in motion forces that, at war's end, would quickly erase its achievements. Among those it prompted into action at the time were Rockefeller and King.

Late in October 1917, King made one of his whirlwind visits to New York. By prearrangement, Jesse Welborn was also visiting the city, and the two men, along with Rockefeller and Clarence Hicks, met to discuss developments at C.F. & I. In a continuing display of concern for the effectiveness of their invention, some minor changes in the working of the representation plan were agreed upon. King adamantly refused, however, to agree to one change that the others supported. They wanted to institute individual agreements wherein each miner would pledge to abide by the representation plan as a condition of continuing employment. This was tantamount to a yellow-dog contract, under which workers signed away, on pain of discharge, their right to join unions. Although such contracts were legal according to a recent ruling of the Supreme Court, King pointed out that unions, and most fair-minded people, found them offensive and condemned them. For, after all, they were expressive of the employers greater power and contempt for the workers. King's impassioned opposition won him his point. He could not help but wonder, however, at the lack of understanding that his colleagues revealed.

A similar lack seemed evident later the same day, when Rockefeller asked him what he meant by self-government in industry. King explained that workers would have to play a progressively broader role in the conduct of industry, if warfare between labor and capital was to be avoided. This led to a discussion of King's future relationship to Rockefeller and to the decision to postpone making any plans until after the Canadian election in December. Before the conversation drew to a close, Rockefeller said some things that caused King to spend the next several days brooding about his future.

King was particularly offended by a question Rockefeller asked about the source of his livelihood before their association. To be sure, Rockefeller had politely asked permission to put a personal question, but King felt that the question could only have been aimed at exposing his financial vulnerability. If it was Rockefeller's intention to make him feel subordinate and obligated, King vowed he would not continue to advise him. He told himself that their professional association had to be one of mutual advantage or not at all.

Perhaps King sensed how greatly he was deluding himself in looking for mutual advantage, for his very next thought was that his rightful place was in Canadian politics. But he could not bring himself to admit that his relationship with Rockefeller had undergone a metamorphosis and that the passing of Rockefeller's once desperate need for his counsel and encouragement had reduced him from deliverer to advisor, from equal to hired man. Moreover, what mutual advantage could be found in the exchange of his ideas for Rockefeller's money? The greater value of the former, especially now that King was less hard up financially, unbalanced the transaction to his disadvantage. In this way, too, he was subordinated and more nearly indistinguishable from a hireling.

As was his wont, King found coincidental confirmation of his judgment ready to hand. Seeing a Broadway play that evening, in which George Arliss portrayed Alexander Hamilton, he concluded that "more than ever politics was my right field—the only real one for true and full expression."[5] Two days later, on the train trip back to Ottawa, a grand sunrise evoked a reaffirmation of his faith in Canada and in his political future. He characterized himself in his diary as "a Sir Galahad"[6] prepared to fight for the right.

> It is Faith or Fear, and I am putting my all on Faith, with just enough worldly wisdom to see where my livelihood for the next year or two remains secured. I have never had mental rest since the association with the Rockefellers was formed, tho' it has been providential as a means to an end.[7]

Glancing out the window at the dawn-painted countryside, his love for Canada welled up within him and put his doubts to rest. In that roseate light, his opportunism was indistinguishable from his idealism.

In the following months, he and Rockefeller reached a mutually satisfactory understanding about their future relationship. King severed his connection with the Rockefeller Foundation, except for his continuing obligation to complete his book. He was left free to seek a commercial publisher of the book and proceeded to do so. To supply him with income, Rockefeller retained his services as an adviser at $6000 per year for one-third of his time. Under this arrangement he was at liberty to continue to maintain his Canadian residence and political involvement. He was also able, even encouraged, to sell his services as an industrial counselor to companies that requested his advice.

It was a perfect arrangement from King's point of view, particularly since his political fortune was at such low ebb. It also served to dispel much of the hostility that just a few months earlier had colored his thoughts of Rockefeller. Indeed, by spring 1918, King was caught up in the heady wave of optimism engendered in no small part by President Wilson's idealistic Fourteen Points.

Like many of those who wanted change, King came to believe that in the maelstrom of war the pace of social change had been speeded up. Most obviously, this was true of labor reform. Having come to a clear understanding of society's dependence upon labor in production and in the trenches, workers would never permit a return to prewar conditions. Their newly gained self-respect—all segments of society acknowledged the critical role of labor— would lead them to insist with greater force that they play a larger role in the direction of industry. Industrial democracy was in its birth throes.

King was by no means alone in this reading of the times. Intellectuals of varying political persuasions and on both sides of the Atlantic increasingly regarded the war as the climacteric of laissez-faire capitalism. The status and power of labor were clearly on the rise. In addition, it was difficult to believe that governments would retreat entirely from the much enlarged roles that the conduct of the war had imposed upon them, or that popular sentiment would tolerate such a retreat in the face of the unity and coherence that war planning had brought.

The shock waves emanating from the Russian Revolution also

had to be taken into account, for combined with the war, the over-throw of czarism raised telling questions about the integrity of all undemocratic regimes. The Bolshevik seizure of power, more-over, made the trajectory of the future more uncertain than ever. A workers' regime in Russia could provide so irresistible a model that workers in other countries might rise up in emulation. Alter-natively, western capitalists might find themselves compelled to introduce far-reaching industrial reforms in order to forestall rev-olution. In either event, the old order of things was, if not doomed, bound to be transformed. Democracy was the wave of the future. The Fourteen Points made this clear in the international sphere, and labor's growing power presaged a similar result in the con-duct of industry. Apparently, few Americans found the repres-sion of the I.W.W. incongruous with these developments.

So charged was the atmosphere with apocalyptic visions that spring, that with easy consciences, King in Ottawa, Raymond Fos-dick in Washington, and George E. Vincent, director of the Rocke-feller Foundation in New York, conspired to push Rockefeller into the leadership of capitalist reformers. Early in April, Fosdick addressed a "Personal and Confidential" letter to King in which he described a recent meeting with Rockefeller.

> I seized the opportunity to impress upon him as far as I could the fact that the war is going to revamp and reshape our whole conception of living, in a way that we do not dream of at the present time, and that unless we are clear-eyed to these changes and are ready to accept them as part of the new order, the pe-riod of transition, instead of being evolution, will be revolution. I particularly tried to impress upon him the fact that men who have fought and suffered for democracy on European battle-fields will not willingly return to an industrial autocracy. In other words, I tried to get across the idea that the idea of de-mocracy can never be limited to things merely political or even social; that it is irresistibly making its way into the whole indus-trial order; and that he, as the heir to the richest man in the world, has a big part to play in aiding its evolution. Whether that evolution is peaceful or bloody depends largely upon men of his class.[8]

Fosdick went on to relate that Vincent had quite independently been talking to Rockefeller along the very same lines and had given him a copy of the reconstruction program of the British Labour Party. Since Rockefeller would soon be visiting with King in Ottawa, Fosdick asked if he would not join him in the effort to "mold the man who, by reason of his position as the titular head of the capitalist class, can be a powerful influence in helping to liberalize his fellows."[9]

King immediately responded to the effect that he was in complete sympathy with Fosdick's perceptions and with his prescriptions. He, too, looked upon the reconstruction program of the British Labour Party as the best design for the future. Its main thrusts, industrial democracy and the creation of the welfare state, were as desirable as they were inevitable. Of course, he would join forces with Fosdick and Vincent. He confessed that he had always supposed that he could do more to advance the causes of labor and liberalism by influencing Rockefeller than in any other way open to him.

Several of the topics that Rockefeller brought up during his visit to Ottawa provided King with ready opportunities to express his point of view. Rockefeller reported that he had recently proposed to the officers of C.F. & I. that they buy shares of the company's stock at forty dollars per share. (The stock was then trading at sixty dollars.) He would lend them the money, if necessary. He had also pledged himself ready to buy the stock back at forty dollars if its price ever fell below that level. The officers had eagerly accepted his offer. When King asked if he had a similar plan in mind for the workers, Rockefeller asked if he wouldn't attempt to work one out. Many such schemes looked good in theory, he asserted, but none of them seemed to work well in practice.

King was even more mindful than Rockefeller of the practical difficulties involved in stock ownership and profit sharing schemes, for he had just completed a review of the pertinent literature. He greatly admired men like Robert Owen who, in their relations with workers, had been motivated by the desire to enhance the lives and character of their employees. This kind of cooperative effort—true copartnership—seemed to him to contain the only answer to industrial unrest. Yet, in the months ahead, he would devote little time to working out a solution to the problem Rockefeller had posed. It was not simply a matter of being too busy with other things, for the chapters he would work on in his book dealt with copartnership. He believed that the joint ownership of industry lay in the distant future. The first step toward this end was to be found not in profit sharing or money arrangements but in raising the status of labor through employee representation.

The two men also had occasion to discuss events in Russia and their likely impact upon the West. Rockefeller left with King several letters written by an American in Russia that described and reflected on the Bolsheviks in power. In returning these letters to Rockefeller, King took the opportunity to state his view that

> Bolshevism and I.W.W.ism are pretty much one and the same thing. These movements will gain support from the ranks of Labor wherever it becomes possible to point to autocracy in the government of industry. They will fail of support by Labor to the degree to which the right of Labor's voice to a control in its working and living conditions is recognized.[10]

Like many of his reform-minded contemporaries, King often employed the Bolshevik revolution as a bogey man, threatening that a similar fate for this country was to be avoided only by adopting the reforms he favored. This reasoning did not grow out of the Russian situation. King had used the same argument well before the overthrow of the czar. He did not need an actual revolution to sustain his judgment any more than he required an agreement with Raymond Fosdick to articulate his particular point of view. Two generations earlier, Karl Marx had unleashed the specter of proletarian revolution. His vision had diffused so widely that even among non-Marxist intellectuals, revolutionary potential had become the everpresent background noise emanating from capitalist inequalities. They feared—as Marxists hoped— that in time this noise might grow to the volume and pitch that would cause the existing order to shatter. The true menace of the Bolshevik revolution, to men like King and Fosdick, lay not in the activities of revolutionaries, but in its seeming confirmation of Marx's projections. The Russian example gave a profound urgency to the need for reform.

King was decidedly pleased with the results of his talks with Rockefeller. Shortly thereafter, he was himself called on to serve as an active agent of reform. Early in April, Standard Oil of New Jersey had announced the introduction of employee representation plans throughout its many divisions. Such was the temper of the times that even a publication as inflexible on labor matters as *Iron Age* (the voice of the iron and steel industry) bowed in welcome to the news. Standard Oil's action also strengthened Rockefeller's hand in advocating employee representation to the officers of other companies in which his family held an interest. Possibly it was for this reason that the officers of the Consolidation Coal Company decided to follow the lead of the oil company. It is considerably more likely, however, that they were prompted to act by a strike in one of the several coal fields in which Consolidation operated. This factor alone would seem to explain the precipitousness with which the company had a plan designed and approved.

On April 22, Rockefeller wired King asking him to come to New York as soon as possible. Two days later, King arrived and immediately entered into a round of conferences with Rockefeller and officers of Consolidation Coal. By the end of the day, he had produced the draft of an agreement between the company and the miners in its four divisions or districts (Maryland, Pennsylvania, West Virginia, and eastern Kentucky). The agreement provided for the introduction of employee representation. The following day, King traveled to the company offices in Baltimore for further conferences. Talks continued over several days and resulted in various revisions and refinements of the agreement. Satisfied that they had arrived at a final version, King returned to New York.

Two days later, James H. Wheelwright, the president of Consolidation Coal, met in Washington with the U.S. Fuel Administrator, Harry A. Garfield, to request his endorsement of the proposed agreement. The two men went over the document in some detail. When Garfield learned that the miners had not been consulted and knew nothing of the company's proposal, he refused to give it the sanction of his office. He did, however, promise to discuss the matter further with one of his advisors, Rembrandt Peale. The following day, Peale called on Wheelwright and advised that in view of the strike in the Maryland district and the negotiations underway, the Fuel Administration could not give its approval to the company's proposal. Peale indicated that both he and Garfield thought the proposal was admirable in many particulars and that it moved in the direction they would like to see the industry develop, but the timing was amiss. The most pressing matter was to find the terms that would bring the Maryland work stoppage to an end.

As they continued their discussion, one of the two men—it is not clear which from the account Wheelwright rendered to King— suggested that perhaps the Consolidation proposal might be altered to meet the needs of the Maryland situation. They struck out the name of the company wherever it appeared in the proposal and inserted that of the U.S. Fuel Administration. They then redrew the agreement to apply exclusively to the mines in the Maryland district. In this way, the company's proposed provisions guaranteeing the right of union membership without discrimination, and establishing mine committees, dispute settlement machinery, a system of checkweighmen, etc. were transformed into initiatives of the Fuel Administration and became the basis for the settlement of the Maryland dispute.

Peale quickly won Garfield's approval for this strategem. He also won the support of his coadvisor for coal, John S. White, the former president of the United Mine Workers. (Peale represented the operator interests.) When the negotiating committee for the Maryland operators arrived at the offices of the Fuel Administration, a small charade was played out for its benefit. Peale, in the presence of White and the negotiating committee, handed Wheelwright a copy of the proposed agreement to read aloud. The committee eagerly accepted what it took to be the government's proposal and adjourned to carry the agreement back for the approval of the full operators' group. At this juncture, a snag developed. The operators conditioned their acceptance on assurances that the United Mine Workers would drop its bid for recognition.

Wheelwright urgently summoned King back to Baltimore to deal with what seemed to be an impasse. Once the situation was explained to him in detail, King proposed a course of action. In Wheelwright's name, he drafted a letter to Peale and White in which he suggested that the Fuel Administration propose an exchange of written guarantees. The mine workers' union would pledge itself not to press for recognition for the life of the agreement. The operators would pledge to fulfill the terms of the agreement provided the question of recognition did not arise during the life of the contract. Peale and White took up the suggestion and found that both sides were amenable to such an exchange. The Maryland strike quickly ended to the satisfaction of all parties.

King had good reason to be proud of his achievement. The new contract gave the miners everything that the union could have hoped to win for them. The U.M.W.'s acceptance of the agreement signified as much. That the Fuel Administration also had seen fit to adopt his terms as its own, without knowing anything about his involvement, confirmed the wisdom of the policies he advocated. In time, he reasoned, the Maryland operators were also bound to learn from their experience of dealing fairly and openly with their men. The gains from less than two weeks work were clear and substantial: improved living and working conditions for the miners; a system that would permit the amicable resolution of future disagreements; the resumption of vital coal production; and a set of policies that could guide the labor program of the Fuel Administration. King rightly regarded this as war work of the utmost importance.

How he rationalized a quite different action taken on behalf of Rockefeller at this same time is unknown. While on the East Coast in early May, King traveled to Boston to confer with his publisher. Somehow or other Rockefeller had learned that this same publisher was about to bring out a book by one Elizabeth Hasanovitz. At some point in the manuscript, she must have touched on the Colorado Industrial Plan, for otherwise Rockefeller would probably not have intervened. All that survives of the episode is King's report that he had met with the author and succeeded in inducing her to modify portions of the book that were "unhappily phrased."[11] Rockefeller's putative role as the leading reformer of capitalism apparently gave King sanction for meddling of this sort.

A rather different and more wholesome service was exacted of King later in May as he accompanied Rockefeller and Mrs. Rockefeller to Colorado. King served as guide on their tour of inspection of the C.F. & I. mining camps. Rockefeller also counted heavily on his assistance in evaluating the effectiveness of the representation plan and the expenditures made on camp improvements. Unlike the previous visit to Colorado, this wartime sojourn was private, unaccompanied by the press or press agents. Yet the events of the visit were easily as newsworthy and, in one instance, overshadowed in drama and human interest all of the earlier stories.

As the party moved about from camp to camp, King and the Rockefellers talked with miners, their families, and with management people about conditions in each camp. They particularly sought out the elected miner representatives and questioned them about the strengths and weaknesses of the plan. When shortcomings were brought to their attention, they took the matter up with company officials in an effort to bring about correction. For the most part, they were pleased to learn that the plan was working to everybody's satisfaction. King took it as evidence of the plan's effectiveness that in one camp the union had given up its effort to organize. He reflected that, overall, the atmosphere in the camps was positive and relaxed.

To King's way of thinking, the physical environment of the

The Ludlow Monument. By permission of the Colorado Historical Society.

camps was as crucial a factor in shaping their atmosphere as any other aspect of the terms of employment. He therefore carefully observed and reflected on the camp improvements that had been made since his initial survey three years earlier. Since then, Rockefeller and his father had underwritten the construction of numbers of community structures. In addition, the bulk of the rents received from camp houses had been plowed back in the form of improvements. King learned that, in 1917, ninety-one percent of all rent receipts were expended on house repairs and improvements. While rents had been maintained at their 1915 level, wages had since climbed by about fifty percent. All told, in the three years prior to 1918, the company had spent a quarter of a million dollars on capital improvements in the camps. King was told that because of the attractive living conditions and good pay, C.F. & I. was now a preferred company to work for among Colorado miners. He could not help sharing the officers' pride in this achievement. It did not occur to him, however, that the company's generous terms and conditions of employment might have been critical to the success of the representation plan.

On the very first day of the tour, the party drove by Ludlow at Mrs. Rockefeller's urging. She too was drawn, as her husband had been, to the scene of the tragedy. They were surprised to find standing there, under wraps, a large stone monument. That evening King picked up a flyer announcing a Memorial Day ceremony at the site, under the auspices of the United Mine Workers' Union. Union officials would speak and unveil a monument dedicated to the memory of those who had perished in the Ludlow Massacre, four years earlier. The public was invited to attend.

During their tour the following day, King brought up the subject of the memorial. He urged Rockefeller to go to the dedication ceremonies and, if possible, participate in them by addressing the audience. Rockefeller responded that he had been thinking along the very same lines. He agreed that they should give the matter further consideration.

The following morning, the morning of Memorial Day, they renewed their discussion at breakfast in the presence of Mrs. Rockefeller and several company officials. Rockefeller began by expressing his feeling that it was right for him to go to Ludlow. C.F. & I. vice president Weitzel immediately concurred. Mrs. Rockefeller said that she also believed that was the right thing to do and announced that she would accompany her husband.

Later in the morning, when they were alone, Rockefeller talked with King about what he would say if the opportunity to speak arose. As King recorded it in his diary:

> He said he would open by referring to Mrs. Rockefeller being with him; that having noticed the nature of the occasion, they had come to express their respect for the memory of those whose lives had been lost in the unhappy occurrences of four years ago, and their sympathy for the surviving relatives and friends. He would not dwell upon the past, nor was there need now to seek to apportion either blame or praise. Undoubtedly mistakes had been made in which all had shared, and which all regretted; that we could only be true to the best by seeking to profit by mistakes and make impossible their occurrence in the future. Memorial Day had arisen from the Civil War. The armies of the North and South had been in conflict with each other; today they were united in furthering the cause of liberty in the world at large. So, too, he hoped it would be with Labor and Capital in industry. They had been in conflict in the past, and he hoped that the new era was dawning in which they would cooperate . . .[12]

At lunch, it was learned that the union leaders contacted about Rockefeller's attendance at the ceremony were divided about extending him an invitation. Fearful that someone in the audience might say or do something embarrassing or harmful, they wanted to avoid any responsibility. On hearing this, the C.F. & I. officials with whom the Rockefellers and King were lunching, spoke up against his going. But Rockefeller insisted that it was the right thing to do and Mrs. Rockefeller supported him. She urged him to speak as well, saying that attendance alone was of little consequence. Although he then tried to persuade Mrs. Rockefeller not to accompany him, she and King prevailed. The three of them accompanied by a driver drove out to Ludlow, where the ceremonies were already underway.

Mr. and Mrs. Rockefeller remained in the car with the driver while King walked to the speakers' stand and surveyed the scene. Between one thousand and two thousand people were present, many of them picnicking or visiting the refreshment booths. Relatively few were listening to the young man who was speaking either in Spanish or Italian. King wasn't sure which, for a high wind carried off most of the speaker's words. On approaching the side of the stand, he recognized Frank Hayes, the U.M.W. president, and introduced himself. Hayes called over his colleagues, former president John White and vice president William Green. John L. Lewis was also on the platform but he did not participate in the brief conversation that followed.

King informed the unionists that Mr. and Mrs. Rockefeller were present and would like to remain for part of the afternoon. Hayes asked if Rockefeller had it in mind to speak. He went on to say that much as he and his colleagues would like that, they were apprehensive about how the audience would react. They appreciated the spirit he showed in coming to the ceremonies but hoped that he would understand their reluctance to have him speak. King accepted this and then invited the union leaders to come to the car to greet Rockefeller. White, however, demurred and Green and Hayes followed his lead. King returned to the car alone and related the sense of the exchange. The Rockefeller party then drove off to pick up its schedule of camp visits.

All of those privy to Rockefeller's decision to attend the dedication ceremonies had been very much alive to the risks involved. The consequent release of tensions when nothing happened was cathartic. King, in reflecting on the events of the day in his diary that evening, conjured up the worst possible outcome, recalling the assassinations of Presidents Lincoln, Garfield, and McKinley. Yet, he told himself, Rockefeller had *had* to attend. It was the exactly right thing to do even at the risk of his life. As was King's wont, he perceived the hand of God at work, "it was a means which Providence had prepared for enabling him [Rockefeller] to wipe off the slate, as far as he was concerned, the stain against his name and that of his family which the memories of Ludlow had hitherto suggested." [13]

In writing this, King implied that Rockefeller accepted the blame for the Ludlow Massacre, that he felt himself tainted by it and looked upon the dangerous pilgrimage that day as a form of expiation. But none of these things was true. Rockefeller never accepted responsibility for the Colorado strike's violence and deaths. Nor did he hold himself culpable for the massacre. He initially denied that there was a massacre and subsequently could not bring himself to utter the phrase "Ludlow massacre", as if refusing to sound the name would erase the event. He admitted no error, no guilt. From soon after the massacre to the day of the dedication ceremonies, as his proposed speech reveals, he took a position from which he never deviated. He held that it was pointless to look back and try to lay blame; that mistakes had been made on both sides; and that what was important was to ensure against any future recurrence of such strife. By this argument, he avoided both the responsibility and the guilt that everyone else, King included, believed him to hold.

King's misreading of Rockefeller's motivation at such close range makes it easier to understand why both contemporary observers at greater remove, and then historians would draw the same faulty inference. The excitement and tension surrounding the visit to the memorial ceremony appear to have blocked King's usually incisive grasp of events in other ways as well. Whenever he felt extraordinarily pleased with a turn of good fortune, King was likely to blame God. The events of this day prove no exception. As he wrote,

> Hereafter, whenever Ludlow is mentioned, the thought of the people of this continent will go at once to the circumstance that Mr. R. himself went to the memorial services . . . [this] makes it seem that Providence itself has rewarded his effort to wipe out the past by giving him this sublime occasion.[14]

King clearly misjudged the earthly consequences of the day. Among those who know some history, Ludlow remains invariably linked with connotations of Rockefeller wrongdoing. It could be argued that on this occasion Rockefeller's sense for public relations let him down and that, had his presence at the ceremonies been widely publicized, it might have won for him the exoneration King predicted. Yet, for all the thoughts of personal danger and bravery, Rockefeller was hardly present at the ceremonies. By putting himself at the disposal of the union leaders, he ended up waiting in the car while King carried messages back and forth; an unrepentant penitent at an American Golgotha.

Several days after this excitement, Rockefeller and King were galvanized into a different line of action by events two thousand miles away. At breakfast, King brought up a newspaper report of a raging controversy between the National War Labor Board and the Western Union Telegraph Company. He related how the company discharged over eight hundred of its employees simply because they had joined a union. The Board had stepped into the case and recommended that the men be reinstated, which the company refused to do. In consequence, the Board had now brought the dispute to President Wilson and advised him that it lacked further power to compel the acceptance of its recommendation.

King told Rockefeller that Western Union's blatant discrimination against union members could not be tolerated in wartime. Public sentiment aside, it flew in the face of the announced principles of the War Labor Board. He prophesied that the company, and probably other public utility firms as well, would come to rue the day they had forced the government's hand. For there was every likelihood that the government would now push the company further into the arms of the union than was either necessary or desirable. By granting concessions, Western Union might have avoided this and achieved an outcome more to its liking.

Rockefeller proved very receptive to King's analysis. He knew the president of Western Union, Newcomb Carlton, personally and suggested that they get in touch with him. They could explain employee representation and encourage him to introduce a plan at Western Union. They could also allay any fears he might have about conceding the right of employees to join unions by describing their own experience at C.F. & I.

King's initial reaction to this suggestion was that the situation was too dangerous to touch. He may or he may not have been influenced by the knowledge that before coming to Colorado, Frank Walsh, cochairman of the National War Labor Board, had attempted to arrange an interview with Rockefeller. Walsh had wanted to discuss a pressing matter pending before the board, possibly the Western Union case. Rockefeller's nephew, Percy Rockefeller, was a member of the company's board of directors. However, Rockefeller had been confined to his sickbed at the time, so no meeting had taken place. This happenstance left him free to react in any way he chose to the Western Union dispute. But, if Walsh had wanted Rockefeller's help, he might not have been prepared to accept it in the form in which Rockefeller now proposed to give it.

On rethinking the matter later the same day, King changed his mind. He now saw no reason why they should not offer their advice to Carlton. Their intervention might provide the ingredients for a settlement, as it had in the Maryland coal strike, and that, after all, was the main objective of all the parties. Moreover, should Western Union adopt an employee representation plan as a result of their counsel, they would be simultaneously "furthering the Labor movement along safe lines." [15]

He and Rockefeller then collaborated in preparing a telegram addressed to Starr Murphy in New York. They instructed Murphy to call on Carlton and relay their message about the benefits of an employee representation plan. A critical portion of the message read:

> Moreover, we have found that the full concession to employees of right to join any organization, when accompanied by a plan of representation of employees within the company itself, has not in the slightest interfered with the maintenance of an open shop.[16]

The following evening, Carlton responded through Murphy that Rockefeller could help him most by sending King to him immediately. Both Mr. and Mrs. Rockefeller seemed agreeable that he should go, but King dissuaded them. He argued that it would be extremely unwise to accede to Carlton's request. Should his involvement with Western Union become a matter of public knowledge, it would be made to appear that he was acting at Rockefeller's behest to help the company "frame machinery which was intended to defeat trade unionism." King warned that, "should such an impression, though wholly without foundation, ever arise" it would jeopardize everything they had accomplished over the past three years.[17]

But was any such impression "wholly without foundation"? How, without being profoundly hypocritical, could King deny any intention to "defeat trade unionism" when with his previous breath he had proffered the "maintenance of the open shop" as the incentive for adopting employee representation? On the face of it, King seems to have been caught up in a glaring inconsistency.

Being neither a fool nor a hypocrite, he did possess a perspective from which his actions and words made consistent good sense. The trouble was that, like most people, he rarely articulated the basic assumptions that guided his thinking. This difficulty was compounded in the present instance because when King gave expression to these basic assumptions—they would be articulated in his diary and his book—he revealed more ambivalence than he supposed.

King believed that the labor problem would not be and could not be solved in the near future. The employers and the unions were much too far apart for that. Yet, in the long run, he was certain that the unions or something like them were destined to gain their point, for they gave expression to workers' aspirations for industrial democracy. Just as the earlier struggle to enlarge the franchise had marked out the evolutionary development of political democracy, so the development and spread of worker organizations would blaze the emergent trail of industrial democracy. Just as in the past the main barriers to progress had been power and privilege, so in the modern era as well. A class of arrogant capitalists had merely displaced an equally arrogant class of landed aristocrats on the ramparts of the status quo.

King believed that his fortunate liaison with Rockefeller, in a manner of speaking, had thrust him into the headquarters of the enemy camp. He saw himself a uniquely placed agent of change, a labor advocate cast as an advisor to a powerful employer. He regarded Rockefeller as the most benign and well intentioned of the employer class. Had he used his position to tell Rockefeller— and through him, the other employers—that they must accept and learn to live with the unions, they would have distrusted and expelled him. Instead, he believed, he had created in employee representation a device that won him their confidence and simultaneously, led toward their metamorphosis. For, if it did nothing else, employee representation changed employers by teaching them the need for and the benefits of regular contact with their employees. By accustoming employers to having union members in their shops and factories, the nondiscrimination clause contributed to the same end. Employee representation went still further. It led to real improvements in the terms and conditions of employment. It provided workers with organizational skills and lessons in the wisdom of collective action. Unbeknownst to themselves, both the workers and their employers were being schooled for the time when employee representation would evolve into something grander. Then the employers would no longer oppose the organization of their employees because they would have learned that organization was as much in their own interests as it was in the employees'. By then, he believed, the labor unions would also have matured into agencies of cooperation rather than conflict. Peopled by workers skilled in the crafts of industrial democracy, they would hold an honored place in society.

From this perspective, King saw no inconsistency in his advocacy of employee representation. On the contrary, in his view, the threat of paralyzing disputes over union organizing and recognition during the war emergency rendered his position more valuable than ever. It seemed to him that in the Western Union situation, as in the Maryland coal strike, a representation plan coupled with a nondiscrimination clause was the most—indeed the only—effective solution available. He recognized, however, that his position could easily be misunderstood. Union leaders and their allies were not likely to accept an intervention that appeared intended to frustrate them in their objectives. For this reason, he did not want to turn up at Carlton's side in the current strike.

Instead, in a coded telegram in which he became "Nucleoid," King advised the Western Union president to develop a representation plan along the lines of the C.F. & I. model and to include a nondiscrimination clause. He assured Carlton that if he was prepared to take these steps, he would find the government willing to help win guarantees from the union against disruptive activities for the duration of the war. This was the same bargain employed so successfully in the Maryland strike.

By this time, however, Carlton had boxed himself in so badly in his dealings with the War Labor Board that he could not, or would not, follow King's advice. When President Wilson publicly requested the company to comply with the recommendations of the War Labor Board, Carlton again refused. The President then seized the company and placed it under the jurisdiction of the Postmaster General. The long distance intervention King and Rockefeller had attempted had failed.

In talking over the Western Union situation, King pointed out to Rockefeller the altered status of their invention. Up until now, he noted, employee representation had been a sensible step for companies to take if they wanted to avoid labor troubles. It had been a purely voluntary action, lacking in urgency. Sad to say, relatively few firms had shown the foresight or daring to introduce plans. The war and the War Labor Board, he continued, had altered the situation dramatically. Two Board policies were particularly relevant. One ran to the effect that the Board would not intervene in disputes in which the parties had established and not exhausted their own means for settling differences. The other acknowledged the right of employers to deal only with their own employees in situations where some employees were union members and some were not. The effect of these policies was to make the adoption of representation plans much more attractive to firms.

Board policy also strengthened the appeal of the nondiscrimination clause, he pointed out. Carlton had objected to union members among his employees on the grounds that the nature of Western Union's business demanded the undivided loyalty of its employees. This was untenable in view of the right of workers to organize. With a representation plan and a truly open shop with both union members and nonunion employees, the company would have had an internal means for settling disputes. Moreover, it would not have been obliged to deal with employee spokesmen who were not in its employ. King could see no reason why such a compromise would have been against the interests of either the company or the union. Each side would have sacrificed what he regarded as a hollow principle for an effective working relationship.

Though King prided himself on the breadth of his vision and could discourse eloquently on historical parallels and the likely shape of the future, when it came to action his clear preference was almost always narrowly pragmatic. In the context of labor, at any rate, his experiences as a mediator and his overriding concern for conflict resolution, predisposed him to favor short-term solutions, ways to make things work right now. This often blinded him to the longer-term consequences of his position, consequences that many employers and union leaders refused to ignore.

To the employers, letting known unionists into their employ, as King advised, meant complete unionization in the future; it meant the hated closed shop. To many union leaders, foregoing recognition, as he advocated, would have seemed equally suicidal. It meant the absence of the only force capable of pushing for fair and equitable treatment in a sustained way. It meant continuing problems of membership, dues collection, free riders, and discipline, all to the disadvantage of the organization. Thus, where the employers feared the rotten apple, so to speak, the unionists feared an empty barrel. Neither group regarded their principles as hollow.

In the course of their conversation about Western Union, Rockefeller brought out that he had been trying to persuade the president of the New York Standard Oil Company to introduce a representation plan, without much success. In time, he said, he wanted all of the various Standard Oil companies to adopt plans, but he could not push them too far too fast. He noted that even though all of the officers of New York Standard Oil were salaried men and his father held most of the company's stock, his suggestions were often treated with indifference. If King was correct in his appraisal of the situation, and he believed he was, this might be the opportune time to press the matter again. He and King then proceeded to draft a letter addressed to the company president.

That same day they learned from the newspaper that all of the coal companies in the state of Virginia had adopted representation plans like the one Consolidation Coal had introduced in its mines. The following day, an advisor in the U.S. Fuel Administration told them that he anticipated nationwide imitation of the Consolidation plan throughout the coal industry. Once again events confirmed for them the wisdom of their advocacy.

Their tour of C.F. & I. facilities completed, Mr. and Mrs. Rockefeller left for New York, quite satisfied with most of the changes they had observed. King remained behind to help with additional adjustments. He also spent several days in consultation with officers of the Denver-based Great Western Sugar Company. Rockefeller's brother-in-law, S. M. Edgell, was a vice president in the company and provided the connection. King agreed to return in the fall to study working conditions in the company's sugar factories. In the interim, he committed himself to finding suitable candidates for the company's newly created office of employment manager.

As he took leave of Denver and the Welborns, King could not help reflecting that, although he liked Mrs. Welborn very much, what Mrs. Rockefeller had said of her was true. Now that the tension and travail at C.F. & I. had given way to peace and prosperity, she had become self-indulgent. She had lost her concern for the welfare of others. King thought that Jesse Welborn, too, had grown complacent.

This demonstrated the wisdom of something that he supposed he had always known, that the workers were the only ones who could properly look after their own interests. Even in the hands of a well-meaning company officer, they would not expect to gain their proper due. This seemed particularly true in the present instance because the officers were men who rose from the ranks. Mobile men of this sort, he believed, "have a sort of contempt for their fellows." In contrast, managers with a broader background and a liberal education were more likely to understand human limitations. He thought they were also more likely to recognize that the opportunity they had enjoyed was "only an occasion for larger services."[18]

These musings suggest the origins of Rockefeller's earlier remarks to the same effect. They also bear the implication that King did not see himself as one who rose from the ranks but as one whose advantages obligated service. However, consider the inconsistency between his thought that workers alone could defend their interests and the paternalism inherent in his representation scheme. The only way he could bridge the two positions was by telling himself that the C.F. & I. miners weren't yet ready for self-government. His own arguments against closing the camps to organizers, gamblers, etc., logically denied him even this escape. In time, this inconsistency may have helped lead him away from employee representation. For the moment, however, he was one of its two champions.

Hardly had he settled in Ottawa when King received a wire requesting that he come to Bethlehem, Pennsylvania. John M. Larkin of the Bethlehem Shipbuilding Corporation wanted to discuss the introduction of employee representation into the company's shipyards. Larkin had mentioned his interest in the Standard Oil plan to Clarence Hicks, who had referred him to King.

As King had foreseen, the action of government boards, in this instance, the Shipbuilding Labor Adjustment Board, in imposing shop committees where no labor adjustment machinery existed increased the incentive for and interest in employee representation. He advised that he would come to Bethlehem.

On the day of Larkin's wire, King also received a letter from Rockefeller, devoted largely to the recent trip of George Vincent to England. From what Vincent had told him, Rockefeller believed that the future course of industrial relations would be shaped in England within the coming year. He suggested that if King were to visit England sometime within the next six months, he might be able to contribute to the shaping process, on the basis of their experience in Colorado. He could also learn how the British were meeting their labor problems and bring back helpful information. King was thrilled by the prospect of such a trip and arranged to meet Rockefeller immediately after his stop in Bethlehem.

The work for the shipbuilding company proved to be the beginning of a hectic and lucrative period for King. He spent the first two days of July conferring with company officials. On arriving, he learned that they had it in mind to organize some sort of informal employees' society. He argued that a representation plan was much more than that. It created an explicit and formal system of organization and consultation. He went on to explain that its most critical feature was that it enhanced the status of labor by acknowledging its rightful place in the decision-making process. With little difficulty, he persuaded the officers that his was the wisest course for them to follow. Before departing for a Fourth of July holiday with the Rockefellers at Pocantico, he drafted a plan for their consideration and adoption. All of his subsequent dealings with the company were carried on through the mails and telegraph.

On his return to Ottawa, King resumed work on his book. As he wrote, he reviewed the recent literature to learn what other writers offered in the way of suggestions for dealing with labor problems. Throughout the summer, his diary was filled alternately with reflections on his reading and with notes of his comings and goings as a consultant. Very often he found in what he read confirmation for his own point of view. This was particularly true of the second Whitley Councils Report and the writings of Beatrice and Sidney Webb from England, and of Julius H. Cohen's American work *Law and Order in Industry*. Sometimes, however, he found new food for thought. He was surprised to learn, in Earl Dean Howard's work on the labor agreement at Hart, Schaffner and Marx, of a working relationship in which a company effectively cooperated with a trade union. He did not believe that many American companies or unions were mature enough to sustain such a relationship.

In between revisions of the representation plan for Bethlehem Shipbuilding, he concluded that there were three main causes of industrial conflict. Working conditions headed the list, followed by the absence of any means for uncovering and rectifying grievances. The third cause was the absence of joint control, by which he meant the equal participation in the conduct of industry by owners, managers, workers, and representatives of the public. Much of his writing in this period would reveal his absorption with the latter idea. He was obsessed with the idea of equality, without recognizing that he truly meant and much preferred, equity or fairness.

By the time Bethlehem informed him of the introduction of his plan and the first elections under it, King had turned his attention to the considerably more complicated labor situation at the General Electric Company. He had been called in as a consultant by company counsel Guy W. Currier, who knew of his work at Bethlehem.

In some of its plants, G.E. was under fire from the War Labor Board to correct its practices and establish shop committees. In others, spontaneous work stoppages had caught company officials unprepared and unsure about how to respond. In still others, quiet prevailed. From late July through the end of August, King visited the main G.E. plants at Lynn and Pittsfield in Massachusetts and at Schenectady, New York. He learned that at G.E. the plant managers exerted considerable autonomy, and that he would have to persuade them individually of the merits of employee representation. The plants were so autonomous that he was surprised to find in several of them that small clusters of craft unionism had existed for years. The managers in these plants dealt with the unions informally, bargaining in effect but without any show of recognition.

For the benefit of the corporate-level officers with whom he conferred in Boston, and sometimes in New York, King prepared a lengthy memorandum. In it, he described the sources of the company's labor problems, tracing them in each instance to the absence of a system of joint employer–employee committees. He also drafted representation plans, which were eventually adopted in some plants but not in others. When the manager of the Lynn plant, whom he sensed to be an inflexible old liner, installed the plan but without several of its standard provisions, King could do no more than groan in his diary. He may have taken some satisfaction when that particular plant subsequently ran afoul of the War Labor Board.

In the midst of the work at General Electric, King was called upon by the Bethlehem Steel Company. Again, Guy Currier made the contact and the War Labor Board precipitated the company's interest. The Board had recently ordered Bethlehem to alter its practices and create a system of shop committees. King was probably unaware of an added element of tension in the steel industry at the time. In mid-June, the A.F. of L. convention had authorized a nationwide organizing drive targeted at steel workers.

Once at Bethlehem, King met with company officials including president Eugene Grace. Grace informed him that they had examined the plan he developed for the shipbuilding company and had decided to introduce a similar plan into the steel works. Their decision, he asserted, was wholly unrelated to the War Labor Board ruling. Rather, it was a step whose time had come in the evolution of industry. Of course, if in adopting a representation plan the company also satisfied the Board, so much the better. Grace then asked King to explain his ideas about representation, which King was happy to do. Grace listened intently and at the conclusion knew exactly what to say. He told King that, although the idea of representation had first been developed and tested at C.F. & I., it would take hold and diffuse more widely once it was adopted by a major eastern corporation like Bethlehem. King agreed and accepted Grace's offer to go to work immediately.

In just four days, he mastered the structure of the company, conferred with all the relevant officials, and drafted the appropriate memoranda. The first of these memoranda presented an employment contract to be tendered to the employees. Among other things, this contract responded to each of the employment issues raised by the War Labor Board. Either King had persuaded Grace that such a response was necessary or he had known from the outset that Grace had been temporizing in his remarks about the Board. The second memorandum embodied the plan of representation; the third provided a step-by-step procedure to be followed in introducing the plan and the contract. This last document reveals that King's primary purpose was to shield the company from the War Labor Board. It also indicates the lengths to which he was prepared to go to help the company accomplish this end.

The terms and conditions offered by the company in the employment contract that King prepared were not equal to those recommended by the Board. Foreseeing that the Board might press for the adoption of its more liberal terms, King advised that the company might be able to have a group of employees join it "in laying the exact position of [company financial] affairs before the authorities in Washington." [19] In other words, in a period of unprecedented profitability, the company might use its employees to help it cry poor before the Board. The memorandum went on to conclude that in the event the employees refused to cooperate with the company in any way, the company could present copies of its proposed contract and representation plan to the Board in evidence of its efforts to meet Board recommendations.

By the time he left Bethlehem, King was sufficiently troubled not to want to return. Perhaps, he was fearful that his confidential role would come to be known. It is more likely, however, that he sensed that Grace and his colleagues had no intention of seriously consulting with or listening to their employees. Untypically, King did not commit his feelings to his diary.

He had just completed his work for G.E. when he received an urgent summons from J. H. Wheelwright of Consolidation Coal. As a result, he spent several days in Fairmont, West Virginia, conferring with Wheelwright, Clarence Watson, George Watson, and A. R. Hamilton. Clarence Watson was chairman of the board of directors of Consolidation. He was also the Democratic nominee for the U.S. Senate. A. R. Hamilton published a coal industry journal in Pittsburgh. He since has been identified by Dubofsky and Van Tine (1977) as the *eminence grise* of the industry.

It quickly became apparent to King that he had not been summoned to give advice but to receive and transmit a message. Wheelwright and Watson informed him that Consolidation was going to abandon its representation plan and sign a contract with the United Mine Workers. This surprising about-face, they explained, had been brought about as the result of an order of the U.S. Fuel Administration. Henceforth, companies were to cease basing wages on the mine car and would have to pay by the ton. They asserted that under the existing plan, this change would increase wages twenty cents per ton. The union, however, was prepared to sign an agreement by which wages would rise only eight cents a ton. This spread was so great that, in the best interests of the company, they felt duty bound to settle with the union. Hamilton subsequently boasted to King that he had talked the matter through with Frank Hayes and John L. Lewis. That was why they were so sure of the terms on which the union would agree. He also indicated that the company had secured the election as local union officers of men who were known to it and dependable.

King did not believe all of what he was told. He surmised that the true reason for recognizing the union was to win votes for Watson's senatorial campaign. Hamilton was obviously the broker in this deal. From the way these men talked, King concluded they were quite accustomed to buying the support of labor where they could not achieve their ends through force. It followed then, he surmised, that the officers of the U.M.W. were also prepared to make deals of this sort. But King was mistaken in supposing the union leaders to be as venal as the company officers in this affair. The union's primary object in striking a bargain—that it could not keep, as the election results would reveal—was to bring an end to the widespread use of "the bludgeon system"[20] by West Virginia operators.

The thought of being used to carry a message to Rockefeller rankled King. Then, in his last meeting with Wheelwright, the question of his fee came up. He deferred to Wheelwright's judgment and, when the latter suggested $1000, King accepted. The incident brought to the surface his highly ambivalent feelings toward money. His diary entry reads like a tennis match between his conscience and his greater powers of rationalization:

> I thanked him cordially—I did not say it was the easiest $1,000 I had ever made in my life. My feeling was one of sadness that dear father or [brother] Max had not had some such chances. I felt too that corporation money wasted in this manner was wrong. I doubt if I would have agreed to accept it, but for all the work I did earlier in the year & Wheelwright's intention to have this come out of Mr. R.'s retainer. Besides the loss of this week has been serious and it came on top of refusals to go to Lynn, and efforts to keep away from Bethlehem Steel . . .[21]

On returning to New York, King spent an evening at Pocantico. Rockefeller was visibly pleased with the work he had been doing at Bethlehem Steel and General Electric. King passed up the opportunity to unburden himself of his misgivings about the steel company. Instead, he told Rockefeller about developments at Consolidation Coal, which Rockefeller characterized as "base treachery."[22] Rockefeller said he would have preferred to have the company sacrifice the twelve cents a ton difference rather than deal with the union. King understood that his greatest concern was that Consolidation's action might hurt further adoptions of the plan. His own feeling in the matter was that it was to Rockefeller's advantage to have some investments in companies with union contracts. He did not, however, express this thought; nor did he dwell on the degree to which unionism and employee representation were rivals in Rockefeller's thinking.

They dined at Rockefeller Senior's house and King found his host very pleasant, as usual. After dinner, as they walked him to the car, Rockefeller told his father something that pleased King enough to record in his diary. He said "that I had done more for them than they had ever done for me."[23] King needed praise of this sort and, when it was not forthcoming, tended to become petulant and hypercritical. Such feelings were occasioned later that fall, for example, by what he took to be Rockefeller's lack of enthusiasm for his book.

King had hoped to write the last words of *Industry and Humanity* on the anniversary of his father's birth, in mid-September, but he could not. The last touches to the text and the preface were completed on October 3, a day of no auspiciousness. Within less than two weeks, Rockefeller had received and read the galley proofs of the final chapters. King already had some sense that Rockefeller entertained reservations about what he had done, but he could not help feeling hurt by his prefunctory praise for his "bold conceptions . . . and true originality." [24]

The previous December, King had sent Rockefeller the first five chapters of the book. Rockefeller read them and asked Starr Murphy and Rockefeller Foundation president Vincent to read them as well. Vincent had returned critical comments to Rockefeller and subsequently had discussed his evaluation with King. On this latter occasion, King learned that the Foundation would receive his report but would not publish it.

Vincent had told Rockefeller that the opening chapters dealt in broad abstractions and, for that reason, would disappoint those who were looking for concrete programs and policy guidelines. On the other hand, social scientists and other experts would probably fault King's methods and his line of reasoning. Since he had only seen a portion of a larger work, Vincent charitably suggested that it was too soon to render a final estimate. The points he raised, however, were telling.

Even when completed *Industry and Humanity* was hardly a report. It presented no accumulated facts or evidence. It made no pretense to scientific objectivity. Instead, it put foward a curiously old-fashioned polemic based on King's experiences, delivered up as a personal statement on the causes and cures of industrial conflict. Part memoir, part lecture, and part prophecy, the volume attempted to raise the significance of employee representation from the level of an expedient to that of the first step in a grand evolutionary design. If their adventure in Colorado had shifted the arc of Rockefeller's life, *Industry and Humanity* provided the evidence of a similar impact upon King.

He began the book with the argument that the world war and industrial conflict were fundamentally alike: both resulted from mistrust and misunderstanding and both could be cured by building trust through institutionalized channels of communication. In developing the international-industrial parallel, King employed terms borrowed from Louis Pasteur. Although he professed to revere Pasteur, he gave to his words a literal quality that had not been intended. Consequently, King's expansions on the *Law of Peace, Work, and Health* and the *Law of Blood and Death* smacked of pseudo-science, when he simply meant to discuss good and evil. His *Law of Competing Standards* and *Law of Christian Service* were cast in a similar mold. The opening chapters made it clear, as Vincent had recognized, that this was a highly idiosyncratic work.

In seeking to explain the mistrust and misunderstanding that resulted in industrial conflict, King skillfully placed much of the blame with the employers without appearing to do so. Their failure to wield power with intelligence and concern for the consequences had created a labor force dominated by feelings of fear and insecurity. One response to this had been the organization of militant, combative trade unions; another had been to raise demands for public intervention. In both instances, the shortsightedness of the employers fostered attitudes and the growth of institutions that, in seeking to provide workers with some measure of defense or protection, tended also to stand athwart industrial efficiency and growth. This, in turn, provoked the enmity of the employers.

The only way out of this self-destructive cycle was to recognize that industry was necessarily a cooperative undertaking. Its success, therefore, hinged on the ability to elicit the fullest collaboration of all participants. Any technique or institution that hoped to achieve this would have to serve fairly the interests of them all. It was in this context that King put forward employee representation as the crucial first step.

He prophesied that it would take a considerable time for society to evolve the Round Table Conference, at which all four of the partners in industry—capital, management, labor, and the community—were represented and dealt with one another as equals. Drawing a direct parallel between the evolution of industrial democracy and the development of political democracy, he estimated that industrial rights had reached a stage comparable in the history of political rights to the reign of the Plantagenets. Most of his models and precedents (e.g., the Round Table) were English.

To justify the existence of four partners in industry, King began with the usual factors of production, land, labor, and capital. Lumping land and capital together as forms of wealth, he then followed the growing convention of separating management from labor as a distinct factor. Supposing that his contention for a role for the community was the most controversial, he devoted the bulk of his argument to defending this point. He held that in providing the political and social conditions and the institutional framework necessary to industry, the community ranked as a full partner. Overall, however, his factors of production approach was not entirely consistent with the assumption that each of the partners had independent interests. When he discussed the separation of ownership from management in the large corporation in particular, he did so without identifying any significant differences in the purposes or objectives of the two groups. If there were none, it was not clear why both capital and management were entitled to seats at the Round Table. With interests that were substantially the same, these two partners would commonly work as one.

Here, as elsewhere in the volume, King appears to have been heavily influenced by his experience at Colorado Fuel & Iron. Given Rockefeller's determination not to replace the managers who had misled him during the strike, one of King's very first tasks as his advisor had been to develop a rationalization for intervening over the heads of Welborn and Bowers. At the time, King had argued that managers tended to be too close to the situation to have a healthy perspective on labor matters. For that reason, capital had to assume an independent responsibility toward labor. This flimsy argument alone underpinned the notion that capital and management were distinct and independent partners in the large corporation.

When he turned to a discussion of the proper role of the community in labor matters, King took a very long-term perspective. He ruled out any perpetuation of laissez-faire capitalism. He also rejected the collectivist variant of socialism, by which he meant a society that permitted no private property and in which economic activity was dominated completely by the State. Two other variants of socialism seemed to him far preferable. One of these he identified as Christian Socialism, which looked to worker ownership and operation of industry with little or no need for State involvement. The other, which he called Municipal or State Socialism, involved public ownership and direction only of vital industries such as transportation, communications, food, natural resources, and utilities. Under such a regime, the State would also be responsible for ensuring that no citizen fell below an agreed upon minimum standard of living. King clearly sympathized with the goal of Christian Socialism, but he also hailed the reconstruction program of the British Labour Party as the most advanced expression of the State Socialism model.

His preference for State Socialism over Collectivism, as he distinguished them, derived from the ample room the former preserved for private property and individual initiative. He preferred Christian Socialism to Syndicalism for similar reasons. While these two systems seemed bound for the same end result of worker-owned industry, the former proposed to achieve its aims through the thrift and the growing education and understanding of workers. In contrast, the Syndicalists advocated class warfare and fostered sabotage and violence. In addition, the Syndicalists held private property in contempt. In this, he believed, they were as misguided as the Collectivists.

The most difficult point to discern from King's treatment of the four partners idea was the role he prefigured for the labor movement. He argued that the works committees created under the Whitley Councils plan were identical to the shop committees established under the Colorado plan. He also acknowledged the role played by the unions in the British scheme. He did not, however, explain the differences between British and American unions that necessitated works committees, nor did he indicate what role American unions might play in the shop committee system. Apart from defending employee representation against the charge that it was designed to frustrate unionism—he cited in evidence the nondiscrimination clause in the Colorado plan—he had remarkably little to say about what role, if any, organized labor would play in the world of his Round Table conference. In places, his argument seemed to suggest that he entirely approved of unions, particularly British unions. But at other points, he indicated that existing (American) unions would eventually give way to more cooperative, less combative agencies.

King's ambiguity on so central an issue undoubtedly reflected the compromising position he had made for himself in advocating employee representation. While he had been advising Rockefeller and helping companies install representation plans, he lived with the knowledge that only the workers themselves could effectively defend their own interests. For this purpose, they alone could organize themselves—no one else could do it for them.

Earlier, at C.F. & I., King had convinced himself that the miners were too new to the country, too diverse in language and background, and too intellectually limited, to organize themselves. Therefore, he had told himself, it was all right for the employer to provide the organizational initiative and leadership. He now made the same argument implicitly in his book, even providing by way of illustration the frequency distribution of nativities and races among C.E. & I. miners in 1915. Then as now, he overlooked the fact that company policies had been more instrumental than language or nationality differences in blocking worker organization.

Quite possibly, somewhere in the back of his mind, King had the picture of an ideal working class, one composed of able, literate, self-respecting men and women capable of coming together to influence and even control their destiny. The British working class (like most things British) came closer to this ideal than did the American. Perhaps that was why he found British unions so acceptable and why, in contrast, he regarded the efforts of the United Mine Workers to organize the polyglot miners of Colorado as sheer demagoguery. King may also have idealized the British unions because he did not have to deal with them. Given his great aversion to conflict, he thought less of American unions because they seemed so eager to throw down the gauntlet. Even though, by his own argument, American unions *had* to be more combative, he held it against them that they were.

The guiding premise of *Industry and Humanity* resided in the assumption that the parties to industry had overriding common interests that they failed to perceive. Since King regarded labor and government as reactors to the initiatives of employers, the employers would have to change their ways first. He believed that they should do so because it was the socially responsible thing to do. (In a communications failure model of conflict such as his, once the right message is sent, there is a presumption that the receivers will adjust their behavior accordingly.) To make the change still more attractive, King held out the prospect that reform would result in increased productivity and economic gains for all concerned. Higher productivity would permit higher returns to owners, managers, and workers at no one's expense. The community also would benefit, either because the same resources would be used to produce a greater volume of output or because some portion of the productivity gain would be passed on in the form of lower prices.

In explaining how this increased productivity would come about, King argued that once employers began to foster a spirit of genuine cooperation, the workers would reciprocate in kind. The resulting meetings, understandings, and mutual trust would open the way for the introduction of many of the productivity enhancing techniques presently blocked by labor's opposition. He envisaged workers eagerly accepting incentive wage payment systems, scientific management practices, and all forms of technological change. Evidently, no thought was given to the possibility that many of these so-called best practices had been designed, as scientific management had been, to squeeze productivity out of recalcitrant workers. To elicit the willing support of equals, of partners, might require something quite different. The point is that King had based so much of his thinking on management reform and employee representation that he ended up too neglectful of unions, work, and workers.

Perhaps it was only natural that, since much of what he had to say in the book was tied up with Rockefeller, King expected Rockefeller to respond with enthusiasm for what he had written. When, instead, Rockefeller returned the galley proofs with few comments and fewer compliments, King was hurt. He thought Rockefeller undervalued the merits of his arguments and insights. His hurt grew. Then, from another quarter entirely it was relieved.

King called on Sir Wilfrid Laurier in mid-October 1918. Part of his purpose was to report on a feeler he had received the month previous from the ruling Union Government. It had been intimated to him that the Labour portfolio was his for the asking. He told Sir Wilfrid that he had made no response at the time nor since. He reaffirmed that he would not join the government, as some Liberals had done, over the objection of the party leadership. Sir Wilfrid flattered him by saying that, of course, the Union Government wanted him: he was the best man for the job and they knew it. He went on to discuss the future prospects of the Liberal Party and mentioned his intention to retire from the leadership in the near future. He told King that he was in every way fit to succeed him and pledged him his support. King barely contained his excitement until the end of the interview. He then dashed home to record the conversation in his diary, as if writing it down made it more believable. His lifelong ambition to lead Canada had suddenly become a very real possibility.

So, in spite of his disappointment with Rockefeller over the book, an elated King left Ottawa for Denver. This was at the end of October and he was on his way to conduct previously arranged field surveys for the Great Western Sugar Company. En route he stopped in Chicago to consult with the officers of the International Harvester Company about adopting a representation plan and to meet with a vice president of the Youngstown Sheet & Tube Company for the same reason. The president of International Harvester, Cyrus H. McCormick, Jr., had decided to introduce plans into the company's various plants and had previously contacted King through Rockefeller. In this instance, the company drafted a plan on its own, following the C.F. & I. model, then relied on King for criticism and revisions. The Youngstown officer wanted more of King's time immediately, but that could not be arranged. King was committed to conferences with Great Western officials and to visits to the company's various plants.

On arriving in Denver, King launched into the agreed upon program of consultation and site visits. Within a week, Youngstown officials pleaded for a meeting. A vice president and the assistant to the president for industrial relations came out to Denver to confer and have King draft a plan. In the midst of this activity, without any warning whatever, the great war ended.

Notes

1. W.L.M.K. Diary, 4/16/17. W.L.M.K. Papers, Series J13, p. G2711.
2. Louis B. Wehle to Woodrow Wilson, 11/11/17. W.W. Papers, Case File 4341, Series 4. Wilson's address appears in American Federation of Labor (1917).
3. William L. Hutcheson, president of the Brotherhood of Carpenters and Joiners.
4. W.H. Taft to T. Roosevelt, 3/11/18. W.H.T. Papers.
5. W.L.M.K. Diary, 10/29/17. W.L.M.K. Papers, Series J13, p. G2822.
6. Ibid., 10/31/17, p. G2823.
7. Ibid.
8. R. G. Fosdick to W.L.M.K., 4/5/18. W.L.M.K. Papers, Series J1, vol. 39, p. 34384.
9. Ibid.
10. W.L.M.K. to J.D.R., Jr., 4/17/18. W.L.M.K. Papers, Series J1, vol. 41, pp. 36033f.
11. W.L.M.K. to J.D.R., Jr., 5/9/18. Ibid.
12. W.L.M.K. Diary, 5/30/18. W.L.M.K. Papers, Series J13, pp. G2887, 86f.
13. Ibid., 5/30/18, pp. G2887, 95.
14. Ibid., pp. G2887, 100.
15. Ibid., 6/13/18, p. G2887, 119.
16. Ibid.
17. Ibid., p. G2887, 121.
18. Ibid., 6/17/18, p. G2887, 178.
19. Memorandum Respecting Suggested Procedures in Inauguration of Representation of Employees. W.L.M.K. Papers, Series J4, File 190, pp. 25347–28352.
20. Mooney (1967), p. 60.
21. W.L.M.K. Diary, 8/30/18. W.L.M.K. Papers, Series J13, p. G2918.
22. Ibid., p. G2919. Quotation marks in the original. See also W.L.M.K. to J.D.R., Jr., 8/31/18 and J.H. Wheelwright to J.D.R., Jr., 9/16/18, J.D.R., Jr. Papers, Consolidation Coal Company File, Business Interests, Box 34.
23. Ibid., p. G2918.
24. Ibid., p. G2944, 109.

12. Chaos and Constancy

If the outbreak of the world war had found Mackenzie King in distress over the low ebb in his fortunes, the war's end found him bouyed up by a tide of achievement and bright prospects. The completion of *Industry and Humanity* and its impending publication, his challenging work as a consultant, and the promised mantle of Liberal Party leadership, each provided an independent source of gratification. And, at year's end, when he added to his retainer from Rockefeller the consulting fees received from various corporations, he was quite proud that they totalled $22,000. This princely sum, he noted, had come to him for less than six months work and without any effort on his part to solicit business. In his exultant mood, he could hardly have anticipated that the coming year would yield still grander opportunities.

The fortunes of John D. Rockefeller, Jr. (without reference to the sixty million dollars worth of stock his father gave him in 1919), were equally in the ascendant. The pall cast over the family name by the violence of the Colorado strike had dissipated sufficiently by the end of the war to permit him to assume a new role in society. Within a year of the armistice, he would be regarded widely as the leading spokesman of the liberal point of view toward labor among American businessmen. This transfiguration of his basically conservative stance owed nothing to the public relations efforts of Ivy Lee, now more than ever relegated to the role of message carrier. It owed little even to Mackenzie King, who throughout the year tried to pull Rockefeller to the left without success.

Simply by continuing to advocate employee representation as he had for the past three years, Rockefeller came to appear more and more progressive. At first, this feat of seeming to move while actually standing still was an illusion, a mirage created by the chaotic rightward drift of a nation on the verge of panic. In time, however, as the political spectrum of the country shrank to the narrowest band of tolerance, the illusion became increasingly real. In a business environment presided over by the great steel industry Babbit, Elbert H. Gary, Rockefeller *was* something of a very modest liberal—but this anticipates too much. The setting for these broad changes as well as for the activities of Rockefeller and King first requires some elaboration.

The events of 1919 present a formidable challenge to any interpreter. Names, dates, and places are as accessible or inaccessible as in any neighboring year. But the frames of mind and dispositions stimulated by the conjuncture of events in 1919 seem to defy explanation. Just as we cannot explain with any finality the great depression or, closer to home, those feelings of imminent social collapse that gripped segments of the American population in 1973, so with 1919. Such periods have the shapelessness of chaos, when the touchstones of normal behavior seem either wholly inappropriate or altogether out of reach. It is as if, on board a ship in turbulent seas, each and every instrument for reckoning and steering suddenly becomes useless. Just when bearings are most desperately needed, none are available.

One common explanation of the turmoil of 1919 holds that the American people were committed so emotionally to the war that they could not easily adjust to the abrupt victory. Unspent psychic energies, in this view, carried over to find their outlet in superpatriotic hysteria. Another hypothesis holds that periodic bouts of panicky xenophobia are endemic to American political life. In this view, mass anxiety and the suppression of rights was engineered by a political elite that found itself challenged. Whatever plausibility these hypotheses have, however, loses its force as soon as one looks beyond American borders. Almost all of the industrial countries of the world looked into the face of chaos in 1919. Among these were a number of war-weary nations whose patriotic emotions had been taxed to the fullest. Victorious and defeated alike, devastated and unscathed, democratic and monarchial, all with only slight variations in detail experienced the crisis.

Looking back, it seems almost as if, while the dogs of war were being leashed, the four horsemen of the Apocalypse broke loose. The red scare was but one of these four. The others were influenza, inflation, and industrial conflict. Some countries also were visited by food shortages, massive unemployment, and race riots. But the four horsemen were quite sufficient to spread panic in their wake.

Upwards of twenty million people are estimated to have perished in the influenza pandemic that started on the battlefields of northern France late in 1918 and ran a worldwide course by the end of 1919. It exacted a far higher toll of life than the war and touched all classes and groups. At about the same time, inflation struck at often staggering rates (twenty-nine percent in the United States). Everywhere, the anchor given to daily life by customary prices was sharply eroded. In some countries, the resultant hardships led to rioting. Simultaneously, strike activity climbed to historic peaks as workers struggled to catch up with the rapidly rising cost of living. Many workers also struck to redeem the promises of a better life and a wider role in decision making that had been held out to them during the war. At the same time, nations as different in their circumstances as Japan, Italy, the United States, and Britain experienced a red scare. That is to say, many people believed their society in imminent danger of a Bolshevik inspired revolution. However farfetched in reality, such fears were fed and made more potent by actual uprisings in Germany and Hungary. The red scare, taken together with the strike wave, the inflation, and the influenza pandemic, magnified and distorted all the anxieties and uncertainties accompanying the reconversion from war to peace.

Perhaps none of the problems of reconversion was so thorny as the altered status of labor. To win worker support during the war, governments had made many concessions. Improvements in wages and hours were often accompanied by the growth of worker organization and by increasing acceptance of organized labor in national affairs. During the reconversion, market forces were expected to adjust wages to labor supplies. The terms and conditions of employment, in other words, would be modified appropriately by the forces of competition. No comparable force, however, was at hand to adjust the status of labor. In the United States, for example, government agencies had created hundreds of shop committee systems in various industries. Would these continue once the backing of the government were withdrawn? More broadly, would the right to organize and the public influence of labor lead to a new era in industrial relations?

The armistice was only two days old when the gauntlet was thrown down by a spokesman for American employers. Speaking in New York to the members of the National Founders' Association, an employers' group over which he presided, William H. Barr asserted:

> There is no one who will seriously contend . . . that with the return of peace we can continue to operate our mines and facto-

ries and compete in the world of trade if we are to operate on a national eight hour day and pay the wages which have been imposed during the stress of political opportunity. . . . The vogue of those who have strange solutions for our social and industrial problems, and who are willing to experiment with a sorely tried nation in the midst of its great crisis, will cease.

Referring to the labor movement, Barr ominously predicted that

The present determination on the part of certain forces among the workers to attempt to cling to all that union labor has gained on an unsound basis during an abnormal and artificial period will doubtless occasion some trouble and friction.[1]

Four days later, the *Times* carried a response from Samuel Gompers:

Notice is given here and now that the American working people will not be forced back by either Barr, his association, or all the Bourbons in the United States.

The time has come in the world when the working people are coming into their own. They have new rights and new advantages. They have made the sacrifices, and they are going to enjoy the better times for which the whole world has been in convulsion. . . . And the Barrs . . . must understand that their day of absolutism in industry is over . . .[2]

A *Times* editorial on this exchange of views was remarkably temperate, even sympathetic, toward Gompers' position.

In the weeks and months following the armistice, numerous conferences were convened to discuss postwar problems. Labor relations figured prominently on every agenda. It was generally assumed that the federal government would direct the reconversion for some time, and many of the conferences were aimed at influencing its policies. President Wilson, however, had little interest in shaping a reconversion program or in guiding postwar developments. He became preoccupied with the Paris peace talks and then fell critically ill. As a result, domestic affairs were consigned by inattention to a course of masterless drift. Worse still, the precipitate demobilization of the American war machine exacerbated the problems of readjustment. Since, in effect, no one was listening, the many postwar conferences had little effect.

Several of these conferences did, however, provide forums for King and Rockefeller. The parts they played and the positions they took served to establish long-lasting images in the public mind. King's reputation in Canada as a friend of labor and advocate of greater social equality was burnished to a high gloss. Rockefeller's reputation in his country was made over.

Prior to his departure from Ottawa, in late October 1918, King had been requested by Sir Wilfrid Laurier to prepare a resolution on postwar labor relations. Sir Wilfrid intended to present the resolution to a Liberal Party policy meeting in mid-November. His aim was to have it adopted as a plank in the party's reconstruction platform. King responded with what was the thesis of his book, namely that there were four parties to industry, each of whose interests had to be represented if industrial peace was to become a reality. He was in Colorado consulting for the Great Western Sugar Company when he learned that his resolution had been adopted. He also learned that Sir Wilfrid had announced his intention to retire and to call a party convention to elect a new leader. King felt that with the acceptance of his resolution and Sir Wilfrid's backing, he was in a splendid position to win the leadership.

Little more than two weeks later, on December 5, Rockefeller addressed the Reconstruction Conference of the U.S. Chamber of Commerce in Atlantic City. Speaking on "The Personal Relation in Industry,"[3] he advocated employee representation as the best means of bridging the gap between employers and employees in large-scale industry. With fine impartiality, he defended the rights of both capital and labor to organize and urged that the shortcomings of *some* members of either group was no basis for condemning the entire group. He noted that, since so few workers belonged to unions, employee representation was the sole means available to ensure that labor, as one of industry's four partners, was adequately consulted.

Most of what Rockefeller said he had said before. But on this occasion, he was able to point to the wartime labor policies of the federal government as an example of the kind of partnership embraced by employee representation. He implied that voluntarily adopting representation was simply a way of perpetuating those eminently successful policies. The audience proved highly receptive to his reasoning.

As he had on the occasion of his second appearance before

the Commission on Industrial Relations, Rockefeller concluded his speech with a series of credos. At that time, there had been seven statements of belief, now there were ten, only one of which was a direct carry-over. He was immensely gratified when the U.S. Chamber of Commerce voted to adopt his creed as its own platform a few days later. The second credo was excluded because it was thought to be redundant, whereas the eighth was dropped as merely procedural. Even in this amended form, the adoption of the creed by the U.S. Chamber of Commerce meant national recognition and endorsement for employee representation. Rockefeller had won. His was the only new position available to employers who were unwilling either to return to the prewar open shop or to cede the field of industrial relations to the unions. At his direction and expense, 1.25 million copies of his address were distributed.

Although some union advocates were already referring pejoratively to representation plans as company unions, Rockefeller's continued advocacy of them did not impair his standing with various labor leaders. Quite the contrary. Soon after the Atlantic City conference, he and King met for talks with Samuel Gompers. Concerned that the wartime gains of labor were too new to survive any adversity, Gompers wanted to build as many defenses as he could. He was not at all interested in employee representation but in Bolshevism, the A.F. of L., and Rockefeller money.

The first of several meetings was arranged by Captain C. R. Dickinson of military intelligence. In addition to Gompers, Rockefeller, and King, Dickinson and Robert Maisel, the director of the American Alliance for Labor and Democracy, were present. Gompers was seeking support for this latter organization.

Gompers related how the Alliance had been created in July 1917, bringing together elements of the trade union movement and a number of leading prowar socialists. Its goal had been to offset the antiwar propaganda aimed at workers by the radical opponents of the war. At the time, the government had feared an all-out effort on the part of the I.W.W. to hinder the war effort. Gompers had won the support of the President and Secretary of War for the Alliance. Funds had been channeled covertly, and the activities and publicity efforts of the Alliance had quietly been directed by the government's main propaganda agency, the Committee on Public Information. Since the armistice, however, government funding for the Alliance had been meagre. To permit it to continue to function effectively, Gompers explained, private sources of support were now being sought.

Rockefeller and King were given to understand that the peacetime mission of the Alliance would be to work against the spread of Bolshevism among American workers. It was on this basis that Rockefeller subsequently weighed lending his support. But Bolshevism was only one of Gompers' concerns at this time; he was at least as anxious over the ability of the labor movement to withstand the attack by employers he believed would come as government withdrew its benign influence. Contrary to his show of confidence in the exchange with William H. Barr in the *New York Times,* Gompers thought many of labor's recruits too green and many of the gains too newly won to have much staying power. Thus, a critical function of the Alliance would be to "act as an A.F. of L. propaganda agency."[4] Robert Maisel was to serve as his Ivy Lee.

Gompers was not deceiving Rockefeller when he projected the Alliance as a bulwark against Bolshevism. Strengthening the A.F. of L. and fighting radicalism were to him the opposite sides of a single coin. He undoubtedly told Rockefeller that if the conservative trade unions were beaten or frustrated, American workers would of necessity turn to more radical, even revolutionary groups for leadership. To avoid this outcome, it was in the interests of employers to make concessions and find some way to accomodate to the unions. By this reasoning, any activity that strengthened the labor movement served to weaken the appeal of Bolshevism. Moreover, the Alliance had already achieved a reputation for opposing the new Soviet regime. It was thus particularly well placed to carry on the fight for the loyalty of American workers.

Rockefeller, for his part, was decidedly interested in fending off Bolshevik influence in the United States. Why he believed that such influence was either significant or growing is not clear. The Bolshevik revolution had stirred up considerable ferment in American radical circles but it was a ferment largely of words and ideology rather than of action and influence. King shared his views on the Bolshevik danger and proved of little help to him on that account. Perhaps European developments swayed their thinking.

King remained in New York through the Christmas holidays. He undoubtedly saw Felix Frankfurter's estimate of employee representation, for it came into Rockefeller's hands at this time.

Frankfurter, the director of the War Labor Policies Board, had written:

> Mr. Rockefeller's "creed" undoubtedly looks in the right direction, but the French are right, the emphasis makes the song. And the emphasis in industrial relations must be upon thorough-going cooperation—a ready recognition of labor's independent responsibility in working out the problems . . . and not the concession made by management, however, wholeheartedly made or generously conceived.[5]

Frankfurter went on to suggest that the Whitley Councils, based on trade union organization, provided a more appropriate model.

King was given something considerably more exciting than this to think about during the holidays. On the day he was to leave the city, he was asked to call on the Andrew Carnegies. King had been introduced to Mr. and Mrs. Carnegie the previous year. They had taken an immediate liking to him and had since invited him into their company several times. Convinced of his abilities and integrity, they now offered him the directorship of their main philanthropic organization, the Carnegie Corporation. He would preside over an endowment of $130 million and direct the expenditure of the endowment income. He would also have a large influence in other Carnegie philanthropies, including the Carnegie Peace Foundation and the Carnegie Foundation for the Advancement of Learning. His salary would be twenty five thousand dollars a year. There was also the prospect of writing Carnegie's official biography, for which he estimated he would probably be paid one hundred thousand dollars. Since there was no pressing need to fill a vacancy, King was asked to consider the offer at his leisure. He left for Ottawa filled with the certainty that his character assured him a worthy future.

King knew from the outset what his answer would be. In the choice among a life in Canadian politics, in industrial relations, or in philanthropy, he far preferred the first. The second genuinely interested him, but he doubted if he could continue his association with Rockefeller. The third possibility was the most distant from his desire to be of service. As he mulled over the Carnegie offer in early January, he wrote:

> Against both the Rockefeller and Carnegie connections I have the feeling of dislike to associations with wealth, save enough

for an independent political career and to enable me to marry and have a family. I believe there is a handicap to the highest service in the industrial world thro' either of these associations.[6]

When he discussed the Carnegie offer with Sir Wilfrid, he found his preferences reinforced. Sir Wilfrid took it for granted that he would reject the offer to devote himself to the Liberal Party and Canada. He reaffirmed his intention to have King succeed him in the leadership, averring that were King now in Parliament, he would immediately resign the leadership in his favor. King, he ventured, would now have an added luster for party members and voters, once it became known that he had passed up so rich a personal opportunity to serve his country.

King also discussed the offer with Mr. and Mrs. Rockefeller on his return to New York in mid-January. They were quite surprised by his news and even a trifle resentful that their rival in philanthropy should attempt to lure talent away from them. They mounted a host of arguments against accepting the position. Among other things, they asserted that he would not be challenged and that he would have a larger and more satisfying impact in either his industrial relations work or in Canadian politics. As if to make it plain how strongly Rockefeller wished to preserve their relationship, he talked about how it might be made more financially attractive to King.

Every opinion pointed him in the same direction. Yet, since King was under no obligation to give the Carnegies an answer, he gave none. When they met again, after he had talked with Carnegie Corporation officials, he spoke candidly about his life interests and ambitions. He was flattered to have the parallel drawn between himself as their "Philanthropic son" and Charles Schwab as their "Business son."[7] But he came away convinced that Mrs. Carnegie understood his preferences and the likelihood that when the time came, his answer would be no.

As he left New York for Chicago with the Carnegie position still his for the taking, he reflected that the Liberal Party leadership was within his grasp and that Rockefeller seemed as keen as ever on retaining his services. Never in his life had he confronted such splendid alternatives. During the following weeks, his thinking and his perceptions were influenced powerfully by these opportunities. He came to feel himself more of a free agent than he had been for some years. This much became evident as he went about examining the working conditions and facilities of Standard Oil of Indiana in his capacity as an industrial relations consultant.

As was his practice in such consulting ventures, King first worked to dispell any misapprehension that he might be an impractical idealist. He assured Robert W. Stewart, the chairman of the board of directors, that he intended to make a thorough examination of existing practices before making any recommendations. For the benefit of the company president, he denied having any preconceived ideas that he wished to impose. He would conduct his survey as unobtrusively as possible, and any suggestions he made for changes would be offered to the company to accept or reject. Stewart was relieved by King's assurances and related how, when Clarence Hicks had come from Standard Oil of New Jersey to talk about employee representation, he alarmed many management people by giving the impression that representation would be forced upon them. Stewart pledged the full cooperation of the company and instructed King to include all departments, plants, and mines in his survey. King went to work immediately.

The oil industry was new to him and he found it fascinating. As he went through the Indiana refinery, from process to process and among departments, he talked with supervisors and workers, asking questions and noting conditions. For the most part, he found excellent working conditions presided over by sensible young managers with college training. The company had introduced the eight-hour day before the war, largely at the initiative of a worker petition. It had also established a central personnel department, which King thought important in reducing the arbitrary exercise of power by petty bosses. These two features, the eight-hour day and a central personnel department, seemed to him the vital requirements of the postwar readjustment. They demonstrated tangibly the employer's respect and concern for labor. Combined with good working conditions, they constituted the best practice of the day. All that was missing, he noted, was the active participation of workers in many of the decisions affecting them.

King found most of the managers with whom he talked alert to the radical upheavals occuring in Europe. Most of them agreed that these troubles pointed up the need in this country for granting labor a more consequential role. Yet, King observed, within their own company, there were no joint committees and hardly any precedent for worker–management cooperation. He was surprised to learn that there were several unionized groups with which the company dealt in a quiet and informal way. The company went so far as to enter into memoranda of understanding with the boilermakers' and the pipefitters' unions. Delegates from these unions represented their members in handling grievances with the managers. The total number of union members, however, was a small part of the entire workforce of four thousand. When the company could keep unions out, it did so. He learned that an organizing drive by the machinists' union several years earlier had been roundly defeated. All of the direction within the company flowed down from the top.

These were among the impressions fresh in King's mind when he received, in rapid succession, a wire and two letters from Rockefeller. Rockefeller had been invited to participate in a joint meeting of representatives of the New York State Chamber of Commerce and the New York State Federation of Labor. He wanted King's advice on whether he should accept the invitation and serve as chairman of the chamber's committee. He also wanted to know what King thought of the labor leaders he might have to deal with, and whether any such meetings might not serve to confer recognition on the unions. In two separate wires, King urged Rockefeller to look upon the conference as a positive opportunity to help shape postwar industrial relations. He advised him not to become involved in any of the committee work, however, and promised to elaborate on his views in a letter later that day. King could not have foreseen how powerfully his response would be influenced by several conversations held in the course of the day.

The first of these occurred in the offices of Standard Oil, when Stewart, the board chairman, mentioned that Rockefeller was thinking of donating a YMCA building to the town in which the refinery was located. He asked King what he thought of this and of welfare work in general.

King had to admit that he and Rockefeller disagreed about the "Y." He thought that companies should avoid any direct connection with religious associations lest they inadvertently infringe on workers' rights or offend their sensibilities. He could not bring Rockefeller around to a full appreciation of the potential danger, however. Presumably, his allegiance to the "Y" was too strong to override. If it were up to him, King asserted, he would see a self-governing community center as a more appropriate gift.

Warming to his subject and to the opportunity to express his opinions, King proceeded to deride corporate welfare work for being both unilateral and gratuitous. Companies decided what workers needed or wanted and then gave them as much of it as they saw fit. But such programs rarely addressed the problems that most concerned workers. Nor did they create a means whereby the misunderstandings that naturally crop up in an organization could be aired and possibly resolved.

If employers truly wanted to improve relations with their employees, King continued, they would insist on formal contracts, with collective bargaining and grievance machinery. He pointed out to Stewart how easy it would be within his own company to include worker representatives in the weekly meetings of department heads. How, by expanding the practice of worker representation, "much that is being done from above might be made a matter of joint relationship."[8] He left Stewart to think over his remarks and departed to keep an appointment at the executive offices of the International Harvester Company.

King had previously corresponded with the International Harvester Company, as it moved to develop and implement its own employee representation plan. The process of drafting the plan was now in its final stages and, because he was in Chicago, he was asked to confer about several outstanding points. One of the officials present, Arthur H. Young, had recently come to Harvester from Colorado Fuel & Iron through the courtesy of Rockefeller. Young had replaced Clarence Hicks at C.F. & I. (who, it will be remembered, Rockefeller had hired from Harvester) and was now the head of the new industrial relations department. Partly because of his familiarity with the Colorado plan, Young dominated the company's thinking about representation. Yet, King found him both overly legalistic and insensitive to the need to introduce change without setting off power struggles. His disagreements with King were a little like those of a disciple attempting to upstage his master.

But the man whose remarks had the greatest effect on King, was another International Harvester official, Alexander Legge. Legge only recently had returned from Europe, where he had been a food administrator. He impressed King with his report that the continent was in the grip of a reign of terror. To avoid a similar fate, he argued, American employers would have to give up any idea of returning to the autocratic role of the prewar era. They would have to adopt some means that would permit labor a greater say in shaping its fate. King agreed wholeheartedly.

On returning to the Standard Oil offices later that afternoon,

King composed the promised letter to Rockefeller. Emboldened by his acknowledged disagreement with Rockefeller and by his intensified sense of the gravity of the times, he wrote as forcefully as he dared. That evening he would boast in his diary "that no such letter was ever written to a Rockefeller from any of the precincts of the Standard Oil."[9]

In four and a quarter pages, single spaced, he enumerated the reasons why Rockefeller should participate in the joint meeting and advised on the strategy that should be followed. Organized labor, he wrote, no longer could be ignored; the war had seen to that. Since the unions stood ready to meet, talk, and hammer out agreements, the future was in the hands of Capital. If Capital accepted Labor and was prepared to work with it cooperatively, a new era of industrial peace would follow. But if Capital refused Labor's proferred hand of friendship, an era of conflict would ensue. In that event, he warned, "America may not escape the reign of terror which even now Europe is witnessing."[10]

As the foremost industrialist in the country, he argued, Rockefeller had an obligation to pursue industrial peace. He should therefore welcome every approach by labor and enter into cordial relations with it. If the meeting in New York proved successful, other states would probably hold similar meetings. The result might be the drawing together of the U.S. Chamber of Commerce and the A.F. of L. at the national level. But whatever the result, trying to work together at present was more important than anything else. Hoping to offset Rockefeller's cautiousness in making new commitments, King told him that he would have to accept the union leaders at face value. For, however honest or effective they might be in representing the interests of their members, they were the leaders and the only ones to deal with.

Turning to the question of Rockefeller's own interests, King wrote, "I think you personally and your industries have everything to gain and nothing to lose by an immediate contact and association with the recognized labor leaders."[11] King chided him for worrying too much about conferring recognition on the unions. The unions after all encompassed the only organized groups of workers, King noted. It was the unorganized workers who represented the real danger. They were the ones most likely to fall under the spell of the Bolsheviks or the I.W.W.

As to the working of the conference itself, King warned Rockefeller that, above all, he must avoid giving any impression that he wished to push the representation idea. (Left to his own devices, that is exactly what King expected Rockefeller would do.) Should such an impression gain any credence whatever, King argued, the labor people would become hostile and probably withdraw. They would fear that employee representation was aimed at supplanting unionism, even though that was not so. Therefore, forebear, King urged. Let any proposals emanate from labor and have capital play the part of giving labor's suggestions serious consideration. In good time, King prophesied, the representation idea would emerge and win supporters because of its inherent value.

His day's work complete, King prepared himself for a relaxing Saturday evening on the town. He dined with a lady friend and went on to the theater. The play troubled him. Entitled *Happiness,* it placed the virtues of workers in counterpoint against the vices of the idle rich. The dramatic action incorporated the death of a young girl's beloved mother. The themes of social justice, mother, and death, he told himself, were too close to his own thoughts and feelings to be either edifying or entertaining. Later that evening, as he recounted the events of the day in his diary, his recollection of the enervating drama prompted him to a remarkable outpouring. He wrote:

My mind these days is filled with the whole question of my own personal obligation to the social problems of our times, and turning over in my mind the course it is wisest to pursue, in the alternative careers which seem to lie before me and with respect to which I must soon make a decision. Of one thing I am certain, and that is that the accepted practices incidental to the accumulation of wealth under existing conditions are wholly wrong, and that my part in life must be along the direction of exposing what is in error fundamentally, and in helping to bring about such changes in the relations of Labor and Capital as will secure greater justice to the worker. I am certain in my own mind that the revolution which time will effect, which we are at the beginning of already, is one which will wholly reverse the positions of Labor and Capital, and will give to the return upon investment . . . a consideration secondary to that which is given to the conditions under which men and women are called upon to labor . . . As matters now stand, Capital now robs Management, Labor, and the Community of a large part of what each ought, in any system of rewards through social service, to be justly entitled.[12]

King's attitude amounted to a prejudgment of the career choices before him. He would have subjected himself to considerable strain if, in view of his feelings, he subsequently had chosen to remain with Rockefeller or accept the Carnegie offer. Nonetheless, in spite of his feelings, he continued to give Rockefeller the best counsel of which he was capable. Simultaneously, in the days and weeks ahead, he displayed particular sensitivity to the shortcomings of Capital.

The very next working day, for example, as he completed his survey of the Indiana refinery, King found two occasions for further criticism. One involved the employment of a group of women at tasks he thought too arduous, such as lifting sixty-five pound cartons. The other involved the need for still cleaners to work at temperatures of three hundred degrees simply because the company wouldn't invest in more stills. He concluded in both instances that it was the duty of the State to protect workers from the health hazards to which Capital heedlessly subjected them. His reflections on the still cleaners read like perfect arguments for the Occupational Safety and Health Act, adopted two generations later.

Rockefeller responded to King's letter of January 25 by indicating that he was now inclined to accept the chairmanship of the Chamber of Commerce committee. However, he remained of the opinion that the planned conference with labor leaders would prove useless unless aimed at some mutually acceptable plan of action. King understood from this that Rockefeller still hoped to use the conference as a platform from which to advocate employee representation. He wrote again, at even greater length, hoping to sway him from that intention.

He reiterated his belief that the only thing such a conference could agree upon would be broad statements of principle, as had happened at Atlantic City. Any attempt to press the adoption of a more concrete program would prove divisive and, ultimately, destructive. Should the New York state conference succeed in adopting a set of principles, King reiterated, similar groups in other states would undoubtedly hold conventions and adopt similar statements. In time, Rockefeller might find himself with Samuel Gompers at the head of a broad national conference dedicated to building industrial peace. And, if all along the line the same principles were accepted by employer and labor groups, they would guide federal and state governments in the design of legislation. In this fashion representation, collective bargaining, and grievance machinery would be widely instituted and any threat of warfare between Capital and Labor dissolved.

Attractive though it was, King's scenario was both surprising and misleading. Surprising in that he expected Rockefeller, and Americans generally, to have as few qualms about a role for government in industrial relations as he himself had. Misleading in that the scenario left no room for any initiatives on the part of the labor leaders at the conference. King sagely advised Rockefeller that his dealings with union leaders would probably lead him to change his mind about a number of things. But he neglected the point that, if there was to be representation, bargaining, and grievance machinery, the unions entertained no doubt about the proper agency. This would become painfully obvious when, laying aside his work at Standard of Indiana for a few days, King traveled to New York and, with Rockefeller, met the leaders of the State Federation of Labor.

King had several opportunities during the weekend to talk with Rockefeller prior to the Monday afternoon meeting. At lunch on Saturday, they were joined by Carl R. Gray, a new member of the board of directors of Consolidation Coal. In bringing them news of the company, Gray reported that the unionization of the mines in the Maryland district probably was not far off. Those on the scene believed that it would be impossible to resist. This would mean the end of the representation plan there. King advised Rockefeller of how wrong it would be to oppose unions at this time, or in the future. Gray seconded his opinion, noting that during his wartime service on the Railway Adjustment Board, a joint committee had rendered unanimous decisions in all of the cases brought before it. The union leaders who served on the committee had proved themselves perfectly responsible representatives.

Rockefeller responded by saying that employee representation had never been intended as a bulwark against unionism. Its sole purpose was to establish closer contact between employers and their employees. That, he confessed, was all that he was interested in. It was up to the managers and workers within any company to decide whether the representation would be carried out through a union.

King did not challenge this last statement. Either he did not question the right of managers to intrude upon the workers' right to organize or he chose not to raise the issue. Instead, he was pleased, perhaps even relieved, to hear Rockefeller say that he had no intention to oppose unions or the signing of contracts with unions. King had previously told him about the arrangements with the two unions at Standard of Indiana, and Rockefeller had seemed to agree when he argued that if the company was going to deal with unions, it should do so openly, as party to a formal contract.

On Sunday morning, King ate breakfast with Captain Dickinson, late of military intelligence. Dickinson informed him that he had taken an office on Madison Avenue to make his living as a publicist of joint capital–labor relationships. He was preparing articles that he hoped would be published in popular magazines, and he was also angling to have movies made that carried the same message in a dramatic way. He wanted King's advice, but even more, he wanted him to intercede with Rockefeller on his behalf. If Rockefeller would give him $1500 to get started, there were one or two other backers likely to do the same.

So few people had dared to use King to get to Rockefeller's money that he was not troubled by this request. He admired Dickinson's energy and enthusiasm and, for a time at least, thought his cause a worthy one. Later that day, he passed the request along to Rockefeller. Wholly accustomed though *he* was to approaches of this sort, Rockefeller nonetheless gave the matter serious thought. Eventually, he would refuse.

Following the meeting with Dickinson, King attended church and called at the Rockefeller home. For several hours after lunch, the two men carefully reviewed the A.F. of L's reconstruction program. King came away confident that Rockefeller had found nothing in the document to which he took great exception. The way thus seemed clear for a successful, precedent-setting conference under Rockefeller's leadership.

By midafternoon the following day, all of their expectations had been shattered. King may have prepared Rockefeller to accept unionism, but no one had prepared the union leaders to accept employee representation. From the moment the three unionists arrived for a preliminary meeting, they spoke as if the only possible form of worker organization was an A.F. of L. union. King and Rockefeller were bowled over. Because they placed so high a value on representation plans, it was incomprehensible that the unionists should reject them out of hand. King entirely failed to appreciate that no one excepting Rockefeller and himself saw the plans as other than an attempt to evade unionism.

Feeling that he could not leave Rockefeller alone to deal with such a disagreeable situation, King cancelled plans to take an afternoon train to the West. He remained throughout the meeting but argument failed him. Instead of suggesting that perhaps representation plans might be employed to the advantage of millions of as yet unorganized workers, he became petty. One of the union leaders made a cutting reference to the Ludlow Massacre. The meeting was a disaster.

Crestfallen, Rockefeller decided, by the time they returned to the office, that he would not participate in the conference. Several times he remarked that it was "a tragedy, a tragedy" that the venture had failed.[13] King attempted to comfort him, but was himself saddened by the outcome.

Across the continent in Seattle, Washington, that day, a general strike proclamation appeared in the newspapers. Three days later, the city would be brought to a standstill as unionists and sympathizers walked out en masse in support of striking shipyard workers. In many quarters, this event marked the onset of morbid fears of imminent revolution. The red scare had begun.

As he left New York bound for a Standard Oil of Indiana facility near St. Louis, King occupied himself reading the latest work of Arthur Henderson, a leader of the British Labour Party. As usual, he found himself in complete sympathy with Henderson's program and objectives. His only reservation, which he took to be a minor matter, concerned the issue of government ownership of industry. Unlike Henderson, he believed that public ownership was not necessary, that control through regulation was adequate to the same end.

The sharp contrast between the radical position King took when he thought about British affairs and the conservatism of his positions on American affairs was never clearer. In contemplating British politics, he admired and supported the trade union movement, the Labour Party, and the basically socialist outlook that they projected. But in America, as the events of the previous day had shown, he could not even bring himself to accept the existing unions. And, whether he intended to or not, he also denied the crucial premise that worker organizations should be independent of employer influence. For that was all that the state A.F. of L. leaders had assumed when they dismissed employee representation as an alternative to unionism.

In King's mind, these divergent opinions were sanctioned by the belief that Britain was a more advanced country than the United States. Given fixed and immutable stages in the evolution of industrial society, it made sense to have one politics in one society and a different politics in the other. But such a schema also left room for equivocation. Consistency toward the evolutionary model would have required him to believe that American development would replicate the British experience. There would then have been no place for employee representation, only for unions. Instead, he convinced himself that this country and Canada weren't ready for full-blown unionism and that, therefore, representation had an important role to play.

Had King been more introspective on this occasion he also might have discerned how greatly his feelings influenced his judgment. The unionists encountered the previous day had actively grated on his sensibilities. Perhaps, had they shown the proper respect and deference, he could have found a way of working with them. But they had not. Cocksure that the future lay with A.F. of L. unions operating under their leadership, they had been aggressive, even patronizing. Their manner quite as much as their position had shaped his response. As an intellectual, however, King could not admit that his judgment was grounded in personal sentiment, any more than as a liberal, he could admit to class prejudice.

In any event, the stubborn issue of unionism would not go away. On touring the Wood River and Sugar Creek refineries in Missouri, King again found Standard Oil of Indiana dealing with unions without the benefit of contracts. Again, the finding made him uneasy. A visit to the company's only coal mine brought the issue into sharp relief. He grasped what was wrong and, in setting about to correct it, adopted a bold position.

When Standard Oil of Indiana had purchased the coal mine at Carlinville, Illinois, it continued to honor the contract under which the mine was operating. This contract, King was informed, had been drawn between the Operators' Association of Illinois and the United Mine Workers. Subsequently, Indiana Standard Oil had neither joined the former organization nor signed a new agreement with the latter one. But it had, he learned, bound itself to observe the terms of the contract to the letter, even to the point of checking off union dues and requiring new employees to join the union. Most recently, the company had hired an official of the state mine workers' organization, with the consent of the organization, to serve as its personnel manager.

In sorting out his thoughts that evening, King concluded that the company had probably been wise to remain outside the Operators' Association. Some operators might resent its aloofness, but at least the company could not be dragged into or made the scape-goat in any future labor troubles. The company's failure to sign a new agreement, on the other hand, struck him as unwise. Know-ing that the company had no policy barring agreements with unions, he reasoned that the prevailing arrangement had prob-ably originated with the mine manager. From what he knew of this man, King surmised that he had steered clear of a written con-tract so that if the need arose, he could violate the one under which he tacitly was operating.

But what, King asked himself, must the union think? Either that Standard Oil of Indiana was opposed in principle to dealing with unions or that some other force—Rockefeller—restrained the company from having such dealings. So the mine manager would act to suit himself, while the responsibility for his actions would be laid either to Standard Oil or Rockefeller.

King concluded that both the company and Rockefeller should take steps to reduce the jeopardy in which they were placed by this and similar situations elsewhere. Certainly, he would not rec-ommend the introduction of a representation plan at the mine, be-cause "It would provoke conflict, and moreover, with a man like Fisher administering it, would not be successful. What is needed at Carlinville is open and straight dealings with the union."[14] He went on to reflect that a union contract also would demonstrate that Rockefeller's support for the Colorado plan was not aimed at excluding unions.

At the Sugar Creek, Missouri, refinery the following day, King found a manager much more to his liking, a man he thought sen-sitive to labor problems, fair, and open minded. Eight different unions had members among the refinery work force and the manager had understandings, but not written contracts, with each of them. He and King discussed the advisability of creating a de-partment of industrial relations. In talking about the introduction of a representation plan, King revealed for the first time how he thought a plan could coexist with unions. The unions would have to be consulted and permitted to name their own representatives to all joint committees. The policy areas covered by the joint com-mittees would be areas not normally covered in union contracts. King enumerated these as sanitary conditions, safety, and "more in the way of personal contact between the management and the employees."[15] This design suggests that King's thought was to enhance those conditions of work often marginal to the interests of unions but critical to the employer in striving for harmonious employee relations.

King's thinking about the report he was preparing for the executive officers of Standard Oil also was influenced by more distant events. The Seattle general strike in particular was very much in his mind. Accepting the widespread but erroneous characterization of this strike as a radical I.W.W. and Bolshevik action—it was actually led and supported by A.F. of L. unions—he concluded that the greatest need of the day was to bring the leaders of the conservative trade unions into closer contact with business managers. In this way, both sides would come to recognize their common interests and find a way of working together. If this did not happen, he believed, revolutionary unrest would be unavoidable.

For many years, King had used the threat of revolution as an argument in support of reform. This was not a rhetorical device with him. It followed directly from his sense of the drift of history. He believed that the claims workers made upon employers for greater fairness and equality were both morally justified and irresistible. Right and the course of social evolution were on the workers' side. Consequently, employer efforts to frustrate or evade these claims provoked outrage and also thwarted the natural forces of progress. Under such circumstances, workers became increasingly likely to heed the siren song of the revolutionaries. But if, instead, the employers responded to worker discontent with understanding and appropriate reforms, violence would lose its appeal. Progress would follow the calmer path of life enhancement and enrichment through cooperation.

In presenting his report to an assemblage of Standard Oil officers and directors, King discussed the issue of unionism with all of the tact at his command. He described the company's relations with the United Mine Workers at the Carlinville mine, and urged his listeners to consider the situation very carefully. He refused to recommend a specific course of action to them. Instead, he offered it as his personal opinion that the company ought to sign a formal agreement with the union as soon as possible. As Rockefeller's representative, he sensed that his advice absolved the officers of any blame should something adverse arise from the action he suggested. The responsibility, he believed, was his not theirs. The officers and directors listened sympathetically and thanked him warmly at the end of his presentation. He was sure that they would follow his suggestion.

As on many other occasions, King attached momentous significance to his action and its outcome. Such dreams of glory both fed and rewarded his ambition. If Standard Oil signed a contract with the U.M.W., he believed that

> I will have done more to bring together Organized Capital and Organized Labor in America than can be done by all the speeches that all the speakers in the country are making at the present time. I believe, moreover, I shall be doing more for Mr. R. Jr. and his future, and the future of his family, by this step than would be possible in all the counsel and advice I could give him as to the means of circumventing it or in other ways.[16]

Later the same day, King had another opportunity to discuss his report with board chairman Stewart. The latter indicated that the company would probably heed King's advice about dealing with the union. He confessed, however, to a personal reluctance to become party to a closed shop agreement. It struck him as somehow un-American and unmanly to compel miners to join the union if they wanted to work for the company.

King pointed out that the company had been following this practice from the day it took over the Carlinville mine. He wasn't asking the company to adopt a new policy but simply to acknowledge openly its relationship with the union. Stewart conceded that he was correct, but on the following day, he again voiced his reticence about signing a contract that barred the employment of nonunion workers. King patiently explained the issue from the perspective of the union miners. The nonmembers, he pointed out, were quite prepared to accept all of the benefits that came their way through the efforts of the union but avoided paying dues or contributing to the strength of the organization. This was seen as unfair by most union members, and for that reason, they sought to compel membership. Stewart agreed that there was some sense in their position and, grudgingly, dropped the matter. King left him with the expectation that the company would sign the contract and, at its refineries, would introduce representation plans. The following day, he left for Youngstown, Ohio.

King's consultations with officers of the Youngstown Sheet and Tube Company were cut short when he chanced to read in the evening paper that Sir Wilfrid Laurier had suffered a stroke. As speedily as arrangements could be made, he departed for Ottawa. A morning paper purchased enroute, in Buffalo, told him that

Laurier was dead. He returned home to mourn his political mentor and to deal with the very real possibility that he would soon become the leader of the Liberal Party. He confided to his diary:

> This begins a new chapter in my life, a chapter of great responsibilities & I believe great opportunities. Had Sir Wilfred lived there is no question that his guiding hand would have secured me the leadership of the Liberal Party at the convention in June. In his death I lose a political father as well as a great leader.[17]

King thought it important that he remain in Canada for the next few weeks. Some friends and political allies urged him to make an active campaign for the leadership, but he refused. Instead, he increased his visibility. He postponed several consulting jobs south of the border and turned down an offer to travel to Hawaii to consult for the Sugar Planters' Association. Speaking engagements during the following weeks took him to Toronto, Montreal, and Quebec. In each instance, he spoke on the four partners to industry as the pathway to postwar industrial peace.

Every passing day found him more convinced than ever that revolutionary turmoil would erupt if the relations between employers and their employees were not altered in a fundamental way. Possibly he was influenced by a remark President Wilson made at this time, during his brief return from the Paris peace talks: "We are running a race with Bolshevism and the world is on fire."[18]

In any event, King believed it imperative that concessions be made to labor. He wrote to Rockefeller urging him to take the lead in this. Pointing to the situation he found at Standard Oil of Indiana, he recommended that Rockefeller advise the managers in all of his holdings that he did not wish them to withhold union recognition where they had enduring relations with responsible unions. The absence of recognition, he explained, exposed both Rockefeller and the companies involved to misunderstanding and misrepresentation. Open dealings with unions would both preclude mischance and provide graphic evidence of Capital's willingness to work in harmony with Labor. Even companies with representation plans, King continued, ought to find it possible to live with unions in some of their divisions, as was true at C.F. & I. in its railway division. There could be no better proof of the compatibility of employee representation with unionism.

King's about-face on the importance of recognition, which he had more than once derided as hollow, stemmed mainly from his waxing fear of upheaval. In a theme common to his letters to Rockefeller at the time, he wrote:

> I think it cannot be too clearly seen that this is a period of transition in which Organized Labor is bound to come in for an ever increasing measure of recognition. The path of wisdom on the part of management seems to me to be that of bringing about the necessary adjustments in the most natural way and the one least liable to lead to friction.[19]

Although Rockefeller shared King's concern over the possibility of revolutionary upheaval and considered a stream of proposals for meeting this threat, he did not much care for King's suggestion. There was nothing personal in his rejection, for at just this time he made an offer for King's future services that he hoped would counter the Carnegie offer. (The offer provided that either as a member of his staff or as a free-lance consultant, King would be guaranteed a salary equal to what Carnegie had offered, $25,000 per year.) He informed King that he had discussed his recommendation with officers of Standard Oil of New Jersey and with Clarence Hicks. Any effort on his part to press for the recognition of unions, they had told him, would probably backfire. The managers would think that he had reversed his position and now favored unions over employee representation. Yet, interest in representation had never been greater. His action might inadvertently block many adoptions. In addition, they counseled, his advocacy of so radical a step would create resentment and "tend to lessen the confidence of these gentlemen in my leadership."[20] Since these lines of argument were entirely consistent with his own thinking, Rockefeller found them persuasive.

Neither Rockefeller nor King, then or subsequently, recognized that they had reached a turning point in their relationship. Their personal feelings toward one another continued unchanged, and for some months to come, King would give advice that Rockefeller sought and heeded. But their differing judgments about how to deal with the imminent social crisis marked the beginning of the end of Rockefeller's intellectual dependence upon King. No doubt Rockefeller foresaw and was preparing for the changed relationship that surely would follow King's more active role in Liberal Party affairs. Yet, the substantive issue over which they divided exerted by far the more powerful force. As King more unequivocally embraced the position that Capital must concede and learn to live with unionism, Rockefeller resolved that the major antidote to revolutionary upheaval lay with the spread of employee representation.

Where King could only advise, Rockefeller could act. In March, he oversaw the distribution of a quarter of a million copies of his Atlantic City speech "Representation in Industry;" another million copies would be distributed in June. Unsolicited agents meanwhile carried his message to the country and to the distant corners of the world. The head of the International Committee of the YMCA informed Rockefeller that he was boosting employee representation up and down the country and everywhere he went, including China and Japan. "Solving Labor Problems with the Colorado Representation Plan" by Edward S. Cowdrick, assistant to the president of C.F. & I., was published in an iron and steel trade journal.[21] In early April, Clarence Hicks presided over the creation of the Special Conference Committee, which brought together representatives of ten large companies[22] for regular exchanges of information about labor policies and labor market conditions. At about the same time, Rockefeller chose, from among a number of proposals offering to combat domestic Bolshevism, to support the one program oriented most positively toward representation. This involved providing financial backing to Sherman Rogers (nee Carl Van Hemert), a former lumberjack who wrote magazine articles and toured the country speaking on Americanism and the Colorado plan.

By early April, King was prepared to resume his activities as an industrial consultant. The Liberal Party conference scheduled for June had been postponed until August. He decided that he would carry on with his American work and make his visit to England as planned. Believing his chances of being elected party leader were very good, he resolved to let the party come after him. He would not seek the post.

On April 8, on the first leg of his journey south, he stopped at Youngstown, Ohio, to meet with officers of Youngstown Sheet and Tube. Among other things, he learned that the company expected to be struck as part of a nationwide effort to organize and gain union recognition for steel workers. He was informed that the company was prepared to fight. He counseled against "open warfare" if it could be avoided.[23] Privately, he thought that the workers were in an unenviable position in view of the sizeable layoffs that had occurred and the sharp fall in the demand for steel.

The next two weeks were spent touring the mines of the Consolidation Coal Company in West Virginia, Pennsylvania, and Maryland. As usual, when on such tours, King made copious entries in his diary and later referred to these in preparing his report to the company. He reflected on the conditions he observed, the people he met, and the information that came to him.

King sensed that he put Consolidation Coal officials a little off balance by consistently showing greater interest in the living conditions provided for the miners and their families than in the mines, the equipment, and working conditions. He believed, however, that in towns where a company owned all of the property, it had an obligation to provide and maintain facilities that were *above* the average. Part of his reasoning was defensive. As a monopolist of the land in a company town, any standard lower than the one the miners would have adopted had they owned their own homes, provided the basis for justified dissatisfaction with the company. In the dozens of camps visited, King saw both company-owned towns and larger settlements in which the miners owned their own homes. He concluded and reported that the latter were better appointed and maintained on the average, than company housing.

King also advocated high standards out of his conviction that the physical environment decisively influenced the tenor of life carried on within it. When, for the first time, he passed through the Connellsville coke region in Pennsylvania, he compared it with the Black Country of England. So much of the ground was covered with soot and slack that the region was depressingly "bleak, dreary, and dehumanizing."[24] Surely, the workers in the area deserved better. And when he saw the magnificent Carnegie Library building in Connelsville, it struck him as cruel that philanthropy should come at the expense of so debasing an environment for workers and their families. He had similar misgivings when, toward the end of his travels, he passed the former Carnegie steel mills in Homestead. No doubt his sensibilities were heightened in both instances by the connection with Carnegie. He was storing up additional reasons for rejecting his offer.

The inordinate attention that King gave to housing, gardens, company stores, and the need for social centers may also have owed something to the fact that they were a path of least resistance. They provided the easiest means within the power of the owners (Rockefeller) to reduce the likelihood of industrial strife. Had King been actively interested in improving the conditions under which the miners worked, he would have had to confront the technical and economic arguments that mine managers would undoubtedly have raised in opposition. Their costs of production would have been at stake and, therefore, their effectiveness as managers. In contrast, the community improvements that interested King could all be covered out of profits. So long as Rockefeller was prepared to accept a slightly lower return on his investment, equipping and prettifying the mining towns was less of a problem for management. A Consolidation Coal official informed King that the company had spent more than the sum of all its rents on improvements last year. The rent for a substantial five-room house in the Connellsville region at the time was $7.75 per month or $93 a year.

It did not surprise King to learn that the miners themselves showed less of an interest in physical amenities than he did. In the West Virginia district, where the company's mines worked under a union contract, the union representatives concentrated their energies exclusively on the terms and conditions of employment. He understood this emphasis—with the appropriate terms and conditions the miners could look after themselves. But he still thought it vital for companies to reduce the potential for discontent by providing adequate and attractive housing and community facilities. In the West Virginia setting, he thought that a system of employee representation could be established to deal with issues of this sort, leaving the work-related questions to the union.

The relationship between the company and the miners naturally absorbed most of his attention. He found that Consolidation Coal followed different policies in each of the three districts visited. In West Virginia, the company worked under a union contract. In Maryland, an employee representation plan prevailed. The company had no structured relationship whatever with the miners in its Pennsylvania operations. It amused King to note that each district manager thought the situation in his district preferable to any other. He discerned that this was not merely some conservative quirk of nature. Each manager had accommodated company policy to the policy set by the operators' association in his district.

King perceived that as the largest producer in each of the fields, Consolidation Coal sometimes could bend the operators' associations to its will. This was true in both the Maryland and West Virginia districts but much less so in Pennsylvania. In the latter district, the operators were rabidly opposed to unions. He learned that, over the past several years, they had spent some $30,000 combatting a union organizing drive. Consolidation, he was told, had paid its pro rata share of these expenses. The operators were so nervous that, when the company had broached the idea of introducing a representation plan into its mines, they had banded together to importune against such a step. They were fearful that any organization of the miners would be captured by the union and provide a footing for the unionization of the entire district. As a result, Consolidation Coal had agreed not to introduce a plan. King found the situation highly reminiscent of Colorado.

Seeing the full range of possible relationships spread before him in Consolidation Coal's three districts, King's judgment in favor of unionism took on added strength. He deplored the dictatorial rule exercised in the Connellsville district. Of the Maryland district, he concluded that the domination of all of the employee committees by unionists meant the equivalent of a union contract. The West Virginia situation, with open and thorough dealings with the U.M.W. was clearly the best situation, and not only for the miners. He saw that in West Virginia, the managers and foremen could devote themselves to coal production, while in Pennsylvania, they had to devote vast amounts of time and energy to guarding against unionism.

By coincidence, King received a letter from Ivy Lee at this time. Lee, in England, sent along a number of newspaper clippings dealing with the work of the British Coal Commission. The clippings indicated that the British were considering only two equally far-reaching proposals for restructuring their coal industry. One called for the nationalization of the mines, the other for joint union–management control, with the unions rather than the companies owning the housing and community facilities. King thought he saw in these ideas a wholly new viewpoint emerging. Labor should be given control over its living and working conditions, while Capital should be relegated to the more purely economic aspects of the industry. Connecting this thought to his own position, he wrote:

> As one goes about these camps, so numerous that one can scarcely remember them, and sees the enormous wealth controlled by a handful of capitalists, one cannot but feel that the system which permits this sort of control is absolutely wrong, unjust, and indefensible; and that there will not be an end to social unrest until the transition is made to a joint control, with

a restoration to the community of much that today is in private hands. My task seems to be that of trying to bring about the change by an evolutionary method, and avoiding revolution and its attendant evils.[25]

In the following days, in his talks with various company officials, King found himself repeatedly holding up to them the threat of nationalization, saying that if the company did not make this or that class of improvements, it would have to bear the consequences in nationalization. Was he being hypocritical, he wondered? Since he thought that the nationalization of the industry was probably desirable, should he delay its advent by encouraging improvements; and was it honest of him to threaten with something of which he approved? He satisfied his conscience with the argument that his primary goal was to ameliorate the conditions of working people. It therefore mattered less that nationalization might be delayed than that the improvements be made. Concrete, short-term gains thus seemed of greater importance to him than longer-term structural changes in the organization of industry and society. He did not recognize that he sometimes reversed himself. Nor did he grasp that the tension between opportunism and idealism was the mainspring of his being.

At the end of his tour of Consolidation Coal, King traveled to Hot Springs, Virginia, to meet Rockefeller, confer, and relax. He gave considerable thought to how far he could go in recommending changes. He knew that he could not advocate the unionization of the Pennsylvania district. Neither the company people there nor Rockefeller were already for such a step. He could, however, recommend the introduction of a representation plan. That would go at least some way toward reducing the arbitrary rule exercised by the company. And Rockefeller would support such a move.

What King did not know was that Rockefeller had opened himself again to the counsel of Starr Murphy on labor matters. King saw Murphy as uninformed, unsympathetic to labor, and overly conservative. Rockefeller, on the other hand, depended upon Murphy's judgment in many of his other activities. He probably wanted to hear his message now because it conformed so completely with his own views.

As if to steel Rockefeller against the force of King's arguments, Murphy wrote out his advisory on the day the two men were to rendezvous in Virginia. He knew his words would have greater impact in written form than delivered orally. Flatly contradicting

John D. Rockefeller, Jr., and Starr Murphy (right), October 1919. By permission of the Rockefeller Archive Center.

King, he declared that unionism and employee representation were diametrically opposed ideas. Unionism, he argued, assumed the existence of an unending conflict of interest between the employer and his workers. Largely in consequence of this, the unions regarded the closed shop and the strike as acceptable weapons of combat. By doing so, they were rendered both monopolistic and coercive. Employee representation, in contrast, assumed that the parties in industry were bound together by a community of shared interests. It stood for democracy and freedom by including all of the workers while permitting them to join or not join unions, as they saw fit. Employee representation alone made for genuine collective bargaining, he asserted. Given these differences, he advised Rockefeller, "you must be very careful, as to committing yourself to the labor union program. It is better to place your emphasis on the Plan of Representation."[26] Since King was not prepared to recommend anything different from what Murphy and Rockefeller preferred, no problems arose.

In the three weeks between the Hot Springs meeting and his visit to New York City, King arranged his affairs, wrote up his survey for Consolidation Coal, and packed for his journey to England. In the same period, a series of violent incidents added to the growing fear that the United States was under attack from within. On April 28, a bomb was delivered through the mails to the mayor of Seattle, most recently involved in that city's general strike. The device was discovered before it could do any damage. But on the following day, a similar device exploded on opening at the home of a former U.S. Senator from Georgia. News of these incidents including descriptions of the packages, prompted a New York City postal clerk to recall a number of similar packages he had held up for inadequate postage. Sixteen mail bombs were found still at the post office and eighteen more were recovered after other stations were alerted. The bomb targets included cabinet officers, immigration officials, several Supreme Court justices, and two capitalists: J. P. Morgan and John D. Rockefeller.

Coming on the eve of May Day, the bomb plot was assumed by many people to be the work of radicals. As a result, May Day paraders in Boston, New York, Cleveland, Chicago, and Detroit were assaulted by mobs of uniformed service men, veterans, and others. In several cities, the mobs also wrecked the offices of organizations thought to be radical. In most cities, those arrested by the police were usually the victims. Just a few days later, in Washington, D.C., a soldier shot a man who remained seated during the playing of the "Star Spangled Banner." The American Legion was organized two days later on a platform of 100 percent Americanism.

When King arrived in New York toward the middle of May, he found Rockefeller weighing various schemes for thwarting the spread of Bolshevism. Schemes and schemers seemed to abound to King. It transpired that Robert Maisel, the director of the American Alliance for Labor and Democracy, had continued to solicit funds from Rockefeller well after Samuel Gompers had asked him to resign. Several others who approached Rockefeller for support also struck King as opportunists, more interested in promoting their own careers than anything else. He marveled at Rockefeller's ability to resist growing cynical in the face of repeated encounters of this sort. Somehow, he maintained his ability to say no without becoming jaundiced in his view of people.

Sympathizing with Rockefeller's desire to be of some service in combatting Bolshevism, King advised that he should become involved only in a broad national movement, as one of many sponsors. If such a movement were to appear with the aim of educating public opinion, that would be worthy of his support. There were too many hidden dangers in backing individuals or narrow groups. Rockefeller agreed but then gave him a copy of John Spargo's recent book, *Bolshevism*, to read during his trip. He wanted to know if it was the sort of thing he might help to circulate.

After dinner at the Rockefeller home that evening, they were joined by Ivy Lee, newly returned from several months in Europe. Lee reported that England stood on the brink of revolution. Conditions everywhere were chaotic. He thought it inevitable that the coal industry would be nationalized. On learning that Rockefeller was considering an autumn visit to Britain and the continent, he urged against it. In both England and France, he reported, the Rockefeller name was a favorite target of abuse. When in Paris, he had found Upton Sinclair's novel about the Colorado strike, *King Coal*, serialized in the left-wing press. He warned that Rockefeller would not be safe in so supercharged an atmosphere.

The next day, King's last before sailing, was filled with activity and reward. As they drove to 26 Broadway, Rockefeller talked about the report on Consolidation Coal that he had now had an opportunity to read. He expressed complete satisfaction with the document, though he supposed parts of it would greatly embarrass the officers. He was alluding, no doubt, to King's depiction of the company's relations with the miners in Pennsylvania. King had written with perfect candor of finding

an attitude on the part of Capital and Management toward Labor which has been provocative in the past of the most bitter
industrial warfare, and which could not be publicly defended
for an hour in the changed order which the War has helped
bring into being . . . I believe it is true that intimidation is the
method relied upon by the officials of the company to prevent
organization and to secure compliance . . .[27]

When the car brought them to Wall Street, the two men parted
company briefly while King went to keep an appointment with
Senator Watson, the president of Consolidation Coal. Watson
seemed sincerely pleased with his report and discussed several aspects of it. He told King that some of his fellow mine operators
boasted that it was enough to give the miners shanties to live in,
that their operations went as smoothly if they entirely ignored
many of the things King wanted Consolidation Coal to spend
money on. To which King responded that Consolidation Coal was
too large and powerful to escape from public notice as some
smaller operators might. It therefore had an obligation to place
itself above criticism.

Although King saw Watson as an old line Tory, accustomed to
having his way, he could not help being touched by his reference
to the difficulty the older managers would have in trying to catch
up with the rapid changes occurring all around them. King supposed that he was bemoaning his own fate quite as much as that of
the older managers and, for that reason, obliged himself to be especially kind in his responses. At the same time, he could not help
thinking how fortunate it was that such men and their ways of
conducting business were being outmoded. When the senator
asked him to maintain contact with the young man they were
going to place in charge of industrial relations, King promised
that he would. He also cleared his conscience when the question
of his fee arose. Watson offered to pay whatever figure he named,
but King demurred, saying he would accept whatever the company thought appropriate, provided that the $1000 paid him in
August be taken into account, for he believed that he had done
nothing to earn the money.

As he walked to the office at 26 Broadway, King reflected on
how well the interview had gone. A real service had been performed for Consolidation Coal. He had revealed Rockefeller's attitude toward labor to the officers, and they in turn must now
strive to reveal that attitude to their subordinates and to the min-

ers. It struck him that this was the clearest example of what the personal element in industrial relations amounted to—the documents and the machinery were less important than the spirit of the people who worked with them.

After reporting on the interview to Rockefeller, the two traveled uptown to pay a call on Samuel Gompers. Rockefeller had suggested and arranged the visit after informing King that Gompers had recently been in an automobile accident. He was still recuperating, and theirs was in the nature of a courtesy call.

They found the ailing labor leader seated in his dressing gown for the interview. King was shocked at how greatly he had aged since their last meeting. Almost immediately, Gompers began to recount and bemoan, Job-like, his many recent misfortunes. Within the year, he related, while completely absorbed first in war activities and then in peace efforts, his dearest daughter had been carried off in the influenza epidemic, his wife had suffered a paralyzing stroke, and now he had become the victim of this accident. Worse still, his sight was failing him and he feared he would soon be blind.

Rockefeller tried to cheer him by suggesting that his eye problems were probably a temporary result of the accident that would go away as he regained his strength. Insensible to Gompers' atheism, he urged him to keep his faith as he struggled through his troubles.

Rockefeller also thanked the unionist for the very kind words he had spoken about him to Ivy Lee when they had met in France. Gompers replied that his Atlantic City speech had made a profound impression, not only in this country but all over Europe. King then asked what he would think about their distributing copies of the address among American workers, and Gompers responded by suggesting as wide a circulation as possible.

Rockefeller next brought up the questions he had about Maisel's status and his solicitations. Gompers was clearly irritated by what he learned and promised to ensure against any further embarrassment. Rockefeller concluded by suggesting that once he had fully recovered they would discuss a proposal for the Rockefeller Foundation to develop a research program in industrial diseases. He thought it important to have the backing of labor in such an effort.

While Rockefeller moved off and engaged in a conversation with Gompers' nurse, King had a few minutes alone with him. Knowing that King was bound for England, Gompers asked if he would not do what he could to stop the forthcoming visit of Arthur Henderson of the British Labour Party. He was concerned that Henderson would stir up class feelings at the worst posible time. Alluding to his own growing inability to contain the militancy of many unionists and organizers, he confessed, "We are having our problems, and all we can do to keep the movement from going too far at the present time."[28] King did not indicate what response he made. Since he greatly admired Henderson's ideas, the suggestion that he help keep him out of the country must have caused him to feel the burden of living with two political time tables, one for England and another for North America.

They came away feeling that they had visibly cheered Gompers and were pleased that he, in turn, had been so cordial to them. Rockefeller reported that the nurse believed that the accident had saved Gompers' life. He probably would have died of diabetes had he not been compelled by his injuries to take a complete rest. The nurse had also told him of the great quantities of flowers that were delivered every day and of how Mr. Gompers kept only one or two blossoms for himself and had the rest distributed in the hospitals. King, like Rockefeller, attached considerable importance to such gestures.

They met George W. Perkins at the Whitehall Club for lunch. Perkins, a director of United States Steel and International Harvester, was most closely associated with Rockefeller as a supporter and director of the YMCA. He had just returned from an inspection tour of "Y" activities in Europe. The apparent purpose of the lunch was to provide him the opportunity to share his findings informally with Rockefeller. In discussing European conditions, Perkins concurred with Ivy Lee's judgment that it would be unsafe for Rockefeller to visit at this time. On the other hand, he thought King could not have picked a better moment to visit England, since industrial questions and proposals of all sorts were being examined as never before.

At one point, Perkins brought up the idea of profit sharing through stock ownership, of which he was a foremost advocate. Given this particular audience, he took the occasion to do a little soft selling. Over sixty thousand workers at U.S. Steel had bought shares in the company last year, he boasted. That was about one out of every three in the work force. He described how some workers participated in the annual stockholders' meeting and may have mentioned his unsuccessful efforts to have a worker named to the board of directors. Rockefeller suggested that if the steel workers continued to absorb shares year after year, they would in time come to own the company. Perkins agreed. All three men then agreed that such a result was desirable.

On returning to the office, Rockefeller and King met for a second time with Carl Gray of Consolidation Coal, who gave them a glowing account of his visit to C.F. & I. He and his party of fellow officers from Consolidation and Davis Coal & Coke had been very favorably impressed by all they had seen. They found the mining camps in excellent condition, so attractive in fact, that one of his colleagues had despaired of ever bringing Consolidation Coal up to such a standard. But, when it was pointed out that his company's camps were now in better shape than those of C.F. & I. when the improvements had begun, he took heart. They also had been impressed with the smooth and effective operation of the employee representation plan.

Because of these features, they had been told, C.F. & I. was making considerable savings in its labor costs. The company had become so desirable a place of employment that no money had to be spent on worker recruitment. Job applicants regularly exceeded the number of vacancies. Turnover in some of the camps was as low as 5 percent, which Gray contrasted with rates of 60 percent at Consolidation Coal for a comparable period. When Rockefeller asked whether the plan seemed like a paying proposition insofar as dividends were concerned, Gray responded that it seemed to pay in every direction. The only criticism he voiced had to do with the YMCA management of some of the community centers. It appeared that some "Y" staff people were more interested in recruiting members than in providing services to the miners. King thought to himself that all organizations were flawed in this way. He did not lay the problem to Rockefeller's insistence on involving the "Y" in this way, as he might have in a less charitable mood.

Both he and Rockefeller were highly pleased with Gray's assessment. It seemed a fitting climax to their day and for their leave-taking. King had one remaining piece of business, which he completed over tea with the Carnegies. They graciously accepted his refusal of their offer and bade him come to visit them on his return. He left them with no regrets.

In recounting the events of the day in his diary, King made evident the deep sense of fulfillment they had brought him. Hearing Gray describe their success in Colorado "was like completing the circle which we started to trace before the war commenced. . . .

After what has been accomplished in Colorado, nothing is impossible in any industrial situation if the right spirit can be put into it."[29]

Now Consolidation Coal and Standard Oil of Indiana would move along the same path, touched by the same spirit. Perhaps most gratifying of all was the meeting with Gompers. As always, King's thoughts carried him back to his first association with Rockefeller:

> Could anyone have imagined Mr. R. going to call on Mr. Gompers at that time, or believed that the day would come so soon that these two men would recognize in each other fellow workers in a common cause. But that was the significance of our visit this morning, their joint obligation to humanity, each controlling mighty forces, both desiring to use them for the common good. When one thinks here of the chasm that has been bridged which might have widened indefinitely, who can say what service may not have been rendered the world thereby.[30]

Here, it would seem that vanity got the better of King's judgment. Neither Gompers nor Rockefeller occupied the leadership positions he ascribed to them, except in the most figurative sense. With the end of the war, the ailing A.F. of L. leader lost practically all of the very considerable leverage that the government, in its need for uninterrupted production, had conferred on him. As for Rockefeller's influence over industry, King knew from experience it was often more nominal than real. Nor had their meeting erected a bridge strong enough to carry anything save courtesy. Gompers regarded employee representation as an evasion, and Rockefeller still looked on unions as antagonistic and coercive. Sometimes, as in this instance, the afterglow of King's achievements obscured the grasp of reality in which he prided himself. At other times, and this was particularly true of his misreading of the revolutionary potential of American society in 1919, his lifelong fear of disorder led him astray.

Of course, many, many people shared King's misapprehensions about the likelihood of revolution. Few of them, however, were as well read or as experienced as he in the study of social movements and social conflict. Moreover, his fears had not emerged just that spring and summer, when the most graphic evidence of social stress burst into the public consciousness. His revolutionary anxieties predated the red scare by a considerable margin. They were permanently ingrained in his constitution. This was why he was a liberal: the radicals promoted revolution by advocating expropriation, while the Tories threatened the same result by practicing it. Liberalism alone offered a path to the future in which the astute use of the State balanced contending interests and forces in such a way as to produce orderly progress.

On the day King sailed, a general strike broke out in Winnipeg, Manitoba. Normally, such an event would have attracted little notice to the south but, in a time of troubles when everyone is searching for some clue to the future, all signs are read for possible meanings. As with the Seattle general strike, the Canadian breakdown both testified to the combative militancy of workers and lent added credence to fears of an impending, irreconcilable, class conflict. More ominously, two weeks later, bombs exploded within the same hour in eight different American cities. Two people were killed, including one of the bomb throwers who apparently tripped as he approached the home of U.S. Attorney General A. Mitchell Palmer, in Washington. The subsequent identification of the bomber as an alien Italian anarchist from Philadelphia helped to convince numbers of people of the existence of a coordinated nationwide revolutionary conspiracy.

Writing from England on the same day as the bombings, King urged Rockefeller to do everything he could to prevent the outbreak of any major strike at this time. Such a contest, coming in so inflammable an atmosphere, he feared, might provoke a more general conflagration.

The May and June bomb episodes spurred a number of state legislatures to enact laws against criminal syndicalism. At the Justice Department, the Attorney General, and his aides mapped plans for the round up and deportation of alien radicals. In New York, an investigation into Bolshevik propaganda and influence was launched under the chairmanship of state senator Clayton R. Lusk. The Lusk Committee, as it came to be called, aped the tactics previously used by the federal government in the suppression of the I.W.W. In conjunction with public hearings, it sponsored a series of well-publicized raids aimed at collecting incriminating materials and disrupting radical organizations. On June 12, a combined force of state police and agents of the Justice Department raided the office of the Russian Soviet Bureau in New York City. Several tons of files and materials were seized and the head of the bureau brought before the committee to testify. Nine days later, three additonal raids were carried out and more organizational papers and propaganda taken. In the wake of these raids, committee members and their staffs helped to circulate exaggerated estimates of the size and potency of revolutionary radical forces. Although the raids were ostensibly aimed at frustrating the designs of the enemies of the nation, they did more to feed and perpetuate the growing political frenzy.

Toward the end of June, Starr Murphy reflected on King's letter by pointing out to Rockefeller that the recent strike at Western Union had come and gone without touching off a revolution. Evidently, he suggested, the current situation was not as volatile as King supposed.

Even false alarms were to be endured. Acting on what it claimed was reliable information, the Justice Department alerted police chiefs around the country to the likelihood of violent disturbances on the Fourth of July. The Department advised that the Bolsheviks planned to turn Independence Day into a nationwide day of terror. When the holiday passed without incident, it was not entirely clear whether the Justice Department had been mistaken or whether its warning had caused the reds to alter their plans.

Fed by such alarums, by the antiradical activities of many state legislatures, and by the mysterious bombings, tensions mounted as the summer progressed. Adverse economic developments that touched many more households in a direct way, added to the disquiet. Strikes, unemployment, and prices rose sharply through the spring and summer. The high cost of living became a source of grave concern, vying even with Bolshevism for attention. In Washington, Attorney General Palmer divided his time between developing plans for dealing with alien radicals and for combating rising prices. Antitrust suits, raids on speculative hoarders, and an extension of the President's wartime powers over foodstuffs and fuels made up the program of action he proposed in July.

At the very moment the President's Cabinet was examining these plans, the streets of Washington were given up to mayhem. A race riot gripped the capital. For three days violence flared in various parts of the city, leaving seven dead. Order was restored only by calling up federal troops. Several days later, racial warfare broke out in Chicago and continued for almost two weeks. Thirty-eight people were killed in the fighting. These were the two largest, but not most deadly, of the twenty-six race riots that spring and summer.

Mackenzie King returned from England during this riotous period and began preparing for the Liberal Party convention. While Chicago streets ran with blood, he appeared before convention committees in support of the reconstruction platform he had helped to write. While union organizers in Pittsburgh, Gary, and other steel centers, polled steel workers on their willingness to strike to enforce their demands, he attempted to offset Lady Laurier's effort to block his accession to the leadership. Happily for him, the party delegates were not swayed by her counsel. They elected King their new leader on the third ballot.

He wired the news to Rockefeller the same day. A few days later, he wrote that he could no longer accept the retainer they had agreed upon. He would continue to give advice whenever called upon, but he would do so as a friend. Rockefeller responded with a deeply appreciative letter of thanks.

As the war had intervened to give the idea of employee representation a life of its own, so King's elevation, for better or worse, left Rockefeller on his own.

Notes

1. *New York Times* (November 14, 1918), p. 3.
2. *New York Times* (November 17, 1918), p. 3.
3. Reprinted in Rockefeller (1923).
4. Grubbs (1968), p. 130.
5. Felix Frankfurter to John H. Sleicher, 12/23/18. J.D.R., Jr. Papers, Friends and Services, Box 20.
6. W.L.M.K. Diary, 1/1/19–1/14/19. Quoted in McGregor (1962), p. 276.
7. W.L.M.K. Diary, 1/14/19–1/21/19. Quoted in McGregor (1962), p. 274.
8. Ibid., 1/25/19, p. G2986.
9. Ibid., p. G2987.
10. W.L.M.K. to J.D.R., Jr., 1/25/19. J.D.R., Jr. Papers, Friends and Services, Box 72.
11. Ibid.
12. W.L.M.K. Diary, 1/25/19. W.L.M.K. Papers, Series J13, p. G2988.
13. Ibid., 2/3/19, p. G3001. Quotation marks in original.
14. Ibid., 2/7/19, p. G3010.
15. Ibid., 2/8/19, p. G3015.
16. Ibid., 2/14/19, p. G3020.
17. Quoted in McGregor (1962), p. 323.
18. Quoted in Smith (1964), p. 48.
19. W.L.M.K. to J.D.R., Jr., 3/4/19. Quoted in Fosdick (1956), p. 170.
20. J.D.R., Jr. to W.L.M.K., found among undated scraps in W.L.M.K. correspondence file for 1918, p. 35939. The timing of King's proposal would mark this letter as having been written in late February, 1919.

21. *Iron Trade Review* (May 1, 1919). Charles R. Towson to J.D.R., Jr., 5/23/19. J.D.R., Jr. Papers, C.F. & I. File, Business Interests.
22. Bethlehem Steel, E. I. duPont de Nemours, General Electric, General Motors, Goodyear Tire and Rubber, International Harvester, Irving Trust, Standard Oil of New Jersey, United States Rubber, and Westinghouse Electric and Manufacturing.
23. W.L.M.K. Diary, 4/8/19. W.L.M.K. Papers, Series J13, p. G3061.
24. Ibid., 4/14/19, p. G3069.
25. Ibid., 4/16/19, p. G3076.
26. Starr Murphy to J.D.R., Jr., 4/25/19. J.D.R., Jr. Papers, Economic Reform Interests, Box 14.
27. "Memorandum Respecting Survey of Industrial Relations. The Consolidation Coal Company," 5/9/19. J.D.R., Jr. Papers, Business Interests, Box 34.
28. W.L.M.K. Diary, 5/14/19. W.L.M.K. Papers. Series J13, p. G3083.
29. Ibid., p. G3083, 10.
30. Ibid., p. G3083, 14.

13. On His Own

The end of summer brought with it no relief. Strikes and riots continued to erupt, chipping away at confidence in the received order of things. The rush of events dwarfed and threatened to overwhelm all those involved, frightening them with the suggestion that the powers of reason and civilization somehow had been rendered impotent.

On September 1, President Wilson announced his intention to hold a national industrial conference. Equal numbers of labor, employer, and public representatives would be invited to Washington to help formulate the principles that would guide postwar industrial relations. The current strike wave and the impending threat of a nationwide steel strike made such a conference seem timely and appropriate. The British and Canadian governments had previously announced plans for similar meetings. The American press gave Wilson's action its hearty approval.

However, just a few days earlier, the President had made known his plan to tour the country speaking in support of the peace treaty. On September 3, he left Washington, scheduled to make thirty speeches in as many cities. Those who supposed that he would use these speaking opportunities to spell out his ideas about labor policy were destined for disappointment. Wilson neither possessed clear policy preferences nor displayed enough interest to even seek out assistance in developing a policy. In view of the very considerable pressures to which he and his administration were being subjected by labor disputes, his extreme disinterest in "urgent domestic problems"[1] bordered on the self-destructive. Wilson was apparently prepared to shunt the burden of labor problems onto his as yet unnamed conferees, while devoting himself exclusively to his fight for the peace treaty.

From London, Raymond B. Fosdick wrote to the White House to urge that John D. Rockefeller, Jr., be invited to the President's conference. In informing Rockefeller of his action, Fosdick both paid him tribute and expressed a point of view he expected Rockefeller to share. He had nominated Rockefeller, he wrote, because I think that your liberal point of view can aid immeasurably in laying the foundations of the industrial democracy of the future. The old era that existed before the war is dead. Whether we agree with it or not, labor in the future is going to have a great deal to say not only about working conditions and wages, but about management and the division of profits, and I am confident that your influence can help to shape the introduction of this new age so that it can be brought about normally and peacefully. The changes that are coming are going to call for radical readjustments in the attitude of many of our friends such as Judge Gary and others. The currents of the world's industrial thinking are rushing like a mighty Niagara, and while they can be controlled, they cannot be stopped or dammed. I am so confident of your openmindedness, and I believe so sincerely in your fearless adherence to the thing that is *right*—even if it involves a break with the past—that I attach really great importance to your being connected with this Commission . . .[2]

The thought that Rockefeller would be prepared to support trade unionism, and at the expense of employee representation, was an illusion. In time, Fosdick would come to understand, as he did not when he wrote his letter, that Rockefeller tended to become "evangelical in his commitments."[3] When he gave himself over to a particular cause, he closed his mind to alternatives. Fosdick, and Mackenzie King as well, also failed to perceive how profoundly Rockefeller's self-esteem was bound up with the Colorado industrial plan. He could not abandon employee representation without endangering the personal independence or the leadership standing he had gained as its advocate. What they saw as a social issue was deeply vested in Rockefeller as a personal matter. He could not compromise the representation scheme wthout compromising himself. As the fight over unionism intensified in the months ahead, he would find himself compelled to make his stand.

During the first weeks of September, along with its coverage of the President's tour, the *New York Times* carried daily reports on the pending steel strike. The anticipated confrontation between the foremost bastion of the open shop and the combined forces of the A.F. of L. easily overshadowed the host of lesser local strikes and lockouts. Since the President had intervened in late August to prevent a nationwide strike of railway workers, many people assumed that he would likewise intervene to prevent a steel strike. Reports indicated that Samuel Gompers and the leaders of the steel workers' organizing drive were meeting with government officials with just this object in mind. Into this setting, the alarming news of the Boston police strike exploded like a bomb.

Stunned readers across the country read of mobs rampaging through Boston streets, breaking windows and looting shops. America's most proper city had fallen victim to a barbarism that conjured up images of the sacking of Rome. No strike of the period was so widely reported in the press nor condemned so vociferously and universally.

More than any other event of the era, the police strike forced people to think about unions. It did so in a context that was devastating to the interests of the labor movement. The Massachusetts governor dispatched five thousand state guardsmen to the beleaguered city. In the three days of the strike, eight deaths were reported and estimated property damage exceeded a quarter of a million dollars. From Montana, President Wilson denounced the walkout as "a crime against civilization."[4]

Gompers, who chanced to be in Massachusetts for the funeral of his father, moved as quickly as he could to stem the backlash of the strike. He persuaded the police to return to work while efforts were made to arrange a settlement. Then, he wired the Boston Police Commissioner and Governor Calvin Coolidge asking that the men be allowed to return to their posts and that outstanding differences be arbitrated. The commissioner refused both requests and was supported in this by the governor. The latter's response to Gompers so captured the sentiment of the country that Coolidge became something of a national hero overnight. His reply contained the memorable statement "There is no right to strike against the public safety by anybody, anywhere, any time."[5]

While attention was riveted on the unfolding tragedy in Boston, the threatened steel strike moved along its course. When the leaders of the organizing drive learned that the government's latest efforts to arrange a joint conference had failed, they set the strike date for September 22. Unaware of this action, President Wilson wrote to ask that the strike be postponed until after his industrial conference had met. Gompers also went to work for a postponement.

Gompers had learned from Bernard Baruch, the President's emissary in private talks with steel czar Elbert Gary, just how intransigent the steel makers were. He also claimed to possess confidential information to the effect that the open shop forces of the country had pledged their full support to Gary. Because they were "tired of the domination of labor,"[6] these employers wanted the steel industry to set an example that would reverberate throughout the economy. Given this information and knowing how green and untried the steel workers' organization was, Gompers held out little hope for a strike victory. He preferred instead to go along with Baruch's plan to postpone the strike and use the President's conference to engineer a settlement. Both Baruch and Gompers apparently supposed that the public exposure of Gary's blind refusal to countenance the right either to organize or to bargain collectively would prove so embarrassing that he would be forced to come to terms. The wartime policies of the War Labor Board and the exemplary service of American workers were still fresh enough in the public mind to make such a strategy seem plausible.

It proved impossible to revoke the strike order, however. When queried, organizers from many different steel-making districts reported that the workers would strike on September 22, with the union or without it. Like characters in a Greek tragedy, Gompers and the strike leaders were helpless to avoid their fate. The organization and the militancy their efforts had called to life would be consumed in a strike they knew was likely to fail.

On Mackenzie King's recommendation, Rockefeller called on Gary and Henry Clay Frick on September 17. Frick, still notorious for his leading role in the Homestead strike of 1892, was on the board of directors of U.S. Steel. Rockefeller found him perfectly immovable, entirely unsympathetic to any form of collective bargaining or employee representation. Having learned only how to wear his iron fist beneath a velvet gauntlet, Frick again was prepared to bare his hand. The almighty Gary proved equally deaf to counsel. Rockefeller described for him the successes of representation plans at such places as Colorado Fuel & Iron, Bethlehem Steel, and Midvale Steel. But the willful autocrat would have none of it, such schemes were the entering wedge of the closed shop. The principle of representation, he warned Rockefeller, was both dangerous and unsound.

In reporting the exchange to King the following day, Rockefeller wrote:

> The interview was most pleasant and he was glad to talk and was very courteous. I said in leaving that I hoped the situation would work out. . . . He replied: "If it does not, it will be be-

cause you and others are advocating representation and collective bargaining". To which I replied, "With every courtesy and fullest respect, Judge Gary, I might say that if the outcome of the present situation is not as you and I both hope it will be, it will be due to the fact that you and other employers are unwilling to recognize and adopt the fundamental and just principle of representation and collective bargaining".[7]

Rockefeller came away without having had any effect. But what did he mean when he associated himself with the outcome Gary wished for? One reading is that they both wished for a peaceful settlement. Both knew, however, that this could occur only if the union miraculously evaporated. Gary and his minions would not concede anything unless compelled by superior force. Possibly, Rockefeller's remark was a rhetorical flourish. More likely, it meant that he joined Gary in wishing that the steel industry would escape unionization. He must have told Gary that representation plans rendered unions unnecessary. This would have been his main talking point, and the one for which he could adduce hard evidence in the experience of C.F. & I.

Ironically, at the same moment that Rockefeller was probably advancing this line of argument in New York, King was denying it in Ottawa. At the Canadian National Industrial Conference (September 15–20) to which he was a delegate, a union delegate alleged that King had developed the Colorado Industrial Plan to help Rockefeller avoid unionization. This he flatly denied. He told the conference of his talk with the national officers of the U.M.W. and of their expressed belief that neither recognition nor a union contract was possible at that time. They had requested only that C.F. & I. recognize the right of the miners to join unions, and this had been done. The plan had thus been accepted by the top leaders of the union. It represented in every way a real advance over the situation that existed prior to that time. In buttressing his case, King went on to note that he subsequently had counseled Rockefeller in favor of union recognition in his dealing with the miners employed by Standard Oil of Indiana.

Rockefeller was chagrined when he subsequently learned of this reference to Standard Oil of Indiana. He believed King had overstepped the bounds of their confidential relationship and would so inform him when next they met. Before that could occur, however, Rockefeller endured a greater disappointment from a different quarter. When steel workers around the country struck on September 22, most of the men at the Pueblo mills of C.F. & I. joined them. This marked the first strike in a facility with a representation plan.

C.F. & I. president Jesse Welborn had been so confident that *his* steel workers would not strike, that he had taunted a union organizer with "All the men on the outside on Monday will be yours and all those on the inside will be mine."[8] Upwards of ninety-five percent of the company's sixty-five hundred man work force stayed away from work that day. They constituted one of the smaller divisions in the army of a quarter of a million steel workers that struck, about half of the total industry work force.

Both Rockefeller and Welborn had counted on the representation plan to immunize C.F. & I. from the strike. Reassuring one another, they had reasoned that the plan gave their workers some say in working conditions and provided a means for dealing with grievances. When, in 1918, the elected representatives had asked that the eight-hour day be adopted, the company had acquiesced. The men thus had concrete evidence of the effectiveness of the plan in gaining benefits. Moreover, because of its concession, C.F. & I. was the only steel maker that had already satisfied the key strike demand for the eight-hour day. Such reasoning led Rockefeller and Welborn to conclude that the workers in the Pueblo mills had little or nothing to gain from striking. Consequently, when the walkout occurred, both men found it unaccountable. Their thoughts were tinged with feelings of betrayal. Much as the sanctimonious Gary did, they were prepared to blame the steel workers for not knowing what was good for them.

From the onset of the strike, the *New York Times* reverted to its strident prewar antiunionism. Editorially, the paper declared that the true object of the strike was "to destroy the principle of the 'open shop', and upon that point the employers cannot yield save at the cost of grave injustice to their men, a great majority of whom, they declare, do not desire to join the outside organization."[9]

For so long as organs of public opinion like the *Times* were unprepared to assess critically the real world of industrial relations, blind sentiment would continue to call their tune. That the steel companies, so nobly engaged in defending their men from the "grave injustice" of having to join a union. were interested only in the one right that accrued to their own advantage and that they were prepared to violate all other worker rights in the process was simply ignored. The company spies, armed guards, blacklists, and the coercion and intimidation on and off the job were still perceived too dimly to produce a public outcry. Such practices made a mockery of Gary's concern for the individual steel worker's right to work. But no one arose to point the finger at the naked steel potentate. On the contrary, the law enforcement officers and military intelligence agents who knew of "the under-cover reports of the great corporations"[10] were grateful for the information they received as a result. They were also prepared to use these spy reports to the advantage of the companies. The strike meetings dispersed, the pickets arrested, the raids and the shootings—in fact all of the violence and disorder associated with the strike—were attributed by police and Army intelligence officers to reds and revolutionaries. Such authorities and the steel spokesmen were taken at their word and assumed to be blameless.

Mackenzie King happened to address a letter to Rockefeller on the first day of the strike, when its outcome was still very much in doubt. His primary purpose in writing was to report on the Canadian industrial conference that had just ended. He wanted to convey some sense of what had taken place and of the role he had played in the deliberations. Mindful that Rockefeller would participate in similar proceedings in the near future, he closed the letter with some advice. It was not so much counsel as exhortation, remarkable for its bold evangelism. It indicated that the knowledgeable, rational expert relied on faith above all else.

> Take every chance that offers to meet with the heads of the unions. . . . If there is ever to be peace instead of war in industry, it will come only through the attitude of organized groups of Capital and Labor ceasing to be one of militancy and becoming one of cooperation. There is nothing Christian in the militant attitude. Christianity, as you and I know, offers the only final solution to these great problems. Can you imagine our Saviour, with the power that Judge Gary has had, permitting a situation to develop which leads, in the first few hours, to violence and bloodshed? "Let the mind which is in Christ be also in you." No other attitude can be assumed by anyone who professes to be a follower of Christ. The times are demanding that some of us unfurl the standards of Christianity in His name.[11]

Three days after the strike began, President Wilson's speaking tour brought him to Pueblo, Colorado. Although many of those who turned out to hear him were affected in one way or another

by the shutdown of C.F. & I., he did not diverge from his prepared address to discuss the strike. He never had another chance.
Later that night he suffered a stroke. The balance of his tour was
abruptly cancelled and his special train hurriedly carried him
back to Washington. One week later, he suffered a second stroke.
The steel strike was fought out during his incapacity. The industrial conference would convene and collapse while he struggled
for life. He never fully recovered. For the next several months,
those of his duties that were not entirely neglected, were fulfilled
in his name by Mrs. Wilson and his secretary Joseph Tumulty.
Few people knew the President's actual condition or of the extent
of Mrs. Wilson's assumption of power.

One week before the conference was to get underway, King
came to New York at Rockefeller's request. He found him seriously contemplating whether he shouldn't excuse himself from
the conference. Between the steel strike and the President's illness, the situation seemed so confused that he did not see what he
might contribute. King allayed his fears by reminding him of his
leadership responsibilities. More than ever, in view of the circumstances, his willingness to do the right thing was needed by the
country. The upshot of their talk was that Rockefeller asked him to
read over and revise a speech he had prepared for the conference.

Starr Murphy joined them, and as they drove to the Rockefeller
estate in Tarrytown for the day, they discussed the steel strike.
Murphy supported the companies and thought they were fighting
the good fight against the closed shop. King tried unsuccessfully
to get him to admit that many of the grievances voiced by the
unionists were justified. Murphy also refused to concede that the
professed fear of the closed shop just possibly might be more a
matter of employer self-interest than of principle. The exchange
only confirmed King's judgment that, in labor matters, Murphy
was a poor advisor for Rockefeller.

Rockefeller described at some length his meetings with Frick
and Gary. He had been most impressed with how immovable they
were. Their "jaws were set," as he put it.[12] He believed they were
completely in the wrong in refusing to bargain collectively with
their own men. The steel workers at Pueblo, he said, had been
wrong, too, for having answered the union's strike call when their
own relations with C.F. & I. had been so amicable. His mind loved
to strike balances like this, but it was very poor accounting, for as
in this instance it led him to equate liabilities that in their weight
and consequence were highly unequal.

In their discussions of the upcoming conference, King took every opportunity to impress upon Rockefeller how important it would be to avoid any advocacy of representation plans "as a device for a company union."[13] He urged him to shun comparisons or contrasts; to support the idea of employee representation without indicating or limiting who the representatives might be. The challenge of the times, he advised, was to recognize that unionism was here to stay and find some way to transform its militant attitude into a more cooperative one.

Events were racing by so quickly that in one day they barely had time to discuss and make sense of them. The shutdown of the British railways by a strike, the Senate hearings on the steel struggle, the Rockefeller gift of $20 million for the support of medical schools, the President's illness, the racial violence in Omaha—all within the past three days—merited their attention. Most of these events, their outcomes and consequences unknown, only increased anxieties about what lay ahead. King undoubtedly praised the Rockefellers' act of philanthropy because it expressed a positive and hopeful attitude toward the future. He came away believing that he had helped labor by helping Rockefeller to a clearer understanding of his position toward unionism. He also reflected on the changed quality of their encounter, "It was gratifying too, seeing Mr. R. again & especially being my own master & being in a position to meet him on entire equality."[14]

Shortly after his return to Ottawa, King received a letter that alarmed him. It contained further revisions of the speech Rockefeller planned to make at the conference that King thought revealed "an inclination to revert back to a reactionary position."[15] He carefully designed his response to have the greatest effect. By the time his letter arrived, the conference was already underway.

The conference began under a number of handicaps. The President's absence, though felt by everyone, was not among them. If anything, the President was the handicapper. He had agreed to Baruch's plan to use the conference as an arena for settling the steel strike but failed to inform the participants of this, which set many of them on edge. Gary, for example, was prevailed upon to participate as a public representative, but would almost certainly have refused had he known the role intended for him. Only Baruch, and Gompers and his colleagues, were privy to the strategy. The fact that the strike had not been postponed did not cause them to alter their plan.

The composition of the public group also suggests that Wilson

Left to right: Franklin K. Lane, Elbert H. Gary, Samuel Gompers, William B. Wilson, and John D. Rockefeller, Jr. at the President's Industrial Conference, October 1919. By permission of the Rockefeller Archive Center.

counted upon a miracle such as the War Labor Conference Board had provided. None of the many men who had served so effectively on the various wartime labor boards were invited. By this stroke, their experience and grasp of conditions and issues were forsaken. To counsel with professional labor leaders and committed business leaders, he named a hodgepodge of public representatives, few of whom possessed either much experience or understanding of industrial relations. No one could fathom why men like Gary and Rockefeller were named to represent the public. Naming public delegates also resulted, inexplicably, in delegations of unequal size. The consequences were disastrous.

When the conference convened, it was discovered that seventeen business and seventeen labor delegates were present, whereas the public was represented by twenty-two men plus three representatives of the interests of women. Had the original announcement of equal delegations been adhered to, it would have increased the likelihood that majority rule would have prevailed. In the face of unequal groups, however, bloc voting was adopted. A proposition could express the will of the conference only if approved by a majority of the votes cast in each of the three groups. Since no proposition of consequence could muster this kind of support, the voting rule sealed the fate of the conference.

In reviewing the record of the sessions, there is a great temptation to suppose that if only some wonderfully charismatic figure had emerged to speak for the public interest, differences might have been resolved. The conflict of ideas and interests that surfaced at the conference, however, required power, not charisma, if they were to be overawed.

Rockefeller innocently introduced one of the first resolutions at the conference. He called upon the body to accept the principle of employee representation. Hoping to attract support from all sides, he had drawn his resolution very broadly. To his pleasant surprise, no one seemed to oppose him. Philosophically, everyone agreed that workers had a right to organize. The divisive issue centered on the form of their organization. In his motion, Rockefeller had left this up to the parties in each firm to settle. The labor men at the conference prevailed upon him to amend his language to permit the employees alone to decide how they would be represented. This change proved unacceptable to the employer group.

Rockefeller's motion was subsequently displaced by one developed within the public group and presented several days later.

The right of wage earners to organize in trade and labor unions, to bargain collectively, to be represented by representatives of their own choosing in negotiations and adjustments with employers, and in respect to wages, hours of labor, and relations and conditions of employment is recognized.

This must not be understood as limiting the right of any wage earner to refrain from joining any organization or to deal directly with his employer if he so chooses.[16]

Rockefeller was the first to speak in favor of the motion. He read the speech that King had revised for him. Substantial portions of what he said were lifted verbatim from his Atlantic City address the previous December. Consequently, many of his remarks were more germane for their spirit than for their substance. Such were the dynamics at work within the conference, however, that the position he supported outweighed his reasons for doing so. He sat down to the thundering applause of the labor and public delegates.

Both at the conference and afterwards, rumors circulated to the effect that Ivy Lee had written his speech. This was but one piece of the mistaken role that outsiders attributed to Lee and that did so much to inflate his reputation. Rockefeller was sufficiently aware of Lee's limitations as a publicist that he had not even thought to show him the speech. Subsequently, he saw to it that Lee distributed copies of his remarks as widely as possible. This was more nearly Lee's true role in recovering the reputation of the Rockefellers.

The leading spokesman in opposition to the motion was Frederick P. Fish of Boston, president of the National Industrial Conference Board. He presented a number of arguments but concluded with two major reservations. One was that it was wrong to oblige employers to deal with representatives of their employees who were not themselves in his employ. Union leaders, he argued, had interests and aspirations different from those of the men they were supposed to represent. They placed the union's interests before those of the workers and therefore might act in ways inimical to the interests both of a firm and its employees. His second reservation took the form of a sweeping assertion that in view of the diversity of size, character, and existing employee relations among firms, it was wrong to impose upon them a single system of relations.

Counterarguments were offered. It was pointed out that companies routinely hired outside experts to represent them in legal matters, for example. Why shouldn't workers have the same advantage of skilled advocates? Henry S. Dennison, a model employer sitting as a public representative, argued that it was part of his responsibility as a manager to work with whomever his employees chose to represent them.

The employers' group insisted that if employees were conceded the right to organize and bargain collectively, the employer must be granted the correlative right "to deal or not to deal with men or groups of men who are not his employees."[17] The other groups rejected this argument and voted down the employers' substitute motion. The original motion was then put to a vote and supported by labor and the public, but opposed by the employers. The motion therefore failed.

By this time, the plan to use the conference to settle the steel strike had also come undone. Gompers had moved that the conference create a six-man, tripartite, arbitration panel, empowered to resolve the strike. Gary, in his only speech before the body, reiterated the steel makers' intention to deal only with their own employees as in the past. Instead of resenting Gary, many of the delegates took exception to what they saw as Gompers' attempt to introduce a controversial and divisive issue into their deliberations. His motion was defeated. The strike was left to run its course.

On what was to prove to be their final day of meetings, the delegates were read a message ostensibly from President Wilson. It asked them to renew their efforts to find a basis for agreement. Gompers called for a recess. When the delegates reconvened, he presented a new resolution that read:

> The right of wage earners to organize without discrimination, to bargain collectively, to be represented by representatives of their own choosing in negotiations and adjustments with the employers in respect to wages, hours of labor, and relations and conditions of employment, is recognized.[18]

This new wording avoided any mention of unions. By implication, it meant that the labor group was prepared to accept any form of employee organization. But, again, Fish rose in opposition. He contended that the words did not mean what they said, that lurking behind those words was the intention to compel unionization and collective bargaining throughout the economy. He asserted that he would not approve of any resolution that did not grant to employers the right to refuse to deal with representatives of their employees who were not themselves employees of the firm.

Two other employer spokesmen also took the floor to oppose the resolution. One of them quoted a resolution passed at the most recent convention of the A.F. of L. in June. This ran to the effect that many companies had introduced schemes of collective bargaining "akin to the Rockefeller plan"[19] into their plants. The resolution condemned all such "company unions" and asserted that the trade union was the only kind of organization fitted for bargaining.

Gompers was queried on this point and asked to square the meaning of the A.F. of L. resolution with the one now under consideration. He protested that it was unfair to drag in a convention resolution that represented an expression of preferences and goals. It was true, he admitted, that organized labor would continue arguing and persuading in favor of trade unions against company unions, but that was not inconsistent with the motion before the house. In the voting that followed, a majority of the public and labor groups supported the motion while the employers divided 10 to 7 against. The motion, therefore, lost. Following a brief and bitter speech, Gompers led the labor delegation from the conference.

The collapse of the conference was such an important event that little notice was taken of Rockefeller's vote on the last motion. As he wrote that same day, he had supported the right to organize and collective bargaining in the earlier resolutions. But once it had become clear that the labor people believed that only trade unions could properly represent workers, he no longer could go along with them. He had voted against the motion.

The break-up of the conference prompted a *Times* editorial writer to wish that some commanding figure might have emerged from the public group "who could have compelled both parties . . . to compose the differences."[20] But since many of the public members *were* forceful personalities accustomed to leadership, it appears more likely that the differences were unbridgeable. In their last motion, the union leaders had cut their demands to the bone. The employers could not yield the final inch. They could not bring themselves to say that if their employees elected to have unions represent them, they would deal with them. They could not because they did not want to live with that result and because, just then, Gary and the steel industry were locked in combat over precisely this issue. They could not let their champion down.

The members of the public group met alone during the next two days to draft a report and make recommendations to the President. Rockefeller chaired the committee that recommended that a second conference be convened as soon as possible, with fewer participants and no group identifications.

As they met, Gary appeared before the annual meeting of the Iron and Steel Institute. He received a standing ovation. The steelmen applauded his handling of the strike and were grateful that he had conceded nothing at the President's conference. He acknowledged their fealty with a brief homily on the dangers of the closed shop. With all the pedantry at his command, he reminded his listeners of the great trust that was theirs in protecting the rights of the workers. He concluded by exhorting Institute members to do their part in the fight against Bolshevism and un-American propaganda.

The steel strike—whether by company design or not, it is impossible to say—rekindled the languishing fires of the red scare. In either event, a critical role was played by the United States Army. The Wilson Administration in its rush to dismantle the war machine had unwisely chosen to preserve its domestic spying operations. Fearful of the threat of revolutionary subversion, the government wanted listening posts, and military intelligence agents provided them.

With a military network spanning the country and private sources of information available through local police, companies, and members of the American Protective League, intelligence agents fed the growing hysteria of official Washington and the daily press. Rumors of the great influence of radicals in the steel strike were circulated widely. Several military intelligence officers appeared before Senate committee hearings and gave the distinct impression that plots and revolutionary conspiracies abounded. A series of riots in Gary, Indiana, and the exposure of a revolutionary pamphlet, written in 1911 by one of the leaders of the strike, seemed to comport with this testimony.

Late in October, as the red scare revived and the industrial conference moved toward impasse, Secretary of Labor Wilson informed the cabinet that efforts to avert a nationwide coal strike had proved unsuccessful. Unless some action was taken, he advised, the miners would walk out on November 1. The country would then face the unprecedented condition of two massive strikes at the same time. Panicked by the thought that this constellation of events might put an unbearable strain on the country, the cabinet resolved to act decisively.

Efforts to head off the strike through court injunctions, however, proved unsuccessful. Federal troops were soon deployed in West Virginia coal fields, while state militias moved into mining districts in several other states. Quite independent of these events, on November 7, Justice Department agents raided the offices of the Russian Workers' Union in twelve cities. These were the first of the Palmer raids.

The national coal strike provided the second test of the Colorado Industrial Plan within two months. C.F. & I. officials were naturally very eager to avoid a second embarrassment at the hands of their employees. Armed with the intelligence that the coal union intended to convert the national strike into a local struggle to displace the representation plan, Welborn and his subordinates acted to isolate the coal camps. For the first time since the plan had gone into effect, union organizers were denied entry. Union members among the employees were refused access to company buildings for meetings. In several camps, union activists were discharged and given notice to vacate company housing, although only one man was actually forced to move. Company officials also visited the camps and talked with the men in an effort to discourage any strike sympathies. They asked the men, and their wives too at some of the meetings, to vote by show of hands whether they wanted to strike or not. Not surprisingly, most men and women publicly indicated that they had no desire to strike. Convinced that their miners were contented and that every precaution had been taken to shield them from the threats and appeals of union organizers, the managers confidently awaited the strike deadline.

Four out of every five C.F. & I. mine workers stayed out when the strike began. Had the mines closed because of the steel strike been working, the proportion would have been higher still, since those mines were heavily unionized. There were, however, sizeable defections from the strikers' ranks as time passed. On the last day of the strike, only slightly more than half of the work force remained out. This declining support, coupled with the votes in their prestrike polls, led company officials to contend that many of the men had stayed out only because they were fearful of what might happen if they tried to work. Welborn would take this position in his annual report to the stockholders. He attempted to buttress his argument by implying that the strike was least effective in the district where the state militia had provided protection for those who wished to work. He did not point out, though, that the district involved was the one least organized by the union.

In keeping with their efforts to portray both the steel and coal stoppages as the work of outside agitators who had the help of only a few insiders, company officers took steps to make examples of those few. Some miners were refused reemployment. Among these were twenty activists whom Welborn characterized as Bolsheviks or I.W.W. types. Numbers of union members were reemployed but reassigned to the disadvantage of their earnings. Members of this group protested to the union, which in turn brought the matter to the attention of both the U.S. Attorney General and the Colorado Industrial Commission. The latter agency conducted an inquiry and found the company blameless. More persistent investigators happened to be on the ground, however, and they concluded that the company was indeed taking reprisals.

The day the strike ended, posters went up in all of the camps reiterating the nondiscrimination clause in the plan and asserting the company's intention to continue to honor it. After condemning the leaders of the United Mine Workers union and those among its employees in coal and steel who wished to impose the closed shop, the poster went on to applaud the loyalty shown by most of the mine workers. It concluded by stating that "Those who are disloyal to our country or the company, or who engage in efforts to disturb harmonious relations within the company, will neither be retained in our service, nor allowed on our properties."[21]

Returning employees were also asked to sign the following declaration:

> As an employee of the Colorado Fuel and Iron Company, I know that it is operated as an open shop under the Plan of Representation of Employees of which I have received a copy. I will cooperate in maintaining the rules and agreements relating to my service and the laws of my State and Country.[22]

Through union channels, the introduction of this loyalty card, as the miners called it, was brought to the attention of the Attorney General. The union argued that the company was using the card as a device to discriminate against unionists and thus impeding the production of coal. Palmer's office asked C.F. & I. for an explanation and Welborn responded with a denial. Only a few men had been refused reemployment, he asserted. They had interfered with others who wanted to work during the strike.

Welborn also communicated with the Secretary of Labor in an effort to rebut charges that returning strikers had been made to renounce their union membership. He informed Washington that C.F. & I. had not swerved from its policy of nondiscrimination. Locally, however, union leaders disputed his assertions. Had it not been for the presence of a neutral observer, it would have been difficult to decide who to believe.

Several months before the strike, Rockefeller had been asked by the director of the Russell Sage Foundation if a researcher on his staff might undertake an examination of the workings of the plan at C.F. & I. The Sage group was studying distinctive efforts by individual companies to improve their industrial relations. Rockefeller eagerly agreed to the undertaking and readily won Welborn's consent.

Such visitations were not at all uncommon at C.F. & I. From the very start, the company had served as the showcase for representation. When Rockefeller wanted to familiarize any of his staff, or when companies asked to see at first-hand how a plan worked, C.F. & I. served as the training ground and model. Thus, it happened that at the time of the strike, Benjamin Selekman was on hand to observe and report on developments. In most instances he confirmed the existence of the practices that Welborn denied. The latter was not being dishonest; most often it was a case of his interpreting his directives in one way while his subordinates enforced them in another. Welborn was still not in control of his company. However, since Selekman's report was to remain unpublished for a number of years, no immediate consequences flowed from it.

Throughout the strike, Welborn sent a steady stream of telegrams to the New York office. In this manner, Rockefeller was informed of every development. Yet, when he wrote to King during the strike, he did not dwell on the disappointment the strike caused him. Nor did he relay any of the criticisms he heard because of the plan's failure to prevent strikes.

Instead, he paid warm tribute to King and responded in kind to the prayerful letter King had written prior to the President's conference.

How often during these past weeks have I wished that we might be in frequent conference as of old, and that I might have the benefit of the illumination and help which always come from my talks with you on these subjects of which you have thought and studied so deeply. May I speak especially of the closing paragraph of your letter, which so truly sets forth the only solution to all these problems. May the Christ spirit ever continue to guide both of us as we seek to serve our fellow men and to grapple with problems, however knotty and difficult.[23]

On the first anniversary of the armistice, Walter Lippmann captured the temper of the times in a brilliant essay in the *New Republic*. Surveying the past year, he wondered how such a shambles had been made of reconstruction. He answered the question by pointing to the President's abdication from domestic affairs well before his illness and to the helplessness of the cabinet in the ensuing leadership vacuum.

Lippmann thought the red hysteria a direct by-product of industrial conflict. Much of the strife that fed the scare, he believed, was provoked intentionally by the more reactionary businessmen. Gary, to his mind, led these forces. He wrote:

It is an open secret, for example that many powerful business men have been saying for months that there was needed a "show-down" with labor. It was commonly said before the steel strike that Mr. Gary was ready and that it would be an excellent opportunity to smash the overweening pretentions of the A.F. of L.[24]

From Lippmann's vantage point, it seemed incredible that Gary should have been asked to represent the public at the industrial conference. He argued that the President's obsession with the peace treaty might at the very least have led him to propose acceptance of the treaty's labor provisions as a condition of membership. This would have blocked Gary's participation and increased the likelihood that positive results would have emanated from the conference. Not even so perceptive an analyst as Lippmann could understand the design behind the invitation to Gary.

Lippmann twice mentioned Rockefeller in favorable contrasts with Gary. It had been proper to name Rockefeller as a public member, he asserted, since by his actions he had revealed his disinterestedness. Gary, on the other hand, could not rise above his own interests "because for him the issues of the conference were an incident in the labor policy of his corporation."[25] The identical statement could have been applied to Rockefeller's position had his own ambiguity not shielded him from discovery. Hence, when Lippmann bemoaned "the unfortunate fact that Mr. Gary rather than someone like Mr. Rockefeller is leading the employers of the country,"[26] he may not have appreciated how narrow a difference separated the two men. Lippmann had, however, sensed Rockefeller's desire to be conciliatory. It was this spirit of compromise that distinguished him from Gary, and resulted in his ambivalence. Rockefeller was prepared to accept and even support change. His problem was that he could not find a common ground between his position and that of the unions. His acceptance of unionism was predicated on their acceptance of employee representation. Gary, in contrast, scorned any change whatever in the unilateral control of his industry.

Rockefeller's attitude led him to regard the poststrike allegations of antiunion behavior on the part of C.F. & I. as potentially more damaging than the strike itself. Consequently, he arranged to have King come to New York for consultation.

During this one-day visit, they talked over the Colorado situation and King urged him to put an end to the signing of loyalty cards. Such cards, he explained, would be regarded as individual contracts having only one aim, to frustrate unionism. They also discussed the industrial conference at some length. Rockefeller told of enjoying his meetings and dinners with some of the labor leaders. Overall, the conference had accomplished very little, but he was pleased to have been involved. He remarked that in the end Gompers had proved to be a false friend; he was prepared to tolerate representation only if it was provided by unions.

Following their talk, Rockefeller took King with him to a luncheon meeting of the Board of Trade. They heard Ole Hanson, the red-baiting, former mayor of Seattle, speak. King found Hanson "a jingo and sensationalist," overly impressed with his own notoriety.[27] King did not reflect on the picture of the sober and conservative businessmen of New York opening themselves to the rantings of such a demagogue.

Although Rockefeller subsequently took King's advice and asked Welborn to abandon the loyalty cards, he had to be prodded to do so. One week after his visit, King wrote to urge him again to act in the matter, but still another week passed before

Rockefeller contacted Welborn. In contrast, on the very day in late November when Mother Jones called to ask Rockefeller to bring about arbitration in the coal and steel industries, Welborn was notified. The office feared that he might misunderstand if word of her visit became public. He was informed that Rockefeller had told her that, in the absence of dissatisfaction at either the C.F. & I. steel mills or coal mines, there was nothing to arbitrate. These actions suggest that Rockefeller was more concerned about being misunderstood by Welborn than in exerting leadership either within C.F. & I. or in the larger arena of public opinion affecting the two struck industries. He kept acting timidly while King expected him to rise to the immense challenge of the times.

As the flattery in Lippmann's article eventually reached Rockefeller, so the advice he had offered eventually reached the Wilson Cabinet. Rockefeller's committee, it will be recalled, had concluded the business of the first industrial conference by advising the President to assemble a second conference as soon as possible. The cabinet endorsed this recommendation and announced that sessions would begin on December 1. Fifteen prominent men from various professions were chosen to serve. In both a message delivered to the Congress in President Wilson's name and in developing the conference agenda, the labor provisions of the peace treaty were given a prominent place.

After a fashion, Lippmann's wish for the leadership of someone like Rockefeller was also realized. The major recommendations that emanated from the conference represented a triumph for King's ideas and Rockefeller's preferences. Even if publicly unacclaimed, the two men were the leaders of the hour.

When the conference got underway, its energies were directed to the task of designing dispute resolution machinery. Agreement was quickly reached on a system of twelve tripartite regional boards, capped by an appellate national tribunal. The regional boards were to act as arbitration panels when the parties to a dispute agreed to such a step. Should either or both parties refuse to arbitrate, the boards were to act as investigative panels that, equipped with subpoena powers, would inquire into the facts in the dispute and make a public report of findings. This last portion of the design was modelled consciously on King's Industrial Disputes Investigation Act.

A preliminary conference report was issued at the end of December for public consideration and comment. Individual conference members also solicited the views of colleagues, experts, and others who might offer informed opinions on the merits of the proposed scheme.

Conferee Julius Rosenwald, the president of Sears, Roebuck & Company and a fellow philanthropist, had asked Rockefeller for his counsel even before the conference convened. He now passed along a copy of the interim report and asked for his opinion of it. Rockefeller transmitted the report to King for his comments and, with King's permission, passed them back to Rosenwald. King's views were then shared with other conference members when they reassembled in January. (Quite independent of these events, Raymond Fosdick had written to the conference asking that King be invited to give his views. Such an invitation was tendered, but King declined because of other commitments.)

King advised Rockefeller that the scheme proposed in the preliminary report was a composite of the War Labor Board and the Disputes Investigation Act. He felt optimistic about its chances for success. Rosenwald, in his letter thanking Rockefeller, remarked of King's assessment that "the opinion of no one would have been more highly regarded."[28]

The conferees received many different expressions of opinion during the recess. Labor spokesmen vociferously opposed any system of dispute settlement based upon arbitration rather than collective bargaining. They, along with a number of others, argued that the conference was putting the cart before the horse in focusing on dispute settlement rather than the underlying cause of disputes. The right of workers to bargain collectively was put forward as a prerequisite of industrial peace. This right naturally raised questions about the collateral right of workers to organize.

Conference vice chairman Herbert Hoover, on his own initiative, invited a number of business leaders to meet with him. From the list of those known to have attended—executive officers of Standard Oil of New Jersey, General Electric, Bethlehem Steel, and U.S. Rubber, each accompanied by his director of industrial relations—it appears that Hoover met with the members of the Special Conference Committee. This secret organization, it will be recalled, had been organized in April with Rockefeller's blessing to facilitate the exchange of information about the personnel practices and labor markets of its ten member companies. An executive in one of these companies, Owen D. Young of G.E., was also an appointee to the second conference. Another executive, Cyrus H. McCormick, Jr., of International Harvester, had been offered a seat in the conference but had declined. Either of these connections, or some other, could have brought Hoover and the Special Conference Committee together.

At their meeting, Hoover reviewed the current unsettled condition in the country and argued that business leaders could help usher in an era of stability and progress if they would get behind the second conference and support its recommendations. He went on to speak from personal experience of the great confidence he placed in the wise and constructive leadership of Samuel Gompers. If progressive and highly visible companies like those present would support collective bargaining and open up relations with Gompers and the A.F. of L., he believed the basis for a lasting industrial peace would be established. Hoover, at the height of his prestige because of his splendid war relief work, was prepared to spend some of his reputational capital in advocating so daring a proposition.

Members of his audience figuratively ran for cover. They pointed out that, since most of their employees did not belong to unions, Gompers was in no position to speak for them. On the other hand, if Hoover's proposal implied that they should encourage their employees to join unions, such a step was neither desirable nor necessary. Many of their employees were reluctant to have anything to do with unions, and it would be wrong to compel them against their wishes. Moreover, in employee representation, most of their companies already possessed a perfectly satisfactory system for dealing collectively with their workers. As one of the participants recalled the meeting, Hoover's "idea got a very cold reception."[29]

Just as Hoover's initiative provoked a strong defense of employee representation, so an article written by Henry R. Seager, the executive secretary of the conference, may have provided the clinching argument in its favor. Writing from his wartime experience with shop committees under the Shipbuilding Labor Adjustment Board, Seager noted that

the psychology of collective bargaining through shop committees is predominantly cooperative; that of collective bargaining through trade or labor union officials predominantly contentious. . . . Concessions made by the employer to his shop committee are credited to him and serve to increase the loyalty of his employees to the business. Concessions made by the employer to a union negotiator are credited to the organization and serve to strengthen the loyalty of members not to their employers but to the union.[30]

Although Seager went on to support the long-term need for trade unions, his characterization of the difference between them and representation plans proved highly instructive to conference members. As professional men, they were less committed to unions than to the goal of industrial peace. Consequently, when they reconvened late in January, they conceded a union point by giving their endorsement to collective bargaining rather than to arbitration. But they would not concede that the right to organize meant unionization. Instead, they recommended to the employers and workers of the country that they develop employee representation plans.

When the final report of the conference became available in March, Ivy Lee took the rather foolish view that the conference "strikes me as a mountain which has labored and brought forth a mouse."[31] He believed the section on employee representation so noncommittal that it would be overlooked. In fact, the conference endorsement was the most prominent feature of its report and a triumph for Rockefeller. Under his sponsorship, King's invention had been elevated well beyond its initial use, beyond even the wartime emergency adoptions. In this most recent conference it had found acceptance at the highest levels of national policy making.

Discounting the strikes at C.F. & I. as minor incidents, Rockefeller took the opportunity to send along a copy of a recent glowing report on the Colorado Industrial Plan to Gary. As he innocently informed go-between George Perkins, a close reading of the report would change Gary's "whole attitude in regard to the value and importance of . . . such a plan."[32] More likely his action would infuriate the implacable Gary. For, as Walter Lippmann cast them, Rockefeller had become the leader of the liberal wing of business with Gary as his conservative rival. He recognized as much when he politely refused to attend a conference board dinner honoring the business representatives at the first conference, of which Gary was a sponsor.

On every side, in addition to the second conference report, there was evidence that employee representation now stood on its own merits. Many more companies than ever were experimenting with plans. Newspapers and magazines regularly featured articles describing individual plans or discussing representation's place in modern industry. Various professional societies devoted portions of their local and national meetings to papers on the subject. Scholars began to give serious consideration to the implications of the spread of representation plans for unions. The first of many surveys aimed at gauging the variety and number of plans appeared.

In addition to the satisfaction he took from the conference endorsement, little can have pleased Rockefeller more than the story of Hoover's meeting with Special Conference Committee companies. The executives had pointed in self-defense to their representation plans, plans that he had cajoled and urged them to adopt. In this way, they had acknowledged their debt to his leadership. Perhaps, this role of the industrial leader was the one Rockefeller coveted more than any other. He now had good reason to believe that he had attained it, and on his own terms. That those terms, centered on employee representation, were narrow and self-serving escaped him. The broader, more daring social leadership role to which King and Fosdick encouraged him to aspire was something he never fully comprehended.

Notes

1. Justice Louis Brandeis to Mrs. Brandeis, 12/2/18, quoted in Mason (1946), p. 527. In addition to memoirs of Wilson's cabinet members and the House Papers, the following accounts proved useful for the postwar period: Baker (1939), Blum (1951), Grayson (1960), Smith (1964), and Weinstein (1981).
2. R. B. Fosdick to J. D. R., Jr., 9/5/19. J.D.R., Jr. Papers, Friends and Services, Box 19.
3. Typescript. "Conversation with John D. Rockefeller, Jr.", R. B. Fosdick memorandum dated 5/25/53. Ibid.
4. *New York Times* (September 12, 1919), p. 1. See also Murray (1964), Chapter 8.
5. *New York Times* (September 15, 1919), 1.
6. Quoted in Mandel (1963), p. 469. Coit (1957) makes no mention of Baruch's role, but see the authoritative account in Brody (1965), pp. 103f.
7. J.D.R. Jr., to W.L.M.K., 9/18/19. Reproduced in Fosdick (1956), p. 174.
8. Quoted in Brody (1965), p. 112.
9. *New York Times* (September 22, 1919), p. 10.
10. Quoted in Gall (1982), p. 252. See also Preston (1963).
11. W.L.M.K. to J.D.R., Jr., 9/22/19. J.D.R., Jr. Papers, Economic Reform Interests, Box 15.
12. W.L.M.K Diary, 9/29/19. W.L.M.K. Papers, Series J13, p. G3195. Quotation marks in the original.
13. Ibid.
14. Ibid.

15. Ibid., 10/6/19, p. G3202.
16. *Proceedings of the First Industrial Conference,* p. 141.
17. Ibid., p. 158.
18. Ibid., p. 250.
19. Ibid.
20. *New York Times* (October 24, 1919). See Hurvitz (1977) for a different reading.
21. Cited in Selekman and Van Kleeck (1924), pp. 333–45.
22. Ibid., p. 329.
23. J.D.R., Jr. to W.L.M.K., 11/7/19. J.D.R., Jr. Papers, Economic Interests, Box 15.
24. Lippmann (1970), p. 282.
25. Ibid., p. 284.
26. Ibid., p. 287.
27. W.L.M.K. Diary, 11/17/19. W.L.M.K. Papers, Series J13, p. G3246.
28. J. Rosenwald to J.D.R., Jr., 3/9/20 and W.L.M.K. to J.D.R., Jr., 2/2/20. J.D.R., Jr. Papers, Economic Interests, Box 15.
29. Cyrus S. Ching to Herbert Hoover, 5/14/53 and Hoover to Ching in response, 5/16/53. I am grateful to T.T. Thalken at the Herbert Hoover Presidential Library, West Branch, Iowa, for making copies of this correspondence available.
30. Seager (1920), p. 234.
31. Ivy Lee to J.D.R., Jr., 3/18/20. J.D.R., Jr. Papers, Economic Interests, Box 15.
32. Quoted in Brody (1965), p. 83. See also J.D.R., Jr., to L. F. Loree, 3/19/20. J.D.R., Jr. Papers, Economic Interests, Box 15.

Epilogue

Confident of his own grasp of industrial relations, Rockefeller made no effort to replace Mackenzie King. Instead, he hired A. H. Lichty, a former YMCA official, in a much narrower capacity and at a fraction of King's retainer. Rockefeller personally trained Lichty. He reviewed with him the company surveys that King had prepared and instructed him as to what would be his primary concerns. Lichty was then dispatched to Colorado Fuel & Iron to acquaint himself with the workings of the representation plan. While there, he made a trial survey of the mining camps and examined the current state of company relations with its employees. His survey and report concluded with recommendations for improvement.

Evidently, Lichty passed this first test with high marks, for he was quickly sent on to Standard Oil of Indiana, then to International Harvester, Bethlehem Steel, and a number of other companies, where he made similar surveys and reports. He was then offered a position as vice president at C.F. & I., which he accepted with Rockefeller's blessing.

On broader industrial relations questions, Rockefeller turned to Raymond B. Fosdick for counsel. Fosdick eventually would head the Rockefeller Foundation and remain one of his closest associates to the end. Through Fosdick and his ties to Princeton University, Rockefeller found a replacement for Lichty. Professor Robert F. Foerster was retained to carry on the same sort of survey report work. He, too, was sent to C.F. & I. as part of his training.

Rockefeller was troubled, however, by the prospect of having repeatedly to search for qualified men. In the summer of 1921, he invited Fosdick to visit with him at Seal Harbor, Maine, to discuss Fosdick's suggestion for dealing with this problem. Mackenzie King arranged to join them. To give continuity to the survey work and to follow current developments in industrial relations, it was agreed that Fosdick's law firm, Curtis, Fosdick, and Belknap, would establish and maintain a group of labor specialists in its offices. Rockefeller would then draw on the services of this group as he saw fit.

This new arrangement began in January 1922. Surviving two transfigurations, it continues at this writing. In the spring of 1926 the labor group was spun off from Curtis, Fosdick & Belknap to become Industrial Relations Counselors, Inc. Subsequently, the present name, Organization Resources Counselors, Inc., was adopted.

While the group was located within Fosdick's firm, it devoted most of its activity to Rockefeller interests under his retainer. It undertook individual company surveys, followed current developments, and when deemed advisable, recommended actions or statements for Rockefeller's consideration. The group also sent representatives to various professional meetings and conferred with government agencies, employer groups, and other groups interested in labor issues. Led initially by George J. Anderson, who soon became a vice president of the troubled Consolidation Coal Company, the group consistently advocated employee representation and what it took to be a liberal point of view. Anderson was succeeded by Arthur H. Young, who came to the position from International Harvester, and C.F. & I. before that, and would remain at the head of the organization through the balance of the decade.

When Industrial Relations Counselors was formed, Rockefeller continued to underwrite its expenses. The hope was that eventually enough other clients would be found to make the venture self-sustaining. Much of the work, however, contnued to be related to Rockefeller interests and to the advocacy of the view that "sound human relationships and a heightened morale within a company must be the achievement of its officers."[1]

The group was surprised to find its liberal attitudes progressively transformed into something almost bizarre by the deeply conservative drift of the times. In 1920, even that most retrograde employers' association, the National Association of Manufacturers, had been prepared to endorse employee representation. By mid-decade, however, things were quite different. Cyrus Ching of U.S. Rubber liked to tell the story of how, on completing a talk on employee representation before a group of businessmen, he and Arthur Young were chastised by the meeting's chairman for disseminating communist ideas!

Opposition of this sort had the unintended but quite natural effect of fostering a siege mentality. It helped to sustain the conviction of the counselors that they were missionaries contesting against mighty odds. Interestingly enough, when Mary B. Gilson, one of the few women counselors, returned from a period spent abroad, she was so offended by the smug self-righteousness of the group that she quit. In part, her distance had enabled her to see what Arthur Young, Cyrus Ching, Clarence Hicks, and Rockefeller were never prepared to admit, that representation simply was a scheme for avoiding unions.

Industrial Relations Counselors was only one of several means by which attempts were made to further Rockefeller's perspective on industrial relations. Following up on a suggestion from Clarence Hicks (or, possibly, from Fosdick) in 1922, he began to provide sums of $15,000 to $25,000 per year to each of six universities that agreed to establish Industrial Relations Sections. In exchange, Princeton, the University of Michigan, Stanford, M.I.T., CalTech and Queen's University (Ontario) consented to augment their faculties, course offerings, library holdings, and research activity in the field of labor. Rockefeller regarded this penetration of the universities as a vital way of bringing employee representation to the attention of more potential managers and employers. Most of the Industrial Relations sections continue to exist and have thus demonstrated a durability comparable to that of Industrial Relations Counselors. No one has ever investigated the extent, if any, to which they were reliable agents of Rockefeller's point of view.

In contrast, the men who participated in the Special Conference Committee, including Hicks, Young, and Ching, were thoroughly reliable agents—true believers. The committee, it will be recalled, had brought together the industrial relations heads of its ten member companies for regular discussions of labor market developments, union activity, and personnel practices. Whatever impact this collusive arrangement may have had on wage rates and employment practices is unknown. It is clear, however, that the individual members of the committee were esteemed highly by their professional peers and that they exerted considerable influence among them. They frequently served as officers or executive board members in their professional associations and saw that employee representation was talked about regularly and considered. The Committee still survives as the "Cowdrick Group" within Organization Resources Counselors.

Despite the proselytizing efforts of these various agents and agencies, employee representation failed to gain more than a foothold in American industry. The rate of adoption peaked in 1922, when some 385 companies had plans in effect in one or more of their plants. During the twenties, the maximum number of companies with plans in any one year was 432, in 1926. Subsequently, a decline set in, so that by 1928 the number had slipped under 400. At the time, there were about 30,000 manufacturing firms with fifty or more employees.

Larger firms, with 250 or more employees, were more likely than smaller ones to adopt plans and, of course, such firms lent greater visibility to their plans. A 1926 survey reported that the average number of employees per company with a plan was 3169. Ignoring the likelihood that this average was probably based on total employment rather than on a smaller number of covered employees, it remains that in 1929 only 9 percent of all larger (250 employees or more) firms had plans in operation. Probably, no more than ten percent of all workers in manufacturing and mining were covered by "works councils," as they were then designated.[2]

Contemporary analysts were apparently misled by the high visibility of the firms with company unions. From about 1925 onward, many labor specialists, both within and outside academia, accepted the ideas that company unions had become a permanent feature of American industrial relations and that they were spreading. Even so astute an observer as H. B. Butler, an English labor expert, misread the trends when he reported on American labor for the International Labor Organization in 1927.

But it wasn't only the size of the trees that obscured the dimensions of the forest. Another issue, the unprecedented failure of the labor movement to grow during a period of prosperity, beclouded the matter. Taken in conjunction with the very low levels to which strike activity had declined, the stagnation of the labor movement presented a real puzzle. Of course, the boosters and the Babbitts had a ready explanation: American employers had finally learned how to handle labor. Consequently, a new era of industrial harmony had dawned. As they pictured it, considerate, generous employers, and contented, loyal workers collaborated in the most productive and prosperous economy the world had ever seen. It looked very much like the end of the rainbow.

Without accepting this ballyhoo, most serious students of labor nonetheless concluded that the assumed spread of company unions explained the observed decline in worker organization and militancy. But, the domain of the company union, best exemplified in the Special Conference Committee companies, had never been union territory and would not become unionized until the upheavals of the 1930s—or ever, in the cases of Dupont and Standard Oil of New Jersey. As Wolman's data (1936) revealed, the decline of unionism occurred mainly in the sectors of its wartime growth and not in the sectors that adopted company unions.

That cause and effect should be reversed seems evident both from what we have learned in this study of King and Rockefeller and from the subsequent history of company unions. King introduced representation plans mainly in companies under threat either of union organization or War Labor Board–imposed shop committees. Subsequent surveys by French (1923) and Miller (1924) also concluded that the main motive behind the organization of company unions was "to head off trade union organization."[3] And Bernstein (1970) has shown that the union threat embodied in the National Industrial Recovery Act of 1933 led to the organization of company unions in unprecedented numbers. Thus, the evidence suggests that the threat of unions was more critical for the creation of company unions than the latter were for the decline of trade unions.

The truth of the matter seems to be that most American employers rejected the idea of company unions, except under threat from outside, because their disadvantages loomed so large. The most obvious employer reservation sprang from inertia: "if it ain't broke, don't fix it." Ruling by exception, they had little reason to anticipate labor troubles. This position was reinforced by the second reservation, which stemmed from fear of a backfire. Once organized, what was to ensure a company that its union wouldn't turn independent or be captured by an outside union? The absence of organization, in contrast, provided no toehold for hostile forces. Finally, the widespread employer rejection of collective bargaining rendered worker organization largely pointless. Most employers believed that the liberty of contract doctrine to which they subscribed worked equally to the advantage of themselves and their workers, particularly the better and more ambitious workers. Hence, they saw no need to self-inflict the constraints (e.g., standardized wages, strict seniority, etc.) likely to accompany collective bargaining.

The company unon was thus regarded by most employers as a negative alternative. It assumed positive proportions only in the face of the still more undesirable alternative of unionization. Undoubtedly, a few companies embraced representation schemes in the absence of such a threat. And, as Nelson (1982) has shown, there were also companies, and groups of workers, that came to regard their company unions as effective and worth sustaining. Indeed, in a world where companies shaped their responses to unionism on a number of bases (e.g., the political opportunism of Consolidation Coal), such variations were bound to arise. These exceptions, however, should not be permitted to obscure the general proposition: to most users, company unions were a lower-risk escape route from unionization. Nor should evidence of the users' pride in their liberality—and the plaudits they won—distract attention from the main point. Company unions perpetuated management's unilateral control of industrial relations.

Because he could not comprehend this, Rockefeller never understood the union opposition to representation. Supposing that the plans fostered genuine collective bargaining—hadn't the steel workers at C.F. & I. asked for and been granted the eight hour day?—he stubbornly discounted evidence to the contrary. He also naively assumed that other plan users were as sincere in their commitment to representation as he. When he read criticisms of the operation of the plan at C.F. & I., he objected that the authors were biased from the outset in favor of unions. In one instance, he embroiled himself in a protracted effort to block the publication of a Russell Sage Foundation report that he thought prejudiced but that was both accurate and fair.

In defending his actions vis-à-vis the Sage Foundation report, Rockefeller revealed his pretentions to authority in the field of industrial relations. As he saw it, his basic difference with critics of the plan sprang from his belief that the interests of employers and employees more often coincided than conflicted. Hence, effective industrial relations were not contingent on conflict and power plays but on channels of communication and mutual understanding. To demonstrate that he was fully aware of the criticisms commonly lodged against employee representation, he enumerated them. But they held no weight for him. His sense of the correctness of his own views "had been strengthened year by year by my observation of the working of the plan in Colorado."[4] He confessed that he could not understand why his assumptions and point of view were not as valid as those of the critics.

On a previous occasion, Rockefeller had been even more explicit about the legitimacy of his position. Writing in 1921, at a time when the open shop movement was at its height, he deplored the virulent antiunionism of many employers and asserted:

The position which I have always taken with union leaders, of whom I know many most pleasantly, is that I believe that they and I are conscientiously seeking the same end; namely a fair deal for the working man; that while they may be approaching that end by one means and I by another, that that is no reason why we should distrust each other or work against each other, that the best results can only be obtained by our being tolerant, respecting each the other's sincerity of purpose.[5]

Blind to the noblesse oblige at the heart of employee representation, Rockefeller lacked all sense of how transparent that motivation seemed to others. He saw himself a crusader, fighting an uphill battle against recalcitrant managements within companies in which he had some influence. Little of this activity, however, was public knowledge. Even the academic investigators who studied and compared representation plans in the early twenties, failed to recognize their common link to Rockefeller. The Special Conference Committee remained secret until exposed by the LaFollette Committee in the 1930s. Links with Fosdick's law firm, with Industrial Relations Counselors, and with university industrial relations sections were not known widely. Hence, Rockefeller's public stance as an advocate of employee representation hinged exclusively on his support of the plan at C.F. & I. Few beyond his immediate circle of friends and agents could have imagined that anyone named Rockefeller might be seriously interested in organizing his own labor organization.

And, of course, he did not seek as he claimed, "a fair deal for the working man." His interest in employee representation can most charitably be characterized as one of industrial peace at any price, save unionization. He did not care for workers or their welfare but only for their acquiescence.

Raymond B. Fosdick, in his largely uncritical biography of Rockefeller, characterized him as a man given to enthusiasms. He loved to throw himself into one cause or project after another, and always with complete sincerity and seriousness of purpose. Prohibition, the reconstruction of colonial Williamsburg, and the creation of Rockefeller Center were just a few of his many enthusiasms. In view of the variety of his undertakings, it may seem presumptuous to claim priority of one over all of the others. Yet, it seems evident that Rockefeller's relationship with King and employee representation was unique in its personal consequences. In this one instance, his enthusiasm provided him with a cause that simultaneously freed him from his father's dominance and equipped him with an independent standing as a business leader.

The personal resonances of employee representation probably account for his inflexible attitude toward it. When Fosdick questioned him about representation in 1953, Rockefeller still supposed it the best system of industrial relations ever invented. Despite the great growth of the labor movement that had occurred, he could not let go of his plan. Nowhere else was he so intellectually rigid. Once he came to recognize the negative social consequences of Prohibition, for example, he bravely spoke out against it, despite his long-standing commitment and advocacy. Similarly, when a decade-long experiment in providing low-cost worker housing in Bayonne, New Jersey, failed to earn the targeted return, he admitted defeat and called a halt to the effort. His attachment to employee representation, in contrast, held too important a piece of himself in it for him to abandon it.

Practically, however, he did abandon it. As other enthusiasms captured his attention, he gave less and less thought to industrial relations. After 1925, he delegated much of his interest into the hands of his eldest son, John, who prior to entering the office had studied industrial relations at Princeton. Consequently, there is no record of Rockefeller's response to a 1925 report on C.F. & I Prepared by one of Fosdick's experts, this recommended that the company be made to introduce modern managerial practices. It also called for the replacement of president Welborn.

Finding the company's wage scale above the local market, and significant overmanning, the consultant concluded that "The policy, so far as there is evidence of one, has been to manage the capital invested in the corporation for the benefit of the workers rather than anyone else."[6] Nothing was done, however, until after a strike in 1927. (There had also been strikes in 1919, 1921, and 1922.) Acknowledging that C.F. & I.'s plan "has in many ways lapsed into innocuous desuetude,"[7] the New York staff recommended a broad survey of the latest developments in industrial relations. Thus, at the very moment that many labor experts were announcing the triumph of company unions, ways were being sought to salvage the original model. Apparently Rockefeller's staff dared not recommend that the plan be buried. Their call for further study helped maintain the fiction that it hadn't died. At the time, periodic reports from industrial spies were being received from Colorado. . . .

Notes

1. Arthur H. Young in "Report for 1924." J.D.R., Jr. Papers, Box 16, Economic Reform Interests. See also J.D.R., Jr., to R.B. Fosdick, 5/7/26 and response, dated 5/20/26. Ibid.
2. National Industrial Conference Board (1929), p. 20 and (1933), p. 16.
3. French (1923), p. 87. See also Miller (1924) p. 162.
4. J.D.R., Jr to C. W. Eliot, 2/17/25. J.D.R., Jr. Papers, Business Interests, Box 16. All of the documents pertinent to the fight over the Sage Foundation report are in this box. The report eventually appeared in the form of two volumes, Selekman and Van Kleeck (1924) and Selekman (1924).
5. J.D.R., Jr. to E. A. Van Valkenburg, 6/28/21. Ibid.
6. Mark M. Jones to Arthur Woods, 9/26/25. Ibid.
7. Memorandum, Arthur Woods to Thomas M. Debevoise, 1/20/28. Ibid.

Bibliography

Personal Papers and Manuscript Collections

American Federation of Labor Papers. Wisconsin Historical Society, Madison. (Cited as A.F. of L.)

American Management Association Historical Files. Held at the Association, New York.

Cyrus Ching, Reminiscences. Oral History Collection, Columbia University, New York.

Cleveland Chamber of Commerce Papers. Western Reserve Historical Society, Cleveland.

Walter Drew Papers. Bentley Historical Library, Ann Arbor.

Felix Frankfurter Papers. Library of Congress.

Justice Department, General Records. Records Group 60, National Archives, Washington, D.C.

William Lyon Mackenzie King Papers. Public Archives of Canada, Ottawa. (Cited as W.L.M.K.)

Labor Department, General Records. Records Group 174, National Archives, Washington, D.C.

Ivy Lee Papers. Princeton University, Princeton, N.J.

William M. Leiserson Papers. Wisconsin Historical Society, Madison.

Seth Low Papers. Butler Library, Columbia University, New York.

Charles McCarthy Papers. Wisconsin Historical Society, Madison.

National Civic Federation Papers. New York Public Library, New York.

National Industrial Conference Board Papers. Hagley Museum, Greenville, Del.

Robert Ozanne, Notes from the Chicago Office Files of the International Harvester Company. Held by Professor Ozanne.

John D. Rockefeller, Jr. Papers. Rockefeller Archives Center, Tarrytown, N.Y. (Cited as J.D.R., Jr.)

David Saposs Papers. Wisconsin Historical Society, Madison.

Shipbuilding Labor Adjustment Board Papers. Records Group 32, National Archives, Washington, D.C.

William H. Taft Papers. Library of Congress, Washington, D.C. (Cited as W.H.T.)

U.S. Commission on Industrial Relations Papers. Wisconsin Historical Society, Madison.

Frank P. Walsh Papers. New York Public Library, New York. (Cited as F.P.W.)

War Labor Policies Board Papers. Records Group 1, Series 2, National Archives, Washington, D.C.

William B. Wilson Papers. Pennsylvania Historical Society, Philadelphia. (Cited as W.W.)

Hearings, Reports, and Proceedings

American Federation of Labor. *Report of the Proceedings of the Annual Convention* 1914–1919.

National Association of Corporation Schools. *Convention Proceedings,* 1913–1921.

New Jersey Bureau of Industrial Statistics. *Thirty-Eighth Annual Report;* 1916.

Proceedings of the First Industrial Conference. Washington, D.C.: Government Printing Office, 1920.

Report of Industrial Conference Called by the President. Washington, D.C.: Government Printing Office, 1920.

Report of the President's Mediation Commission, January 9, 1918. Washington, D.C.: Government Printing Office, 1918.

U.S. Bureau of Labor Statistics. *History of the Shipbuilding Labor Adjustment Board, 1917–1918.* Bulletin No. 283, 1921.

———. *Proceedings of the Conference of Employment Managers' Association of Boston, Mass.,* 1916.

U.S. Commission on Industrial Relations. *Final Report and Testimony.* Eleven volumes. Washington, D.C.: Government Printing Office, 1916.

U.S. Congress, House of Representatives. *Hearings Before a Subcommittee of the Committee on Mines and Mining.* Two Volumes. Washington, D.C.: Government Printing Office, 1914.

———. *Report of the Colorado Coal Commission on the Labor Difficulties in the Coal Fields of Colorado During the Years 1914 and 1915.* Washington, D.C.: Government Printing Office, 1916.

———. *Report on the Colorado Strike Investigation.* Washington, D.C.: Government Printing Office, 1915.

———. Committee on Labor. *Hearings on a Bill to Regulate the Method of Directing the Work of Government Employees.* Washington, D.C.: Government Printing Office, 1916.

U.S. Congress, Senate, Subcommittee of the Senate Committee on Education and Labor. *Violations of Free Speech and the Rights of Labor.* Part 45. Washington, D.C.: Government Printing Office, 1939.

West, George P. *Report on the Colorado Strike.* Washington, D.C.: U.S. Commission on Industrial Relations, 1915.

Western Efficiency Society and the Society of Industrial Engineers. *Report of the Proceedings of the National Conference.* Chicago, March 1918 (N.p., n.d.).

Newspapers and Serials

American Labor Year Book, 1916–1926.
The Annals, vol. 81, January 1918.
Colorado Springs Evening Telegraph, 1915.
National Association of Corporation Schools, *Bulletin,* 1914.
National Civic Federation Review, scattered issues, 1914, 1918–1920.
The Survey, 1914–1916.

Books and Articles

Adams, Graham. *Age of Industrial Violence, 1910–1915.* New York: Columbia University Press, 1966.

Baker, Liva. *Felix Frankfurter.* New York: Coward-McCann, 1969.

Baker, Ray Stannard. *Woodrow Wilson: Life and Letters,* vol. 7 of 8. New York: Doubleday, Doran, 1939.

Barnett, George E. "The Present Position of American Trade Unionism." *American Economic Review* XII:1 (1922).

Beaver, Daniel R. *Newton D. Baker and the American War Effort, 1917–1919.* Lincoln: University of Nebraska Press, 1966.

Bell, Daniel. "The Background and Development of Marxian Socialism in the United States." In D. D. Egbert and S. Persons, eds., *Socialism and American Life,* vol. 1. Princeton, N.J.: Princeton University Press, 1952.

Bernstein, Irving. *The Lean Years.* Boston: Houghton Mifflin, 1960.

———. *Turbulent Years.* Boston: Houghton Mifflin, 1970.

Beshoar, Barron B. *Out of the Depths; The Story of John R. Lawson a Labor Leader.* Denver: Colorado Historical Committee & Denver Trades & Labor Assembly, 1942.

Best, Gary Dean. "President Wilson's Second Industrial Conference, 1919–1920." *Labor History* 16:4 (Fall 1975).

Bing, Alexander M. *War-Time Strikes and Their Adjustment.* New York: Dutton, 1921.

Blum, John M. *Joe Tumulty and the Wilson Era.* Boston: Houghton Mifflin, 1951.

Boemke, Manfred F. "The Wilson Administration, Organized Labor, and the Colorado Strike, 1913–1914." Unpublished Ph.D. dissertation, Princeton University, 1983.

Brandes, Stuart D. "Welfarism in American Industry, 1880–1940." Unpublished Ph.D. dissertation, University of Wisconsin, 1970.

———. *American Welfare Capitalism, 1880–1940.* Chicago: University of Chicago Press, 1976.

Brody, David. *Labor in Crisis.* Philadelphia: J.B. Lippincott, 1965.

———. *Workers in Industrial America.* New York: Oxford University Press, 1980.

Brown, Waldo R. *What's What in the Labor Movement?* New York: B. W. Huebsch, 1921.

Butler, H. B. *Industrial Relations in the United States*. Geneva: International Labor Organization, 1927.

Carnegie, Andrew. *The Gospel of Wealth*. Cambridge: Harvard University Press, 1965. Originally appeared in *North American Review* (June, December 1889).

Chase, Mary Ellen. *Abby Aldrich Rockefeller*. New York: Macmillan, 1950.

Ching, Cyrus S. *Review and Reflection*. New York: Forbes, 1953.

Clarkson, Grosvenor B. *Industrial America in the World War*. Boston: Houghton Mifflin, 1923.

Coben, Stanley. *A. Mitchell Palmer: Politician*. New York: Columbia University Press, 1963.

Coit, Margaret. *Mr. Baruch*. Boston: Houghton Mifflin, 1957.

Commons, John R. *Myself*. Madison: University of Wisconsin Press, 1963.

Cowdrick, Edward S. "The New Freedom for Labor." *Leslie's Illustrated Weekly* (October 21, 1915).

———. *Industrial History of the United States*. New York: Ronald, 1923.

———. *Manpower in Industry*. New York: Henry Holt, 1924.

Craven, Paul. *"An Impartial Umpire": Industrial Relations and the Canadian State, 1900–1911*. Toronto: University of Toronto Press, 1980.

Crunden, Robert M. *Ministers of Reform*. New York: Basic Books, 1982.

Daniels, Josephus. *The Cabinet Diaries of Josephus Daniels*, edited by E. David Cronon. Lincoln: University of Nebraska Press, 1963.

Dawson, Robert M. *William Lyon Mackenzie King 1874–1923*, vol. 1. Toronto: University of Toronto Press, 1958.

Doubleday, F. N. *The Memoirs of a Publisher*. New York: Doubleday, 1972.

Douglas, Paul H. et al., eds. *The Worker in Modern Economic Society*. Chicago: University of Chicago Press, 1923.

Draper, Theodore. *The Roots of American Communism*. New York: Viking Press, 1957.

Dubofsky, Melvin. *We Shall Be All*. New York: Quadrangle Books, 1969.

Dubofsky, Melvin, and Warren Van Tine. *John L. Lewis: A Biography*. New York: Quadrangle Books, 1977.

Dunlop, John. *Industrial Relations Systems*. New York: Henry Holt, 1958.

English, John, and J. O. Stubbs, eds. *Mackenzie King: Widening the Debate*. Toronto: Macmillan of Canada, 1978.

Feldman, Herman. *Survey of Research in the Field of Industrial Relations*. New York: Social Science Research Council, 1928.

Fetherling, Dale. *Mother Jones, The Miners' Angel*. Carbondale, Ill.: Southern Illinois University Press, 1974.

Fitch, John A. "What Rockefeller Knew and What He Did." *The Survey* 34 (August 21, 1915).

———. "Two Years of the Rockefeller Plan," *The Survey* 39 (October 6, 1917).

Fosdick, Raymond B. *John D. Rockefeller, Jr., A Portrait*. New York: Harper, 1956.

French, Carroll E. *The Shop Committee in the United States*. Baltimore: Johns Hopkins University Press, 1923.

Gall, Gilbert, Jr. "Heber Blankenhorn, the LaFollette Committee and the Irony of Industrial Repression." *Labor History* 23:2 (Spring 1982).

Garraty, John A. *Right-Hand Man: The Life of George W. Perkins*. New York: Harper and Brothers, 1957.

Gibb, George S., and Evelyn H. Knowlton. *The Resurgent Years, 1911– 1927*. Volume 2 of *History of the Standard Oil Company (New Jersey)*. New York: Harper, 1956.

Gilson, Mary B. *What's Past Is Prologue*. New York: Harper, 1940.

Ginger, Ray. *The Bending Cross*. New Brunswick, N.J.: Rutgers University Press, 1949.

Gitelman, H.M. "Being of Two Minds: American Employers Confront the Labor Problem, 1915–1919." *Labor History* 25:2 (Spring 1984).

———. "Perspectives on American Industrial Violence," *Business History Review* 47:1 (Spring 1973).

Gompers, Samuel. In *American Federationist* 21 (November 1914).

Grayson, Cary T. *Woodrow Wilson, an Intimate Memoir*. New York: Holt, Rinehart and Winston, 1960.

Green, Marguerite. *The National Civic Federation and the American Labor Movement*. Washington, D.C.: Catholic University Press, 1956.

Grubbs, Frank L., Jr. *The Struggle for Labor Loyalty: Gompers, the A.F. of L., and the Pacifists, 1917–1920*. Durham, N.C.: Duke University Press, 1968.

Gulick, Charles A., Jr. *Labor Policy of the United States Steel Corporation*. New York: Columbia University Press, 1924.

Hardy, H. Reginald. *Mackenzie King of Canada*. New York: Oxford University Press, 1949.

Harvey, Katherine A. *The Best-Dressed Miners: Life and Labor in the Maryland Coal Region, 1835–1911*. Ithaca, N.Y.: Cornell University Press, 1969.

Hicks, Clarence, Jr. *My Life in Industrial Relations*. New York: Harper, 1941.

Hiebert, Ray E. *Courtier to the Crowd: The Story of Ivy Lee and the Development of Public Relations*. Ames: Iowa State University Press, 1966.

Hoagland, H.E. "Closed Shop Versus Open Shop." *American Economic Review* 8 (December 1918).

Houser, J. David. *What the Employer Thinks: Executives' Attitudes Toward Employees*. Cambridge: Harvard University Press, 1927.

Hoxie, Robert F. *Trade Unionism in the United States*. New York: Appleton, 1924.

Hurvitz, Haggai. "Ideology and Industrial Conflict: President Wilson's First Industrial Conference of October, 1919." *Labor History* 18:4 (Fall 1977).

Jensen, Joan M. *The Price of Vigilance*. Chicago: Rand McNally, 1968.

Jensen, Billie Barnes. "Woodrow Wilson's Intervention in the Coal Strike of 1914." *Labor History* 15:1 (Winter 1974).

Kopald, Sylvia. *Rebellion in Labor Unions*. New York: Boni and Liveright, 1924.

Kurland, Gerald. *Seth Low*. New York: Twayne, 1971.

Lane, Anne W., and L.H. Wall, eds. *The Letters of Franklin K. Lane*. Boston: Houghton Mifflin, 1922.

Lange, William H. *The American Management Association and Its Predecessors*. New York: American Management Association, 1928.

Laslett, John. *Labor and the Left*. New York: Basic Books, 1970.

Lauck, W. Jett. *Political and Industrial Democracy, 1776–1926*. New York: Funk and Wagnalls, 1926.

Leiserson, William M. "Constitutional Government in American Industries." *American Economic Review* 12:1 (1922).

Levinson, Edward. *I Break Strikes!* (New York: McBride, 1935.

Lewisohn, Sam A. *The New Leadership in Industry*. New York: E. P. Dutton, 1926.

Link, Arthur. *Woodrow Wilson and the Progressive Era*. New York: Harper, 1954.

Lippmann, Walter. *Early Writings*. New York: Liveright, 1970.

Litchfield, Paul W., *The Industrial Republic* Boston: Houghton Mifflin, 1919.

Lorwin (nee Levine), Louis. "The Development of Sydicalism in America." *Political Science Quarterly* 28 (September).

Loth, David, *Swope of G.E.* (New York: Simon and Schuster, 1958.)

Lynd, Robert S. "Done in Oil." *The Survey* 49:3 (November 1, 1922).

Mandel, Bernard. *Samuel Gompers*. Yellow Springs, Oh.: Antioch Press, 1963.

Marot, Helen. *American Labor Unions*. New York: Henry Holt, 1914.

Marshall, Leon C. "A Missing Chapter in Our War-Labor Policy." *Journal of Political Economy* 27:5 (May 1919).

———. "The War Labor Program and Its Administration." *Journal of Political Economy* 26:5 (May 1918).

Mason, Alpheus T. *Brandeis: A Free Man's Life*. New York: Viking Press, 1946.

MacIver, R. M. *Labor in a Changing World*. New York: E. P. Dutton, 1919.

McGovern, George S., and Leonard F. Guttridge. *The Great Coalfield War*. Boston: Houghton Mifflin, 1972.

McGregor, F. A. *The Fall and Rise of Mackenzie King*. Toronto: Macmillan, 1962.

McNeill, William H. *Plagues and People*. Garden City, N.Y.: Anchor Press, 1976.

Merritt, Walter G. *Destination Unknown. Fifty Years of Labor Relations*. New York: Prentice-Hall, 1951.

Miller, Earl J. *Workmen's Representation in Industrial Government*. Urbana: University of Illinois Press, 1924.

Milton, Charles R. "The Development of Philosophies of Personnel Administration." Ph.D. dissertation, University of North Carolina, 1960.

Mitchell, John. *Organized Labor*. Philadelphia: American Book and Bible House, 1903.

Montgomery, David. *Workers' Control in America*. Cambridge: Cambridge University Press, 1979.

Mooney, Fred. *Struggle in the Coal Fields*. Morgantown: West Virginia University Library, 1967.

"Mr. Rockefeller's Concessions." Letter to *New York Evening Post* (May 1, 1914).

Murray, Robert K. *The Red Scare*. New York: McGraw-Hill, 1964.

———. *The Harding Era*. Minneapolis: University of Minnesota Press, 1969.

National Industrial Conference Board. *Experience with Works Councils in the United States.* New York: Century, 1922.

————. *Industrial Relations Programs in Small Plants.* New York: National Industrial Conference Board, 1929.

————. *Collective Bargaining.* New York: National Industrial Conference Board, 1933.

Nelson, Daniel. *Managers and Workers.* Madison: University of Wisconsin Press, 1975.

————. "The Company Union Movement, 1900–1937: A Reexamination." *Business History Review* LVI (Autumn 1982).

Nevins, Allan. *Study in Power: John D. Rockefeller, Industrialist and Philanthropist.* New York: Charles Scribners, 1953.

Noble, David F. *America By Design.* New York: A. A. Knopf, 1977.

Ozanne, Robert. *A Century of Labor–Management Relations at McCormick and International Harvester.* Madison: University of Wisconsin Press, 1967.

Perlman, Selig. *A Theory of the Labor Movement.* New York: A. M. Kelley 1928 (1949).

Preston, William. *Aliens and Dissenters.* Cambridge: Harvard University Press, 1963.

Pringle, Henry F. *The Life and Times of William Howard Taft.* New York: Farrar and Rinehart, 1939.

Ramirez, Bruno. *When Workers Fight.* Westport, Conn.: Greenwood Press, 1978.

Raucher, Alan R. *Public Relations and Business, 1900–1929.* Baltimore: Johns Hopkins University Press, 1968.

Ripley, Charles M. *Life in a Large Manufacturing Plant.* Schenectady, N.Y.: General Electric, 1919.

Rochester, Stuart I. *American Liberal Disillusionment in the Wake of World War I.* University Park: Pennsylvania State University Press, 1977.

Rockefeller, John D., Jr. *The Personal Relation in Industry.* New York: Boni and Liveright, 1923.

Rosenblum, Gerald. *Immigrant Workers: Their Impact on American Radicalism.* New York: Basic Books, 1973.

Russell, Bertrand. *Power.* New York: W. W. Norton, 1938.

Salvatore, Nick. *Eugene J. Debs: Citizen and Socialist.* Urbana: University of Illinois Press, 1982.

Scheinberg, Stephen J. "The Development of Corporation Labor Policy, 1900–1940." Ph.D. dissertation, University of Wisconsin, 1966.

Seager, Henry R. "Company Unions vs. Trade Unions." *American Economic Review* 13 : 1 (March 1923).

Seidman, Joel. *The Yellow Dog Contract.* Baltimore: Johns Hopkins University Press, 1932.

Selekman, Ben M. *Employes' Representation in Steel Works.* New York: Russell Sage Foundation, 1924.

Selekman, Ben M., and Mary Van Kleeck. *Employes' Representation In Coal Mines.* New York: Russell Sage Foundation, 1924.

Slichter, Sumner H. "The Current Labor Policies of American Industries," *Quarterly Journal of Economics* 43 (May 1929).

Smith Gene. *When the Cheering Stopped.* New York: William Morrow, 1964.

Soffer, Benson. "A Theory of Trade Union Development: The Role of the 'Autonomous' Workman." *Labor History* 1:2 (Spring 1960).

Songs of the Workers. 29th ed. Chicago: Industrial Workers of the World, 1956.

Stacey, C. P. *A Very Double Life; The Private World of Mackenzie King*. Toronto: Macmillan, 1976.

Steigerwalt, Albert K. *The National Association of Manufacturers 1895– 1914*. Ann Arbor: University of Michigan Bureau of Business Research, 1964.

Stephenson, John J. "Labor and Capital," *Popular Science Monthly* 84:5 (May 1914).

Taft, Philip. *The A.F. of L. in the Time of Gompers*. New York: Harper, 1957.

Taft, William H. "Justice and Freedom for Industry." *The Square Deal* 16: 120 (July 1915).

Tarbell, Ida M. *Owen D. Young, A New Type of Industrial Leader*. New York: Macmillan, 1932.

Taylor, Albion G. *Labor Policies of the National Association of Manufacturers*. Urbana: University of Illinois Press, 1928.

Tead, Ordway, "Trade Unions and Efficiency." *American Journal of Sociology* 22:1 (July 1916).

Tedlow, Richard S. *Keeping the Corporate Image: Public Relations and Business, 1900–1950*. Greenwich, Conn.: JAI Press, 1979.

Valentine, Robert G. "The Progressive Relation Between Efficiency and Consent." *Bulletin of the Society to Promote the Science of Management* 1:6 (November 1915).

Veblen, Thorstein. *The Engineers and the Price System*. New York: B. W. Huebsch, 1921.

Wakstein, Allen M. "The Open Shop Movement, 1919–1933." Ph.D. dissertation, University of Illinois, 1961.

Watkins, Gordon S. *Labor Problems and Labor Administration in the United States During the World War*. Urbana: University of Illinois, 1919.

Wehle, Louis B. *Hidden Threads of History*. New York: Macmillan, 1953.

———. "War Labor Policies and Their Outcome in Peace." *Quarterly Journal of Economics* 33 (February 1919).

Weinstein, Edwin A. *Woodrow Wilson: A Medical and Psychological Biography*. Princeton, N.J.: Princeton University Press, 1981.

Weinstein, James. *The Corporate Ideal in the Liberal State*. Boston: Beacon Press, 1968.

White, Alfred T. "Seth Low." *The Survey* XXXVI (September 30, 1916).

Wiebe, Robert H. *Businessmen and Reform*. Cambridge: Harvard University Press, 1962.

Wolf, Harry D. *The Railroad Labor Board*. Chicago: University of Chicago Press, 1927.

Wolf, Howard, and Ralph Wolf. *Rubber: A Story of Glory and Greed*. New York: Covici, Friede, 1936.

Wolfe, A. B. *Works Committees and Joint Industrial Councils*. Philadelphia: United States Shipping Board, 1919.

Wolman, Leo. *Ebb and Flow in Trade Unionism*. New York: National Bureau of Economic Research, 1936.

Index

Abratani, Jiro, 206
Advisory Commission (to the Council of National Defense), 224–26, 228
Agent 426, 209
King Albert (Belgium), 97
American Alliance for Labor and Democracy, 269–70, 295
American Anti-Boycott Association, 26, 79
American Association for Labor Legislation, 8
American Federation of Labor (A.F. of L.), 26, 58, 80, 82–85, 87, 164, 223, 227–30, 269–70, 276, 280–82, 300, 306, 318, 327
American Federationist, 58
American Legion, 295
American Protective League, 319
Anarchists, 30, 105, 301
Anderson, George J., 332
Anthracite Coal Commission, 229
Anti-unionism, 5, 26, 30, 58, 68, 79–80, 93, 111, 150, 158, 163, 166, 208, 210, 212–14, 227, 231
Arliss, George, 232
Assassination, 105, 243, 294, 301
Atkinson, the Rev. H. S., 35
Atlantic Monthly, 200, 211
Attorney General, 54, 301–02, 321

Baker, Newton D. (Secretary of War), 229, 269
Baldwin-Felts Detective Agency, 3, 130, 142
Barr, William H., 266–67, 270
Baruch, Bernard, 307–08, 313
Bedford, A. C., 218–20
Beeks, Gertrude, 156, 172
Belmont, August, 69
Benchley, Robert, 59

Berkman, Alexander, 30
Bernstein, Irving, 335
Bethlehem Shipbuilding Co., 251–52
Bethlehem Steel Co., 253–54, 256, 308, 326, 331
"bludgeon system", 255
Bolshevism, 234, 236, 269–70, 276, 284, 286, 295, 301–02, 319, 321
Bombings, 294, 301–02
Boughton, Lt. Col. Edward S., 27
Bowers, Lamont M., 10–16, 21, 25, 116, 124, 131, 135, 137–38, 143, 259
Brandeis, Louis D., 223
Brewster, James H., 125
Brisbane, Arthur, 29
British Coal Commission, 291
British Labour Party, 234–35, 281, 298
British trade unions, 225, 261, 281
Brooks, John Graham, 44
Brown, James P., 29
Brown University, 5, 9, 49, 58, 60
Bulletins, 33–35, 58–60
Butler, H. B., 334

Calloway, A. W., 213
Canadian National Industrial Conference, 309
Carlson, Governor, 131
Carlton, Newcomb, 245–46, 248
Carnegie, Andrew, 7, 69, 190, 271–72, 278, 287, 289, 299
Carnegie Corporation, 271–72
Carnegie, Mrs. Andrew, 271–72, 299
Casson, Herbert, 29
Chatauqua, 200
Checkweighmen, 2, 107–08, 191, 204, 238
Chicago Civic Federation, 83

Ching, Cyrus, 332–33
Christian Socialism, 40, 44, 259
Cohen, Henry, 122–23
Cohen, Julius H., 252
Collective bargaining, 37, 51–52, 61,
    70, 72, 87, 107, 111, 149, 158, 177,
    193, 214, 230, 275, 278–79, 294,
    312, 317–18, 326–28, 335
Collectivism, 259–60
Colorado Federation of Labor, 18
Colorado Fuel and Iron Co. (C.F. &
    I.), 3–4, 9–11, 16–17, 37, 51–56,
    65, 68–75, 92–97, 101–09, 114–
    15, 123–27, 130–36, 139–45,
    153–59, 163–79, 181–96, 200,
    202–08, 210–11, 213, 215–16,
    219–20, 231, 235, 241–42, 245,
    250–51, 254, 259, 262, 275, 288,
    299, 308–10, 320–22, 332, 336–38
Colorado Industrial Commission, 191,
    203, 321
Colorado Industrial Plan, 192, 199–
    200, 202–03, 226, 239, 260, 306,
    328
Colorado Militia, 1, 17–18, 22–
    24, 27
Columbia University, 85, 227
Committee on Industrial Relations,
    209
Committee on Public Information,
    269
Commons, John R., 43–44, 96, 205
Company union (see also Employee
    representation), 1, 313, 318,
    334–36
Conflict, theories of, 119–22, 261
Congressional investigating commit-
    tee, 14, 20, 58, 105, 111, 183
Consolidation Coal Co., 237–38, 250,
    254–56, 279, 289–96, 299–300,
    332, 336
Consumers League of Massachu-
    setts, 40
Coolidge, Calvin, 307
Cornell University, 200, 216–17
Costigan, Edward, 94, 116
Council of National Defense, 85, 224–
    25, 228
Cowdrick, Edward S., 9, 185, 288
Cowdrick Group, 333

Craven, Paul, 44
Currier, Guy W., 252–53
Curtis, Fosdick, and Belknap, 331–32

Davies, Hywel, 56
Davis, Coke and Coal Co., 212–14,
    299
Dennison, Archie, 182
Dennison, Henry S., 317
Denver Chamber of Commerce, 193
Denver Post, 139
Dickinson, Capt. C. R., 269, 280
Dos Passos, John, 59
Doubleday, Frederick N., 32
Dubofsky, Melvin, 255
Dunne, Finley, 78
Dupont Co., 335
Duty, 16–17, 47

Easley, Ralph, 84, 86–87, 156–57,
    160, 164, 172
Edgell, S. M., 250
Eight-hour day, 2, 198–99, 230, 267,
    273, 310, 336
Eliot, Charles W., 29, 99–100, 104,
    164
Ely, Richard T., 44
Employee representation, 51, 66, 71,
    74–75, 78, 95, 124, 129, 143, 145,
    150–53, 158, 166–67, 173, 177,
    182–83, 185, 187–92, 195, 200–
    04, 206–08, 210–14, 219–20,
    226, 236–37, 239–41, 245–58,
    260, 262–64, 268–70, 273–83,
    286–94, 299–300, 306, 308–10,
    313–15, 321, 324, 327–29, 332–38
Fabian Society, 43
Farr, Jeff, 127, 131, 133, 139
Federal Council of Churches, 35, 61
Fish, Frederick P., 316
Fitch, John A., 24, 159–60
Flexner, Dr. Simon, 29, 215
Foerster, Robert F., 331
Ford, Henry, 69
Fosdick, Raymond B., 9, 29, 47, 222–
    24, 234–36, 305–06, 326, 329, 331,
    337–38
Foster, Martin (Congressman), 20–21,
    105–06

Fourteen Points, 233–34
Frankfurter, Felix, 223–25, 270–71
French, Carroll, 335
Frick, Henry C., 308, 312
Fuel Administration, 237–39, 250, 255

Garfield, Harry A., 237–38
Gary dinners, 4
Gary, Elbert H., 199, 265, 306–15, 317–19, 323–24, 328
Gates, Frederick, 4–10, 17, 28, 32, 49, 55–56, 99, 104–05, 161
General Electric Co., 198, 252–54, 256, 326
Gilday, Patrick, 64, 106–07, 202–03
Gilson, Mary B., 333
Gompers, Samuel, 58, 83, 85, 87, 157, 164, 175, 191–92, 224–25, 228–29, 269–70, 278, 295, 297–98, 300, 307–08, 313, 317–18, 324, 327
Grace Episcopal Church, 212
Grace, Eugene, 253–54
Gray, Carl R., 279, 299
Great Western Sugar Co., 250, 262–63, 268
Green, William, 169–75, 243
Greene, Jerome, 4, 26, 29, 36, 45, 56, 61, 97, 99–100, 105, 110, 164
Grey, Sir Edward, 100
Guggenheim, Daniel, 226
Guggenheim, Simon, 123, 125, 136

Hamilton, A. R., 255
Hanson, Ole, 324
"Happiness", 277
Harriman, Mrs. E. H., 101, 104
Harvard University, 29, 33, 39–40, 224
Hasanovitz, Elizabeth, 239
Hawaiian Sugar Planters' Association, 286
Hawkins, Horace, 138–44, 192–93
Hayes, Frank J., 17, 152, 243, 255
Henderson, Arthur, 281, 298
Hepburn, A. Barton, 97
Herrington, Cass, 124, 126–28, 130–31, 135, 141–42, 154
Herrington, Fred, 126, 131, 141–42, 154

Heydt, Charles O., 99, 115, 145
Hicks, Clarence J., 155–56, 163–69, 206, 208, 219–20, 231, 251, 273, 275, 287–88, 333
High cost of living, 302
Home Defender, 26
Hoover, Herbert, 326–27
Howard, Earl Dean, 252
Huerfano County, 123, 131, 209
Hull House, 39
Hutcheson, William, 230

Independent, 159
Industrial Disputes Investigation Act, 40, 57, 92–93, 140, 144, 205, 325–26
Industrial Relations Counselors, 332–33
Industrial Relations Sections, 337
Industrial violence, 1, 3, 14, 17–20, 159, 311
Industrial Workers of the World (I.W.W.), 81–84, 234, 269, 276, 284, 301, 321
Industry and Humanity, 256–57, 261, 265
Inflation, 266
Influenza pandemic, 265–66, 297
International Harvester Co., 155–56, 168, 262, 275, 298, 326, 331–32
International Labor Organization, 334
Interstate Commerce Commission, 33, 34
Iron Age, 236
Iron and Steel Institute, 319

Johns Hopkins Medical School, 215
Joint ownership of industry, 235, 298–99
Judson, Harry P., 99, 104–05
Justice Department, 301–02, 320–22

Kirby, John, 84

Labour Gazette, 40
Labour portfolio, 37, 40, 262
LaFollette Committee, 337
Lane, Franklin K., 27
Larkin, John M., 251

Las Animas County, 123, 131, 193
Lauck, W. Jett, 227
Laurier, Lady, 303
Laurier, Sir Wilfrid, 262, 268, 272, 285–86
Lawson, John R., 92–96, 106, 112, 116, 122, 129–30, 133, 137–45, 148–49, 158, 170, 175, 182, 191–93
Lawson, Thomas W., 46
Lee, Ivy, 1, 29–30, 32–35, 37, 52–56, 58–60, 95, 100, 108, 110–11, 137–38, 141, 146, 156–58, 160, 163–69, 185, 199, 218, 264, 291, 297–98, 316, 328
Legge, Alexander, 275
Leiserson, William, 44
Leslie's Weekly, 185
Lewis, John L., 243, 255
Liberal ideology, 91, 301
Liberal Party, 37, 262, 264, 268, 272, 286–88, 303
Liberty Bond drive, 226
Lichty, A. H., 331
Lincoln, Abraham, 243
Lindsey, Judge Ben B., 28, 125
Lippmann, Walter, 21, 75, 323–25, 328
Little Red Songbook, 81
Lloyd, Henry D., 46
Low Commission, 64–66, 68, 84, 93, 96, 102, 106–10, 112, 127, 137, 157–58, 164, 172, 174–75, 200, 202–06
Low, Seth, 64, 84–86, 102, 106–08, 110–11, 157–58, 160, 164, 202–05, 227
Loyalty cards, 321–22, 324
Ludlow Massacre, 1, 17–20, 22–24, 68, 241–43, 283
Lusk, Clayton R., 301

MacGregor, Francis, 114–16, 135–36, 140, 145
Macy, V. Everit, 226–27
Maisel, Robert, 269–70, 295
Marshall, Leon C., 223
Marx, Karl, 236
McCarthy, Charles, 58–60, 65, 94
McCormick, Cyrus, 155, 326

McCormick, Harold, 29, 155–56
McHarg, Mr. 138
McLennan, Mr., 152
Midvale Steel Co., 308
Miller, Earl, 335
Mills, Charles W., 64, 203
Minnepaqua Steel Works (C.F. & I.), 4, 165, 202, 310, 312
Mitchell, John, 85, 157, 161, 172–76, 192
Morgan, J. P., 69, 294
Mother Jones, 75–77, 92, 116–19, 140, 143, 325
Murphy, Starr, 4, 25, 29–30, 55–56, 95, 97, 99, 103, 110–11, 132–33, 146, 154, 157, 163, 169–71, 246, 257, 312

National Association of Manufacturers, 26, 79–80, 84, 332
National Cash Register Co., 86
National Child Labor Committee, 8
National Civic Federation, 64, 83–87, 155, 157, 164, 172, 205, 226, 229
National Founders' Association, 266
National Industrial Conference Board, 223, 229–30, 316
National Industrial Recovery Act, 335
National War Labor Board, 81, 231, 244–45, 248, 252–54, 308, 326, 335
Neill, Charles P., 56, 97
Nelson, Daniel, 335
New Republic, 75, 323
New York Evening Post, 24–25
New York State Chamber of Commerce, 274
New York State Federation of Labor, 274, 279–81
New York Times, 54, 68, 159, 181, 185–86, 267, 270, 306, 310
Northcutt, Jesse, 123–24, 127, 129–33, 135, 139
"Nucleoid," 248

Occupational Safety and Health Act, 278
Ogburn, William F., 227
Open shop, 14–15, 61, 70, 176, 210, 246, 248, 269, 310, 336

Organization Resources Counselors, 332–33

Osgood, John C., 53, 55, 119, 122–24, 126, 130, 135, 139, 143, 154–55

Owen, Robert, 235

Palmer, A. Mitchell, 301–02, 320–22

Parker, Carleton H., 227

Pasteur, Louis, 257

Peale, Rembrandt, 237–38

Pennsylvania Railroad, 29, 33, 37

Perkins, George W., 298–99, 328

Philanthropy, 4–8, 36, 78, 98–99, 101–05, 129, 165, 185, 195, 211, 219, 271–72, 289, 313

Pittsburgh Survey, 133

Pope, Horton, 123–27, 130, 138

Popular Science Monthly, 30

Postmaster General, 248

Powderly, Terence V., 117

Pratt and Whitney Co., 198

President's Industrial Conferences, 305, 313–19, 325–28

Princeton University, 56, 331, 333, 338

Profit sharing, 235, 298

Progressives, 84, 93

Public relations, 28–29, 32–35, 181, 184–86, 244

Pueblo Star-Journal, 186

Pullman, George H., 86

"Pure and simple unionism," 83

Race riots, 302–03, 305, 313

Railroad Adjustment Board, 279

Rea, Samuel, 29

Recognition strikes, 44, 247–49

Red scare, 260, 281, 294–95, 301–02

Religion, 7, 22, 38–39, 47, 117, 121, 174, 194, 311, 323

Republic Steel Co., 198

Revolution, 81, 124, 144, 270, 284, 287, 295, 300–02, 319

Robinson, Helen Ring, 125

Rockefeller, Abby Aldrich, 49, 61, 103, 114, 130, 195–96, 199, 217, 239–43, 246, 250

Rockefeller, David, 199

Rockefeller Foundation, 7, 29, 45, 57, 60, 62–63, 71, 94–95, 97–100,

103–05, 129, 161, 164, 169, 175, 185, 209, 218, 222, 233–34, 257, 331

Rockefeller, John D. (Senior), 1, 4–7, 20–22, 32, 49, 63, 66, 69–71, 93, 104–05, 176–79, 185–86, 193–96, 210, 212, 216–17, 219, 249, 256, 264, 294

Rockefeller, Sr., Mrs., 5, 16, 47, 49,114

Rockefeller, John D., III, 338

Rockefeller, Percy, 185, 245

Rockefeller, William, 185

Rogers, Sherman, 288

Roosevelt Administration, 84

Roosevelt, Franklin D., 227

Roosevelt, Theodore, 230

Rose, Wickliffe, 97–99

Rosenwald, Julius, 326

Royal Canadian Mounted Police, 51

Russell Sage Foundation, 322, 336

Russian Revolution, 233

Russian Soviet Bureau, 301

"Sacred Thirty-Six," 119

St. Patrick's Cathedral, 105

Sandburg, Carl, 59

Schwab, Charles, 17, 272

Scientific management, 261

Seager, Henry R., 327

Sears, Roebuck and Co., 326

Selekman, Benjamin, 322

Service, 88, 121, 194

Shibusawa, Baron Yei-ichi, 199

Shipbuilding Labor Adjustment Board, 226–27, 251, 327

Shop committees, 224–25, 227–28, 252–53, 335

Sinclair, Upton, 20, 77, 295

Socialism, 42, 81–82, 201, 222–23,259

Socialist Party, 82

Spargo, John, 295

Special Conference Committee, 326–27, 329, 333–34, 337

Spies, 142–43, 191, 208–09, 215, 310–11, 319, 338

Standard Oil of Indiana, 273–76, 278–86, 300, 309, 331

Standard Oil of New Jersey, 46, 59, 64, 159, 215–20, 227, 236, 273, 287, 326, 335

Standard Oil of New York, 249
Stephenson, John J., 30
Stewart, Ethelbert, 13
Stewart, Robert W., 273–75, 285
Strikes: Colorado Coal, 1–5, 17–20; Anthracite, 84, 172–74; Grand Trunk Railway, 117; Standard Oil, 159, 215–16; 1919, 266, 302, 305; Seattle, 281, 284; Winnipeg, 301; Boston, 307; Coal, 319–22; C.F. & I., 310, 320–21, 338
Survey, 159
Syndicalism, 81–82, 259–60

Taft, William H., 80–81, 229–30
Tarbell, Ida, 46
Temperance movement, 7, 338
Tories, 91, 139, 301
Toynbee, Arnold, 44
Trinidad Chamber of Commerce, 103
Tumulty, Joseph, 150, 312

Union Government (Canada), 262
Unionism, 16, 37, 43, 52, 61, 69–70, 72–73, 78–81, 149–53, 171, 176, 184, 203–04, 214–15, 256, 260, 276–88, 290–94, 306–07, 309, 313–18, 324, 327
United Mine Workers Journal, 191
United Mine Workers Union, 1–2, 10, 16–17, 21, 53–55, 59, 65, 77, 87, 92–94, 106, 122, 125, 141, 144, 153, 161, 163–64, 167–69, 172–74, 177–78, 184, 191–92, 203, 205–06, 212–15, 238, 241, 255, 261, 309, 321
U.S. Chamber of Commerce, 268–69, 276
U.S. Commission on Industrial Relations, 4, 27, 57–62, 64–66, 68–75, 84, 87, 90, 93, 96–98, 111–12, 116, 122, 124–25, 137–38, 143, 146, 148–54, 159–61, 168–69, 171–72, 193, 201, 209, 229, 269; *Final Report,* 159, 161
U.S. Rubber Co., 326, 332
U.S. Steel Co., 298
University of Chicago, 7, 39

Valentine, Robert G., 44, 200

Van Tine, Warren, 255
Victor-American Fuel Co., 53, 123
Vincent, George E., 234–35, 251, 257

Walsh, Frank P., 58–60, 65, 68–69, 71–75, 78, 81, 87, 94, 109, 116, 137–38, 140, 145–46, 149–54, 159–61, 164, 177, 209, 229–30, 245
War Department, 222, 229
War Labor Conference Board, 229–31, 315
Watson, Clarence, 255
Watson, George, 255
Webb, Beatrice and Sidney, 252
Weitzel, E. H., 131–32, 134–35, 143, 206–08, 241
Welborn, Jesse, 11–14, 21, 26–27, 52–56, 66, 95–98, 101–03, 106–09, 115, 124, 126–35, 139, 141–45, 154–56, 163–69, 186–87, 202, 207, 216, 231, 250, 259, 310, 320–22, 324–25, 338
Welborn, Mrs. Jesse, 95, 98, 102–03, 115, 127–30, 250
Welfare work, 86–87, 156, 274–75, 298
Weller, F. W., 215–16
Western Federation of Miners, 122
Western Union Co., 244–49, 302
Westinghouse Electric Co., 198
Wheelwright, James H., 237–38, 254–56
White, John S., 169–75, 238, 243
Whitley Councils, 225, 228–29, 252, 260, 271
Willets, Joseph, 44
Wilson Administration, 1, 58, 84, 223, 228–29, 231, 319, 325
Wilson, William B., 13–14, 54, 108–09, 111–12, 205, 229, 319, 322
Wilson, Woodrow, 20–21, 27–28, 53–57, 64–65, 68–69, 148–50, 203, 205, 222, 227–28, 233, 245, 248, 267, 269, 286, 305–07, 311–13, 323, 325
Wilson, Mrs. Woodrow, 312
Wolman, Leo, 335
Women's Justice League, 182
Workmen's compensation, 86, 108

Works committees. *See* Shop committees

World War, 62, 97, 198, 219–20, 222–24, 233, 263, 265

Yale Law School, 229

Yellow-dog contract, 231

Young, Arthur H., 275, 332–33

Young, Owen D., 326

YMCA, 155–56, 165, 206, 210, 212, 217, 219, 226, 274, 288, 298–99, 331

Youngstown Sheet and Tube Co., 262–63, 285, 288